Praise for *The New Nuclear Danger*

"Dr. Helen Caldicott has the rare ability to combine science with passion, logic with love, and urgency with humor. . . . At the dark dawn of another war without end, it is once again time to listen up as she sounds the global alarm." —NAOMI KLEIN, author of *No Logo*

"What a contribution to the planet! Helen Caldicott's . . . untiring commitment to the public's health is hastening the end of the nuclear madness." —BEN COHEN, co-founder of Ben & Jerry's

"Helen Caldicott has done it again. Now, more than ever, her voice is crucial. . . . Read this." —ROBIN MORGAN

"Helen Caldicott reminds us that the world still possesses thousands of warheads, enough to blow up the world many times over, and that policy remains inordinately influenced by the manufacturers of weapons rather than the makers of peace."
—DANIEL HIRSCH, President, Committee to Bridge the Gap

"No one has worked harder and longer to prevent human extinction than Helen Caldicott." —PATCH ADAMS, M.D.

"Dr. Helen Caldicott speaks the truth . . . and her command of the medical consequences of nuclear warfare communicates with visceral force the ultimate madness of those leaders who seek security and safety with nuclear weapons." —ADMIRAL GENE CARROLL

T0151977

THE NEW NUCLEAR DANGER

George W. Bush's Military-Industrial Complex

HELEN CALDICOTT

THE NEW PRESS

NEW YORK
LONDON

This book is dedicated to Scott Jeffrey Powell, without whose unswerving perseverance it would never have been written.

© 2002 by Helen Caldicott
Introduction © 2004 by Helen Caldicott
All rights reserved.
No part of this book may be reproduced, in any form, without written permission from the publisher.

Original edition published by The New Press in 2002
This edition published in the United States by The New Press, New York, 2004
Distributed by W. W. Norton & Company, Inc., New York

ISBN 1-56584-878-0 (pbk.)
CIP data available

The New Press was established in 1990 as a not-for-profit alternative to the large, commercial publishing houses currently dominating the book publishing industry. The New Press operates in the public interest rather than for private gain, and is committed to publishing, in innovative ways, works of educational, cultural, and community value that are often deemed insufficiently profitable.

The New Press
38 Greene Street, 4th floor
New York, NY 10013
www.thenewpress.com

In the United Kingdom:
6 Salem Road
London W2 4BU

Composition by dix!

Printed in the United States of America

10 9 8 7 6 5 4 3 2 1

CONTENTS

Acknowledgments vii
Preface ix
Introduction to the 2004 Edition xxi
1. The Tragedy of Wasted Opportunities 1
2. The Reality of Nuclear War 7
3. It's a Mad, Mad World: Nuclear Scientists and the Pentagon Play with Deadly Gadgets 13
4. Corporate Madness and the Death Merchants 24
5. Manhattan II 43
6. Star Wars: The Story of National Missile Defense Systems 71
7. Space: The Next American Empire 115
8. Nuclear War in the Gulf and Kosovo 145
9. The Lockheed Martin Presidency and the Star Wars Administration 162
Appendix A: Major U.S. Nuclear-Weapons Makers 189
Appendix B: U.S. Nuclear-Weapons Control Centers, Government Authorities, and Nuclear War Plans 209
Appendix C: Locations of the Majority of Usable U.S. Nuclear Weapons 219
Appendix D: Major Antinuclear Organizations in the United States, Europe, Russia, Japan, and South Asia 223
Appendix E: Media 243
Notes 255
Index 278

ACKNOWLEDGMENTS

WITH GRATEFUL THANKS to all who helped to assemble and organize the information for this book:

Bruce Gagnon, whose prophetic work first inspired the notion of this project; Mary Cunnane whose support and advice was ever present; Diane Wachtell, my excellent editor; Faith Hamlin, my wonderful and persistent agent; Scott Powell, whose meticulous research provided some of the data and all the reference lists; Karl Grossman, Bob Alveraz, and Jacqui Cabasso at Western States Legal Foundation; Hugh Gusterson, MIT; Robert Aldridge, Pacific Life Research Center; Admiral Eugene Carroll, Center for Defense Information; William Hartung and Frida Berrigan, World Policy Institute; Richard Marek and Bonnie Urfer, Nukewatch; Gregory Talmadge, The Center for Responsive Politics; Stephen Schwartz, Bulletin of the Atomic Scientists; Bill Sulzman, Katya Komisaruk, and Jack Cohen-Joppa, The Nuclear Resister; and Maria Gilardin, TUC Radio.

Discretionary Budget, Fiscal Year 2001

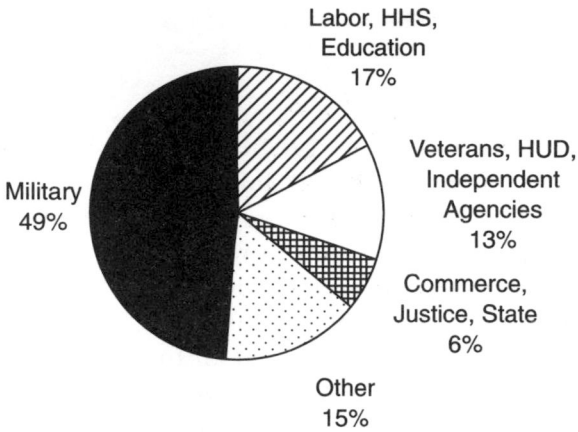

The pie chart shows discretionary spending for Fiscal Year 2001, which runs from October 1, 2000 to September 30, 2001. This is the last discretionary budget settled under the Clinton presidency. Discretionary spending refers to the part of the federal budget that is up to the discretion of Congress. Entitlement programs such as Social Security and Food Stamps are non-discretionary; Congress can restrict or expand eligibility, but cannot directly determine the level of spending. Pentagon spending still consumes almost half of discretionary spending while education takes up only about 7%. (*Source:* © 2001 National Priorities Project, Inc.)

PREFACE

On September 11, before much of the world was even aware of what had happened in New York, Washington, and Pennsylvania, the Bush administration had raised the country's nuclear alert codes from defcon 6 to defcon 2—the highest state of alert before the launch code is operable.* Russia, the country with the second largest nuclear arsenal in the world, almost certainly responded in kind. As a result, thousands of nuclear weapons stood poised on hair-trigger alert, ready to be launched by the president of either country with a decision time of just three minutes. The intercontinental nuclear-armed ballistic missiles controlled by these codes have a thirty-minute transit time from Russia to America or vice versa. They cannot be recalled. And they pose an ever-present threat of global nuclear holocaust.

In the months since the terrorist attacks, Secretary of Defense Donald Rumsfeld and others in the administration have also used September 11 to justify everything from pursuit of a missile-defense shield (even though such a shield would be utterly useless against suicidal men armed with boxcutters and plane tickets) and abandonment of long-standing weapon-control treaties, to massive increases in defense spending. While most Americans desire an increased sense of security in a newly destabilized world, many do not realize that the new "security" measures and the "conventional" war the United States has waged against Afghanistan are intimately connected to the enormous nuclear threat posed by the current American posture. Aggressive militarization under the rubric of defense against terrorism threatens to provoke a chain reaction among nuclear nations, big and small, that, once set in motion, may prove impossible to control. No

* It is not known how long this situation was maintained.[1]

military confrontation anywhere in the world is free from this ominous and ever-present danger.

The U.S.'s own behavior in Afghanistan has veered frighteningly close to deployment of nuclear weapons, which could easily have engendered a nuclear response. In addition to deploying the most horrific conventional weapons known to man (even though there were very few targets of military significance), the defense department recommended the use of tactical nuclear weapons,[2] while some members of Congress strongly advised the use of small nuclear "bunker busters."[3] Bush advisors, including Stephen Hadley, Deputy National Security Advisor Stephen Cambone, and William Schneider, also advocated the use of nuclear weapons.[4] The founder of the neutron bomb, Samuel Cohen, even postulated that his weapon might be appropriate for Afghanistan.[5] (The neutron bomb has a relatively small blast effect compared with its radiation, hence it tends to kill large numbers of people with horrendous radiation illness while leaving buildings intact.) Although the U.S. has previously been clear that it would attack only nuclear-armed countries with nuclear weapons, Secretary of Defense Rumsfeld consistently refused to rule out the use of nuclear weapons in Afghanistan, which is not nuclear-armed.[6]

Some of the conventional weapons America used to support the Northern Alliance during their advances on the Taliban were so powerful that they are described by the Pentagon as "near nuclear" weapons. They are as follows:

15,000-POUND FUEL AIR EXPLOSIVES (FAEs): In military jargon these are referred to as "Daisy Cutters." The Foreign Military Studies Office at Fort Leavenworth says "A fuel air explosive can have the effect of a tactical nuclear weapon without the radiation."[7] There are many different varieties of FAEs, but they typically consist of a container of fuel and two separate explosive charges. Dropped by parachute from a huge MC-130 Combat Talon plane, they detonate just above the ground, creating a wide area of destruction.[8] The first explosion bursts the container at a predetermined height, disbursing the fuel, which mixes with atmospheric oxygen. The second charge then detonates this fuel-air cloud, creating a massive blast that kills people and destroys unreinforced buildings. Near the ignition point people are obliterated, crushed to death with overpressures of 427 pounds per square inch, and incinerated at temperatures of 2500 to 3000 degrees centigrade. Another wave of low pressure—a vacuum effect—then ensues. People in the second zone of destruction are severely burned and suffer massive internal organ injuries before they die. In the third zone, eyes are extruded from their orbits, lungs and ear drums rupture, and severe concussion ensues. The fuel itself—ethylene oxide and propylene oxide—is highly toxic.[9] Up to 200 civilians died 20 miles away from the cave complex in Afghanistan where Osama bin Laden was thought to be hiding at Tora Bora when U.S. planes attacked. They suffered blast trauma—ruptured lungs, blindness, arms and hands blown off, almost certainly from FAEs.[10]

CLUSTER BOMBS: These have been used extensively in Afghanistan by the U.S. Terrifying and deadly, each bomb is composed of 202 bomblets, which are packed with razor-sharp shrapnel dispersed at super-high speed over an area of 22 football fields, ripping into human bodies. These weapons are prohibited by the Geneva Protocol.[11] Civilians were inevitably killed throughout Afghanistan by these illegal and dreadful weapons. On one documented occasion, the U.S. bombed a mosque in Jalabad during prayer and while neighbors were digging out 17 victims, additional bombs killed more than 120 people.[12]

Historically, between 5 and 30 percent of these bomblets fail to explode initially, lying around the countryside as mines that explode with violent force if touched, tearing their victims to pieces. Tragically, the bomblets are colored yellow and shaped like a can of soft drink, and therefore attractive to children.[13] The food parcels containing peanut butter, Pop Tarts, rice, and potatoes dropped throughout Afghanistan by the U.S. are also yellow and the same size and shape as the munitions. (Some of these food drops themselves went astray, destroying houses and killing more people.[14]) Human Rights Watch estimates that over 5000 unexploded cluster bomblets may be littered across Afghanistan, adding to the hundreds of thousands of mines left after the Russian–American war of 1979 to 1989.[15] Afghanistan is currently the most heavily mined country in the world.

GUN SHIPS: These lumbering C-130 planes built by Lockheed Martin have been converted to airborne gunships, capable of firing a fearsome array of weapons, inflicting the most devastating damage, and leveling an area of several football fields, with up to 2000 rounds per minute. They are armed with 25mm Gattling guns, which fire 1800 rounds per minute; 40mm Bofors cannons, which fire 120 rounds per minute; and 105mm Howitzer cannons, which fire 8 to 10 rounds per minute.[16] Secretary of Defense Rumsfeld said Afghanistan is not a "target rich" area, and many analysts felt that these attacks far exceeded their expectations. On October 22, in the village of Chowkar-Karez, scores of civilians were mown down by these gunships. CNN quoted an "unnamed" Pentagon official as saying "The people are dead because we wanted them dead."[17] Almost certainly, many civilians therefore were wounded and killed.[18, 19]

BUNKER BUSTERS: Dropped from B-1 or B-2 planes, these 5000-pound behemoths are made from the gun barrels of retired naval ships and are so heavy that they burrow 20 to 100 feet into the ground before their high-explosive materials detonate. Most are laser guided, but some use Global Positioning satellites for guidance.[20]

CARPET BOMBING: This means dropping tons of bombs from B-52 planes at a 40,000-foot altitude: high enough to protect pilots but too high to protect civilians. This is indiscriminate bombing, and the pilots have no idea on whom their bombs are landing. In 1969 carpet bombing used in Cambodia by Kissinger and Nixon during the Vietnam War induced the total destruction of the ancient irrigation system and water supply and most of the rice-growing areas of the country and, as a secondary effect, caused the absolute disintegration of Cambodia's culture. The bombing runs were called "breakfast," "lunch," and "supper."[21]

UNMANNED DRONES. These are pilotless planes armed with Hellfire missiles, guided by the Global Positioning System, allowing the military to reduce the time between "identification and destruction of a target."[22] Clearly these planes pose no threats to pilots but terrible threats to civilians on the ground, who may live next to or within a certain "military target," which could be a factory, an electricity generator, or a railway station.

The U.S. has not announced whether or not it used depleted uranium weapons in Afghanistan (as it has done elsewhere in recent wars), but it is quite possible that it did. We will not know for sure until independent sources can enter the war zones and test for this radioactive element.

During the first four weeks of the war, half a million tons of bombs were dropped on Afghanistan, 20 kilos for every man, woman, and child.[23] During eight and a half weeks of U.S. bombing, a documented 3,763 civilians were killed.[24]

WHAT ARE THE INTERNATIONAL RAMIFICATIONS OF THIS BEHAVIOR LIKELY TO BE?

Pakistan has been deeply involved in Afghanistan since the 1979–1989 U.S.–Russian war, when America channeled weapons, training, and funding through the Pakistani military and intelligence services to the mujahadeen, the Taliban, and Osama bin Laden to fight the Russians. After September 11, America changed sides, pressuring Pakistan to ally with the U.S. against their previous friends and allies, the Taliban, bin Laden, and al-Qaeda, because the U.S. needed Pakistani airports to fight their war—a move that was anathema to thousands of Pakistani supporters of bin Laden and the Taliban. These supporters include many members of the Pakistani military, who could well rebel and gain control of the army and its 20 to 50 nuclear weapons, passing these on to the Taliban and al-Qaeda in Afghanistan or to their global networks.

The use of Pakistani nuclear weapons could trigger a chain reaction. Nuclear-armed India, an ancient enemy, could respond in kind. China, India's hated foe, could react if India used her nuclear weapons, triggering a nuclear holocaust on the subcontinent. If any of either Russia or America's 2,250 strategic weapons on hair-trigger alert were launched either accidentally or purposefully in response, nuclear winter would ensue, meaning the end of most life on earth.

OTHER NUCLEAR THREATS

TERRORIST NUCLEAR WEAPONS

Up to 100 small suitcase Russian nuclear weapons have been lost over some years. Al-Qaeda network may now possess several of these, which could well be smuggled into America on a small boat or overland, from Canada or Mexico, in a truck. Nuclear Oklahoma Cities are not beyond question. Immediate deaths would number in the tens of thousands, while tens of thousands of cancers would incubate quietly among the survivors over decades. Britain, Europe, and Australia, among other places, will not remain immune.

DIRTY NUCLEAR DEVICES

Hundreds of tons of highly carcinogenic plutonium and enriched uranium stand unguarded in Russia. From 1993 to 2000, the UN International Atomic Energy Agency—which monitors nuclear security—documented 153 confirmed cases of theft of nuclear materials.[25] Some of this material could be obtained by terrorists to make primitive nuclear weapons, or "dirty" bombs. There would be no nuclear explosion, but conventional explosives would be used to scatter plutonium or uranium across a wide area, contaminating all in the pathway with these carcinogenic elements. Other radioactive elements from reprocessed nuclear fuel, such as cesium-137, strontium-90, and cobalt-60, could also be deployed.[26]

Terrorists could, with some difficulty, manufacture their own nuclear devices from stolen plutonium or uranium. The design for a primitive weapon can be found on the internet. The possibilities for nuclear terrorism seem endless.

NUCLEAR MELTDOWNS

Terrorists do not actually need nuclear weapons. They have been conveniently supplied with 103 nuclear power plants scattered throughout the United States (438 of these deadly facilities exist throughout the world).[27] A planned meltdown at one of these facilities would make the World Trade Center attacks seem like child's play. The massive concrete containers protecting the reactors are not strong enough to withstand the impact of a jumbo jet.

Alternatively, an infiltrator working as an operator could engineer a meltdown by taking over the control room, as the hijackers on September 11 took over the planes. They could also disrupt the water supply (one million gallons a minute is needed to cool a reactor core) or the external electricity supply. Either event would induce a meltdown within hours. The spent-fuel cooling pools adjacent to the reactor contain 20 to 30 times more long-lived radiation than the actual reactor core.[28] (A 1000 megawatt nuclear reactor contains as much long-lived radiation as that released by the explosion of 1000 Hiroshima-sized bombs).

Here is the medical description of the meltdown of a 1000-megawatt nuclear power plant near New York City (there are two reactors at Indian Point, 35 miles north of Manhattan):

> With ten million people at risk, 3300 people would die from severe radiation damage within several days; 10,000 to 100,000 would develop lethal acute radiation sickness within 2 to 6 weeks of exposure; 45,000 would become short of breath from lung damage caused by inhalation of intensely radioactive gases; 240,000 would become hypothyroid, with accompanying symptoms of weight gain, lassitude, slow mental functions, loss of appetite, constipation, and absent menstruation; 350,000 males would be rendered temporarily sterile, while the remaining sperm would be genetically mutated; 40,000 to 100,000 women would stop menstruating, many permanently. Up to 100,000 babies would be born as cretins, mentally retarded, as radioactive iodine destroys their thyroid glands (imperative for neurological development), and there would be 3000 deaths in utero. Five to sixty years later, 270,000 people would develop cancers of various organs, and there would be an estimated 28,800 cases of thyroid malignancy.[29]

Apart from the nuclear power plants, there are many military-related nuclear facilities in the United States with massive quantities of nuclear waste, all vulnerable to terrorist attacks.

Since September 11, the FAA banned all aircraft flying within 12 miles of any nuclear facility. The Nuclear Regulatory Commission (NRC) advised all reactors to go on the highest state of alert,[30] and for the first time, the NRC is investing 800,000 dollars to stockpile massive quantities of potassium iodide tablets to be made available to the public in case of a meltdown. Specific states will need to request the tablets, and this medicine must be taken within hours of a meltdown to block the uptake of radio-iodine by the thyroid gland. (This measure may not be adequate, however, because over one hundred different deadly radioactive elements are also released during a meltdown, and these concentrate in other bodily organs.[31])

POLITICAL IMPLICATIONS

The scope of U.S. retaliation for September 11 may be as important a factor in international response as the nature of the weapons the U.S. employs. In Washington, the Bush administration is experiencing its own internecine warfare around this topic. On the one hand, Secretary of State Colin Powell and the state department put together a harmonious if tenuous international coalition with Europe, Russia, China, and the Arab nations to "battle" terrorism in Afghanistan only. But the defense department has been taken over by unreconstructed, Reagan-era cold war warriors, intent on moving the war from Afghanistan to other states.[32]

This policy is extremely dangerous. Vice President Cheney has listed fifty states or countries that could be targeted by the U.S. for military, financial, or diplomatic action, including North Korea, Somalia, Yemen, Iran, the Sudan, Libya, Syria, Lebanon, Indonesia, the Philippines, Saudi Arabia, and countries in South America. Victoria Clarke, a Pentagon spokeswoman, warned, "The war on terrorism neither begins nor ends with Afghanistan. The president will decide the next target."[33]

Iraq tops the list. Ever since the U.S.–Iraqi war in 1991, when America "failed to eliminate Hussein," a right-wing putsch has been eager to finish the job. The excuse: Iraq will not allow weapons inspectors to enter the country, barring them since December 1998 from checking for nuclear, biological, or chemical weapons activities. (However, Iraq's foreign minister, Naji Sabri, said in late November 2001, "We will consider a return of monitoring [of weapons] after the lifting of sanctions."[34]) Deputy Secretary of Defense Paul Wolfowitz is spearheading the Iraqi attack movement along with his close colleague Richard Perle, who was Reagan's undersecretary of defense.

Perle chairs an unofficial bipartisan group called the Defense Policy Board, which is vigorously promoting the overthrow of Hussein, even though there is no evidence linking him to the September 11 attacks.[35,36] (The Defense Policy Board meets in a room adjacent to the secretary of defense's office, and includes such luminaries as Henry Kissinger, former secretary of state; Harold Brown, former secretary of defense; Newt Gingrich, former house majority leader; and R. James Woolsey, former director of the CIA. The group has assumed a quasi-official status with the imprimatur of Secretary Rumsfeld.) This attitude seems to be prevailing within the administration, and Powell appears to be losing his authority, although the international community is outraged by these proposals.

An attack on Iraq would infuriate Arab populations, the U.S.-led alliance against al-Qaeda[37] would dissolve, and the world would descend into a terrorist-ruled chaos. A veteran of the CIA's Directorate of Operations said "The agency as an institution would never offer up a view of these people [Perle, et al.], but if you ask individuals, they think these guys are more than a little nuts." Another longtime case officer at the CIA said, "Attack these places and there will be consequences that we simply will not be able to deal with. But Perle and Wolfowitz are absolutists, and they're stupid."[38]

Meanwhile, other destabilizing plans are afoot in the Bush administration:

- The administration will aggressively pursue testing of its missile defense system, a.k.a. Star Wars, even though Russia and China are adamantly opposed. After the cordial Bush-Putin meeting at Crawford Ranch in Texas in November 2001, National Security Advisor Condoleezza Rice said, "The timeline has not really changed. The president continues to believe that he has got to move forward with the testing program in a robust way, so that we can really begin to evaluate the potential for missile defenses." What she means is that the U.S. will withdraw from the seminal Anti Ballistic Missile Treaty (ABM) with six months notice.[39] Such a move will destabilize global arms control and the associated treaties, and induce a massive new nuclear arms race.
- The Bush administration boycotted the Comprehensive Test-Ban Treaty Conference (CTBT) at the United Nations in November

2001 and had the audacity to remove its nameplate from its seat in the conference room. A week before, at a General Assembly meeting, the U.S. was the only country to vote against placing the CTBT on the General Assembly's agenda for 2002. Washington has signed, but the Senate has not ratified the treaty, which would ban all above- and below-ground nuclear testing. As a group of non-government organizations said, "Failure to act may lead to a cascade of proliferation events that will enable future terrorists to use nuclear weapons."[40]

- There is a strong move by Bush's people to resume nuclear testing at the Nevada Test site because, as Secretary of Defense Rumsfeld said, "we may need to develop new nuclear weapons." This could stimulate Russia, China, India, and Pakistan, among others, to resume nuclear testing, leading to a new nuclear arms race.[41]
- In July 2001, the U.S. prevented the UN conference on curbing small-arms exports from convening by insisting that it was a threat to the Second Amendment.
- Also in July 2001, after ten years of negotiations, the U.S. refused to endorse a protocol on a compliance to ban biological weapons, saying it would put at risk national security and confidential business information.
- In February 2001, the U.S. delegate at a UN debate to combat terrorism said such a conference would have no practical benefits.[42]
- In November 2001, Congress cut 69 million dollars from a program designed to safeguard Russian nuclear materials in order to prevent terrorists stealing plutonium and enriched uranium to build their own nuclear bombs. Bush wanted to reduce the program still further by 29 million dollars.[43]
- Simultaneously, Congress increased the funding for U.S. nuclear weapons by 300 million dollars and granted 8.3 billion dollars for missile defense.[44] As Joseph Cirincione of the Carnegie Endowment for International Peace said, "Tragically some are using the terrible tragedy [September 11] to justify their existing programs, slapping an 'anti-terrorist' label on missile defense and military budget increases."[45]
- The terrorist attack has provided a great fillip for the military-industrial complex. The military budget is expected to reach 375 billion dollars in 2001, a 66 billion dollar increase from 2001, and

Deputy Secretary of Defense Paul Wolfowitz said that these appropriations will "just be a down-payment" toward the major long-term increases the Pentagon will need to fight its new kind of war[46] which Vice President Cheney says "may not end in our lifetimes."[47]

- The war in Afghanistan is costing 1 billion dollars a month,[48] while two-thirds of the world's children are malnourished and starving.

Loren Thompson, defense analyst from the Lexington Institute said, "The whole mindset of military spending changed on September 11. The most fundamental thing about defense spending is that threats drive defense spending. It's now going to be easier to fund almost anything." Indeed, Lockheed Martin stocks rose from $39.39 on September 11 to $48.11 by November 12, 2001. The Pentagon is to receive 20 billion dollars of the 40 billion dollars allocated by congress for antiterrorist activities, an amount to be added to 343.2 billion dollars for fiscal 2001, already the largest military budget since Reagan's at the height of the cold war—greater than 50 percent of all discretionary funding for domestic needs. Among the firms already benefitting from this extraordinarily extravagant and unnecessary largesse are Lockheed Martin, Grumman, Raytheon, and Boeing. Most of this money will not be used for the war in Afghanistan, but for new fighter planes like the F/A-18E/F, the F-22, and the Joint Strike fighter, for a new Virginia class submarine designed to trail now-extinct Soviet subs around the globe, and for 12 more Trident D5 submarine ballistic missiles. In this context it is interesting to note that the Afghanis had very few planes to speak of, and that these were destroyed by massive U.S. bombing within the first few days of the war. Paul Nisbet, another defense analyst said, "With the [Bush] administration, we will see a rebuilding of the military to bring it back to where it was eight years ago. We will see a considerable appreciation in defense stocks as we saw in the Reagan years."[49, 50]

RECENT INTERNATIONAL WEAPONS DEVELOPMENTS

People may feel reassured that President Bush, meeting in Texas in November 2001 with President Putin, offered to reduce America's stockpile of strategic weapons from some 7000 down to 2220–1700 over the next ten years. But this offer was made without the guarantee of any formal written treaty and can therefore be abandoned or reversed at any time. Without verification, it will be impossible to confirm that cuts are actually carried out, while the ten-year duration gives much latitude for reversal and change.

In fact, although the cuts look good on paper, they mean nothing. The U.S. will still have plenty of weapons to maintain its first-strike winnable nuclear war policy, and none of the weapons will be dismantled, but will be stored, awaiting possible future use. The reductions do not include the removal of multiple warheads on missiles required by the START II Treaty (the Russians have a monstrous ten-warheaded SS-18 missile, code named "Satan"). And the U.S. Trident submarine fleet, with their invulnerable first-strike arsenal, will be exempt, as will weapons on long-distance bombers being overhauled, and all tactical nuclear weapons.[51]

In truth, if Russia comes to the party, such bilateral reductions will make it easier for the U.S. to win a nuclear war against Russia, because there will be fewer targets, and the missile-defense system now under construction will mop up any Russian missiles that escape the initial surprise attack. U.S. antisatellite weapons under construction will also be necessary to destroy the "eyes and ears" of the Russian early-warning system. This is a terrifying but realistic scenario, a logical extension of the Pentagon's current policy to "fight and win" a nuclear war.

So Bush's unilateral reductions proposal is a ploy to divert the world's attention away from his Star Wars project, which Simon Tisdall of the London *Guardian* called "a reckless act of weapons proliferation," which will provoke an international arms race, entangle third parties such as Britain and Australia, and, as this book makes clear, lead directly to the militarization of space if it does not cause nuclear winter first.

Tisdall warns that "the highly contentious military and geostrategic foundations of the 21st century are being laid—and hardly anybody is watching."[52]

That is why I wrote this book.

INTRODUCTION TO THE 2004 EDITION

Why, of course people don't want war. Voice or no voice, the people can always be brought to the bidding of their leaders. . . . All you have to do is tell them that they are being attacked and denounce the pacifists for lack of patriotism and exposing the country to danger. It works the same in any country.

—Hermann Goering at the Nuremberg Tribunal

AN ELEVEN-YEAR MARCH TO WAR

Although the majority of Americans believe the 2003 attack on Iraq was a direct response to the 2001 Al Qaeda attack on the World Trade Center and the Pentagon, in fact the Iraq war was in the planning stages at least eleven years earlier. Preparations for the second U.S.-Iraq invasion (the first invasion had taken place in 1991) were started in 1992 by a small group of "defense intellectuals"—some in the first Bush administration, others outside—who founded an organization that came to be known as the Project for a New American Century (PNAC). They met in the editorial offices of William Kristol, chief editor of *The Weekly Standard*—a magazine owned by Rupert Murdoch.

The group included Paul Wolfowitz, Douglas Feith, R. James Woolsey, and Richard Perle, whose subsequent roles in the second Bush administration are described below. During the early 1990s, they began to publish a series of letters in *The Weekly Standard* calling for another U.S. invasion of Iraq, as well as advocating support of Israel's campaign against the Palestinians and warning about the rising power of China.

In 1992, then-Secretary of Defense Dick Cheney instructed Wolfowitz, who had disapproved of the "premature" end of the 1991 Iraqi war[1] and who was then Undersecretary of Defense for Policy, to draft a Defense Policy Guidance document that called for a second military intervention in Iraq to assure "access to vital raw material, primarily Persian Gulf oil." The document also called for preemptive U.S. attacks against nations—even friendly nations who are potential rivals—and advocated ad hoc coalitions, though it said that the U.S. should be prepared to act alone if necessary. It stated that the primary goal of U.S. policy should be to prevent the rise of any nation that threatened the primacy of the U.S.[2] The ideas promulgated in this document were not well received by the U.S. establishment at the time. The *New York Times* ran a large front-page story and a scorching editorial saying that the "go-it-alone" attitude was "downright perverse," and Senator Robert Byrd called the recommended strategy "myopic, shallow and disappointing."[3]

In 1996, David Wurmser, Douglas Feith, and Richard Perle coauthored a report calling for "reestablishing the principle of preemption" and noting that "This effort can focus on removing Saddam Hussein from power in Iraq. . . . Iraq's future could affect the strategic balance in the Middle-East profoundly."[4] According to William Pitt, editor of truthout.org, a website devoted to exposing truth in reporting, PNAC openly advocated the capture of Iraq for the purposes of:

- acquiring control of the oil heads so as to fund the entire enterprise
- firing a warning shot across the bow of every leader in the Middle East
- establishing in Iraq a military staging area for the eventual invasion and overthrow of several Middle Eastern regimes, including some allies of the U.S.[5,6]

In 1998, a group from PNAC including Richard Armitage, Richard Perle, John Bolton, Elliott Abrams, Donald Rumsfeld, and Paul Wolfowitz wrote to President Clinton asking him to "aim at the removal of Saddam Hussein from power "; and in September 2000 PNAC issued a report called "Rebuilding America's Defenses: Strategy, Forces and Resources for the New Century," which went on to call for a permanent Gulf military presence "should Saddam pass from the scene" (because "Iran may well prove as large a threat").[7]

Upon the November 2000 Republican presidential coup, Vice

President Dick Cheney—a founding member of PNAC—wasted no time staffing the Bush administration with PNAC-ers, where they immediately took advantage of Bush's inexperience in international matters to implement their neoconservative agenda. PNAC members appointed to official positions include: I. Lewis Libby, Cheney's top national security assistant and chief of staff; Secretary of Defense Donald Rumsfeld; Paul Wolfowitz, Deputy Secretary of Defense (whose aggressive eleven-year advocacy for the overthrow of Hussein has been instrumental in his becoming "probably the best-known deputy secretary of defense in recent history"[8]); Elliot Abrams, a member of Bush's national security council, pardoned by Bush Senior for his role in the Iran/Contra scandal; John Bolton, specifically assigned to the State Department to counteract moderate Colin Powell;[9] Richard Perle, former head of the Defense Policy Board; Randy Scheunemann, president of the Committee to Liberate Iraq, who was Trent Lott's national security aide and who advised Rumsfeld in 2001 on Iraq; Bruce Jackson, former vice president of Lockheed Martin and chairman of PNAC; and Douglas Feith, Undersecretary of Defense.

Since 2000, these neoconservatives have fundamentally controlled the White House, the Pentagon, the Defense Department, the armed forces, and the intelligence communities, with a compliant, nonquestioning, Republican-dominated Congress and senate supporting almost every item on their wish list.[10] The Defense Policy Board (DPB), established in 1985 to provide the Secretary of Defense "with independent, informed advice and opinion concerning major matters of defense policy," has morphed under the Bush II administration into a PNAC spin-off.[11] And Wolfowitz's 1992 master plan, including his notion of using U.S. preemptive force throughout the world, repudiated by Bush the first, has now become U.S. strategic doctrine.[12]

A 2000 PNAC report dolefully noted that "the process of transformation, even if it brings revolutionary change, is likely to be a long one, absent some catastrophic and catalyzing event. . . ."[13] The appearance of Osama Bin Laden on the international scene on September 11, 2001, however, offered just such a convenient catalyst.

SELLING WAR ON IRAQ TO THE AMERICAN PEOPLE

Only days after the World Trade attack, Richard Perle convened the Defense Policy Board, which dispatched James Woolsey to Europe to look for evidence that Saddam Hussein was linked to Al Qaeda. Simultaneously his colleague and close friend Wolfowitz urged President Bush to expand the war on terrorism to Iraq.[14]

When the official U.S. intelligence agencies failed to endorse Wolfowitz's assessments of Iraqi "weapons of mass destruction" and Saddam Hussein's "connections with Al Qaeda," Wolfowitz, in an unprecedented move, created the Office of Special Plans (OSP) within the Pentagon, an alternative entity to offer separate analyses to the CIA.[15] Abram Shulsky, the director of the OSP, had worked for the RAND Corporation and had served under Richard Perle when Perle was Assistant Secretary of Defense for Reagan. Reporting in to Undersecretary of Defense William Luti, an advocate of military intervention in Iraq, the OSP took close advice from members of the Iraqi National Congress and Iraqi defectors.[16, 17]

Despite intelligence reports to the contrary, OSP touted connections between Hussein and Al Qaeda, and made public claims that the Iraqis were using aluminum tubes meant for artillery rockets to enrich uranium, that Iraq had purchased uranium from Niger, and that Iraq had obtained magnets to enrich uranium. In an October 7, 2002, speech in Cincinnati, President Bush said, "The evidence indicates that Iraq is reconstituting its nuclear weapons program. Iraq has attempted to purchase high-strength aluminum tubes and other equipment used for gas centrifuges, which are used to enrich uranium for nuclear weapons." He also said that through its ties to Al Qaeda, Iraq could use biological or chemical weapons against the U.S.[18] As recently as March 2003, Vice President Cheney went on NBC's *Meet The Press* to announce, "We believe [Saddam Hussein] has, in fact, reconstituted nuclear weapons."[19] (Wolfowitz admitted after the invasion was over that, "For bureaucratic reasons we settled on one issue, weapons of mass destruction, because it was the one reason that everyone could agree on."[20])

The International Atomic Energy Commission officially informed the U.S. that these claims were untrue. And an official from the National Security Council characterized most of the evidence for an Iraqi reconstituted nuclear program, thriving chemical-biological production, and an Iraqi connection to Al Qaeda as "a classic case of rumit—rumor-intelligence plugged into various speeches and accepted as gospel."[21]

Although calls in the Congress for investigations followed, Cheney visited a GOP senators' lunch on June 4 and instructed his Republican colleagues to block any investigation.[22]

President Nixon was almost impeached for a burglary at the Democratic Headquarters; President Clinton was impeached for having sex with an intern. But President George W. Bush lied to the Congress and the nation, instigated an illegitimate war that killed thousands of people, invaded a sovereign nation, and violated international law. No president has ever provided such indisputable grounds for impeachment.

A CENTURY OF OIL AND WAR IN THE MIDDLE EAST

The history of the Middle East was forever altered after the First World War, when Britain conveniently appropriated Iraq and installed a king of Britain's own choosing. By the mid 1920s, Iraqi oil production was controlled by British Petroleum, Exxon, Mobil, and Shell of the U.S., and TotalFinaElf of France.[23] [24]

Eventually the British-installed Iraqi monarchy was overthrown in a bloody assassination on July 14, 1958, and General Abd al-Karim Qasim, became prime minister of Iraq. Qasim proceeded to severely antagonize the U.S. and the UK by nationalizing parts of the Iraqi Petroleum Company, by withdrawing from the anti-Soviet Baghdad Pact, and by purchasing arms from the Soviet Union.[25]

In response, the CIA formed a team to assassinate Qasim in 1959. This action failed, but the CIA cabal included one potentially important member: Saddam Hussein.[26] Following the attempted assassination, Hussein escaped to Beirut, where the CIA paid for his apartment and gave him a brief training course. The CIA then sent him to Cairo. Hussein was not a person uniformly admired by his employers. As a former U.S. official said, "He was known as having no class. He was a thug—a cutthroat."[27]

Qasim was finally killed in a Baath Party coup in July 17, 1968,[28] an action almost certainly organized by the CIA, who then provided the Iraqi National Guard with lists of suspected communists who were jailed and summarily executed. These mass killings were presided over by Hussein and were seen as a great victory by the CIA. Hussein was then installed as head of a secret intelligence wing of the Baath Party, al-Jihaz a-Khas.[29]

Despite this brief confluence of interests, in 1972 the Baath Party finally nationalized the oil holdings of British Petroleum, Exxon, and Mobil, and the U.S. and Britain lost control over Iraqi oil.

In 1979 Hussein took power in Iraq.[30]

Meanwhile, to hedge their bets, the U.S. administration was simultaneously jockeying for oil in Iran. The exceedingly popular Iranian Prime Minister Mohammed Mossadegh's first action when he took office in 1951 had been enforcement of the Oil Nationalization Bill. On August 19, 1953, the CIA and British secret intelligence service, MI6, succeeded in a coup against Mossadegh, replacing him with another CIA puppet, Shah Reza Pahlavi, who returned from exile in Italy for twenty-five years of despotic rule in Iran.[31] The Shah then invited U.S. and British oil companies back into the Iranian oil fields.[32]

But things did not proceed according to plan for the U.S. in Iran either. In 1978, the Ayatollah Khomeini, a Muslim cleric based in Paris, fomented an Iranian revolution by sending thousands of anti-American, anti-shah audiotapes to Iran. A group of Iranian students took over the American embassy on November 4, 1979, blindfolding and taking hostage some U.S. employees.

In 1980, the U.S. responded to this extremely provocative action by orchestrating a war between Iran and Iraq, in which Iraq's Saddam Hussein was called on to act as a surrogate for a vengeful U.S. administration. The Iraqi military was armed and funded by America, and the Pentagon supplied logistical support. The CIA delivered battlefield intelligence to assist the Iraqi armed forces and used a Chilean conduit to increase Hussein's supply of cluster bombs. (It must be noted, though, that the Defense Intelligence Agency (DIA) and the CIA simultaneously provided satellite intelligence to *both* Iraq and Iran, thereby inducing a kind of military stalemate.[33])

By November 1983, Reagan's Secretary of State, George Schultz, was receiving daily reports that Hussein was using poisoned gas against Iran, a violation of international conventions that Schultz sanctioned by his silence. Despite these reports, in December 1983, Schultz sent Donald Rumsfeld, then the CEO of Searle Pharmaceuticals, as an official envoy to meet with Saddam Hussein. Rumsfeld was sent specifically to promote the construction of a billion-dollar oil pipeline from Iraq to the Jordanian port of Aqaba. In a stunning conflict of interest, the pipeline in question was to be built by Bechtel . . . of which Schultz was the former president and CEO; after his term expired with the Reagan administration Schultz *returned* to Bechtel as a member of the board of directors![34] (While in office, Schultz also assisted Bechtel in China by offering to provide U.S. technology in exchange for U.S. companies to share in China's estimated 20 billion dollars' worth of nuclear power plant construction, and during a 1983 visit to India, he smoothed the way for Bechtel to participate in India's nuclear program after such cooperation had been cancelled by President Jimmy Carter. Schultz's Bechtel history began in 1974, after he left the Nixon administration as Secretary of the Treasury to become Bechtel's executive president in May 1974, at a salary of 400,000 dollars per year with a stock purchase plan that made him a multimillionaire. Shortly before he joined the Reagan team in 1982, this figure increased to 600,000 dollars with more stock options, making him one of the highest paid executives in the country.)[35]

By March 28, 1984, just as the UN was officially verifying Hussein's use of poisoned gas, Rumsfeld returned to Baghdad a second time to lobby for the Bechtel project. Despite this intense U.S. pressure for the pipeline, Hussein eventually rejected the idea. (He said that the pipeline was too close to Israel and could be damaged by military action, and that Bechtel had overpriced the deal.[36]) Hussein subsequently arranged oil deals with France, Russia, and China, severely antagonizing Bechtel and the Reagan administration.

Throughout the 1980s, in order for Iraq to be adequately armed to fight Iran, the U.S. Commerce Department encouraged U.S. companies to export 1.5 billion dollars' worth of goods capable of military applications to Iraq, while the Agriculture Department oversaw a government-guaranteed loan program that provided Hussein with billions of dollars with which to pay for weapons.[37] (The Italian Banca Nazionale del Lavoro also contributed more than 4 billion dollars in loans to Iraq in the 1980s.[38]) When Paul Freedenberg, chief export-licensing official at the U.S. Department of Commerce, asked for official guidance about the licensing policy toward Iraq when it was clear Hussein was using chemical weapons in Iran and against the Kurds, the National Security Council told him to treat these exports as "normal trade."[39]

Many U.S. exports to Iraq were even more sinister. Between the years 1985 and 1990 the United States approved 771 licenses to export biological agents (bacteria and viruses), in addition to high-tech equipment and military materiel, to Iraq. The U.S. Center for Disease Control and Prevention in Atlanta in 1985 sent Iraq three shipments of West Nile Virus for "medical research,"[40] and between 1985 and '89 the American Type Culture Collection (ATCC)—which routinely supplies bacteria and viruses to companies, academic institutions, and governments throughout the world—was given official permission to export to Iraq a variety of anthrax bacteria and other bacteria that cause meningitis, influenza, and tetanus.

The U.S. Departments of Defense, Energy, Trade, and Agriculture were also involved in arming Iraq, as were the U.S. nuclear-weapons labs—Lawrence Livermore, Los Alamos, and Sandia—which arranged visas for three Iraqi nuclear scientists, assisted with Iraq's nuclear-weapons program, and provided non-fissile explosive material.[41] According to a report issued by Dennis Kucinich, U.S. companies under permits from the first Bush administration exported to Iraq parts for a new nuclear reactor. (Nuclear reactors make plutonium, which can be used as the fuel for nuclear weapons.)[42]

As late as 1989 to 1990, live bacteriological cultures were still being sent to Iraq from the States for germ-warfare research, while American companies including Bechtel helped to construct a chemical-weapons factory and also exported hydrogen cyanide precursors. Dow Chemical sent large quantities of pesticides and chemical toxins, all precursors for chemical warfare, and Alcolac International, Inc., a Maryland company, exported thiodiglycol, a chemical used to manufacture mustard gas.[43]

OPERATION DESERT STORM

When Saddam Hussein invaded Kuwait in 1990, accusing Kuwait of drilling for oil beneath Iraq's border and of inducing low oil prices through overproduction,[44] the first Bush administration responded with a short but devastating invasion of Iraq in 1991.[45] Specifically, the U.S. launched a massively destructive attack on the infrastructure of Iraq—bridges and roads were shattered, 158 ministry buildings were bombed and destroyed, as well as power plants, water supplies, hospitals, and schools. 18,898 targets were hit from the air, fewer than 10 percent directly related to the leadership or military command.[46] This deliberate targeting and destruction of Iraqi societal infrastructure by U.S. bombs, together with UN-imposed sanctions, imposed great hardship and suffering on Iraqi citizens. According to the World Health Organization, some 5,000 Iraqi children have perished every month since the 1991 war, from malnutrition, waterborne disease, and lack of medicines. Childhood cancer induced by radioactive uranium weapons was not included in these statistics.

OPERATION IRAQI FREEDOM

Fast forward to August 2002 and the beginning of the debate about whether or not Iraq had weapons of mass destruction. Why did the Bush administration maintain so adamantly that Iraq had WMDs? *Because America supplied them.* In 2003, when Iraq finally declared its weapons inventory to the UN Security Council, it released a 12,000-page document including a list of 150 international companies that had armed Iraq for the Iran-Iraq war of the 1980s (during which over a million people were killed). Of these companies, eighty were German, fifty were subsidiaries of foreign companies that operate their weapons business out of the U.S., and twenty-four were American.

The U.S. corporations include Hewlett-Packard, DuPont, Eastman Kodak, Spectra-Physics, Honeywell, Rockwell, Tectronics, Bechtel, International Computer Systems, Unisys, Sperry, and Ti-Coating. These companies provided materials for Iraq's rocket program, planned their conventional- and nuclear-weapons program, and provided military logistics, supplies, and materials for building weapons plants.

In a 1987 statement whose irony quotient grows with each passing decade, Assistant Secretary of State Richard Armitage stood by the American decision to supply Iraq with weapons of mass destruction: "We cannot stand to see Iraq defeated."[47]

THE ECONOMICS OF WAR

OR THE CHARMED CIRCLE OF AMERICAN CAPITALISM

In the counsels of government, we must guard against the acquisition of unwarranted influence, whether sought or unsought, by the military industrial complex. The potential for misplaced power exists, and will persist. We must never let the weight of this combination endanger our liberties or democratic processes.

—President Dwight Eisenhower, January 1961

Without stretching very hard at all, the 2003 invasion of Iraq can be seen as a business deal—a kind of private economic stimulus package—orchestrated by and for Bush ideologues and their corporate friends in the military-industrial complex. In this charmed circle of American capitalism, Lockheed Martin-, Boeing-, and Raytheon manufactured munitions destroy Iraq; George Schultz's Bechtel Corporation and Dick Cheney's Halliburton rebuild Iraq; and Iraqi oil pays for it all.[48]

Looking first at the arms bazaar that has pumped new vigor into the moribund defense industry, consider:

- The U.S. Apache helicopter shot down by Iraqi farmers cost 22 million dollars
- Each Bradley Infantry Fighting Vehicle cost 1.2 million dollars
- Each Tomahawk cruise missile cost 1 million dollars

Talk about economic stimulus. Bombing the infrastructure and people of Iraq makes tax rebates and fiddling with interest rates look like games for children. First, there's the guarantee that replacement orders will promptly be put in for all expended weapons. And then there's the free publicity and marketing! What better way than an actual war for weapons manufacturers to demonstrate the mighty and effective killing power of their "products." (These latest weapons would normally have been featured at the arms bazaar of the Paris Air Show in June 2003, however U.S. corporations and government felt obliged to boycott the show because of the French reticence to support their illegal Iraqi invasion.[49])

The already-inflated Pentagon budget rose from 294 billion dollars in 2000 to 392.2 billion dollars in 2003, *without including the costs of the Iraqi conflict.* President Bush asked Congress for an additional 75 billion dollars to finance the Iraqi invasion, an amount projected to cover only the first six months in Iraq; a more realistic estimate to cover the whole event—destruction and reconstruction—is nearer 200 billion dollars. In fact, as the Iraq quagmire drags on, estimates for the monthly occupation were increased in July from 2 billion to 4 billion dollars per month, with no end in sight.[50]

Jeff Madrick of the *New York Times* wrote, "even before the war started, the Defense Department has been spending money so fast it can't keep track of it." Since Bush took office in 2001, military spending has grown almost 20 percent.[51] From generating surpluses of 5 to 6 trillion dollars over ten years, the U.S., because of massive military spending (and huge tax cuts for the very rich), could end up with a deficit of almost 2 trillion dollars by 2013.[52] (These estimates became worse when a study released in March by the General Accounting Office found that the Pentagon could not account for more than one trillion dollars, and the army had lost track of fifty-six planes, thirty-two tanks and thirty-six Javelin missile command launch units.[53]) Senator Robert Byrd has noted that the United States spends more on defense than "all other 18 members of NATO, plus China, plus Russia, and plus the remaining rogue states combined." Byrd continues, "In an age when we talk about smart bombs and smart missiles and smart soldiers, any talk of smart budgets has gone out the window."[54]

The U.S. armament industry is the country's second most subsidized industry next to agriculture. And most of the weapons sold throughout the world to friend and foe alike are manufactured in the

U.S. (Of the world's ten major purchasers of U.S. weapons, five are from the Middle East—Egypt: 1.1 billion dollars, Kuwait: 1 billion dollars, Saudi Arabia: 885 million dollars, Oman: 826 million dollars, and Israel: 885 million dollars.)[55]

A quick look at three of the major military corporations readily illustrates the economic bonanza the war in Iraq represents to them.

LOCKHEED MARTIN

Lockheed Martin, the world's largest weapons contractor, made the F-117 stealth attack fighter that participated in the opening salvo of "Operation Iraqi Freedom" by bombing leadership targets. Its new Paveway II bomb, guided to its target by a sensor, was showcased in this attack, as well as its PAC-3 Patriot missile. In early March 2003, just before the Iraqi invasion, the army gave Lockheed Martin 100 million dollars for 212 PAC-3s to be used in Iraq.

Not coincidentally, Lockheed Martin played a significant role in organizing the Iraqi invasion. Bruce Jackson, former LM vice president, chaired the 2002 Coalition for the Liberation of Iraq, formed with the explicit support of the Bush administration. Jackson also helped draft the statement signed by the ten "New Europe" members in support of the war, deriding France, Germany, and other members of "Old Europe" because they would not support Bush's push to invade Iraq. Lockheed Martin receives, on average, 105 dollars annually from each U.S. taxpayer to support its weapons construction.[56]

BOEING

The world's second largest weapons maker made the updated B52 used to deliver both smart bombs and the precision-guided missiles in Iraq. They made the Joint Direct Attack Munitions (JDAM) at 22,000 dollars each, and converted older "dumb" bombs into smart bombs by adding guidance devices. (Officials estimated that 80 percent of the bombs used in the 2003 Iraqi invasion were precision-guided bombs.)[57]

Boeing spokesperson Robert Algarotti said that from September

2001 to October 2002 their JDAM program earned them more than 1 billion dollars in Pentagon contracts (clearly in anticipation of the war), and they planned to increase JDAM production 40 percent by summer 2003. (Boeing also sells these bombs to five other countries.[58]) Boeing's C-17 transport plane was used extensively in 2003 to lift tanks, helicopters, Humvees, and Bradley fighting vehicles. The company has since been awarded a contract to build sixty more C-17s at a cost of 9.7 billion dollars.[59]

RAYTHEON

Another huge military contractor, Raytheon is involved in 4000 different weapons programs. It provided the Tomahawk missiles at a cost of 600,000 dollars each for the 2003 Iraqi invasion. At 1,000,000 dollars each, their AIM-65 Maverick air-to-surface missile is, according to Raytheon, the most widely used precision-guided munition in the free world. Raytheon also makes the AIM-9 Sidewinder air-to-air missile and the AIM-120 Advanced Medium Range air-to-air missile, all of which were used in Iraq.

Raytheon specializes in radar, surveillance, and targeting systems used extensively on most U.S.-produced combat aircraft. It makes the 5000-pound "bunker buster" GBU-28-most notoriously used in efforts to "neutralize" Osama Bin Laden in the underground caves where he was thought to be hiding—and the TOW, Maverick, and Javelin missiles, which were all used in Afghanistan. It also built the sensors and radars for the unmanned and manned reconnaissance planes used in Afghanistan and Iraq.

Because they benefit so inordinately from belligerent U.S. foreign policy, firms like Lockheed Martin, Boeing, and Raytheon cultivate ties to the administration that ensure the orders for new weapons keep flowing. They essentially lobby for war, perpetually.

DEFENSE POLICY BOARD ADVISORY COMMITTEE

The Defense Policy Board Advisory Committee offers an excellent example of the invasive and malignant influence that military corporations exert on government policy. The composition of the Board demonstrates the synergistic nexus between the conservative right or PNAC members in the Bush administration and the military corporations.

Douglas Feith, a former Reagan administration official and a member of PNAC, selected the thirty members of the present Defense Policy Board,[60]—originally designed to offer impartial analysis of defense issues to the administration. Of these thirty, nine have significant affiliations with companies that collectively took 76 billion dollars in military contracts during the years 2001–2002. Four of the members are registered lobbyists; one of these represents two of the three largest military contractors in the country. These board members disclose their business interests to the Pentagon each year, but the public has no access to these records.[61]

The DPB was chaired by Richard Perle, a close advisor to Donald Rumsfeld, until March 2003, when Perle resigned under allegations of conflict of interest because he represented companies doing business with the Department of Defense.[62] The influential DPB meets only two days every three months and neither writes reports nor votes on issues. However it does advise on Pentagon weapon purchases. The board's general defense and weapons reports are classified and summarized for the Secretary of Defense.[63]

Prior to the second Bush administration, the board was relatively bipartisan and advisory. Under Bush II and Donald Rumsfeld, it quickly became heavily involved in actual policy decisions, despite the fact that it is not mandated with an official role.[64] Topics discussed range from intelligence briefings delivered by the Defense Intelligence Agency (DIA), to the Defense Advanced Research Project, the Total Information Awareness project that the Pentagon seeks to establish to spy on American citizens (research for this project is being conducted by private contractors, some of whom have ties to individuals on the Defense Policy Board), to North Korea and Iran.[65] While members are not directly paid for their time, the financial benefits of membership are incalculable—as are the opportunities for clear judgment to be lost amidst opportunities for personal gain.

Richard Perle himself offers the most obvious example:

At the time he chaired the Defense Policy Board, Perle was also employed as an advisor and paid 750,000 dollars by a soon-to-become-bankrupt telecommunications company called Global Crossing Ltd. Based in Bermuda, Global Crossing wanted the Committee on Foreign Investment in the United States (CFIUS) to approve sale of Global Crossing's overseas subsidiaries to a Chinese consortium.[66] The FBI and Pentagon opposed this sale, as the company's fiber-optics network would then be placed in Chinese hands; the decision about whether to block the sale on national security grounds ultimately rested in the hands of the CFIUS, where it could be strongly influenced by the Defense Policy Board, *chaired by Perle.*[67]

- Perle is also employed by Goldman Sachs to advise its clients on "investment opportunities" in postwar Iraq, making Perle's consistent and persuasive advocacy of the Iraq invasion look anything but objective, and his close relationship with Secretary of Defense Donald Rumsfeld seem self-serving at best.
- Perle's venture-capital company, Trireme partners, invests in defense products and homeland security. Trireme has raised 45 million dollars in capital, almost half of which comes from Boeing.
- Perle is a director of the British-based Autonomy Corporation, which manufactures a high-tech eavesdropping technology capable of monitoring hundreds of thousands of e-mail messages and telephone conversations simultaneously. The Department of Homeland Security, the Secret Service, and the National Security Agency, among others, have all given Autonomy huge contracts. Perle also owns 75,000 shares of Autonomy Corporation.

Unabashedly touting his ability to help his corporate clients, Perle stated in an affidavit on March 7, 2003, that his position on the Defense Policy Board gives him "unique perspective on and intimate knowledge of the national defense and security issues that will be raised by the CFIUS review process." Subsequently, however, under scrutiny by *New York Times* reporter Stephen Labaton, Perle said, "I am not using public office for private gain, because the Defense Policy Review Board has nothing to do with the CFIUS process." When Labaton asked him about his "unique perspective and intimate knowledge," Perle replied disingenuously that he had not noticed that phrase—that it "was drafted by lawyers, and frankly I did not notice it."[68]

Other significant players on the Defense Policy Board include:

Retired Admiral David Jeremiah, former vice chairman of the Joint Chiefs of Staff. A director or advisor to five major corporations that received over 10 billion dollars in 2002 Pentagon contracts, he also sat on the board of Getronics Government Solutions, which was bought by DigitalNet in December 2002. Richard Perle is a director of DigitalNet Holdings Inc.

Retired Air Force General Ronald Fogleman. Fogleman sits on the boards of directors of various companies allied to the Pentagon, including Rolls-Royce North America, North American Airlines, AAR Corporation, and the MITRE Corporation—the latter has longstanding ties to the U.S. air force and other Defense Department branches and profited from more than 900 million dollars in Pentagon contracts in 2002.

Retired General Jack Sheehan. With 35 years of Marine Corps service including stints as NATO's Supreme Allied Commander Atlantic, and Commander in Chief, U.S. Atlantic Command, Sheehan retired in 1997 and joined Bechtel in 1998 as a senior vice president. One of the largest construction firms in the world, Bechtel was awarded over 1 billion dollars in defense contracts in 2002 and was awarded the major government contract worth 680 billion dollars to rebuild Iraq after its devastation. Sheehan supervises Bechtel's extraordinary global outreach, operating in Europe, Africa, the Middle East, and Southwest Asia.

James Woolsey. A PNAC member and former CIA director, Woolsey is a principle participant in the Paladin Capital Group, a venture capital firm that resembles Perle's Trireme Partners. The Paladin Group solicits investment for homeland security firms. Since July 2002, Woolsey has also been vice president of Booz Allen Hamilton, which obtained 680 million dollars in Pentagon contracts that same year.

Woolsey originally worked for the law firm Shea & Gardner, a registered agent for the Iraqi National Congress (INC), the group of Iraqi expatriates Pentagon-picked to govern Iraq under U.S. control after the invasion ended.[69] Woolsey lobbied for the passage of the Iraq Liberation Act mandating Iraqi regime change, which was formalized by the U.S. Congress in 1998; 100 million dollars were allocated to the INC.[70]

Woolsey is an extreme example of the influential neoconservatives. Labeling the cold war "World War III," he calls for a World War IV, during which America and England would attack Islamacists, Iranian theocrats, Baath Party "fascists" in Syria and Iraq, Bin Laden of Al Qaeda, Hosni Mubarak of Egypt, and the ruling Saud family in Saudi Arabia.[71] Woolsey consistently repeated on talk shows that Hussein was behind the destruction of the World Trade Center and the anthrax letters to members of Congress, although U.S. intelligence agencies continue to deny those connections. Nevertheless, he actively and publicly cultivated the assumption—held by over half the people in the U.S. by late 2002—that Hussein was linked to the 9/11 attacks and that, consequently, war on Iraq was justified.[72]

William Owen. As former vice chairman of the Joint Chiefs of Staff, Owen was responsible for the introduction of commercial high technology into the U.S. Department of Defense. He sits on the boards of five companies that received more than 600 million dollars in military contracts in 2002. He is president, chief operating officer, and vice chair of Science Applications International Corporation, one of the ten largest military contractors in the world, and is ubiquitously represented on boards of other firms including Symantec, Nortel Networks, ViaSat, and Polycom.

Harold Brown, former Secretary of Defense under President Jimmy Carter. Brown is a partner at Warburg Pincus LLC, a member of the board of Philip Morris Companies—with 146 million dollars in Pentagon contracts in 2002—and a trustee of the RAND Corporation—who won 83 million dollars' worth of contracts in 2002.

James Schlesinger. Former CIA director, Secretary of Energy, and Secretary of Defense, Schlesinger is a senior advisor at Lehman

Brothers and the chair of the board of trustees at MITRE Corporation, which received 474 million dollars in military contracts in 2002.[73]

THE ECONOMICS OF RECONSTRUCTION

OR THE CORPORATE INVASION OF IRAQ

"Any time you have an emergency response driven by time, the opportunity for fraud, waste and abuse is huge. And when the opportunity is that great, it will occur."[74]

—Thomas D. Thatcher II, head of the consulting firm that monitored the integrity of New York's Ground Zero cleanup

Now we will turn our focus from the lucrative destruction of Iraq and redirect it toward the lucrative rebuilding of that desecrated country.

Before the U.S. invasion, the Iraqi people owned their country: their oil, their ministries, their education department, schools, universities, roads, and bridges. Nefarious planning to take control of all of these started well before March 2003. Documents released in July 2003 under the U.S. Freedom of Information Act show that an energy task force organized by Vice President Dick Cheney was already at work in March 2001 *(before the attack on the World Trade Center)* examining Iraq's oil assets. The documents include maps of Iraqi oil fields, pipelines, refineries, and terminals. Another document titled "Foreign Suitors for Iraqi Oilfield Contracts" compiles a list of the countries interested in ownership of Iraq's oil.[75]

After the invasion, as Naomi Klein wrote in *The Nation,* Iraq "is being treated as a blank slate on which the most ideological Washington neoliberals can design their dream economy: fully privatized, foreign-owned and open for business."[76] Immediately after the war's end, a 4.8 million dollar management contract to restore the port of Umm Qasr went to a U.S. company, Stevedoring Services of America, and the country's airports, roads, bridges, printing facilities, water, and oil were put on the auction block. (Klein calls this "mass theft disguised as charity, privatization without representation."[77])

The whole country is now for sale, and corruption and conflict of interest know no bounds. Californian Republican Congressman Darrell Issa, to take but one small example, is pushing for installation of a U.S. CDMA cell-phone system made by Qualcomm—a corporation that is a generous donor to Issa.[78] And, as Klein documents in her *Nation* article, a group of Iraqi exiles have been advising the U.S. State Department on how to implement the privatization of oil so that it appears not to be U.S.-based.[79] (Investors are openly predicting that once Iraqi privatization commences Iran, Saudi Arabia, and Kuwait will be forced to compete by privatizing their oil.) As Klein writes, "America may have bombed its way into a whole new Free Trade Zone."[80]

In the largest reconstruction effort since the post-World War II Marshall Plan,[81] a country pulverized by two massive bombardments twelve years apart, which has suffered from a series of iniquitous sanctions of drugs, food, and equipment imposed by a vindictive U.S.-dominated UN, which has lost approximately 5000 children monthly from malnutrition, waterborne diseases, and lack of medical therapy since the 1991 invasion, is set to be taken over by avaricious multinational corporations who plan to "rebuild" the shattered country to the tune of up to 100 billion dollars and thence to "own" it. The rebuilding will be largely financed by American taxpayers, though Iraqi oil money may also be brought into play. "We're going to use the assets of the people of Iraq, especially their oil assets, to benefit their people," said Secretary of State Colin Powell in March 2003.[82]

Even before the invasion of Iraq commenced, the U.S. Agency for International Development (USAID) secretly asked six companies to submit bids for a 900 million dollar government contract to rebuild Iraq's infrastructure: roads, bridges, ports, hospitals, schools, water systems. These lucky companies—Bechtel Group, Inc., Halliburton Co., Fluor Corp, Louis Berger Group, Inc., Parsons Corp, and Washington Group International—have all contributed significant amounts of money to political parties and politicians in recent years: a combined total of 3.6 million dollars between 1999 and 2002.[83] Confidential documents show that the companies will now be paid on a "cost plus fixed fee" basis—after the cost of a project is established, the contractor is guaranteed to recover the entire cost plus a fee that is a fixed percentage of the cost: 8–10 percent if not more.[84]

This fast-track, noncompetitive construction bidding, orchestrated by the Bush administration, has already been called into question by members of Congress. Congressmen Henry A. Waxman of California and John D. Dingell of Michigan have asked the General Accounting Office to examine the bidding process at USAID, saying that, "Because the administration has released few, if any, details about these contracts, little is known about the authority to enter into the contracts, or whether proper procurement procedures were followed."[85] (Other countries are annoyed that the administration is allocating contracts only to U.S. companies—they also want part of the action. But the decision to use only U.S. contractors was justified by the head of USAID, who cited time constraints and security clearances as reasons for not opening the bidding process up.)

The head of USAID, doling out these dream contracts and endowed with ultimate fiduciary responsibility for the reconstruction, is former Massachusetts Turnpike Authority chair Andrew Natsios, who, from 2001 to 2002, was in charge of the Big Dig in Boston. This project, conceived by former Congressman and House Speaker Tip O'Neil as a legacy to his beloved hometown and involving moving Boston's major highways underground, was originally priced at 2.5 billion dollars in 1985. Actual costs, under Natsios's latter oversight, had reached 14.6 billion dollars by 2003. (Although he was chair of the Massachusetts Turnpike Authority for only one year, Natsios refused to take legal action against the contractor for its misuse of taxpayer money, and he fired the deputy general counsel who recommended that he do so.)[86]

THE LUCKY WINNERS

The top two beneficiaries of the Iraq reconstruction (aka George W. Bush's economic stimulus plan), not surprisingly, have long-standing connections and ongoing business dealings with Natsios and the Bush administration.

Bechtel

The hands-down champion in the Iraq reconstruction sweepstakes is the massive construction company Bechtel, originally scheduled to receive 680 million dollars over eighteen months to "rebuild power generation facilities and electrical grids, hospitals, schools, administrative buildings, major irrigation projects, essential transport links, airport facilities and water and sewage systems" in Iraq. Subsequently they were granted an additional 350 million dollars for the ongoing reconstruction.[87] (Bechtel plans to subcontract more than half of these projects, and, in a feeding frenzy, companies from all over the world are applying for a piece of the action; Bechtel's website explaining the subcontracting process had received 71,000 hits by May 21, 2003.[88])

Bechtel has an interesting and rather dangerous history. A San Francisco-based, privately owned firm with 2002 revenues of 13.3 billion dollars, it has been in the construction industry for 105 years, with a history of 20,000 projects in 140 countries. Interestingly, the Bin Laden family is a substantial investor in a private equity firm founded by Bechtel.[89] It is a major nuclear corporation, originally involved in the Manhattan Project, which made the first three atomic bombs. It constructed the "doomsday town" that was blown apart in a nuclear test. It built and/or designed over half the nuclear power plants in America, and services two thirds of them. It designed the first commercial nuclear reprocessing plant, in West Valley, NY, which proved to be an ecological catastrophe.

Bechtel is currently mining Yucca Mountain in Nevada for possible storage of the country's high-level nuclear waste. It is involved in the construction of two nuclear reactors in volatile North Korea. It manages the Nevada nuclear test site, which may become operational in the near future. And it holds the contract for nuclear waste management and "clean-up" at some of the major DOE sites.[90] Bechtel also built the San Francisco BART rail system, the massive Hoover dam, and is one of the top ten privatizers of water in the world. (Although it is located in a dry and desolate desert region, Iraq has two major river systems—the Tigris and the Euphrates—and a sophisticated system of dams and river-control projects, which might cause one to wonder: Is the "privatization"/theft of water on the Bush agenda along with oil?)

Those who have been following closely know that Bechtel is also the same company responsible for the massive cost overruns on Boston's Big Dig—the company against whom Natsios, much to the annoyance of the Boston establishment, refused to take legal action. George Schultz was a prominent Bechtel board member during most of the Big Dig years. He was Bechtel's CEO during the eight years between his service as Nixon's Secretary of Treasury and Reagan's Secretary of State. Schultz then returned to Bechtel after his Reagan term, as a board member and senior counsel—roles he continues to hold as over a billion dollars in taxpayer-funded business are steered Bechtel's way. Schultz, interestingly, was chair of the Committee for the Liberation of Iraq, a fiercely pro-war group with close ties to the ultraconservatives in the White House. In this latter capacity, Schultz penned a September 2003 *Washington Post* piece titled "Act Now; The Danger is Immediate," a directive that takes on a very different, conflict-ridden meaning when Schultz is wearing his Bechtel helmet.

Schultz is also the chairman of the International Council of JPMorgan Chase, a corporation that lent Hussein's regime 500 million dollars in 1983 for weapons;[91] and Bechtel was one of the U.S. companies that sold Iraq the weapons they bought with this money (specifically equipment for a factory to manufacture precursors for chemical weapons). Thus, Secretary of State Schultz helped craft policy requiring the manufacture of weapons for Iraq; JPMorgan Chase, a company later chaired by George Schultz, helped finance the purchase of these weapons by Iraq; and Bechtel, while Schultz sat on the board of directors, got the contract to "rebuild" Iraq—a one-man show! (Reagan's Defense Secretary, Casper Weinberger, also sits on the board of Bechtel, and so did former and now deceased CIA director William Casey.[92])

Halliburton/KBR

The Halliburton subsidiary Kellogg, Brown and Root (KBR) was awarded an open-ended 7 billion dollar contract by the Army Corps of Engineers to fight oil fires and reconstruct oil fields in Iraq after the invasion. (This despite the fact that only eight gas wells and pipelines had been set ablaze during the conflict, and all but one had already been extinguished by the time the contract was made.[93]) Amazingly, KBR did not need to bid for the contract, perhaps because

KBR itself, a Dallas-based oil company with a 12.5 billion dollar intake in 2002, wrote the army's contingency plan for the Iraqi oil-well repair.

Kellogg, Brown and Root has also been hired to build and maintain temporary military bases in Iraq, and, according to William Rivers Pitt, will almost certainly be contracted to build permanent bases in Iraq, from which attacks on other countries can be launched.[94] (KBR built twelve permanent bases in Kosovo, and the holding pens or cages for political prisoners in Guantánamo Bay at a cost of 300 million dollars.)

But KBR does not just repair oil wells and build bases; it holds another, even more important contract with the Pentagon. In 1992, the Defense Department hired Kellogg, Brown and Root to write a classified report on how private companies could assist the Pentagon logistically in the world. Soon after this report was produced, the Pentagon's Logistics Civil Augmentation Program or "Logcap" awarded the first five-year Logcap contract to KBR, essentially turning KBR into what Dan Baum of the *New York Times* calls, a "for-profit ministry of Public Works for the Army." Under Logcap, KBR is on call to the army to perform nonmilitary functions once conducted by army members: delivering mail, repairing trucks, cleaning up hazardous waste, peeling potatoes, doing laundry, fixing and cleaning sewers, repairing generators, and controlling the airspace overhead. KBR is authorized by Logcap to spend whatever it needs for each job, and to add a profit ranging from 1 to 9 percent on top.

Privatizing by the military is seen by some analysts as good: "You want the 82nd Airborne training to kill people and blow things up, not cleaning latrines or trimming hedges," said one analyst cited in the *New York Times Magazine,* and General Barry McCaffrey said, "I am unabashedly an admirer of outsourcing. There's very few things in life you can't outsource."[95] On the other hand, Representative Janice Schakowsky, Democrat from Chicago, says, "We talk a lot in Congress about how many troops are there and for how long, but not at all about the contractors. They don't have to follow the same chain of command, the military code of conduct may or may not apply, the accountability is absent and the transparency is absent—but the money keeps flowing."[96]

Hundreds of private companies, ranging from small consulting firms to multinationals, are now employed by the Pentagon, at a cost of 100 billion dollars a year to the taxpayers. From 1992 to 2002 the Pentagon entered into 3000 contracts with private firms. Halliburton now provides the logistics for every major American military deployment. (Even the ROTC—Reserve Officer Training Corps programs—at over 200 U.S. universities have been taken over by private corporations.[97])

But private companies provide little quality assurance, and often cut corners to save money. They have also been known to overbill for hours, and to use poorly trained workers, even when lives are at stake.[98] A former DynCorp employee accused the company of cutting costs by hiring waiters and security guards to work as mechanics on army helicopters. Halliburton, which took in 2.2 billion dollars for troop support in the Balkans, boosted its bottom line by charging the army 85 dollars for a piece of plywood that cost 14 dollars, and cleaning offices four times in one day, according to the General Accounting Office.[99]

Whether one agrees with the Logcap/privatization approach or not, few people would feel that the government should allow massive contracts such as KBR's to be signed off on by individuals with a personal stake in the contracted company. And yet that is exactly what has happened. In 1992, Dick Cheney, in his capacity as head of the Defense Department, was responsible for hiring KBR to write the classified report on privatization. In 1995 Cheney became CEO of Halliburton, Kellogg, Brown and Root's parent company, and he remained there until leaving to run as Bush's vice president in 2000. "Clearly Dick gave Halliburton some advantages—doors would open," said Bob Peeler, a Halliburton vice president. Now the country's vice president, Cheney received a "package" of 30 million dollars in stock options upon leaving Halliburton, and the company is paying him up to one million dollars per year in deferred compensation following his resignation as CEO in 2000. (See Chapter 4: Corporate Madness and the Death Merchants for more detail.)[100] (As a side note, between 1997 and 2000, during Cheney's tenure as Halliburton CEO, two of Halliburton's subsidiaries sold Saddam Hussein 73 million dollars' worth of oil-field supplies, in clear violation of

U.S.-imposed sanctions making it illegal for any U.S. company to do business with Iraq.[101])

According to the *New York Times,* much of the business done by Halliburton depends upon foreign customers receiving loans from U.S. banks, and these loans are guaranteed by the U.S. government's trade-enhancing Import-Export Bank. As an illustration of Dick Cheney's ongoing contacts and influence, consider this: In the five years before Dick Cheney became CEO of Halliburton, the IE bank guaranteed loans of 100 million dollars so that foreign companies could buy the services of Halliburton. During his five years as CEO, that figure grew to a massive 1.5 billion dollars.[102] Halliburton is now scheduled to receive 1.7 billion dollars for the Iraqi program, in the no-bid appropriation of contracts by the Bush administration.[103]

And other lucky winners . . .

As mentioned above, Stevedoring Services of America, which made 1 billion dollars in sales in 2002, was awarded a 4.8 million dollar contract by Natsios on March 24, 2003 for "assessment and management" of the vital Umm Qasr port in Southern Iraq.[104]

- International Resources Group, was awarded a 7 million dollar, ninety-day contract to manage relief and rebuilding in postwar Iraq, including education, agriculture, civil society, and infrastructure.
- DynCorp, which donated 100,00 dollars in 2002 to the Republican Party, won a multimillion-dollar contract from the U.S. State Department to train the new Iraqi police force. (The company is hiring only U.S. nationals for the job. There is no stipulation that these employees must speak Arabic.) DynCorp also runs the core of the Bosnian police force, functions as the personnel guard of Afghan President Hamid Karzai, and is in charge of the border posts between the U.S. and Mexico. It polices many of the Pentagon's testing ranges, and it guards the fleet of Air Force One presidential planes and helicopters.[105]

  But DynCorp has an unsavory history. Its personnel in Bosnia contracted to the UN police service were implicated in buying and selling prostitutes, and several employees were accused of videotaping the rape of one of the women. DynCorp has also been heavily involved in spraying vast quantities of herbicides over Colombia to kill the cocoa crops; the pesticides were later implicated in causing illnesses in humans and livestock and killing children.[106]

And running the reconstruction show . . .

The first person chosen by the Pentagon to oversee the transition period in Iraq after the invasion ceased was Lieutenant General Jay Garner, a personal friend of Donald Rumsfeld's, who moved from the military to the presidency of SYColeman, a defense contractor that stood to make profits from the Iraqi war. Garner is an associate of the Jewish Institute for National Security Affairs, a right wing, pro-Likud think tank that has long advocated the overthrow of the Iraqi regime.[107]

The person chosen to take over the management of Iraq when Jay Garner left was L. Paul Bremmer III, who left a new unit of insurance broker Marsh & McLennan, an organization created a month after 9/11 to profit from the new concern around catastrophic risk.[108]

The person chosen to oversee oil production in Iraq is a former chief executive of the Shell Oil Company, Philip J. Carroll. After leaving Shell, he was chairman and CEO of Fluor Corporation, a construction company that will be party to the lucrative reconstruction in Iraq.[109] He is paid more than 1 million dollars a year in retirement benefits from Fluor, and he currently owns one million shares in the company.[110]

The person chosen to head the Iraq Survey Group looking for "weapons of mass destruction" is David Kay, a recent and frequent commentator on U.S. television who called for regime change in Iraq, and former vice president of a San Diego based defense contractor, Science Applications International Corporation (SAIC) which was deeply implicated in the current war in Iraq including a contract of 650 million dollars for services and support of the U.S. army, running a U.S.-funded radio station—Voice of the New Iraq in Umm Qasr—and helping to provide senior advisors to the occupational authorities in Baghdad.[111]

THE WAR AMERICA DIDN'T SEE

As an ex-post-facto justification for the invasion of Iraq, President Bush, as he spoke from the deck of the USS *Abraham Lincoln* in May 2003, invoked the "last phone calls, the cold murder of children and the searches in the rubble" of the victims of September 11, 2001.[112] Leaving aside the specious connection between the World Trade victims and the government of Iraq, what of Iraqi children and civilians? Excerpts from the Australian and British media tell the story that was all but unreported to the American people, who paid for the invasion of Iraq with their tax dollars and were ultimately responsible for the carnage in their name.

According to Robert Fisk in an article in the April 2, 2003, London-based newspaper *The Independent*, in one twenty-four-hour period, the Al Hillah hospital had received thirty-three corpses and 180 injured people. A videotape showed "a father holding out pieces of his baby, shouting 'cowards, cowards,' " while "two lorryloads of bodies including women in flowered dresses could be seen outside the Hillah hospital." Dr. Nazem el-Adeli stated that most of the patients were victims of cluster bombs that were dropped by the Americans. The hospital mortuary was "a butcher's shop of chopped up corpses."[113]

Reporting in the *Sydney Morning Herald* on April 4, 2003, Paul McGeough wrote, "In the operating theatre doctors fought to save three lives—a woman with serious head injuries, a man who had holes the size of bread-and-butter plates in his abdomen, and a man with much of his abdominal organs beside him on the operating table."[114] He quoted an Iraqi civilian as saying, "I could see the American flag on the tank 500 metres down the road from us. There was no warning. There was a noise and a lot of shouting on the bus, then peoples' heads seemed to snap away from their bodies, and many of them were dead. . . . .We don't know what kind of weapon did this. Their bodies were completely destroyed, but the bus wasn't. Peoples' heads were severed and the viscera was outside their bodies; their limbs were cut off."[115]

Charles Hanely wrote in the *Sydney Morning Herald* on April 7, 2003, that doctors were amputating limbs without adequate anesthetics and antibiotics. They were using ketamine, a five-minute anesthetic, to perform amputations. In Baghdad at the height of the slaughter, about 100 to 200 casualties were arriving at the city hospitals each day, and doctors were unable to cope with the burns, severe internal organ injuries and amputations.[116]

Three days later, Paul McGeough reported, "If it is possible to have a nightmare within a nightmare, Kindi Hospital is it. The horror of war in Baghdad is distressing, but it is not possible to walk into this hospital without questioning the very essence of humanity as we know it." A surgeon said that there had been a marked change in the hospital's workload since the U.S. troops had moved into Baghdad: "We're now getting not just shrapnel wounds but pieces of people. These are wounds from missiles and rockets." In the hospital morgue lies a pile of twenty-five to thirty corpses on the floor. Some faces are scorched black, others have "clothes ripped off, their intestines hanging out. Limbs protrude from the pile, lying across the corpses, and it is impossible to tell who is who. . . . Patients keep arriving in a procession of racing ambulances and battered taxis. An army of exhausted, weepy support staff help them onto trolleys, scattering the flies that feed on the blood of the last patient."[117]

According to Bob Graham in the June 19, 2003, London *Evening Standard* in Baghdad, young American troops reached states of panic in the terror of the moment, not able to distinguish between civilians and fighters. The behavior of some became erratic and uncontrollable as they mowed down civilians giving vent to their terror. According to one soldier, "When there were civilians there, we did the mission that had to be done. When they were there, they were at the wrong spot, so they were considered enemy."[118]

(Several U.S. neurophysiological labs funded by federal money are currently working on a morning-after pill that soldiers would be able to take to ablate regret, remorse, pain, or guilt associated with the memory of their killing the day before.[119])

Iraqi Hospitals operated for months after their electricity and water supplies had been destroyed. Many doctors failed to report to work because of random looting and threats to their very survival. Once the official war ended, the hospitals were looted, medical records were stolen, and in some hospitals surgical instruments were taken from operating theaters, even as U.S. troops sat by on their tanks.[120]

Although the USAID paid the World Health Organization (WHO) 10 million dollars to identify the Iraqi peoples' immediate health needs, not even basics such as electrical generators for the hospitals were provided. The WHO has since calculated that an additional 120 million to 180 million dollars will be required to rebuild Iraq's public health system.[121]

How many Iraqi people were slaughtered by the U.S.? General Tommy Franks had the temerity to say "you know, we don't do body counts."[122] However, there is evidence to suggest that 5000 to 10,000 civilians were killed, and tens of thousands were injured.[123] And the figures keep mounting as the fighting goes on. Estimates as late as September 2003 put the Iraqi civilian death toll as high as 37,137.[124] The powerful munitions used by the American and British forces during the official invasion probably left thousands of civilians buried, burned, or pulverized. But, according to Captain Frank Thorp of the Navy, chief military spokesperson at the Central command headquarters, "We cannot look at combat as a scorecard"—lingering on the battlefield to count the enemy dead "is too time consuming and frankly too risky."[125] There are apparently no figures at all for Iraqi military casualties.[126]

In the wake of the war, innocent citizens continue to die. With water and sewage systems destroyed by bombing and looting, most people in Iraq's cities do not have access to safe drinking water; human sewage is contaminating the water and leading to infectious diseases including cholera and typhoid.[127] There has been a doubling of childhood diarrheal-related diseases. And, horrifyingly, unrestrained looting took place at some of Iraq's 1000 abandoned nuclear sites. Up to 400 looters per day sacked the Al-Tuwaitha 120-acre nuclear complex south of Baghdad. They emptied and stole buckets and drums for domestic purposes—milking cows; storing water, milk, and vegetables—containers which had previously held 300–400 kilograms of radioactive natural and low enriched uranium and uranium dioxide. Drums containing deadly thorium, cesium, plutonium, and cobalt were also tampered with. Children bathed in radioactive water, and desperate families took up habitation at the nuclear facilities. According to the International Atomic Energy Agency inspectors, in 1991 this site contained 1.8 tons of low enriched uranium and 500 tons of natural uranium; it is estimated that 20 percent of this material is now gone.[128]

The U.S. did finally allow IAEA inspectors to enter these nuclear facilities, but only to document radiation at the site and to estimate what has been stolen. They were not allowed to survey levels of radioactive contamination in the villages, nor to document the illnesses or to arrange diagnosis and treatment for exposed patients.[129] Among the exposed populations at these nuclear sites, physicians are noting the classic signs of acute radiation symptoms in their patients—shortness of breath, nose bleeds, rashes, and nausea. If these people do not succumb within two weeks of acute radiation illness (massive hemorrhage or overwhelming infections), many of them are destined to develop cancers five to sixty years from now.

Apart from the immediate threat to the health of Iraqi civilians, the enriched uranium from the Al-Tuwaitha site could be processed into weapons-grade material. Another radioactive site that was looted was the Baghdad Nuclear Research Facility, which housed deadly spent radioactive elements: cesium and cobalt. These intensely radioactive materials could be fashioned into dirty bombs.[130] It is hard to see how the Bush administration reconciles leaving these materials unprotected, with their stated goal of preventing nuclear terrorism.

Chapter One

THE TRAGEDY OF WASTED OPPORTUNITIES

The hidden hand of the market will never work without a hidden fist. McDonald's cannot flourish without McDonnell Douglas, the designer of the F-15. And the hidden fist that keeps the world safe for Silicon Valley's technologies is called the United States Army, Air Force, Navy, and Marine Corps.

—Thomas Friedman, *New York Times Magazine,* March 28, 1999

IMAGINE THIS: The cold war is over. A wise and visionary young American president, elected in 1992, decides that now is the time to rid the world of nuclear weapons. Six months into his first term he flies to Moscow to meet with a pliable Russian president, who agrees to sign a treaty to eliminate Russian and American nuclear weapons within five years. The governments of France, China, England, and Israel follow suit. India and Pakistan choose not to pursue the development of nuclear armaments, a path they were about to take. The United Nations is vested by the international community with the authority and funding to prevent lateral proliferation of nuclear weapons. Hundreds of tons of deadly plutonium are removed over the next five years from the world's total of 52,972 nuclear weapons.[1] The overwhelming relief that the world will soon be free from the threat of instant annihilation catalyzes effective international planning and cooperation to solve the problem of where and how to store the plutonium.

American tax dollars are diverted from massive Pentagon and corporate military budgets into projects designed to take care of the nation's people. A government-funded system of universal health care is instituted, and free, state-of-the-art education from kindergarten through college gradually becomes available throughout the nation. Congress passes a law mandating that all cars be built to operate at 80 miles per gallon and appropriates funding for public-transportation initiatives in every state. Legislation is enacted requiring that most buildings be retrofitted to collect solar energy, and that every new building be powered, heated, and cooled by solar energy. Generous safety nets are put in place, providing for the old, the poor, the sick, and the indigent, and the Social Security system remains immune to the work of "market forces." Every American child will be fully immunized, and no child will live below the poverty line.

Almost five decades since the dawn of the atomic age, the United States of America is on the way to becoming truly secure, no longer dependent on a nuclear barricade for its safety. The nation becomes an inspirational example to all other countries as we enter the twenty-first century.

Now blink and reenter reality.

A newly elected young president—touched paradoxically with both hubris and timidity—who had never acquired an in-depth knowledge of matters military or nuclear was handicapped by a severe leadership impediment: He had evaded the Vietnam draft. In his own mind he never overcame this apparent character deficit, and the military that he allegedly commanded made sure that he never forgot it. To exacerbate this situation, several acute personal problems of a deeply embarrassing—not to mention compromising—nature occupied this president, to the point where he contemplated possible resignation and faced actual impeachment.

Partly to compensate for these "deficiencies," Clinton used U.S. military force overseas—in Bosnia, Iraq, and Kosovo, among other places—more frequently than any other U.S. president of the last twenty years. Further, his was the only administration since Eisenhower's that did not negotiate a single significant nuclear arms control treaty.[2]

Bill Clinton's basic disinterest, distraction, draft handicap, and lack of vision allowed the military—Pentagon, nuclear scientists, and military corporations—to move into this presidential vacuum.[3] They wooed, seduced, and bought Congress and the administrative staff, and the opportunity for nuclear disarmament was tragically lost. Ironically, as we enter the twenty-first century, after eight years of a Democratic administration, the world is in a position even more dangerous than it was at the height of Reagan's buildup of nuclear weapons and Star Wars dreams. It is against this unfortunate backdrop that the events of September 11, 2001, took place, adding ominously to the possibility of international nuclear war or nuclear accidents, as the U.S. nuclear arsenal was placed on the highest state of alert and international tensions rose. U.S. nuclear policy and weaponry has never been more aggressive:

- The U.S. currently has 2000 intercontinental land-based hydrogen bombs, 3456 nuclear weapons on submarines roaming the seas 15 minutes from their targets, and 1750 nuclear weapons on intercontinental planes ready for delivery. Of these 7206 weapons, roughly 2500 remain on hair-trigger alert, ready to be launched at the press of a button.[4] Russia has a similar number of strategic weapons, with approximately 2000 on hair-trigger alert.[5, 6] In total there is now enough explosive power in the combined nuclear arsenals of the world to "overkill" every person on earth 32 times.[7]
- The U.S. currently has in place plans to fight and win a nuclear war, and is prepared to use nuclear weapons first if necessary. Winning a nuclear war with Russia, for example, requires the use of antisatellite weapons to destroy Russian early warning systems, a secret preemptive first strike attack to destroy Russian missiles before they can be launched from their silos, and preemptive destruction of Russian nuclear subs in port and at sea, all of which capabilities are currently in place. (Any Russian missiles escaping the initial attack would have to be destroyed en route to the U.S. in space, using a newly developed U.S. ballistic missile defense system.)
- The Pentagon's official targeting plan, the single integrated operational plan (SIOP), has been upgraded since 1989: Instead of a total of 2500 targets there are now 3000. These include 2260 Russian sites, 1100 of which are ostensibly "nuclear facilities," 160 of which are "leadership" targets—government offices and military

command centers (in a country almost devoid of leadership)—and 500 of which are disintegrating factories that produced almost no arms last year.[8]

- China is now included in SIOP for the first time in twenty years, despite the fact that the U.S. Senate moved to normalize relations with China by granting it permanent normal trading relations status (PNTR) in September 2000. (This country of 1.3 billion people, potentially a huge market for the U.S., has only twenty nuclear missiles capable of reaching America.)
- Non-nuclear nations such as Iran, Iraq, and North Korea are also targeted with nuclear weapons for the first time.[9] (Before the nineties, the U.S. had targeted only other countries with nuclear weapons.)
- The U.S. department of energy's nuclear laboratories—Los Alamos and Sandia in New Mexico, and Lawrence Livermore in California—are embarked on a second "Manhattan Project"—a massive scientific undertaking costing 5 to 6 billion dollars annually for the next ten to fifteen years, to design, test, and develop new nuclear weapons under the guise of ensuring the safety and reliability of the U.S.'s current stockpile of nuclear weapons.[10] This is twice the cost of the original Manhattan Project, which developed the first three atom bombs in the early forties, and significantly more than the annual average of 3.8 billion dollars spent on nuclear weapons during the cold war.[11]
- The Bush administration is pledged to fast-track plans for a new national missile defense system. This runs the risk of destabilizing the many arms-control treaties already negotiated between Russia and America.

Who are the enemies that America is so frantically and expensively arming against at the dawn of the twenty-first century? Until September 11, 2001, America had no enemies with the potential to wreak real harm on its land or people. It has friendly countries to the north and south, and vast oceans to the east and west. Under the current configuration, no foreign nation would ever think of invading the U.S. But it is now apparent that America has terrorist enemies—amorphous, difficult to track and locate, and almost impossible to extinguish by firepower or enormous arsenals of weapons.

> The Pentagon and State Department justify the extraordinary U.S. military expenditure—now 310 billion dollars annually—with potential threats from North Korea, Iraq, Iran, China, Russia, and possibly Libya. But of these, only the 5000 strategic nuclear weapons in Russia—half of which could hit U.S. cities thirty minutes after launching—pose a major threat to American security. More relevantly, as recent events have made all too clear, the largest nuclear stockpile in the world can accomplish little in the face of terrorists armed with box cutters, except, possibly, offering the potential for terrifying escalation of any ensuing conflict between nations. America currently spends 22 times as much on its military forces as all the other so-called rogue states or "states of concern"—Iraq, Iran, Syria, North Korea, Cuba, and Libya—put together, when nullification of any threat they might pose could be achieved for a fraction of that amount.[12, 13]

Other possible explanations for America's immense military expenditure include:

- It fattens the coffers of weapons makers.
- It is a direct result of the rivalry between the air force, the army, the navy, and the marines, each of whom want their own weapons systems.
- It elevates the prestige of top lawmakers within Congress and the White House who are the recipients of huge donations from weapons manufacturers as they legislate for more weapons.
- A huge conventional and nuclear arsenal allows America to do what it will around the world with impunity—it is the iron hand in the velvet glove of U.S. corporate globalization.

All of this is why Clinton's failure to seize the opportunity to eliminate or pare down the number of nuclear weapons in the world through rapid and realistic negotiation with Russia—at a time when this was possible—is so deeply tragic. Ironically, it may well be the very fact of the September 11 attack, and the U.S.'s resulting need to adopt a more conciliatory stance toward Russia, that leads George W. Bush to enact the stockpile reductions that eluded Clinton in calmer times.

The nuclear weapons establishment has four arms—the nuclear scientists, the military corporations, Congress plus the White House, and the Pentagon. Subsequent chapters look at each of these in turn. But first, let's set the stage by imagining what nuclear war might really be like.

Chapter Two

THE REALITY OF NUCLEAR WAR

WHAT WILL LIKELY BE the final conclusion to incessant nuclear-war planning? The destruction of the planet. And such an event could be triggered tonight or tomorrow by human or computer error, or even by a terrorist attack.

What would nuclear war be like?

MEDICAL CONSEQUENCES OF NUCLEAR WAR

If launched from Russia, nuclear weapons would explode over American cities thirty minutes after takeoff. (China's twenty missiles are liquid-fueled, not solid-fueled. They take many hours to fuel and could not be used in a surprise attack, but they would produce similar damage if launched. Other nuclear-armed nations, such as India and Pakistan, do not have the missile technology to attack the U.S.) It is assumed that most cities with a population over 100,000 people are targeted by Russia. During these thirty minutes, the U.S. early-warning infrared satellite detectors signal the attack to the strategic air command in Colorado. They in turn notify the president, who has approximately three minutes to decide whether or not to launch a counterattack. In the counterforce scenario the U.S. government currently embraces, he does launch, the missiles pass mid-space, and the whole operation is over within one hour.

Landing at 20 times the speed of sound, nuclear weapons explode over cities, with heat equal to that inside the center of the sun. There is practically no warning, except the emergency broadcast system on radio or TV, which gives the public only minutes to reach the nearest fallout shelter, assuming there is one. There is no time to collect children or immediate family members.

The bomb, or bombs—because most major cities will be hit with more than one explosion—will gouge out craters 200 feet deep and 1000 feet in diameter if they explode at ground level. Most, however, are programmed to produce an air burst, which increases the diameter of destruction, but creates a shallower crater. Half a mile from the epicenter all buildings will be destroyed, and at 1.7 miles only reinforced concrete buildings will remain.

At 2.7 miles bare skeletons of buildings still stand, single-family residences have disappeared, 50 percent are dead and 40 percent severely injured.[1] Bricks and mortar are converted to missiles traveling at hundreds of miles an hour. Bodies have been sucked out of buildings and converted to missiles themselves, flying through the air at 100 miles per hour. Severe overpressures (pressure many times greater than normal atmospheric pressure) have popcorned windows, producing millions of shards of flying glass, causing decapitations and shocking lacerations. Overpressures have also entered the nose, mouth, and ears, inducing rupture of lungs and rupture of the tympanic membranes or eardrums.

Most people will suffer severe burns. In Hiroshima, which was devastated by a very small bomb—13 kilotons compared to the current 1000 kilotons—a child actually disappeared, vaporized, leaving his shadow on the concrete pavement behind him. A mother was running, holding her baby, and both she and the baby were converted to a charcoal statue. The heat will be so intense that dry objects—furniture, clothes, and dry wood—will spontaneously ignite. Humans will become walking, flaming torches.

Forty or fifty miles from the explosion people will instantly be blinded from retinal burns if they glance at the flash. Huge firestorms will engulf thousands of square miles, fanned by winds from the explosion that transiently exceed 1000 miles per hour. People in fallout shelters will be asphyxiated as fire sucks oxygen from the shelters. (This happened in Hamburg after the Allied bombing in WWII when temperatures within the shelters, caused by conventional bombs, reached 1472 degrees Fahrenheit.)[2]

FALLOUT

Most of the city and its people will be converted to radioactive dust shot up in the mushroom cloud. The area of lethal fallout from this cloud will depend upon the prevailing wind and weather conditions; it could cover thousands of square miles. Doses of 5000 rads (a rad is a measure of radiation dose) or more experienced by people close to the explosion—if they are still alive—will produce acute encephalopathic syndrome. The cells of the brain will become so damaged that they would swell. Because the brain is enclosed in a fixed bony space, there is no room for swelling, so the pressure inside the skull rises, inducing symptoms of excitability, acute nausea, vomiting, diarrhea, severe headache, and seizures, followed by coma and death within twenty-four hours.

A lower dose of 1000 rads causes death from gastrointestinal symptoms. The lining cells of the gut die, as do the cells in the bone marrow that fight infection and that cause blood clotting. Mouth ulcers, loss of appetite, severe colicky abdominal pain, nausea, vomiting, and bloody diarrhea occur within seven to fourteen days. Death follows severe fluid loss, infection, hemorrhage, and starvation.

At 450 rads, 50 percent of the population dies. Hair drops out, vomiting and bloody diarrhea occurs, accompanied by bleeding under the skin and from the gums. Death occurs from internal hemorrhage, generalized septicemia, and infection. Severe trauma and injuries exacerbate the fallout symptoms, so patients die more readily from lower doses of radiation. Infants, children, and old people are more sensitive to radiation than healthy adults. Within bombed areas, fatalities will occur from a combination of trauma, burns, radiation sickness, and starvation. There will be virtually no medical care, even for the relief of pain, because most physicians work within targeted areas.

NUCLEAR POWER PLANTS

The United States owns 103 nuclear power plants, plus many other dangerous radioactive facilities related to past activities of the cold war. A 1000-kiloton bomb (1 megaton) landing on a standard 1000-

megawatt reactor and its cooling pools, which contain intensely radioactive spent nuclear fuel, would permanently contaminate an area the size of western Germany.[3] The International Atomic Energy Agency now considers these facilities to be attractive terrorist targets, post–September 11, 2001.

DISEASE

Millions of decaying bodies—human and animal alike—will rot, infected with viruses and bacteria that will mutate in the radioactive environment to become more lethal. Trillions of insects, naturally resistant to radiation—flies, fleas, cockroaches, and lice—will transmit disease from the dead to the living, to people whose immune mechanisms have been severely compromised by the high levels of background radiation. Rodents will multiply by the millions among the corpses and shattered sewerage systems. Epidemics of diseases now controlled by immunization and good hygiene will reappear: measles, polio, typhoid, cholera, whooping cough, diphtheria, smallpox, plague, tuberculosis, meningitis, malaria, and hepatitis.

Anyone who makes it to a fallout shelter, and is not asphyxiated in it, will need to stay there for at least six months until the radiation decays sufficiently so outside survival is possible. It has been postulated that perhaps older people should be sent outside to scavenge for food because they will not live long enough to develop malignancies from the fallout (cancer and leukemia have long incubation periods ranging from five to sixty years). But any food that manages to grow will be toxic because plants concentrate radioactive elements.[4]

NUCLEAR WINTER

Finally, we must examine the systemic global effects of a nuclear war. Firestorms will consume oil wells, chemical facilities, cities, and forests, covering the earth with a blanket of thick, black, radioactive smoke, reducing sunlight to 17 percent of normal. One year or more will be required for light and temperature to return to normal—perhaps supranormal values, as sunlight would return to more than its usual intensity, enhanced in the ultraviolet spectrum by depletion of the stratospheric ozone layer. Subfreezing temperatures could destroy the biological support system for civilization, resulting in massive starvation, thirst, and hypothermia.[5]

To quote a 1985 SCOPE document published by the White House Office of Science and Technology Policy, "the total loss of human agricultural and societal support systems would result in the loss of almost all humans on Earth, essentially equally among combatant and noncombatant countries alike . . . this vulnerability is an aspect not currently a part of the understanding of nuclear war; not only are the major combatant countries in danger, but virtually the entire human population is being held hostage to the large-scale use of nuclear weapons. . . ."

The proposed START III treaty between Russia and America, even if it were implemented, would still allow 3000 to 5000 hydrogen bombs to be maintained on alert.[6] The threshold for nuclear winter? One thousand 100-kiloton bombs blowing up 100 cities[7]—a distinct possibility given current capabilities and targeting plans.

ACCIDENTAL NUCLEAR WAR

On January 25, 1995, military technicians at radar stations in northern Russia detected signals from an American missile that had just been launched off the coast of Norway carrying a U.S. scientific probe. Although the Russians had been previously notified of this launch, the alert had been forgotten or ignored. Aware that U.S. submarines could launch a missile containing eight deadly hydrogen bombs fifteen minutes from Moscow, Russian officials assumed that America had initiated a nuclear war. For the first time in history, the Russian computer containing nuclear launch codes was opened.

President Boris Yeltsin, sitting at that computer being advised on how to launch a nuclear war by his military officers, had only a three-minute interval to make a decision. At the last moment, the U.S. missile veered off course. He realized that Russia was not under attack.[8]

If Russia had launched its missiles, the U.S. early-warning satellites would immediately have detected them, and radioed back to Cheyenne Mountain. This would have led to the notification of the president, who also would have had three minutes to make his launch decision, and America's missiles would then have been fired from their silos. We were thus within minutes of global annihilation that day.

Today, Russia's early-warning and nuclear-command systems are deteriorating. Russia's early-warning system fails to operate up to seven hours a day because only one-third of its radars are functional, and two of the nine global geographical areas covered by its missile-warning satellites are *not under surveillance for missile detection.*[9] To make matters worse, the equipment controlling nuclear weapons malfunctions frequently, and critical electronic devices and computers sometimes switch to combat mode for no apparent reason. According to the CIA, seven times during the fall of 1996 operations at some Russian nuclear weapons facilities were severely disrupted when robbers tried to "mine" critical communications cables for their copper![10] This vulnerable Russian system could easily be stressed by an internal or international political crisis, when the danger of accidental or indeed intentional nuclear war would become very real.

And the U.S. itself is not invulnerable to error. In August 1999, for example, when the National Imagery and Mapping Agency was installing a new computer system to deal with potential Y2K problems, this operation triggered a computer malfunction which rendered the agency "blind" for days; it took more than eight months for the defect to be fully repaired. As the *New York Times* reported, part of America's nuclear early-warning system was rendered incompetent for almost a year.[11] (At that time I was sitting at a meeting in the west wing of the White House discussing potentially dangerous Y2K nuclear weapons glitches. Several Pentagon officials blithely reassured me that everything would function normally during the roll-over. But in fact, their intelligence system had already been disabled.)

Such a situation has the potential for catastrophe. If America cannot observe what the Russians are doing with their nuclear weapons—or vice versa—especially during a serious international crisis, they are likely to err on the side of "caution," which could mean that something as benign as the launch of a weather satellite could actually trigger annihilation of the planet. This situation became even more significant after the September 11 attack.

Chapter Three

IT'S A MAD, MAD WORLD: NUCLEAR SCIENTISTS AND THE PENTAGON PLAY WITH DEADLY GADGETS

We were fascinated by abstract violence on a huge scale. I became addicted to nuclear weapons work. It gave me a sense of great power. I remember dreams about a weapons design that I'd been working on—when it failed it was a nightmare. When it succeeded it was a high—that sense of: I'm good at this. It's my bomb. Except we never called them bombs. We called them gadgets.

—Ted Taylor, former bomb designer

NUCLEAR SCIENTISTS have been called priests or monks by a media and public in awe of their inventions.[1] Most journalists and policy-makers therefore assume that the scientific activities within the weapons labs are sacrosanct and beyond question.[2] Because of the almost mystical power these individuals are granted, they have dominated the national security scene since the Manhattan Project began in 1942. Virtually unimpeded and uncontrolled, over a period of fifty years they designed sixty-five different types of nuclear weapons, exploded 1030 bombs at the testing site in Nevada, and directed the manufacture of over 70,000 bombs.[3] (As noted above, 1000 bombs exploding over 100 cities could induce "nuclear winter" and the end of most life on the earth.)[4]

These scientists have always operated in absolute secrecy, which gave them the anonymity they needed to pursue their work. They used a language that was incomprehensible to all but the most educated, and, like physicians, they hid behind an arcane scientific complexity, never emerging to inform the world what they were doing.

They still operate the three major nuclear weapons labs—Los Alamos and Sandia in New Mexico, and Lawrence Livermore in California. All are currently run by the department of energy (DOE) and overseen by the University of California. (While most Americans know that the DOE supervises U.S. energy policy, few are aware that the same department also oversees all nuclear weapons research.)

At the end of the cold war, nuclear scientists saw their future slipping away from them. The euphemistically named Stockpile Stewardship and Management Program (SS & M), was a way to ensure their continued employment. Ostensibly created to ensure that old weapons will still explode if necessary, the labs are actually designing, testing, and building a variety of new nuclear weapons, many in violation of existing treaties and bans. (See Chapter Five for a full discussion of the SS & M charade.)

At a political level the scientists have been able to associate their work with nationalism and the preservation and protection of the United States. Yet it is doubtful that any of the individuals involved—from the politicians mandated to guide and direct these scientists on our behalf to the scientists themselves, the military personnel, or the businessmen who profit from the nuclear weapons enterprise—understand the philosophical, moral, spiritual, or biological problems engendered by capturing gigantic extraterrestrial forces manifested only in the sun and the stars.

Let us begin with the nuclear scientists: thousands of physicists, chemists, and engineers—the cream of the crop, recruited from U.S. colleges over a period of sixty years—brilliant, rational, careful, strictly scientific, engaged in exploring the very elements of creation, and all committed to the design, construction, and testing of nuclear weapons.

Surprisingly, while many are to the right of the political spectrum, others are liberal in their views. They do not believe that designing bombs is an act of patriotism as the right-wingers do, but are drawn to the culture of low-key "rational-speak" (their term for strictly rational discussion, bereft of emotional overtones) and find joy in scientific problem-solving.[5]

The Lawrence Livermore Lab has a policy that if an employee expresses any concern about the ultimate result of the use of nuclear weapons (i.e., the possible destruction of the world), they are advised—and sometimes required—to see a counselor. In a scenario right out of *1984* (and a classic sign of a cult mentality), anyone giving voice to the stark truth must be counseled to accept the lie of the labs.[6]

Cults also typically withhold information from potential recruits to conceal the true nature of the group or the work with which it is involved.[7] Thus, when Dr. Andreas Toupadakis, a chemist, became an employee of the Lawrence Livermore nuclear weapons lab in 1988, he was led to believe that he would be working on environmental cleanup and nuclear disarmament. In fact, as he gradually realized, he was participating in an ongoing nuclear arms race, and he became agitated and deeply concerned. Toupadakis was advised to see a counselor shortly before he left Livermore Lab in January 2000.[8]

Since the 1940s, the scientific bomb cult has allowed individual scientists to design and test their very own bombs. If the testing proved successful, it was a rite-of-passage for the newcomer. More experienced members have attested to gaining a sense of power over the forces of nature while renewing their stature.[9] Bomb designers often slept alone in a room above the Nevada Test Site with the control mechanisms that would trigger the explosion the next day,[10] like a racing-car driver flirting with death—in this case, not just individual death, but the death of millions, the death of life.

At a more fundamental level, these scientists felt that their technical mastery over the bomb implied that they would then be able to control the impending annihilation that their work signified. But in psychological terms the mastery they had acquired actually implied that they had intense fear of the bomb and of death.[11] Interestingly, the language of the scientists reflects the imagery of birth and new life, denoting more profound psychological dynamics. The first nuclear bomb ever tested in 1945, code-named Trinity (after the Father, Son, and Holy Ghost), was called "Oppenheimer's baby" in honor of the scientific director of the Manhattan Project. The telegram Edward Teller sent to Los Alamos after the first successful A-bomb test in 1945 read "it's a boy."[12] The bomb gets "married" to the diagnostic canister, and as it explodes it "couples" with the ground, making "daughter fission products" that pass through "generations."[13] One of the scientists described the test as "like having a baby" and compared the tenseness he experienced during the test to "whether to push or not."[14] Another bomb designer compared his post-test feelings to a state of "postnatal depression."[15]

The anthropologist Hugh Gusterson, in his book *Nuclear Rites,* surmises that to the scientists, nuclear weapons tests "symbolize not despair, destruction, and death but hope, renewal, and life" and therefore nuclear weapons must be part of the natural order. Perhaps at a subliminal level these scientists—almost exclusively men—are seeking an archetypal understanding of the experience of conception and delivery, otherwise unavailable to them. The ultimate destruction of the creation is, in their minds, analogous to creation itself. Oppenheimer quoted the *Bhagavad Gita* upon witnessing Trinity, the first nuclear explosion: "I am become death, the shatterer of worlds."

On the other hand, unlike the nurturing instincts of a new mother, much of their language reflects their profound dehumanization of people. To them, people are "human resources" and "components" within a system. They describe human communication as "interfacing" and miscommunications as "disconnects." The pain of human injuries is referred to as "damage," and when a human being is killed she is "disassembled."[16] The Pentagon echoes this language, calling targeting of cities "countervalue targeting." People are dubbed "soft targets" (missile silos are hard targets). The 15 million civilians who would initially be killed in a counterforce attack on Russian hard targets are "collateral damage."[17]

As Gusterson writes, "Techno-strategic discourse is characterized by its lack of emotion, its game-theoretical models of human motivation, its fondness for abstraction and for passive sentence constructions, its focus on hardware rather than people. And its fundamental unquestioned and unquestionable assumption that weapons development must continue."[18] As they remove pain and fear from their vocabulary, presumably the scientists are protecting their psyches from the human consequences of their work. At the same time, however, they wax lyrical about their weapons, describing nuclear equipment as beautiful, and their relationships to technology as Zen. Weapons are arms, bombs are warheads, a nuclear attack is a decapitating strike, the strategic nuclear forces have three legs, early-warning satellites are eyes and ears, missiles are covered with skins, and aging weapons grow "whiskers" that can interfere with their "health."[19]

Superimposed upon the humanization of nuclear weapons and the mechanization of human bodies is the culture of careful expert rationalism, very similar to the rational language used by physicians to distance themselves from the almost unbearable human pain and suffering they deal with on a daily basis. One obvious difference, however, is that, while physicians deal with pain already existing in their patients, these scientists create the source of their pain. The psychological pain these scientists must then confront is self-imposed.[20]

MILITARY MADNESS AND THE PENTAGON CULT[21]

You start talking about targeting or strategic command and control and, baby, that's the family jewels.

—General Jack Merritt, former director of the Joint Chiefs of Staff

According to retired admiral Eugene Carroll, interservice rivalry is the real engine of the nuclear arms race—the three services under the direction of the Pentagon, each competing for the nuclear dollar. It's about power building, each wanting and demanding more planes, bombs, and ships.[22]

This competition among the services—a dynamic centered at the mental and psychological age of my grandchildren, aged eight, seven, and five years, who argue continuously and competitively about toys, all wanting their very own and never having enough—may have been socially and politically acceptable during World Wars I and II, in a prenuclear era. In a world bristling with nuclear weapons, such rivalry is calamitous. Any military skirmish in an interdependent world involving the navy, the army, or the air force, could escalate and trigger a thermonuclear holocaust. Indeed, all nuclear war games "played" by the Pentagon end up obliterating both the victors and the vanquished. In this context it is interesting to examine the powerful political role that the Pentagon has played since the cold war ended.

The new international scenario, in which the Pentagon was left without a major national enemy at the end of the cold war in 1989, came as a shock to the entrenched military establishment, which was faced with a kind of post-traumatic stress syndrome. Indeed, many individuals overtly mourned the loss of their once-predictable former enemy.[23]

To the contrary, in the face of newfound opportunity President George Bush displayed commendable leadership, defying Pentagonian pressure and moving decisively and unilaterally to eliminate all ground-based tactical missile bombs, all tactical nuclear weapons from naval vessels, and all hydrogen bombs from long-range bombers. He also cancelled certain land-based missile programs. He de-escalated both as a gesture of goodwill and as a strategic defense maneuver; as he explained to one of his aides at the time: "I want tactical nuclear weapons out of Europe. Gorbachev needs U.S. cover to get their nukes out of the republics before they collapse."[24] At the same time, then–Secretary of Defense Dick Cheney and Chairman of the Joint Chiefs of Staff Colin Powell instigated a full-scale review of the single integrated operational plan (SIOP)—the U.S. nuclear targeting strategy that was the guiding light of the Pentagon, but that had now been rendered obsolete.[25]

Both men were appalled by the subsequent report. Not only was SIOP arcane and hopelessly out of date, it also lacked clear logic and objectives. According to one account, "Cheney concluded that SIOP was not a nuclear war plan . . . it seemed like a jumble of processed data. . . . Every time the Pentagon had bought a new nuclear weapons system to match the Soviets' . . . Omaha [the Strategic Command Headquarters in Omaha, Nebraska] had simply found targets for the added warheads and rearranged the SIOP math formulas. This had gone on for years, as captains and majors who wrote the SIOP plan rotated in and out."[26] This dynamic was so out of control that by 1986, SIOP had targeted 16,000 "nuclear facilities" in the Soviet Union[27] (as a point of comparison, there are only 240 major cities in the entire northern hemisphere). Following the Cheney-Powell review, thousands of targets in the former Soviet republics were removed from the SIOP plans, and all focused targets were now located in Russia,[28] which was fast becoming an ally. The targets still included command and control centers, conventional forces, all war-supporting industries including such things as shoe factories, most other factories, oil and gas facilities, power plants, railroad stations, schools, and universities, in addition to actual nuclear forces—so there was overkill, but less overkill.[29]

Bush continued to take command of nuclear weapons policies, never allowing the military bureaucracy to prevail in decision-making. He counted on his main advisors, who were astute inside players, to carry out his objectives, and they received powerful presidential support in the face of Pentagon opposition.[30]

Prior to the Bush administration, no president, presidential aide, or official from the office of the secretary of defense had been involved in directing or even trying to understand the logic of the SIOP planners in the Pentagon. Indeed, one military official from the Joint Strategic Planning Service charged that officials in prior administrations "were criminally negligent" for their lack of oversight for SIOP, all the details of nuclear targeting strategy having been left to junior officers in the Pentagon.[31]

In *An Elusive Consensus,* Janne Nolan describes the years before the first Bush administration as follows:

> Briefings to senior officials about the SIOP typically were perfunctory and often unintelligible. The thousands of pages of SIOP data and computer codes contained in the plans would be translated into an hour-long briefing and presented in several dozen view graphs. "Generally no one at the briefings wanted to ask questions because they didn't want to embarrass themselves," according to one account, in reference to both military and political authorities. "We would cut deals as junior officers [of the different services] in allocating weapons . . . sometimes this resulted in remarkable changes in the guidance, which should have been reviewed at the highest levels."[32]

Once, while being briefed on the SIOP, then–Secretary of Defense Cheney began squirming uncomfortably in his chair as he watched Moscow—which had been targeted with 200 separate hydrogen bombs, entailing an enormous excess of megatonnage—turn slowly into a solid red mass covered over and again with ludicrous targets.[33]

The Pentagon thinks about nuclear strategy in a strange and pathological way. (One could readily diagnose the attitudes of the Pentagon as clinically sick and suggest that all people who subscribe to these theories need urgent counseling and therapy.) "Aggression" by an enemy will be "deterred" with a threat to vaporize millions of people as Joanne Nolan comments in her book. The rationale is as follows: Officers responsible for nuclear weapons must have the ability to hold "at risk" anything that an adversary would "value most." But because those doing the targeting cannot know what is most valued, almost everything is held "at risk." As one military official was heard to say, "If he values his grandma, we have to target grandmas."[34]

While the Bush administration bequeathed an activist legacy of potent arms control and unilateral disarmament programs to the next president, this tradition was not perpetuated by President Clinton. Clinton vacillated and was ever reluctant to engage himself directly in nuclear issues. And Clinton simply never took command of the Pentagon. As one of Bush's aides said, "Clinton debates objectives with his subordinates. Bush debated tactics but never objectives."[35]

Clinton's first secretary of defense, Les Aspin, the former chairman of the House Armed Services Committee, was highly experienced in the area of nuclear weapons strategies. Aspin had doubts about the relevance of nuclear deterrence in the post–cold war era, noting, "A world without nuclear weapons would actually be better. . . . Nuclear weapons are still the big equalizer, but the United States is not the equalizer but the equalizee."[36]

To this end, Aspin initiated a nuclear posture review, based upon the concepts of "mutual assured safety" and "cooperative denuclearization." The review was to encompass and incorporate policies, doctrines, force structure, operations, safety, security, and arms control and was to include a critique by an outside panel of experts. Aspin specifically planned the review to emphasize the fundamentally political character of nuclear policy. However, there was strong opposition from Pentagon officials who decided that outside participation would not be necessary or desirable. As one commented, "We certainly weren't about to invite any weirdos from ACDA [the Arms Control and Disarmament Agency]."[37]

Aspin resigned in 1994 shortly before he died, and responsibility for the review passed on to Deputy Secretary of Defense John Deutch, a relatively inexperienced man who had recently been appointed from the private military sector. (He was later appointed head of the CIA.) Operational responsibility for the review was shared by Ashton Carter, assistant secretary of defense for national security and counterproliferation, and Lieutenant General Barry McCaffrey[38] (who later became Clinton's drug czar).

Aspin's instruction to the nuclear posture review had been to extricate the entrenched nuclear establishment—including the Pentagon—from its obsolete cold war preoccupations and to foster more appropriate understandings of the post–cold war reality. The military establishment, Aspin believed, needed to accept and understand the enormous dangers of the U.S. nuclear strategy. But in the absence of senior oversight and disciplined leadership once Aspin resigned, the review process failed. President Clinton declined to become involved, Secretary of State Warren Christopher was disengaged, and National Security Advisor Anthony Lake was uninterested. So the job was left essentially to Deutch and Carter.[39]

Carter, who was well intentioned, sincerely believed that a process of logical analysis could alter orthodox military thinking about nuclear weapons strategy. To this end, he established six working groups, staffed by midranking and junior military officers plus career bureaucrats. Most had little background in nuclear strategy, and all met in closed-door meetings within the Pentagon. Their attitude was derisive to any "outsider analysis" and new ideas were given polite but frosty receptions.[40]

The Pentagon personnel overwhelmingly opposed any changes to their triad of nuclear forces, and to the concept of de-alerting their strategic nuclear weapons. The air force also strenuously resisted eliminating their land-based ICBM weapons. The others charged that any change in their strategy of employing a variety of launch options threatened America's ability to respond to nuclear attacks effectively. Some military officials also sensed an assault on their nuclear procedures and their lines of authority. As one midlevel officer asserted: "We know how to produce nuclear war plans. We have the methodology, we can analyze damage expectancies."[41]

The vice chair of the Joint Chiefs of Staff, Admiral William Owens, who oversaw the committees was a potent critic of nuclear weapons, but unfortunately he did not challenge his colleagues when they vigorously opposed the mandate of the review. (Even had consensus been reached by the Pentagon however, the White House never at any stage attempted to engage or educate the Congress about these extraordinarily important issues.) Eventually, after ten months of review process, the working groups sabotaged Aspin's original concept, opposing even minor changes or innovations. Instead they produced analyses and a series of view graphs totally supporting the structure, doctrine, and force levels implicit in the current nuclear doctrine.[42]

Carter became so frustrated that he bypassed the working groups and appointed two outsiders to rescue the process—Steve Fetter, a physicist and professor from the University of Maryland, and Lieutenant Commander Leo Mackay, who wrote his Harvard doctoral dissertation on nuclear strategy. He organized high-level clearances in order to give them full access to the necessary documents. This "counter-review" was specifically structured to analyze the possible removal of land-based ICBMs vulnerable to a first strike, de-alerting of strategic weapons, removal of the remaining U.S. nuclear weapons in Europe (there are still 200), and alteration of nuclear targeting doctrines. Post–cold war, it was obvious, to Carter at least, that America could operate with a much smaller strategic nuclear arsenal, if indeed it needed one at all.[43]

Deutch expressed sympathy with these proposals, but when the Joint Chiefs of Staff got wind of the briefing charts, a revolt was triggered in the Pentagon. Although Carter had been appointed to oversee the nuclear posture review by the office of the secretary of defense, in the end he was abandoned to do solitary battle against the power and might of the Pentagon. A meeting called by regional commanders "to call Ash on the carpet" progressed to a brutal showdown. Carter had no authority to present options to the secretary of defense they said, unless the options had been approved by the "working groups."[44]

Though Carter defended himself, saying that it was not appropriate for colonels and lower-level Pentagon personnel to craft U.S. national policies, the policy that was finally given approval by a disengaged president was a complete triumph for the Pentagon. It called for a "lead and hedge" strategy in which the U.S. would publicly pursue nuclear arms control while at the same time hedging "against . . . a return to an authoritarian military regime in Russia hostile to the United States." In the end, this new policy allowed America to retain its nuclear weapons should the cold war reemerge, to double the number of strategic intercontinental weapons allowed under the START II treaty—from 3000 to 6000—and there were to be no limits on nondeployed warheads (nuclear weapons in storage) or tactical nuclear weapons (tactical nuclear weapons are not delivered by intercontinental missiles or intercontinental planes, but are launched from short-range missiles, cruise missiles, or short-range planes). Finally the policy reinforced the triad of land-, air-, and sea-based weapons. Ashton Carter has since disclaimed that there was really any genuine attempt to alter the U.S. force structure or the overall nuclear policy.[45]

The Pentagon had prevailed. There was no change in nuclear policy, and the status quo of nuclear comfort returned.

When the review was released, one Russian commentator observed, regarding the lack of leadership displayed in the face of the Pentagon's post-review tantrum: "Clinton's foreign policy is determined by immediate reactions to internal, and to a lesser degree, external factors."[46]

Chapter Four

CORPORATE MADNESS AND THE DEATH MERCHANTS

I see in the near future a crisis approaching that unnerves me and causes me to tremble for the sake of my country. . . . Corporations have been enthroned and an era of corruption in high places will follow, and the money power of the country will endeavor to prolong its reign by working upon the prejudices of the people until all wealth is aggregated in a few hands and the Republic is destroyed.

—Abraham Lincoln, November 21, 1864

WHO RUNS THE Congress all these years later? The transnational corporations whose executives wine and dine, woo, bribe, and corrupt the officeholders of the White House and Congress—from the president and vice president to almost all the elected congressional officials. These all-powerful corporations manipulate and control most of the federal legislation, foreign and domestic, that passes through Congress. They do it through a variety of mechanisms: think tanks, corporate mergers, lobbying, and political donations.

THINK TANKS

In the seventies leading international corporations jointly organized and endowed a series of think tanks—their own "battle management organizations"—whose primary purpose was to sway popular and political opinion in directions useful to the think tanks' corporate sponsors. These think tanks are staffed by erudite researchers who produce editorials, TV news pieces, papers, media releases, and legislative material, which are well-conceived, well-researched, well-written, easy to understand, and very acceptable to the media and Congress.[1] Production of this material is orchestrated in a timely fashion to guide specific pieces of legislation. Mostly Washington based, these think tanks also have a pervasive presence in the media, their spokespeople being regular political commentators on the Sunday-morning talk shows and in print.

TREE TOPS PROPAGANDA

If the mass will be free of the chains of iron, it must obey the chains of silver. . . . If it will not love, honor and obey, it must not expect to escape seduction.

—Harold Lasswell, leading American scholar of propaganda, 1939[2]

This broad-reaching, sophisticated, high-level manipulation of the so-called free, democratic media and legislature is known as "tree tops" propaganda, and it has been extraordinarily successful for the sponsoring corporations and the points of view they espouse. Such an approach effectively controls government agendas in many countries—certainly including the United States—and is more effective by far than grassroots organizing, for all but the very few issues around which millions of concerned citizens can be mobilized. The right-wing think tanks almost alone created the new conservative movement of the 1970s.

But these think tanks are neither free nor democratic. They are nonelected, private bodies controlled by wealthy and powerful corporations. In effect they are advertising agencies acting for the corporations that founded and fund them. They represent the corporate philosophy of "economic rationalism," which favors the corporate takeover of all public enterprises, from health care and education to water and electricity, and an agenda that includes decreasing or abolishing government regulation of big business, decreasing corporate taxes and taxes for the rich, destroying the unions, and increasing corporate profits.[3] The IMF, the World Bank, GATT,

NAFTA, APEC, FTAA, and WTO have all taken their cues from these think tanks.*

One of the most influential think tanks is the Heritage Foundation. Funded by transnational corporations and wealthy individuals including Amway, Hyundai, Exxon, Phillip Morris, United Parcel Service Foundation, Joseph Coors, Timothy Mellon and the Sarah Scaife Foundation, the Heritage Foundation's income for 1999 was 43.6 million dollars.[5] The Heritage Foundation established a comprehensive list of agenda items for the Reagan presidency, which they titled "Mandate for Leadership—Policy Management in a Conservative Administration." Items included arming America to fight and win a nuclear war, and to develop "superiority over the Soviet Union." Most of these agenda items became policy.[6] (They followed up by issuing another Mandate for Leadership in Reagan's second term.)

THINK TANKS AND THE MILITARY-INDUSTRIAL COMPLEX

The think tanks exert a huge amount of influence on behalf of the military-industrial complex. The Heritage Foundation is still very much involved in promoting the nuclear arms race in all arenas, and actively lobbying for Star Wars.[7] Other powerful right-wing think tanks that involve themselves in American "nuclear security" include the American Enterprise Institute and the CATO Institute.[8] Yet another think tank, the Center for Security Policy (CSP), serves as the nerve center of the Star Wars lobby. It was organized by Frank Gaffney, a Pentagon official under Reagan and a high priest of mis-

* In January 1998, a chief World Bank economist, Joseph Stiglitz, attracted worldwide attention during a lecture he gave in Helsinki when he criticized this so-called "Washington consensus." Stiglitz pointed out that Washington-inspired austerity, privatization, and deregulation—which has become the standard policy prescription for much of the world—was misguided and often disastrous. He said that market ideologues were using economic crises in various countries as excuses to discredit government intervention and to promote more market liberalization. He argued, contrary to the economic rationalist line, that moderate inflation is fairly harmless, budget deficits are not necessarily evil, privatization is not a panacea, and deregulation of domestic and international financial markets can do serious harm. Not surprisingly, he was fired from the World Bank at the end of 1999.[4]

sile defense. (Gaffney also heads the Coalition to Protect Americans Now, a group that organizes TV ads to promote missile defense and all-out Star Wars. One ad depicts visions of babies in their cradles and children playing baseball, interspersed with missiles falling from the sky, and a caption reading, *Where will you be when the missiles are launched?*).[9]

CSP is funded by military contractors including Lockheed Martin, Boeing, TRW, General Dynamics, Rockwell International, and Northrop Grumman. CSP's board includes six Lockheed Martin executives; members of the Heritage Foundation;[10] President Reagan's science advisor George Keyworth; two staunch Republican supporters of missile defense, Senator John Kyl of Arizona and Representative Kurt Weldon of Pennsylvania; and the notorious—and now elderly—Edward Teller, the inventor of the hydrogen bomb. (Teller calls Star Wars the "third generation" of nuclear weapons, the atomic bomb being the first and the hydrogen bomb the second. For thirty-two years he has urged the nuclear weapons labs to conduct more research on "defensive weapons.") The CSP packs a powerful corporate punch, publishing over 200 press releases a year, euphemistically called national security decision briefs.[11] (In 1998, the Center for Security Policy gave its Keeper of the Flame award to Donald Rumsfeld, former defense secretary under Ford and now secretary of defense in the present Bush administration; other notable recipients of the award have included Ronald Reagan and Newt Gingrich.)

But even as early as 1983, when Reagan—under Edward Teller's guidance—gave his speech advocating Star Wars, most credible scientists knew that the scientific hypothesis upon which the theory was based—that a comprehensive and effective missile shield could be built—was simply unworkable. Seventy billion dollars and a string of uninterrupted technical failures later, the Center for Security Policy, the Heritage Foundation, Lockheed Martin, TRW, Raytheon, and Boeing remain committed to the Star Wars concept and the country is still trying to build a missile shield.

HOW THE THINK TANKS RESUSCITATED STAR WARS

When the Soviet Union collapsed in 1991 it became necessary for the corporations, their think tanks, the State Department, and the Pentagon to invent new excuses to justify this unworkable, enormously expensive military-scientific adventure.

First, a new arch-enemy had to be found, and North Korea (a country unable to feed its own people) was the propaganda machine's number-one choice. Originally labeled (along with Iraq) a "rogue state" by the State Department, and now called a "state of concern,"[12] North Korea does not have a single missile that could hit the U.S., nor any nuclear weapons. John Pike, then with the Federation of American Scientists, commenting on the North Korean missile test site, said, "This facility was not intended to support and in many respects is incapable of supporting the extensive test program that would be needed to develop a reliable missile program." The site has no transportation links, no paved roads, no storage facility for propellant, and no staff housing.[13]

Nevertheless, the ongoing demoniacal representation of North Korea is important to the Pentagon because it has been and is used to justify the only U.S. military deployment on mainland Asia (the U.S. maintains 37,000 troops in South Korea). Adherence to this policy is essential because it gives the U.S. a reason to maintain a military presence and a belligerent policy in an Asian country while it is currently positioning itself to cast China as the next major enemy on the horizon. Though recently Afghanistan has, on an acute basis, replaced China as a major Pentagon focus.

Consequently the Pentagon, State Department, and military industry have worked with the leading think tanks to make the public case for the need to defend the U.S. from this "rogue state." So important has the North Korean "threat" been to U.S. military policy that William Cohen's first question to policy officials when he became Secretary of Defense in 1994 was "How can we change the assumption that U.S. troops will be withdrawn after peace comes to the Korean Peninsula?"[14]

Unfortunately this "enemy" is not behaving according to plan. For one thing, North Korean President Kim Chong-il and South Korean President Kim Dae Jung signed a peace treaty on June 15, 2000, agreeing that they needed reconciliation and the establishment of peace. (A military officer who closely follows the situation noted that "The U.S., in my opinion, is obsessed with the status quo," and said the Pentagon was underestimating the potential for a peace breakthrough and resisting changes in its forces in South Korea that could ease tensions further.)[15] North Korea even informed Russian President Putin that it would abandon its fledgling missile program in exchange for Western aid in building scientific satellites.

But the State Department remains less than convinced. As one department spokesman insisted, "The threat of war is still there. In terms of the [North Korean] military capability, they still have over one million troops ready to go."[16] And in the spring of 1999, despite the "problems" brought on by Korean peacemaking, the Star Wars partisans claimed success. Their prodigious lobbying efforts, corporate political donations, and propaganda exercises persuaded the House and Senate to pass legislation stating that the official policy of the United States government is to deploy a national missile defense as soon as is "technically feasible."[17] A Pentagon intelligence report quoted in the *New York Times* in September 2000 concluded that "North Korea remains a dangerous military threat." And when Kim Dae Jung, a Nobel Peace Prize laureate, visited George W. Bush soon after Bush's inauguration, he was essentially snubbed by the president and his staff.[18]

CORPORATE MERGERS AND NUCLEAR POLICY

The most powerful military corporation on earth, Lockheed Martin, was created in 1993 by a series of corporate mergers. During the eighties and early nineties there were ten to fifteen major U.S. weapons firms. However, in 1993, Secretary of Defense Les Aspin concluded that the Pentagon could no longer sustain the enormous weapons procurement budgets of the lavish Reagan years,[19] and, in an early-1993 meeting, Undersecretary of Defense William Perry bluntly informed industry executives of the new Pentagon policy of encouraging corporate mergers.

That seminal meeting was triumphantly dubbed "the last supper" by Norman Augustine, at that time CEO of Martin Marietta and subsequently the guiding hand behind the mergers. Martin Marietta merged with Lockheed, to become Lockheed Martin, a 35-billion-dollar behemoth, and the number-one contractor for the Pentagon, NASA, and the Department of Energy.[20] Boeing absorbed McDonnell Douglas, and Raytheon bought the military units of Hughes Aircraft and Texas Instruments to become numbers two and three, respectively. Other smaller firms survived, including TRW, Northrop Grumman, and United Defense, but their earnings were significantly lower than those of the big three's.[21] (Ironically, the Pentagon has not closed a single major weapons production line since the mergers were instituted. With a smaller number of corporations now bidding competitively for military contracts, prices have gone up, not down, and, in the end, no actual savings have been passed on to taxpayers.)

Two government officials, William Perry and his Pentagon colleague John Deutch, both of whom were past paid consultants to Martin Marietta, shepherded the mergers through the government bureaucracy. Officially it was against the law for Perry and Deutch to act on behalf of their former employer, but they obtained "conflict of interest waivers" from Defense Secretary Aspin. Perry and Deutch even went so far as to change the Pentagon's contracting rules, thus allowing merging companies to be compensated for costs involved in moving factories, for legal fees, and for executive bonuses (a policy memorably dubbed "payoffs for layoffs" by Congressman Bernie Sanders from Vermont). This type of corporate-orchestrated merger and payoff operation is a classic example of the "revolving-door syndrome": Corporate employment leads to a Pentagon position, where one is then able to featherbed the nest of one's corporate colleagues. Then, when the government term of office expires, some return to private industry equipped with invaluable Pentagon connections.

Lockheed Martin realized a taxpayer-financed windfall from the merger amounting to 1.2 billion dollars. The company also became the single largest advocate of aggressive nuclear development in the country, in a quest to protect its *billions of dollars* worth of government arms contracts (18 billion dollars in 1997).*

* Less than two months after the September 11 attacks, the Pentagon awarded Lockheed Martin a mammoth contract of 200 billion dollars over the next several decades to build 3000 F-35 joint strike fighter planes.[22]

Birth of a Death Merchant

As Lockheed Martin came to power, so did Norman Augustine, CEO of the newly merged company and perhaps the key player on the corporate side of the military-industrial equation. Augustine personally received 8.2 million dollars in government payouts stemming from the merger. As one Pentagon source noted, "If you're concerned about corporate welfare, the one you should look out for is St. Norman Augustine."[23] (Former Tennessee governor Lamar Alexander also got 250,000 dollars for the "hardship" he endured when asked to leave the board of the newly merged company!)

Who is the man who has come to play such a key role in the defense industry?

Originally a forest ranger, Augustine majored in geological engineering. As a first-year graduate student, however, he was "utterly shocked" when the Soviet Union launched *Sputnik*—"I couldn't imagine how we could be number two," he said—and within months he took a job at the Douglas Aircraft Corporation. He has stayed in the weapons industry ever since.[24] He sees weapon production as a patriotic duty, and he refers to the military corporations as "the fourth armed service," noting that increased spending on weapons is a national imperative, not merely a means to increase corporate profits.[25]

While he led the nation's largest corporate military contractor, Augustine was also influential in other areas. As chairman of the Defense Science Board (DSB), a Pentagon panel, he helped to decide for or against multibillion-dollar weapons projects. He was president of the Association of the United States Army, a politically influential group of retired army personnel, and he served as chairman of the Defense Policy Advisory Committee on Trade, a committee that gives confidential guidance on arms exports to the secretary of defense.[26] (Beyond his military credentials, Augustine was also the chairman of the American Red Cross and president of the Boy Scouts of America.)

A hard-driving man conversant with all the major policy and technical issues affecting Lockheed Martin, Augustine was a high-stakes lobbyist and became an unofficial—and intimidating—policy maker, successfully advocating initiatives that yielded billions of dollars in government funding for his corporation.[27] Former government officials declined the opportunity to testify on Pentagon procurement recommendations because "Norman Augustine really wants this." During the summer of 1994, he had become such a presence on the Hill that one staff member referred to him sarcastically as "the secretary of defense."[28] (Augustine continued in his dynamically influential role as CEO of Lockheed Martin until 1998, when he was replaced by Vance Coffman. But Augustine remains on the board, an effective lobbyist for his company, and he continues to participate in military-related activities. He sat on a congressionally mandated bipartisan committee to investigate increasing terrorist threats to the United States. He also participated in a committee in 2001 to assess the efficacy of the ill-fated Osprey helicopter.)[29]

WHAT NORMAN WANTS . . .

One of the ways military corporations curry favor with lawmakers is by employing people in multiple political districts. The legislators express gratitude for increased employment in their districts by enacting legislation that forces the Pentagon to spend money on weapons that it doesn't necessarily want or need.

Lockheed Martin, headquartered in Bethesda, Maryland, has major military research and production centers in eight other states: Moorestown, New Jersey; Marietta, Georgia; Oak Ridge, Tennessee; Colorado Springs, Colorado; Fort Worth, Texas; Albuquerque, New Mexico; Vandenberg Air Force Base and Sunnyvale, California; and at the Nuclear Test Site in Nevada. But actually the corporation maintains facilities in fifty states.[30] As John Pike, formerly of the Federation of American Scientists, said, Lockheed Martin carries a "big political footprint."[31]

Since 1994, when the Republicans gained control of both houses of Congress, billions of dollars beyond Pentagon requests have been added each year to the military budget. For instance, in the years 1996–98, 20 billion dollars extra was added, three-quarters of which was earmarked for weapons that benefited only their corporate producers.[32] Dozens of unnecessary weapons systems were crammed into the Pentagon budget during the Gingrich era in an add-on game called "the waste that keeps on wasting."[33]

An egregious example is the huge C-130 military transport plane, manufactured by Lockheed Martin just outside Newt Gingrich's congressional district in Georgia. Since 1978, the air force has requested only five of these planes, yet Congress built 256—a ratio of fifty for each plane requested! Republican Senator John McCain of Arizona was heard to say that there were so many surplus C-130s that "we could use them to house the homeless." Indeed, the air force was forced to retire more than a dozen C-130s because they had no use for them. (And Congress doesn't even budget for the actual operation of the planes—said to be 1 billion dollars over the next six years.) These C-130s are deployed as trophies with national guard units in the states of key congressional members—for example, more than a dozen C-130s sit at Kessler Air Force Base in Trent Lott's home state of Mississippi.

MERGED MONEY TALKS

Political donations represent even more overt efforts by the huge new military corporations to affect policy. In 1997, for example, the military corporations spent more than 2.4 million dollars contributing to political campaigns and parties. From 1991 to 1997 they surpassed even the tobacco companies in political donations by a margin of 32.3 to 26.9 million dollars. Lockheed Martin led the pack.[34] One Lockheed operator, Bernard Schwartz, a former company board member who owned Loral Industries before it merged with Lockheed in 1996, gave 601,000 dollars to the 1996 Democratic war chest and more than 1.1 million dollars to committees of the Democratic party in 2000.[35] And in just two years—1997 and 1998—America's six biggest weapons makers spent 51 million dollars actively lobbying for their killing weapons. Lockheed Martin alone spent 10.2 million dollars lobbying in 1997 and 1998.[36] (Of course most lobbying activities are tax deductible.)

Lockheed Martin has even installed company people in key positions in Democratic and Republican presidential campaigns. For example, Lockheed's vice president Bruce Jackson served as vice-chair for the Dole fundraising campaign in 1996; he subsequently occupied the same position for Governor George W. Bush in 2000. Lockheed

Martin shared the limelight at the 2000 Republican convention with other notable U.S. corporations, including the United States Tobacco Company, AT&T, Freddie Mac, and Southern Co. Each of these firms contributed 60,000 dollars to Senate Majority Leader Trent Lott for a fifties-style sock hop titled the "Lott Hop." Lockheed then cemented this political connection by pledging 1 million dollars to the "Trent Lott Leadership Institute."[37] Lott, it turns out, had helped to bail out Lockheed's multimillion-dollar F-22 fighter plane project in the late nineties, when it experienced huge cost overruns and was not performing according to specifications. He also helped to fund the construction of many superfluous C-130 planes, and he vigorously supported the theater high altitude area defense project (THAAD), for which Lockheed received 4 billion dollars. (THAAD has failed six of eight tests.)[38]

Lott's generosity did not stop there. In September 2000, he steered a bill through the Senate to provide 4 to 6 billion dollars in tax subsidies to the tobacco, arms, and pharmaceutical industries over the next decade. As William Hartung, a senior fellow at the World Policy Institute, writes, "The provision of the bill that would give double tax breaks to weapons exporters like Boeing, Raytheon, and Lockheed Martin is particularly outrageous. These companies already benefit from over seven billion dollars per year in government grants, loans, and promotional activities designed to promote U.S. weapons exports. . . . If there was ever an example of an industry that emphatically does not need more government subsidies, the U.S. weapons industry is it."[39]

Other corporate-influenced people at the Republican convention included House Majority Whip Tom DeLay, who received the Boeing-Lockheed award with no apparent embarrassment. When DeLay was later questioned about ubiquitous corporate donations, he said, "We're raising money left and right, we'll leave this convention with a significant amount of resources." Then he added "It's cynical for the media to make it like it's bad: it's better to raise money than to have the government pay for elections."[40] While 97 percent of Americans do not contribute to any political party,[41] Lockheed Martin, TRW, Raytheon, and Boeing collectively gave 6 million dollars in campaign contributions during the election year of 2000. (These weapons firms have consistently contributed more to Republicans than Democrats by a 2:1 margin since the Republicans took control of Congress in 1994.)[42]

And the connections don't stop there. George W. Bush attempted to award a contract to Lockheed Martin to run the Texas welfare system! Bush relented in the face of strong public opposition.[43] Lynne Cheney, the wife of the vice president, for years served on Lockheed's board, for which she received 120,000 dollars annually in compensation.

Dick Cheney himself served as secretary of defense under George Bush and was a fellow at the American Enterprise Institute from 1993 to 1995.[44] He scored a 100 percent rating from the American Conservative Union and zero percent from Americans for Democratic Action during the eighties.[45] Appointed chief executive of Halliburton corporation in 1995, he doubled the size of the company both through a series of mergers and through business deals with the Pentagon. Under Cheney's reign, Halliburton became one of the nation's largest weapons contractors, ranking twenty-second in prime Pentagon contracts by January 2001.[46] Cheney organized a 1.1-billion-dollar Pentagon contract for Halliburton to support military operations in the Balkans,[47] and 2.3 billion dollars in government loans, an increase from 1.2 billion dollars received over the previous five years. The company donated a total of 1.2 million dollars to both political parties and congress over five years, and in 1999 it spent 600,000 dollars on lobbying—up from 280,000 dollars in 1996. When Cheney retired to run for vice president, he left with a "package" of 20 million dollars in stock options and an overall worth of 50 million dollars.[48]

His Democratic opponent in the vice presidential race, Joseph Lieberman, is not without corporate taint either. Both Gore and Lieberman were avid solicitors of campaign funds from Lockheed Martin and Raytheon. Lieberman was one of the first Senate Democrats to join Senate Majority Leader Trent Lott and Senator Thad Cochran to support Star Wars. He lobbied extensively for the troubled Lockheed Martin F-22 plane (at 200 million dollars per plane it is the most expensive ever built); the engines are constructed by a branch of United Technologies in his home state of Connecticut. He received over 96,000 dollars in political donations from military corporations in 2000.[49]

Lieberman also supported loan-guarantee programs for countries buying American weapons, and he voted against the arms sale code of conduct—legislation that prevents weapons from being sold to countries with a poor human-rights record or countries that may be working on developing nuclear weapons. He voted consistently against initiatives to reduce the U.S. military budget, and supported programs to prevent transfer of money from military to domestic programs.[50] For the past five years he has served as chairman of the pro-military Democratic Leadership Council with a corporation-friendly, pro-military, fiscally conservative agenda. Although Lieberman was vocal about religion and personal behavior during the campaign, as William Hartung commented, the Democratic ticket demonstrated "a failure of public ethics, not private morality."[51]

TO THE VICTOR GO THE SPOILS

To give some feel for how Lockheed Martin has benefited through lobbying, revolving-door policies, political donations, etc., here is a short list of some of the company's nuclear weapons related contracts:

Lockheed Martin currently produces the Trident II submarine-launched ballistic missile, armed with eight 100- kiloton or 475- kiloton hydrogen bombs. (As a reference, the Hiroshima bomb was equivalent to 13 kilotons of TNT.) Each Trident submarine is equipped with 24 of these missiles. (Eighteen Trident subs, together containing killing power three times the threshold for nuclear winter, glide silently beneath the oceans of the world, invisible to all: a subliminal global holocaust machine.)

But this is not all.

Lockheed Martin has government contracts, all together worth billions of dollars, for:

- The payload launch vehicle for the interceptor system
- The space-based infrared system (SBIRS) "high" component
- The theater high altitude area defense (THAAD)

- The airborne laser (ABL), in partnership with Boeing and TRW
- The navy theater-wide system
- The medium extended air defense system (MEADS), in partnership with Alenia of Italy and Daimler Chrysler of Germany

On the side, Lockheed Martin is also developing the capability to conduct simulated nuclear tests at the Nevada Test Site with the Bechtel Corporation and receives 2 billion dollars a year to run the department of energy's Sandia National Laboratory in New Mexico.[52]

TWO CASE STUDIES

I once naively believed that the administration in power and Congress determined U.S. foreign policy. I was wrong. Here are but two examples of recent foreign policy deals orchestrated by the weapons industry.

NATO EXPANSION

During the cold war years, the North Atlantic Treaty Organization (NATO), was the military bulwark in Western Europe against invasion by the Soviet Union. Western European countries enjoyed "protection" under the American nuclear umbrella: If the Soviets invaded, America would use nuclear weapons to fend off the attack. If necessary, the U.S. would be prepared to absorb a nuclear attack on its own territory to defend its NATO allies. (The U.S. has always controlled the NATO alliance.)

When the Berlin Wall fell, the Bush administration promised Gorbachev that NATO would not expand into Eastern Europe if Russia did not oppose the admission of a unified Germany into the alliance. But when Clinton was elected, he decided to enlarge NATO, in violation of President Bush's agreement. By welcoming the Czech Republic, Hungary, and Poland into NATO, and arming these former Eastern Bloc countries—two of which directly adjoined the Russian border—America reestablished a hostile situation with Russia. The reason given was that free-market democratic reforms would be consolidated, and an expansion of the market into former Eastern Bloc countries would benefit trade and the U.S. economy. But the truth was different. U.S. military corporations knew that NATO expansion presented a huge marketing opportunity—any new NATO country would be forced to upgrade its weapons systems to NATO standards.

Lockheed Martin was well represented among the lobbyists. Bruce Jackson, a vice president, volunteered to become president of the U.S. Committee to Expand NATO, a lobbying and public education organization operating out of the offices of the American Enterprise Institute. This committee ran a series of ads in the congressional magazine *Roll Call*, stating that "Americans agree" on NATO expansion. (The "Americans" they chose were "Stormin" Norman Schwarzkopf and three former secretaries of state, including Henry Kissinger.) The Committee to Expand NATO delivered speeches, gave congressional briefings, published articles, produced white papers, and sponsored ad campaigns within the U.S., all promoting the "widest possible expansion of NATO."

In 1997, Norman Augustine toured prospective NATO countries and enthusiastically supported the entry of Romania into the club—a country that shares a long contiguous border with Russia and to which his company had already sold 82 million dollars in radar equipment. Lockheed Martin, Textron, and McDonnell Douglas funded organizations such as American Friends of the Czech Republic, and foundations promoting Romania's entry into NATO. They also bankrolled a public referendum in 1997 in Hungary on NATO expansion and vigorously worked with the top leadership in Poland, the Czech Republic, Romania, and Hungary to convince them that the best way to gain U.S. support for entry into NATO was to buy American weapons.

Despite official rhetoric to the contrary, the expansion of NATO was entirely about weapons sales, the bill for which will run in the range of 500 billion dollars over twelve to fifteen years—2500 dollars for every American household, since America ends up bankrolling much of this military expenditure. Sales to foreign governments are particularly lucrative for weapons manufacturers, since by the time the weapons are ready for export, all research, development, and initial production problems have been covered by the U.S. taxpayer. But forcing the impoverished nations of the former Soviet bloc to buy sophisticated weapons as they experienced freedom was an act of cynicism and exploitation. Furthermore, it is unethical for any foreign corporation or government to interfere with the domestic politics of other countries. (Remember the furor created when China was said to have contributed to Clinton's reelection campaign in 1996?)

In 1998 the Senate voted 81 to 19 to expand NATO, adding Poland, Hungary, and the Czech Republic (Romania did not make it on this round). Russia was understandably furious, regarding the U.S. as hostile and dishonest, and backed away from talks to reduce nuclear weapons. In April 1999 a lavish event was thrown in Washington, D.C. to celebrate NATO's fiftieth anniversary. International politicians and weapons makers mingled at the party that was funded by Boeing, Lockheed Martin, and United Technologies, each of whom donated 250,000 dollars.

And there was an added cause for celebration: the war in Yugoslavia was at its zenith. Although it would cost U.S. taxpayers about 1 billion dollars per month, it was good for corporate business. Replacement of lost Raytheon-made Tomahawk cruise missiles used in battle (each lost cruise missile costs 1 million dollars to replace) and Lockheed Martin F-16 and F-22 fighter planes would provide billions in new contracts for the weapons makers.[53]

When Bush visited Europe in June 2001, he continued actively to promote NATO expansion.

LIFTING THE ARMS BAN ON LATIN AMERICA AND OTHER FOREIGN MILITARY SALES

For twenty years the United States had a policy banning arms sales to Latin America because it was populated by brutal dictators. However, when the Reagan years ended and the domestic weapons spending bonanza faded, foreign markets were seen as a way to increase corporate profits. Lockheed Martin, Boeing, and others decided to eliminate restrictions based on human rights or the possible nuclear weapon proliferation record of a particular country in order to avail themselves of new weapons "markets." They also decided to organize new government subsidies so that U.S. taxpayer dollars would supply cash to foreign countries to buy weapons.

Clinton's defense secretary, William Perry (formerly Norman Augustine's paid consultant), joined Lockheed Martin to become an advocate within the administration to lift the Latin American weapons ban despite strenuous resistance by the state department. To this end, the air force performed demonstration flights of the F-16 fighter plane at the 1996 air show in Santiago, Chile, and Brazilian generals were invited into the cockpits of F-16 planes to do test flights. Aerospace lobbyists then organized thirty-eight senators and seventy-eight house members to send letters to Secretary of State Warren Christopher (a former director of Lockheed) supporting the abolition of the ban. (This was lucrative work because these legislators subsequently received a total of 1 million dollars in political action committee contributions from the relevant military companies.) A Lockheed Martin brochure was published on their web site and distributed at arms conferences and on the Hill, touting the Latin arms market as a 3- to 15-billion-dollar opportunity over the next ten years.

At the same time, former Costa Rican president and Nobel Peace Prize winner Oscar Arias Sánchez was vigorously promoting a moratorium on sales of advanced weapons to countries in Latin America to promote conflict prevention and force reductions.[54] Yet President Clinton's allegiance was to the weapons industry. (On the contrary, Jimmy Carter displayed moral fortitude in the face of corporate displeasure—one notorious Carter state department cable, which became known as the "leprosy letter," warned its diplomats to shun arms exporters.)[55] In May 1993, Secretary of State Christopher instructed U.S. embassies to assist arms companies in promoting international trade. To consolidate this policy, two years later, in February 1995, President Clinton issued Presidential Directive 41, stating that arms sales were essential for preserving industrial jobs. The directive ordered the diplomatic corps to boost arms sales.[56]

The State Department appointed a semi-official body—the Defense Trade Advisory Group (DTAG) to advise on arms exports. In a direct conflict of interest, its forty members included representatives from Boeing, United Technologies, Hughes, Allied Signal, Litton Industries, Raytheon, General Dynamics, Loral Space Systems, the Electronic Industries Association, and the Aerospace Industries Association.[57] In 1995 the federal government also created the 15-billion-dollar Defense Export Loan Guarantee (DELG) program, together with other financially supportive government programs.

These new weapons export policies are complementary to Article XXI in the General Agreement on Tariffs and Trade (GATT), which directs countries to take any action they consider necessary to protect their essential security interests—actions "relating to the traffic in arms, ammunition and implements of war and such traffic in other goods and materials as is carried on directly for the purpose of supplying a military establishment."[58] The GATT accord was written in 1993 by transnational lawyers, some of whom represented the military-industrial complex.

Lockheed Martin and others benefit hugely from foreign military sales. American firms typically arm both sides in regional conflicts, a practice that is fundamentally good for business. Ancient enemies are armed: Turkey and Greece for their conflict in Cyprus, India and Pakistan, Peru and Ecuador, Taiwan and China, and Israel and every other country in the Middle East—the world's largest arms market. Ironically, if a country previously armed by America—such as Iraq—becomes an "enemy," U.S. troops will be killed by American weapons.

In 1999, America garnered 39 percent of new weapons contracts, deals that netted 11.8 billion dollars—outdoing the sales of Russia, France, Britain, and China combined.[59] Secretary of Defense William Cohen's worldwide travels resembled marketing tours for weapons. He encouraged Chile and Argentina, longtime enemies, to upgrade their arsenals; he pushed weapons in the Persian Gulf states, in Eastern Europe, in Western European countries, in Japan, and in Australia. No country is exempt from the outreach of the United States.[60]

Here is a sampling of weapons sold abroad by Lockheed Martin from 1994 to 2000:

- Advanced gunnery-training systems to Egypt
- Army tactical missiles (ATACMs) and launch assemblies to Greece and South Korea
- C-130 Hercules transport planes and/or associated spare parts to Bangladesh, Brazil, South Korea, Kuwait, Saudi Arabia, and Tai-

wan (Turkey and Zimbabwe also took some spare parts of C-139 airplanes)

- C-130 transport planes to Bolivia, Botswana, Bulgaria, Ethiopia, Greece, the Philippines, Romania, South Africa, Tunisia, and Zimbabwe, and H-30 transport planes to Malaysia
- F-16 fighter jets to South Korea and Taiwan (Turkey and Egypt received upgrades to their F-16s)
- F-16 A/B Fighting Falcons to Bahrain and Jordan; F-16 C/D Falcons and upgrades to Bahrain, Egypt, and Singapore; F-104s to Zimbabwe
- Hellfire II air-to-ground antitank missiles to Egypt, Israel, Kuwait, and Taiwan
- LANTIRN (low-altitude navigation and targeting infrared for night) navigation pods to Egypt, Singapore, and Turkey
- MK-41 vertical-launch system to South Korea
- Multiple-Launch Rocket Systems (MIRSs) to Israel, South Korea, and Turkey
- Multiple-Launch Rocket Systems–Extended Range (MLRS-ER) to South Korea
- P-3B Orion patrol aircraft to Argentina and Greece
- Sharpshooter infantry fighting vehicles to Egypt
- T-33 to Zimbabwe and Turkey
- Walleye missile tube vidicons to Israel[61]

Chapter Five

MANHATTAN II

SS & M is a scientific and technical challenge perhaps as formidable as the Manhattan Project.

—Dr. Victor Reis, assistant secretary
of defense programs at the DOE

IN THE LAST SIX years, the nuclear weapons laboratories—Los Alamos and Sandia in New Mexico and Lawrence Livermore in California—have embarked upon the largest scientific endeavor ever attempted. This new project, the Stockpile Stewardship and Management Program, nicknamed Manhattan II, was ostensibly instituted to ensure the proper functioning of the U.S. stockpile of nuclear weapons post–cold war. But this benign description disguises the truth. Nuclear scientists are actually designing, developing, testing, and constructing new nuclear weapons at an annual cost of 5 billion dollars over the next ten to fifteen years.

Authorization of Manhattan II was the price the department of energy exacted in 1995 for nominally agreeing to extend the nuclear Non Proliferation Treaty (NPT). Officially, the U.S. played a key role in convincing 180 other nations to sign the extension, which reads in part:

> Each of the Parties to the Treaty undertakes to pursue negotiations in good faith on effective measures relating to cessation of the nuclear arms race at an early date and to nuclear disarmament, and on a treaty on general and complete disarmament under strict and effective international control.[1]

In 1996, five nuclear weapons nations—Russia, France, England, China, and the U.S. (excluding India, Pakistan, and Israel)—and forty-four other countries with the potential to construct nuclear weapons, also agreed to abide by the Comprehensive Test Ban Treaty (CTBT). The CTBT preamble states:

> . . . (T)he cessation of all nuclear weapons test explosions and all other nuclear explosions, by constraining the development and qualitative improvement of nuclear weapons and ending the development of advanced new types of nuclear weapons, constitutes an effective measure of nuclear disarmament and nonproliferation in all its aspects . . .

These were noble ideals on the part of the international community and appropriate in the post–cold war era. However, the treaties provoked a major battle for power and control within the U.S. nuclear establishment. In a seemingly irreconcilable irony, the nuclear labs and their overseer, the department of energy, would allow America to be party to a ban on nuclear testing only if the labs were granted funding to expand their nuclear weapons operations. Thus, violation of both international treaties designed to control the spread of nuclear weapons was built into acceptance.

Technically known as the Stockpile Stewardship and Management Program, the new effort was abbreviated to SS & M (amusingly reminiscent of the acronym for sexual sadomasochism, and thus very much in keeping with all the other sexual language of the nuclear labs). According to the labs, the SS & M program is designed to ensure the safety and reliability of the U.S. nuclear stockpile. But, as a February 1996 publication from the DOE makes clear, the labs' real mandate goes far beyond safety and reliability: "Ability to design new warheads will be retained by DOE at its defense programs (DP) laboratories: Los Alamos National Laboratory (LANL), Lawrence Livermore National Laboratory (LLNL) and Sandia National Laboratory (SNL)."[2]

SS & M's real agenda is as follows:

- To expand the scientific knowledge and understanding of nuclear weapons physics and engineering by creating and outfitting a host of new sophisticated experimental facilities

- To model the behavior of exploding nuclear weapons using the world's fastest computers
- To refurbish and modernize all the weapons in the stockpile by replacing components with updated versions and, in some cases, by designing and manufacturing completely *new* nuclear weapons[3]

At the height of the cold war, the U.S. spent an average of 3.8 billion dollars a year on nuclear weapons design, testing, and manufacture. Now, twelve years after the end of the cold war, it is spending 5 billion dollars annually over a ten- to 15-year period on a project that will violate both the Comprehensive Test Ban Treaty and the nuclear Non Proliferation Treaty.[4]* America is engaged in "vertical proliferation"—building more nuclear weapons—which encourages other nuclear countries to do the same. And America is triggering "lateral proliferation," in which nonnuclear nations, emulating its example, will almost certainly develop their own nuclear weapons. Among the side effects of such a wrongheaded effort are the health problems faced by tens of thousands of nuclear industry workers each year and the environmental hazards created by waste products and abandoned sites, discussed at the end of this chapter.

THE INFRASTRUCTURE OF SS & M

STOCKPILED WEAPONS

Nuclear weapons are extremely complex systems composed of more than 5000 parts. Fundamentally they consist of a primary and a secondary mechanism. The primary is usually a hollow sphere of plutonium or highly enriched uranium in some cases, surrounded by conventional explosives. Tritium is injected into the sphere to boost the explosive yield of the primary. The conventional explosives initiate the chain reaction by compressing the plutonium into a critical mass.

* This unstable situation was worsened in 2000 when, to the disquiet of the rest of the world, Jesse Helms, the powerful chairman of the Senate foreign relations committee, convinced the Republican-controlled Senate not to ratify the Comprehensive Test Ban Treaty.

The intense flux of gamma and X rays derived from the explosion of the primary are then reflected and directed into the secondary mechanism composed of uranium, lithium, and deuterium compounds. This induces nuclear fusion. The fusion reaction in the secondary mechanism determines the size of the explosion. Hydrogen bombs are cheap to make—cheaper by far than the cost of deploying troops. They can also be very large—50 megatons or the equivalent of 50 million tons of TNT. (The Hiroshima bomb that destroyed a city was a 13,000-ton equivalent.)

Over the years, the U.S. has built 70,302 nuclear weapons using sixty-five different designs. From 1945 to 1991 the U.S. conducted 1030 tests, while the Soviet Union exploded 715, France 210, China 45, England 45, and India 5.[5]

JUSTIFICATION FOR SS & M

SS & M is ostensibly designed to ensure the safety and reliability of the U.S.'s aging stockpile of nuclear weapons. *Safety* is typically defined as a certified guarantee that a bomb will not inadvertently explode should it be involved in an accident—for example, dropped from a crane, or enveloped in a fire. Safety is not affected by aging of the bomb. In fact, weapons actually become safer as they age because the metals corrode, adhesives degrade, and component parts crack, making them less likely to explode by accident. DOE also found no evidence that aging will make the chemical explosive more sensitive.

Reliability is a guarantee that bombs will explode as programmed.[6] A recent DOE study conducted by the JASONS (a group of distinguished scientists who work for the Mitre Corporation and who advise the DOD and DOE on issues of national security) determined that even if the DOE did nothing to detect and repair defects in bomb components, fewer than 2 percent of the stockpiled warheads would fail to function in the first thirty years after manufacture. They also found no evidence to suggest that the rate of failure would increase for older weapons.[7] In fact, since 1970, no defects have been found in the stockpile of nuclear weapons when they were subjected to underground testing. Since 1991, no U.S. weapon has been retired because of aging.

Many experts concur that 100 hydrogen bombs would suffice to guarantee American deterrence. So even if the present stockpile of over 10,000 bombs were left untouched, only some would degrade, over a long time, and the degradation could easily be detected by physical examination of the weapons. The defective bombs could then be removed from the arsenal.[8]

THE TRUE AGENDA

The Stockpile Stewardship and Management Program is not necessary for reasons of either safety or reliability. Contrary to the DOE's alleged motivations, the scientists involved know that testing has little impact on either of these issues. (Indeed, if weapon designs are altered as a result of SS & M research without the benefit of full-scale testing, safety could actually be *compromised.*[9] So the Manhattan II project stands to endanger the very issue of safety that it is said to protect.) In fact, the real agenda of SS & M is nuclear weapons development, and internal DOE documents make that incontrovertibly clear. According to the Stockpile Stewardship and Management Program released by the DOE's office of defense programs on February 29, 1996, for example, the SS & M program is designed to "maintain a surge capability to rebuild a larger stockpile."

NEW WEAPONS DESIGNS AND MODIFICATIONS

Actually, the scientists have already made a new nuclear weapon, violating the NPT. This is the B61-11 earth-penetrating "bunker buster," the first new weapon produced since 1989, designed to have a variable yield of 300 tons to over 300 kilotons. Twelve feet long and weighing 1200 pounds, this bomb is to replace the old B53, with a 9-megaton yield. It has a casing made of uranium 238 (depleted uranium), which is 1.7 times more dense than lead.[10] Because of its weight it supposedly can burrow 15 to 20 feet into the earth before exploding. It is, the scientists say, "a new way to hold at risk robustly defended, deeply buried targets,"[11]—for example, Saddam Hussein's bunker. (This is one glaring example of excess. Any nuclear weapon exploding at ground level will gouge out a huge crater in the earth. It doesn't need to "burrow." Furthermore, the construction of such small nuclear weapons may make their use "thinkable," breaking the traditional fire wall between conventional and nuclear war.)

Two new bombs are on the drawing board. One is another updated version of the B-61 equipped with wings, which flies after being dropped from a plane, allowing the plane itself to escape from the close proximity of the nuclear explosion. This bomb is called BIOS (bomb impact optimization system).[12] The other is a new warhead for the Trident missiles, but this is cloaked in secrecy.

The labs are also designing new weapons for the Mark 5 missile of the Trident submarine. One will utilize an existing plutonium pit and the other will require a new pit design. (New pit manufacturing is a medically dangerous process exposing workers to carcinogenic doses of plutonium.) Los Alamos National Lab plans to manufacture between 80 and 500 new pits annually—which signifies the addition of 80 to 500 new nuclear weapons per year.[13]

These new Trident weapons are designed to foil the intent of START (Strategic Arms Reduction Treaty) II, which was specifically designed to eradicate first-strike weapons capable of destroying missile silos, or "hard targets." Most of America's hard-target weapons are deployed in ground-based intercontinental missiles, as are the Russian weapons. But by upgrading the Trident missiles to extreme accuracy, the U.S. will retain its hard-target capability after seeming to comply with START II. No wonder the rest of the world views America's nuclear policies with cynicism.

In October 2000 Congress passed an authorization bill for research and possible development of a "user friendly" mini-nuke. Designed to be less than 5 kilotons in size, it will exert a one-mile radius of blast destruction. (The Hiroshima bomb at 13 kilotons experienced a blast radius of one and a half miles.)[14] Stephen Younger, associate laboratory director for nuclear weapons at Los Alamos National Laboratory, wrote that these low-yield weapons offer the "advantage" of "reduced collateral damage"—but only by half a mile. Younger enthused in a paper titled "Nuclear Weapons in the Twenty-First Century" that mini-nukes would not require testing because they could use enriched uranium instead of plutonium and be triggered by a well-known "gun assembly" mechanism—which was deployed in Little Boy, the Hiroshima bomb. (Enriched uranium combined with the gun assembly is a tried-and-true design and does not need to be tested.) Like the bunker buster, mini-nukes would most likely be regarded as weapons on the battlefield to be used to "defeat hardened and deeply buried targets," thus again crossing the fire wall between conventional and nuclear weapons.

Years ago, the military used Davy Crocketts, similar tactical nuclear weapons small enough to be carried into the battlefield on the shoulders of soldiers. Congress was so worried about these weapons that they banned them under a 1994 defense authorization act. But in 2000, championed by leading Senate Republicans, mini-nukes were authorized[15] and another new weapon was spawned under the guise of testing for safety and reliability.

Since the September 11 attack, there have been numerous suggestions both from within and without the Bush administration to use nuclear weapons in Afghanistan. Secretary of Defense Donald Rumsfeld has categorically failed to rule out the use of nuclear weapons in this war, and Andrew Card, White House chief of staff, said, when asked about the possible use of nuclear weapons, "I'm not going to talk about the operations that might be considered by the defense department and the president. But we're going to do everything we can to defend the United States."[16] Specific nuclear weapons suggested for use in this war are bunker busters, mini-nukes, and neutron bombs.[17] The latter suggestion, made by Sam Cohen, the inventor of the neutron bomb, was received sympathetically by some in the Washington establishment.[18]

Other nuclear weapon "upgrades" are being contemplated by the labs. DOE has elaborate plans to replace each of the thousands of parts in every nuclear weapon on a regular schedule, including the plutonium pit. Parts will be refurbished and modernized with new components of new design.[19] A large arsenal of a variety of modernized nuclear warheads, many of low to moderate yield, will be fitted to an array of faster, stealthier, long-range delivery platforms (planes and missiles). These "platforms" will be equipped with sophisticated electronics, and fully integrated into the U.S. military's vision of a twenty-first century battlefield—a battlefield dominated by satellite surveillance, remotely deployed sensor arrays, and precision weaponry.[20] All of this seems to lose sight of the fact that when the first nuclear weapons are detonated, the "battlefield" will disappear.

THE FACILITIES

Twenty-five thousand people are employed in nuclear facilities located in seven states, researching, testing, and producing nuclear weapon components under the guise of SS & M. These facilities include Lawrence Livermore and Sandia National Labs in California, Los Alamos and Sandia National Labs in New Mexico, the Pantex plant in Texas, the Kansas City plant, the Y-12 plant in Tennesee, the Savannah River plant in South Carolina, and the Nevada Test Site (NTS). All of these facilities were used in the past during the cold war to design, test, and build nuclear weapons. They are ostensibly used to support SS & M, but most are currently being upgraded for the new surge in sophisticated nuclear weapons production.

Broadly speaking, the facilities are devoted to a number of related endeavors, including:

- Learning more about the behavior of plutonium: stereoscopic views of imploding plutonium pits are being created, and experiments are being conducted to simulate "virtually" the behavior of this critical nuclear element
- Experimenting with fusion: machines such as the X-1, which can induce fusion, are being built; laser-powered fusion is being explored; and different "igniters" are being tested
- Testing nuclear weapons: subcritical tests that are difficult to detect are being conducted; facilities to resume full-scale testing are being built as the U.S. plans to abandon the Comprehensive Test Ban Treaty within months of September 2001; and virtual testing via elaborate computer models is being undertaken
- Building new nuclear weapons: the next generation of upgrades to nuclear weapon components—including the design, integration, prototyping, fabrication, and qualification of microsystems for weapon components—is being manufactured

LEARNING MORE ABOUT THE BEHAVIOR OF PLUTONIUM

Hydrodynamic and High-Explosive Test Facilities

The term *hydrodynamic* applies to the motion of plutonium in the pit just before it reaches critical mass. As we've seen, it is compressed by conventional explosives under extremely high pressures in millionths of a second, and it apparently acts like a liquid under pressure. Now, high-energy X rays are being tested that will penetrate deep inside the imploding pit, produce visual images, and take electrical and optical measurements. The scientists will then produce images of the exploding plutonium.

Six of these hydrodynamic measuring facilities are already operational. Two new highly sophisticated operations are under construction or planned: a dual-axis radiographic hydrodynamic test facility (DARHT), and an advanced hydrotest facility (AHF). One DARHT has recently been completed at the Los Alamos Lab to provide stereoscopic images of imploding plutonium pits. Equipped with separate beam lines, the machine will take pictures from two directions. A second axis will be added to give stereoscopic viewing (3-D) of imploding pits. This will produce four images of the pit over a period of four nanoseconds.

And as a follow-on to the DAHRT, the AHF will utilize proton radiography to penetrate deeper into the pit. Four axes are planned to provide 3-D images from multiple directions, each axis producing twenty images in rapid succession. AHF will be constructed at Los Alamos or the Nevada Test Site.

Pulse-Powered Facilities

Virtual experiments are currently being conducted to simulate the behavior of plutonium without actually using the element. Short, intense bursts of electrical energy are focused onto targets to induce extremely high temperatures and/or pressures approaching conditions within a nuclear explosion—millions of degrees centigrade and pressures many times above atmospheric pressure. These experiments are designed to test the basic physics of matter at high energy density. The data is used to improve and test computer codes which model nuclear weapons behavior. Seven of these plutonium testing facilities are already operational. A new one is planned.

Joint Actinide Shock Physics Experimental Research (JASPER)

This is to be a two-stage gas gun able to shoot projectiles that travel at 8 to 15 kilometers per second onto plutonium and uranium targets. Operated by the Lawrence Livermore Lab and under construction at the NTS, it is designed to examine the properties of these and other such materials at high pressures, temperatures, and strain rates.

EXPERIMENTING WITH FUSION

Machines that can induce fusion are being built, laser-powered fusion is being explored, and different "igniters" are being tested.

X-I Machine

This machine, to be constructed at a Sandia National Labs facility, is expected to produce temperatures greater than 3 million degrees Kelvin and enough X-ray energy and power to implode fusion capsules of deuterium and tritium to achieve high-yield fusion. The Sandia scientists believe that this machine could be built for "just" 1 billion dollars.

Inertial Confinement Fusion (ICF)

A major DOE program is being designed to study and produce laser-powered, inertial confinement fusion. Multiple intense laser beams are to be focused on targets of tritium and deuterium in order to heat and compress these elements until they fuse to induce an enormous amount of energy. Already fusion has been produced in a primitive fashion, but not actual "ignition," which simulates the actual energy released in the sun and stars. Five such facilities are already in operation at the labs, but this seems not to be enough.

National Ignition Facility (NIF)

This stadium-sized facility is presently under construction at Lawrence Livermore Lab. Designed to be the world's most energetic laser, it was initially pegged to cost 1.2 billion dollars, but it has incurred huge cost overruns—and an enormous degree of controversy. Completion is now estimated at 4 billion dollars. The lifetime cost over thirty years, including disassembly and cleanup, could approach 10 billion dollars.

Saddled with a history of technical mismanagement, aborted and inadequate peer reviews, endless R and D requirements, and spiraling costs, this facility is one of the more expensive components of the SS & M program.[21, 22] Diagnostic costs have not yet been included in the cost estimates.[23]

The NIF will consist of 192 separate laser beams. When focused on a single target, the combined energy released in bursts of just three-billionths of a second will be 1.8 million joules (a measurement of energy). The laser beams will be fired simultaneously to converge on a tiny BB-sized pellet containing the thermonuclear fuel of tritium and deuterium. For a brief instant, temperatures will reach 100 million degrees centigrade, and the pressure will be 100 billion times earth's atmosphere—conditions existing in the center of the sun.

But there is work to be done. A suitable material for ignition-capable targets has yet to be found. Also, when each laser beam is converted to ultraviolet light (third harmonic), it severely damages the expensive optic components, causing them to explode after only a few dozen experiments.

If successful, the national ignition facility could stimulate the development of a pure fusion bomb. If there are no fission products involved in the production of nuclear weapons, their construction cannot be detected by satellites or other technical means. This means that arms-control verification will be nullified.

Ted Taylor, a highly regarded physicist and former bomb designer at Los Alamos, believes the NIF laser could provide the scientific "means" to move the U.S. to the next level of weapons development. If successful, he says, the United States will have unleashed an entirely new threat to the planet's safety.

The NIF laser has absolutely nothing to do with safety and reliability of nuclear weapons. According to Bob Puerifoy, a retired vice president of Sandia National Labs, who for thirty-nine years has been designing, testing, and evaluating nuclear weapons, "NIF is worthless . . . [it] can't be used to maintain the stockpile, period."

When Edward Teller was asked what role NIF would have in maintaining the nuclear stockpile, he said "none whatsoever."

Also, five facilities that are used to *split* atoms—be they nuclear reactors or accelerators—already exist at the nuclear weapons labs; a sixth is about to be built.

TESTING NUCLEAR WEAPONS

Article 1 of the CTBT states, "each state party undertakes not to carry out any nuclear weapons test explosion or any other nuclear explosion and to prohibit any such nuclear explosion at any place under its juristiction or control." Yet subcritical tests that are difficult to detect are being conducted by the U.S. (and probably by other countries as well), facilities to resume full-scale testing are being built, and virtual testing via elaborate computer models is being undertaken.

Nevada Test Site (NTS)

In 1995, DOE awarded a five-year 1.5-billion-dollar contract to Bechtel Corporation to manage the Nevada Test Site for the possible resumption of full-scale underground nuclear testing. Lockheed Martin, as previously noted, has also been involved in the NTS. In the meantime, DOE conducts four underground nuclear tests a year using small subcritical quantities of plutonium. High explosives compress the plutonium and its physical properties are collated and observed when it is "shocked." This data is then incorporated into computer models of nuclear weapon performance.

Since 1996, nine subcritical tests have taken place at the NTS, under DOE code names such as *rebound, oboe, bassoon,* and *holog.* Clearly these tests violate the letter and the law of the CTBT. Difficult to detect because of their size, they complicate seismic verification of the CTB treaty.[24]

It is known that Russia and France are also conducting subcritical tests. Other countries will inevitably follow suit.

The Nevada Test Site is a huge facility. There are more than 1100 support buildings and labs, dozens of holes ready for future underground tests, and extensive equipment and personnel on the ready for the resumption of full-scale nuclear testing. DOE is in the process of renovating 37 miles of roads, and it is currently replacing an electrical supply substation and other electrical facilities.

Los Alamos National Laboratory

Subcritical tests are also being conducted at the Los Alamos National Lab. This program, code named *appaloosa,* is conducted in utmost secrecy, using an eight-foot diameter, two-inch thick, single-use vessel made of special steel developed for submarine hulls.

According to researcher Greg Mello from the Western States Legal Foundation, these Los Alamos tests probably serve several purposes, but one is the unique capability to conduct detailed implosion studies of full primaries using plutonium 242. According to Mello, the tests are the closest thing to an actual nuclear explosion without an actual nuclear detonation. That seems to be the plan for newly manufactured W-88 pits, and for the W-76 replacement warhead, both of which are newly designed bombs.[25]

BUILDING NEW NUCLEAR WEAPONS AND UPGRADING FACILITIES

Camouflaged by "stockpile management" jargon, the next generation of upgrades to nuclear weapon components—including the design, integration, prototyping, fabrication, and qualification of microsystems for weapon components—is being manufactured, and with it, what amounts to brand-new nuclear weapons.

Accelerated Strategic Computer Initiative (ASCI)

A massive undertaking is underway at all three nuclear weapons labs to develop computers with enormous speed and memory capacities far greater than available today.

The computers will be used to model precisely the behavior of an exploding nuclear weapon through all its stages in order to develop extremely complex nuclear weapons codes for virtual testing of nuclear weapons. They will also be used for weapons design, production and accident analysis, for certification, and for the prototyping of manufacturing techniques.[26]

Existing facilities include the ASCI Red Terascale computer, the world's fastest computer, at Sandia Labs; the ASCI Blue Mountain computer, the third fastest computer in the world, at Los Alamos; and the ASCI Blue Pacific computer at Lawrence Livermore Lab, running at 80,000 times the memory of the average personal computer.

The Red Terascale and Blue Mountain computers recently simulated a 3-D explosion in the secondary component of a hydrogen bomb for the first time, and the Blue Pacific simulated a 3-D explosion in the primary plutonium trigger for the first time.[27] So the nuclear establishment is already well on its way into this series of experiments. And more sophisticated computers are planned.

The ASCI Option White TeraOPS computer is currently being built jointly by IBM and the Lawrence Livermore Lab at a cost of 110 million dollars. This will be the world's fastest, most powerful computer. A 30-TeraOPS computer is planned for Los Alamos Lab and a 100-TeraOPS computer for Lawrence Livermore. Each lab, evidently, must have its own.

All of these supercomputers will be manufactured by Intel Corporation, Silicon Graphics Corporation (and its subsidiary, Cray), and IBM.

Other R and D Test Facilities

There are nine major operational facilities at the nuclear weapons labs that work with and on plutonium, tritium, uranium, beryllium, silicon-based microelectronics devices, chemical facilities, flight-test facilities, and high-explosive facilities. All are related to the development of nuclear weapons.

Two more facilities are planned—the first is a chemistry and metallurgy research building (CMR) at Los Alamos, to be constructed for research and experimentation in analytical chemistry, metallurgy, and plutonium and uranium chemistry. The price? One billion dollars. This building will be equipped with hot-cells and glove boxes to handle and machine the plutonium metal with lathes. In all, Los Alamos plans to manufacture 80 to 500 new plutonium pits per year for the equivalent number of hydrogen bombs.[28]

The second is a microsystems and engineering sciences applications (MESA) facility, destined for construction at Sandia. MESA will be used to manufacture the next generation of upgrades to nuclear weapon components, including the design, integration, prototyping, fabrication, and qualification of microsystems for weapon components. The facility will cost 400 million dollars.

Manufacturing Facilities

There are seven huge nuclear weapons complexes, apart from the nuclear weapons labs, which have been operational for decades.

Over many years these facilities have become extremely polluted. They include the Kansas City plant (KCP); the Y-12 plant in Oak Ridge, Tennessee; the Pantex plant in Texas; the Savannah River plant (SRP) in Aikin, South Carolina; the TA-55 plutonium facility at Los Alamos; the nonnuclear manufacturing facilities at Los Alamos; and the neutron generator facility (NGF) at Sandia Labs.

Seven more facilities are planned for the production of ever more hydrogen bombs. These include a tritium extraction facility (TEF) at Savannah River, new uranium enrichment facilities at Y-12, a storage site for enriched uranium, and two other sites to manufacture plutonium pits for bombs. The largest will be the large-scale-pit production facility at Los Alamos at a cost of 3 billion dollars.

It is hard to pretend that any of these activities, let alone all of them, are being undertaken in the name of safety and reliability of already-existing weapons that have been stockpiled.

HAZARDS OF SS & M

COMPUTER CHAOS

In some cases, work that is taking place at these facilities may actually *jeopardize* the reliability and safety of existing weapons. For many years, for example, computer calculations bridged the gap between partial experimental measurements gained from actual nuclear tests and incomplete theoretical understanding of the bomb mechanism. These calculations provided a working predictive capability for the design and production of many generations of nuclear weapons. Obviously, as computers became increasingly sophisticated, fewer actual nuclear tests were needed. Computer codes thus became an integrated compendium of the diverse scientific and engineering knowledge relevant to the construction and function of nuclear weapons, even becoming the principal design tools for specific weapons. The goal of the SS & M program is to construct a three-dimensional, full-physics, full-system computer simulation of the explosion of a nuclear weapon. The problem is that as more new and sophisticated data is fed into these supercomputers, the old nuclear codes derived from nuclear testing become confused. In other words, new data erodes the predictive capability of the old nuclear weapon performance codes. Any change in the proven design of a hydrogen bomb undermines its reliability. Therefore, the greater the number of changes induced by a massive array of experiments, the greater will be the incentive to resort to full-scale underground testing.

ACADEMIC STRATEGIC ALLIANCES PROGRAM (ASAP) AND INTERNATIONAL ACCESS TO WEAPON DESIGN

Perhaps the most dangerous aspect of SS & M is its real potential to put sensitive nuclear weapons data into the hands of nonnuclear nations. By developing alliances with a number of universities and offering their students and staff access to previously confidential material, this program could give foreign nationals free access to U.S. nuclear weapons design for the first time. This situation will expedite the ability of nonnuclear countries to design and build advanced nuclear weapons. (The department of energy actually acknowledges the problem. A 1995 report titled "The National Ignition Facility and the Issue of Nonproliferation," states that "a modern, sophisticated proliferator with access to ICF computer codes and today's computer workstations would have far more tools for designing a secondary [the major component of a hydrogen bomb] than the U.S., U.K., or U.S.S.R. had in the 1950s, or France or China in the 1960s.")[29] This potentially dangerous situation has been alleviated somewhat since the concern at Los Alamos about a potential Chinese spy, Wen Ho Lee, who in December 1999 was charged with downloading sensitive nuclear weapons codes onto insecure computers. He was later cleared of virtually all charges. Since September 11, however, there will almost certainly be stringent conditions imposed upon the ASAP program to prevent foreign students gaining access to sensitive nuclear weapons data.[30]

On July 31, 1997, the DOE announced the award of multimillion-dollar, multiyear contracts to five universities. The purpose was to study basic science, computer science, mathematics, and engineering research for the U.S. nuclear weapons program.[31] Thus nongovernment academic scientists are to be involved in the development of nuclear weapons for the first time since the Manhattan Project.[32]

The lucky campuses are as follows: the California Institute of Technology, Stanford University, the University of Chicago, the University of Illinois at Urbana-Champaign, and the University of Utah. In all, a total of fourteen universities and colleges are already participating to some degree in the ASAP. Each university is to receive 20 to 30 million dollars over a five-year period, possibly to be extended for another five years at another 20 to 30 million dollars.

The universities are establishing "centers of excellence" operating as partners with the nuclear weapons labs in the accelerated strategic computer initiative. This exercise is classified as "level one" funding. Levels two and three are in the pipeline. The schools will work in close collaboration with Los Alamos, Lawrence Livermore, and Sandia on R and D activities in specific areas related to nuclear weapons development as follows:

- The California Institute of Technology (Caltech) will develop a "virtual shock tube," a computer simulation of the detonation of high explosives and the effect of the ensuing shock waves on specific test materials related to nuclear weapons—plutonium and uranium.

  At this stage it is not clear whether data from this virtual shock tube could be incorporated into the labs' supercomputers as a nuclear weapons code. A bomb code would also need to include—

critically—fission and fusion nuclear processes, plus the energy released in the explosion.

Caltech will investigate the combined simulations of high explosives with shocked materials (including plutonium and other materials used in nuclear weapons); it will also investigate the physical dynamics at material interfaces of these metals, plus shock-induced compressible turbulence and the mixing within these test materials.

The Caltech program is ambiguous. On the one hand it will be required to produce unclassified research material and to educate foreign students; on the other, it must produce data relevant to the explosion of nuclear weapons. This means that foreign nationals will have free access to the design of nuclear weapons—previously a closely guarded secret. This posture will obviously induce a conflict of interest for the university and the labs if lateral proliferation of nuclear weapons is to be avoided.[33]

- The University of Chicago plans to simulate thermonuclear processes that operate within the sun and stars. This research could be complementary to the Caltech program.
- Stanford University is to research the dynamics of gas turbine engines, specifically examining turbulence within gaseous and solid states, with specific reference to materials incorporated in thermonuclear weapons.
- The University of Illinois at Urbana-Champaign will conduct research on solid rocket propellants used in missiles. This program will concentrate on broad simulation issues of multicomponent, multiphenomena, and multiscale systems for solid rocket boosters.

  Rocket propellants are complex materials that have many innate problems. The new information will therefore be very useful in new nuclear war planning as well as for the missile defense shield.
- The University of Utah will compile data on fires and explosions specifically related to nuclear weapons accidents.

Scientific Goals of the Academic Strategic Alliances Program

Overall the academic strategic alliances program has been allocated five major goals by the department of energy:

1. Establish and validate the practices of large-scale modeling, simulation, and computation as a viable scientific methodology in key scientific and engineering applications supporting DOE science-based stockpile stewardship goals and objectives
2. Accelerate advances in critical basic sciences, mathematics, and computer science areas, in computational science and engineering, in high-performance computing systems, and in problem-solving environments that support long-term ASCI needs
3. Leverage other basic science, high-performance computing systems, and problem-solving environments research in the academic community
4. Establish technical coupling of academic strategic alliances program efforts with ongoing ASCI projects in DOE laboratories
5. Strengthen training and research in areas of interest to ASCI and SBSS (science-based stockpile stewardship) and strengthen ties among Lawrence Livermore National Lab, Los Alamos National Lab, Sandia National Labs, and universities[34]

This last proviso is specifically meant to recruit a new generation of intelligent young people into the "art" of bomb making. Some programs will be designed so that professors and students may never discover the ultimate applications of their research unless they become intimately involved in classified nuclear weapons work.[35]

The chancellor of the University of Illinois, Michael Aikin, enthusiastically endorsed the notion of SS & M when he wrote, "The national importance of simulation of the science-based stewardship program cannot be overestimated, and it is an area in which we are willing and highly able to contribute. . . . I believe that multidisciplinary research and training partnerships embodied in the DOE academic strategic alliance program and our [Illinois's] proposed center are critical to the development of national defense policy and preparedness, and we are excited about the prospects of working in this enterprise."[36]

The ASAP gives university students unprecedented access to the supercomputers of the weapons labs. It also plans to make available to the public more classified information than ever before. It's worth repeating that although foreign nationals will be prohibited from working in this area, it will not prevent the drift of valuable weapons information into foreign hands, for crucial nuclear design programs will be shared with a wide array of weapon and nonweapon scientists, and the computers will run on standard lines. Therefore information from ASCI will be difficult or impossible to keep secret. This leaky situation will expedite the ability of nonnuclear countries to design and build advanced nuclear weapons.[37]

ENVIRONMENTAL HAZARDS OF SS & M

Plutonium—named after Pluto, the god of hell—remains radioactive and biologically dangerous for 500,000 years. It is acknowledged to be the most carcinogenic substance known to humans—hypothetically one pound, if uniformly distributed, could induce lung cancer in every person on earth. The proliferation of nuclear labs and facilities under the SS & M umbrella poses a relentlessly frightening list of health and environmental issues to human beings working or living near the nuclear plants. Plutonium also causes mutations in the genes of the reproductive cells—the eggs and sperm—posing a genetic risk to all future generations, a kind of random compulsory genetic engineering.

But plutonium is not the only danger. The waste from nuclear weapons production contains other deadly radioactive elements, which bio-accumulate thousands of times at each step in the food chain. Because radioactive elements are tasteless, odorless, and invisible, it is impossible to know whether exposed food is contaminated or not. Cesium 137 concentrates in meat and causes cancers of the muscle; strontium 90 concentrates in milk and induces bone cancer and leukemia; radioactive iodine concentrates in vegetables and milk and migrates to the thyroid gland, inducing thyroid tumors and cancer. Tritium combines with water molecules and is incorporated into the actual genetic structure. It is a potent carcinogen. Many of these elements also remain radioactive for hundreds of years, well beyond our lifetimes.

These materials and others compose nuclear waste—the detritus from weapons production and the generation of nuclear power. Vast quantities of concentrated high-level waste in liquid and solid form lie scattered around the weapons facilities. Indeed, all the DOE weapons-manufacturing plants scattered across the nation are superfund sites leaking and leaching the most extraordinarily dangerous radioactive and toxic chemical contaminants into soil, rivers, lakes, seas, and water supplies.

One particularly vivid example of an intensely polluted DOE site is the old Rocky Flats plant, which from 1953 to 1989 manufactured approximately 70,000 plutonium pits—that is, an average of five pits per day. During a 7.7-million-dollar "cleanup," several men were delegated to excavate 171 drums of uranium from a trench in the ground that hadn't been touched for forty years. One of the men was directed to scoop out an unmarked barrel with a backhoe. It had rotted and uranium sludge oozed from the barrel. Suddenly, there was a blue flash and the ooze burst into flame. The fire had to be extinguished by a dump of sand. As the *Denver Post* wrote, "one drum down, 1,099,956 to go."

The government is attempting to detoxify this nuclear bomb plant, the first such attempt in the history of the nuclear age.

Included in the challenges:

1. To find 1100 pounds of plutonium that were "lost" in the ducts of the plant, drum, and glove boxes (used to machine the plutonium). This is enough plutonium to build 150 Nagasaki-sized bombs. It is also more than enough to reach critical mass (10 pounds is critical mass) and produce a large nuclear explosion, thereby obliterating much of Denver and Boulder, either by blast and/or fallout.
2. To "clean" thirteen "infinity" rooms—so radioactive that monitoring instruments went off-scale. One room in the plant is so hot that managers welded the door shut in 1972. Another room was filled with plutonium-fouled machinery and entombed in concrete.
3. To ship 16,000 pounds of plutonium by truck through Denver to South Carolina. On top of the plutonium shipments, three additional truckloads of radioactive waste must be shipped out per day in order to comply with the 2006 cleanup deadline. The cleanup is costing 2 million dollars a day, and it is two years behind schedule. It will cost twice as much to raze Rocky Flats as it cost to construct the new Denver airport.

A recent report by the National Academy of Sciences notes that two thirds of the government sites involved in nuclear weapons production will never be decontaminated. Long-term stewardship will be required for 100 of the 144 sites, and many will remain dangerously radioactive for tens or even hundreds of thousands of years. These areas will become—or are now denoted—"national sacrifice zones."

In fact, the federal government lacks the technology, money, or management techniques to prevent the spread of contamination. Many radioactive-contaminated plumes in underground water streams have already migrated well beyond the plant boundaries and it is impossible to police the waste properly. For instance, the DOE erected *no fishing* signs at a creek near the Oak Ridge National Lab, but children stole the signs. This occurred in this generation. What will happen long after we are forgotten?

The NAS report also said that any known barriers for radioactive waste, such as concrete and steel, would fail, and that most of what is now known about the behavior of contaminants in air, soil, and water might "eventually be proven wrong."[38, 39] Even the department of energy finally agreed in October 2000 with the Institute for Energy and Environmental Research, that official government data on the volume and radioactivity of buried plutonium and similar materials were "inconsistent and contradictory."

The amount of plutonium and other man-made radioactive elements—from the manufacture of nuclear weapons—that has been released into the soil or buried in flimsy containers such as cardboard boxes is 10 times greater than original estimates.[40] The DOE itself admitted that "there is little or no information on volumes of soil potentially contaminated by leaching of buried solid wastes, nor is there information on hazardous waste components known to have been commingled with the radioactive components." Some of these wastes are explosive materials, making retrieval difficult. This buried waste comprises 30 percent of the nation's radioactivity.[41]

The DOE surveyed production and dumping records at only six sites—Hanford, the Idaho National Engineering and Environmental Laboratory near Idaho Falls, Los Alamos National Lab, Oak Ridge National Lab in Tennessee, the Savannah River site in South Carolina, and the Nevada Test Site.[42]

There is new evidence to show that plutonium moves through the soil at a rate much faster than previously predicted. For instance, the Snake River aquifer lies 590 feet below the Idaho facility. Plutonium that was originally buried twenty feet below the surface has now been found at 240 feet. At this rate it will take only twenty-five years to reach the aquifer and enter the Snake River. Americium, a decay product of plutonium but even more deadly, has already entered the river.[43]

The department of energy recently admitted for the first time that four tons of plutonium were released into the soil at the Nevada Test Site over a period of four decades. Vast quantities of deadly fission products were also released, some of which are moving rapidly in water systems toward populated areas nearby.[44]

Fires at Nuclear Weapons Labs

In a freak of nature—possibly related to the phenomenon of global warming—the contaminated grounds of three of the nation's major nuclear weapons facilities caught fire during the year 2000—at Los Alamos, Hanford, and Idaho.

A total of 6.4 million acres burned throughout the U.S., 3.5 million acres above the ten-year average.

LOS ALAMOS NATIONAL LAB. On May 4, 2000, a fire set by park rangers during protective burn-off in forests near the lab swept through a total of 48,000 acres and burned 7500 acres or one-third of the lab facility. At temperatures of 2000 degrees Fahrenheit, the fire consumed decommissioned contaminated buildings dating from the Manhattan Project, the machine shop for the main research and development facility (DARHT), and storage areas. In all, it destroyed or damaged 112 lab structures and disrupted the operation of 237 facilities. It burned more than 600 waste-disposal and contaminated sites, plus several contaminated canyons running through the lab.

Los Alamos waste areas are contaminated with the deadliest materials—plutonium 238 and 239, americium 241, tritium, uranium, strontium 90, cesium 137, beryllium, and organic carcinogenic compounds (PCBs and solvents). For many years the preferred storage container for much of the lab's waste was the cardboard box. Over 2120 potentially radioactively contaminated sites at the lab could now release radiation. During the fire, the department of energy failed to deploy airborne monitoring systems to measure smoke contaminants, nor did it attempt to monitor possible localized "hot spots."

Firefighters were not equipped with radiation monitors, nor were they carefully protected as radiation workers are—in fact, they were mostly unaware of the dangers they faced. Fires at nuclear facilities present special dangers, first because they disrupt safety systems leading to loss of power and important means of ventilation, and second because the contaminated vegetation has been converted to ashes, and strong winds sweep radioactive elements into the air to be carried great distances. Flash floods sweep vast quantities of radioactive elements from the canyons at Los Alamos into watersheds. These water sources drain into the Rio Grande River, where they pollute drinking and irrigation supplies through New Mexico and Mexico.

Three particular Los Alamos canyons are at risk:

1. The Parajito Canyon—code-named *TA-18*. Facilities here include a defunct and contaminated Omega West reactor, nuclear weapons test facilities (Kivas) that contain "high-energy burst assemblies," and a vault containing large amounts of plutonium and highly enriched uranium. The White Rock community lies directly downstream.
2. The Los Alamos Canyon—code-named *TA-41, TA-2*. Dangerous facilities in this canyon include the defunct and contaminated Omega West reactor. Placed at the bottom of the canyon, it is vulnerable to slope instability, mudslides, and rock falls.
3. The Pueblo Canyon, which contains the Diamond Road crossing and utility facilities for the town of Los Alamos.

Other radioactive canyons—recipients of decades of waste-dumping—include: Mortandad Canyon, DP Canyon, and Acid Canyon. Some of these radioactive canyons are surrounded by communities of Native Americans.

Seventy-seven other waste-disposal sites and contaminated areas at Los Alamos are located on potential floodplains.

Following only a modest postfire rainfall in September 2000, the concentration of cesium 137 in suspended run-off mixed with clay and soil in the water was 5 to 20 times higher than prefire levels, plutonium was 5 to 10 times, and strontium 90 was 2 to 5 times higher.

Flash floods inundate the region almost every year.[45, 46, 47]

HANFORD NUCLEAR RESERVATION. On July 28, 2000, a wildfire near Richland, Washington, sparked by a fatal car collision, burned 190,000 acres, including parts of the Hanford Nuclear Reservation.

An eight-foot wall of fire came to within 400 yards of 330 50-gallon barrels of waste containing uranium powder and chips, and other toxic and hazardous waste material. A single drum, if ignited, could send flames 20 to 30 feet into the air, releasing all the radioactive and toxic contents.[48]

The fires also passed through an area of known radioactive dump sites. The firefighting operation was hampered by lack of adequate maps detailing radioactively contaminated nuclear sites.[49] The fires burned through highly contaminated B/C cribs (storage sites) in the 200 West area, which probably contain more radioactivity than the entire Los Alamos inventory.

Plutonium was detected in air monitors around the area, but the monitoring was inadequate. Because federal officials misjudged the seriousness of the fire, the plutonium measurements were incomplete; the most reliable testing by the EPA was performed after the fires ended. Levels measured at that time were still 100 times the normal amount. It is unknown what the measurements were during the height of the blaze.

Plutonium could potentially enter the lungs of people hundreds of miles away depending on wind direction. One-millionth of a gram of inhaled plutonium is a carcinogenic dose.[50]

IDAHO NATIONAL ENGINEERING & ENVIRONMENTAL LABORATORY. In July 2000, a fire burned 49,000 acres in and around the Idaho National Lab, producing higher-than-normal levels of radioactivity in the air. The fire entered a test reactor area. Evacuation from the facility was ordered.

Another fire in September at the same labs consumed 8000 acres and resulted in an accident that officials admitted was very dangerous. One chamber of an incinerator that was used to "burn" mixed radioactive and toxic waste containing plutonium continued to burn overnight without supervision after worker evacuation. Lab officials claim that workers shut down the incinerator before they left, but one chamber reignited because of the fire. Safety procedures required that the incinerator be attended at all times, but they were not followed. Operated by Bechtel—a DOE contractor—the incinerator has since been closed.[51]

It is evident that radioactive material should never be subjected to incineration, as it is transferred unchanged into the air to be dispersed by the wind.

OTHER NUCLEAR FACILITIES. Several major nuclear weapons facilities were closed over the past ten years, leaving behind large quantities of unguarded, unstable nuclear materials, including 189 tons of combustible, highly enriched uranium at the Oak Ridge Y-12 weapons plant in Tennessee, stored in old wooden buildings. If a wildfire ignited the uranium metal, water used to fight the fire would generate hydrogen, converting the blaze to a small holocaust.[52]

Government Compensation

Thousands of people who once worked in nuclear weapons production plants are, for the first time, to receive compensation from the federal government. These people mined, milled, and enriched uranium, operated nuclear reactors, reprocessed deadly radioactive materials, machined plutonium, uranium, and thorium, and handled radioactive waste. Many have already died; others are now dying of cancers and diseases related to their radioactive and toxic chemical exposure. Yet for sixty years the government stubbornly denied a link between work exposure in the nuclear weapons complex and subsequent disease processes. Very few nuclear workers, if any, were informed of the medical dangers implicit in their work. Rather, the emphasis was on the cold war–related emergency production of nuclear weapons. This was a national security imperative, and the health of the workers was a secondary consideration.

Finally, Congress has offered a one-time 150,000-dollar payment plus free health care to those who have suffered. The total cost to the government is estimated at 1 billion dollars over the next five years, compared with the billions doled out by Congress to the military corporations, the Pentagon, and the nuclear labs.

Another, possibly larger group of people exposed during the forties and fifties were employed by more than 200 private companies across the nation. Ranging from mom-and-pop machine shops to large chemical firms, these facilities were quietly converted to the production of nuclear weapons components. In total ignorance, workers handled tons of dangerous uranium, thorium, polonium, beryllium, and other toxic and radioactive substances.

Most of the factories were located in the industrial belts of New England, New York, Pennsylvania, New Jersey, around the Great Lakes, and through the Ohio and Mississippi River Valleys, as well as in the cities of Detroit, Chicago, St. Louis, and Cleveland. In all these facilities, many thousands were exposed to levels of radiation hundreds of times higher than the arbitrary limits imposed at the time, limits that have since been shown to be many times too high. Workers in the most dangerous jobs were exposed to lung doses of 130 rems or higher—ten times that accepted today. (A *rem* is a biological measurement of radiation.)

No dose of radiation is safe, and radiation is biologically cumulative—each dose adds to the risk of cancer development years later. Some of these workers were so contaminated they were 200 percent more likely than unexposed people to die of radiation-induced cancer. Government reports documenting the medical risks were classified and hidden.

The new Congressional compensation bill applies specifically to government employees, excluding those who were privately employed. Many of the private nuclear companies have shut down, and records have been displaced or lost. The surrounding communities are largely unaware of the permanent radioactive and toxic contamination of their environments—a medically tragic legacy of this secret weapons work. As a single example—one of many—the Harshaw Chemical Company in Cleveland pumped 350 to 500 pounds of radioactive uranium dust from its stacks.

• • •

In light of this ongoing danger, the SS & M program will perpetuate and make worse an already catastrophic environmental and health problem. There is no cold war. There are no enemies except terrorists, and they will not be stopped by the use of nuclear weapons. We the people must demand that the labs cease to function: They are killing us all to make the bombs to kill us all better.

Chapter Six

STAR WARS: THE STORY OF NATIONAL MISSILE DEFENSE SYSTEMS

If the U.S. proceeds to destroy the ABM treaty. . . . We can and will withdraw not only from the START II treaty . . . but from the whole system of treaty relations having to do with the limitation and control of strategic and conventional arms.

—Russian President Vladimir Putin, 2001

Any amendment, or abolishing of the treaty, will lead to disastrous consequences. This will bring a halt to nuclear disarmament now between the Russians and Americans, and in the future will halt multilateral disarmament as well.

—Chinese Arms Control Ambassador Sha Zukang, 2001

AT ROUGHLY THE SAME TIME that nuclear scientists conceived the idea of a "stockpile management program" to prolong their careers after the end of the cold war—and as a cover for development of new nuclear weapons—Bill Clinton and George W. Bush, in response to pressure from weapons manufacturers, worked on a parallel effort to craft a missile defense system. Shaped, as always, by the politics of the day, the plan evolved from Lyndon Johnson's Sentinel to George W. Bush's national missile defense program (NMD), via Ronald Reagan's memorably named Star Wars plan. Each successive incarnation has added new approaches to creating a comprehensive missile shield for the U.S., and it is important to understand both the evolution of missile defense and the various components of the latest plan being put forth by George W. Bush—including his proposal to put nuclear reactors and possibly nuclear weapons in space as well as on earth and in the immediate atmosphere—in order to evaluate the viability and implications of our current policy. This chapter looks at the history of missile defense and its current components. Chapter Seven looks at plans to militarize space.

FROM SENTINEL TO NATIONAL MISSILE DEFENSE

Every military weapon ever built has instigated another weapon to counter it. Ever since scientists designed missiles capable of delivering nuclear weapons through space, the next imperative became an antimissile system. To this end, in 1967 President Lyndon Johnson proposed a system called Sentinel. President Richard Nixon called his hypothetical version Safeguard, and Ronald Reagan's version became known as Star Wars. Eventually, all these plans were abandoned because none of them worked. Building thousands of hydrogen bombs proved far easier than building a system to foil them.[1] Nevertheless, Reagan's charisma and powers of persuasion swayed public opinion in favor of Star Wars—a "shield" to be constructed over the continental U.S. to protect against incoming Soviet ballistic missiles. His Star Wars speech in 1983 gave the imprimatur to a plan recognized by every reputable scientist to be unworkable. Reagan's speech also gave the whole concept of missile defense an indelibly memorable name and many people—myself included—now use the term "Star Wars" for all comprehensive missile defense plans, despite each successive administration's renaming efforts.

Seventy billion dollars later, after enormous amounts of work and research in many of the universities, colleges, and corporations around the nation, none of the evolving technologies has been shown to be effective against incoming ballistic missiles. Following his election in 1992, Clinton directed his defense secretary, Les Aspin, to end the Star Wars program, or the strategic defense initiative (SDI) as it was then called. In May 1993 Aspin created as an alternative a new organization called the ballistic missile defense organization (BMDO). Moving away from the concept of space-based weapons, the new plan was to acquire and develop ground-based systems designed to defend American forces overseas from battlefield missiles. Eighty percent of the BMDO budget was appropriated to "theater" or short-range missile defense; 20 percent for research into national or long-range missile defense.[2] But since the same technology is used to design both short- and long-range systems, the Republican Right was actually quite pleased with Aspin's plan,[3] and Frank Gaffney, former assistant to Reagan's undersecretary of defense, said that Aspin was really just "rearranging the deck chairs."

As early as 1991, the navy, army, and air force had quietly begun to develop their own theater missile defenses. The navy and army worked on two similar systems—a lower-tier defense designed to intercept short-range missiles in the lower atmosphere, and an upper-tier defense designed to intercept missiles in the upper atmosphere.[4] The air force, meanwhile, had been developing several theater missile defense (TMD) programs, including a boost-phase laser system intercept that would be deployed in a piloted plane. Aspin's BMDO specifically endorsed three of these systems—the army's Patriot (PAC-3) lower-tier system, the navy's Aegis program to be based aboard Aegis ships, and the army's theater high altitude area defense (THAAD).[5] (It is a generally accepted notion that theater or short-range missile defense does not violate the Antiballistic Missile—ABM—treaty. However, THAAD operates at altitudes of 40 kilometers, almost outside the atmosphere, so in effect it does violate the ABM.)

But the shock of the political loss of the House and Senate to the Republicans in 1994 had a dramatic effect upon Clinton's opposition to Star Wars. Among the dictates of Speaker Newt Gingrich's "Contract with America" was a provision calling for a "highly effective defense" of the continental United States at the earliest practical date.[6] In order to placate the now-powerful Republican Congress, Clinton specifically embraced the Star Wars issue, retitling it once again, this time as the seemingly more benign national missile defense (NMD).

The American Right remained adamantly wedded to the Star Wars idea, despite the fact that a 1995 U.S. national intelligence estimate found that "no country, other than the major declared nuclear powers, will develop or otherwise acquire a ballistic missile in the next fifteen years that could threaten the contiguous 48 states and Canada."[7] Upset by this report, the Republican-controlled Congress appointed Donald Rumsfeld, secretary of defense in the Ford administration (and now secretary of defense for George W. Bush) to head an "independent" commission to counter the assertions. According to Bob Aldridge's background paper on national missile defense titled "Son of Star Wars," the commission was directed to consider the worst-case possibilities, but to exclude the most likely scenarios in its deliberations.

They were told to assess real or potential threats from ballistic missiles carrying nuclear, biological, or chemical weapons, but were not to decide their probability or feasibility. Nor were they to consider that there could be other easier ways to deliver these weapons. In other words, the commission was directed to find specific threats for Congressional promotion of its NMD ambitions.[8] General Henry Shelton, chairman of the Joint Chiefs of Staff, gave some perspective on the Rumsfeld report in a letter he wrote to Senator James Inhofe on August 24, 1998: "The [Rumsfeld] commission points out that through unconventional, high-risk development programs and foreign assistance, terrorist nations could acquire an ICBM capability in a short time, and that the intelligence community may not detect it. We view this as an unlikely development."[9]

Unfortunately, Shelton's letter arrived just as North Korea launched a Taepo-Dong missile containing a satellite over the Japanese mainland in August 1998, an event that gave new momentum to national missile defense. This missile was based upon primitive scaled-up Scud missile technology, built by a country that has a gross domestic product smaller than Delaware's.[10] (The prestigious journal *Jane's Defense Weekly* said of the North Korean long-range missile site that it looks "more like an abandoned oil derrick than the nerve center for annihilating the 'running dogs of capitalism.' ") Inherently incapable of reaching the U.S. mainland, the primitive Korean medium-range missile crashed into the sea off the coast of Japan. Nevertheless, it provided the American Right an enormous boost of moral ammunition. It also prompted Japan, which had previously been reluctant to become involved with the U.S. on plans for missile defense, to sign a cooperative agreement in August 1999 to develop a theater missile defense.

The Rumsfeld report was now followed by another assessment from the National Intelligence Council, published on September 9, 1999. This new report warned that proliferation of medium-range ballistic missiles, driven primarily by missile sales from North Korea, presented an "immediate, serious and growing threat . . ." (This was not even an allegation that North Korea presented a threat, but that it was selling missile components to *other* countries that *might* be threats.) Among other allegations, the report said that Iran, with the help of Russia, *could* test a missile before 2010 that *could* deliver a several-hundred-kiloton warhead against the U.S.[11] And that over the next fifteen years the U.S. "most likely will face ICBM threats from Russia, China, and North Korea, probably from Iran, and possibly from Iraq."

While these reports were designed to sound comprehensive and authoritative, in their zeal to justify a multibillion-dollar defense program they failed to acknowledge the fact that any country or person in the world could smuggle a nuclear, chemical, or biological weapon into the United States aboard a ship, in a suitcase, or in a small private plane. A truck could be driven in from Mexico or Canada loaded with weapons. A cruise missile flying beneath radar, undetectable by any NMD system, could also be used as a suitable delivery mechanism. Or, as we witnessed on September 11, 2001, American aircraft loaded with civilians and thousands of gallons of jet fuel could be used as ballistic missiles, the primary weapons—simple, inexpensive box cutters. As the *Mercury News* argued on September 10, 1999, attack through these means was much more likely than attack through space.

Joseph Cirincione, the director of the Carnegie Endowment for International Peace, incisively stated that the new report "reflects a lowering of previously established intelligence standards for judging threats." The report arbitrarily shifted the missile threat to incorporate all fifty states instead of forty-eight (as allowed under the antiballistic missile treaty, which excluded Hawaii and Alaska), and it advanced by at least five years the possible date of a "rogue state" long-range-missile deployment. The report itself acknowledged that "some analysts believe the prominence given to missiles countries 'could' develop gives more credence than is warranted to developments that may prove implausible."[12]

Meanwhile, in Washington, an independent review team headed by former air force chief of staff and retired four-star general Larry Welch, and comprised of twelve experts on missile defense, issued another report. This team was touted as "the most experienced collection of civilian and retired military officers to have studied the antimissile effort." They found that the missile-defense program was plagued by inadequate testing, spare parts shortages, and management lapses. The report criticized the government and contractors for exhibiting over-optimism about their ability to develop a reliable missile interceptor. It found failures based in poor design and fabrication, lax management, and lack of rigorous government oversight. The report said that the test schedules had been so compressed that the program was essentially "a rush to failure."[13, 14] The panel also pointed out that an *actual* kill vehicle had not been tested on an *actual* booster (as opposed to prototype warheads and surrogate boosters) and there was major concern that the kill vehicle would not be able to withstand the actual shock loads, because the actual booster is much faster and the loads are "more than an order of magnitude greater than those of the surrogate booster now being used." The panel recommended that Clinton delay his decision to build the national missile defense.[15]

Clinton, however, was under impeachment proceedings in January 1999, and in an exceedingly vulnerable political position. By the end of the month, Defense Secretary William Cohen, acting for Clinton but also agreeing in principle himself, increased the missile defense budget by 6.6 billion dollars over four years and announced a timetable that included a deployment decision before Clinton left office.[16] While the Clinton administration had initially endorsed a modest missile defense system in response to a theoretical small ICBM attack from a "rogue" state, the defense budget increase announced by Cohen allowed the Star Wars lobby to get their proverbial foot in the door, and an animated debate on the efficacy, technical validity, and viability of the proposed NMD ensued. As scientists from both sides of the fence attacked each other, three tests for the missile system failed, North and South Korea made peace overtures to each other, and the rationale for NMD disappeared.

Clinton had originally enumerated four criteria for making the decision about deploying national missile defense: the threat, the cost, the technology, and overall American security. The threat was now gone, the cost was incomparable, the technology did not seem to work, and many felt that American security would be endangered rather than enhanced by deployment of NMD, a view confirmed by a classified intelligence report issued at the time on "Foreign Responses to U.S. National Missile Defense Deployment." The report warned that NMD would prompt China to expand its nuclear weapons arsenal tenfold and cause Russia to place multiple hydrogen bombs on missiles that currently carry only one bomb. The report also stated that if China were prompted to deploy 200 warheads by 2015 (as noted, they currently have only twenty hydrogen bombs capable of hitting America) this would prompt India and Pakistan to respond with their own nuclear buildup.[17]

In response to the report (and with obvious relief), Clinton passed the Star Wars problem on to the next president and thus avoided being labeled the president who destroyed the ABM treaty. (Even as he failed definitively to decide the future of NMD, in typical Clinton fashion he directed his secretary of defense to pursue a "robust program of technological development." So, unofficially, the program proceeded unabated.)

In contrast, George W. Bush now enthusiastically endorses a full-scale, no-holds-barred, multilevel NMD system.[18] The Heritage Foundation has been busy setting the stage and leading the charge, including circulating the following petition during the presidential election year 2000, some months before Bush was declared president:

> Citizen's Petition to Protect America Now
>
> Whereas China and Russia have threatened the U.S. with nuclear attack, and rogue nations such as Iraq, North Korea and Iran have acquired or are acquiring missiles equipped with weapons of mass destruction;
>
> Whereas the United States currently cannot stop even one missile after it is launched;

> Whereas the Administration has declared that it must have the permission of the Russian government before deciding to deploy any missile defense for the United States;
>
> Whereas the limited, land-based missile defense system the Administration says it may decide later this year to deploy will not be able to protect our families until 2005 at the earliest;
>
> Whereas the United States Navy could be ordered to immediately begin the process of deploying a sea-based defense that would provide some missile protection several years before 2005;
>
> Whereas senior Pentagon officials have judged that a comprehensive missile defense with a combination of land-, sea-, air-, and space-based components would offer the American people the most effective protection against missile attack; and
>
> Whereas the Administration is currently engaged in treaty negotiations with Russia that would prohibit the United States from deploying sea-, air- or space-based defenses;
>
> Therefore I, [fill in name] of [fill in state], call upon my elected representatives and candidates for public office to pledge to my family and all of the families of the United States to support immediately beginning the process of deploying a sea-based missile defense as the first layer of protection for America's families; and further to pledge to reject the notion that any other nation may exercise a veto of the U.S. military's ability to offer the American people the most effective protection available.

Jack Spenser and Michael Scardaville, Heritage Fellows, fashioned an op-ed piece for the *Miami Herald* on October 17, 2000, justifying such a commitment to NMD. They reminded readers that Iran tested a Shahab missile with an 800-mile range on September 21, 2000, and announced that Iran is "dangerously close to developing nuclear weapons." They also noted that on September 23, Syria acquired a new model of Scud missile from North Korea, allowing it to attack Israel from bases deep within its own territory. Libya, they said, began receiving North Korean Nodong missiles on September 24, giving Libya the ability to attack Israel and southern Europe. They wrote that Pakistan and India were also planning new missile tests for intermediate-range ballistic missiles, and they ended by stressing that the threat to "our troops and friends abroad is growing," that the U.S. needs an antiballistic missile system, and that reliance upon the ABM treaty is folly.[19]

In response, Steve LaMontagne, a research analyst at the Council for a Livable World, wrote that Spenser and Scardaville omitted the fact that the missile developments of Libya, Iran, and Syria *occurred within a week of and in response to Israel's successful test of its new Arrow 2 anti-tactical ballistic missile system,* and that none of the above-mentioned missiles could reach the U.S. His article pointed out that if—as the Heritage Foundation claimed—antiballistic missile systems deter proliferation, "why do Iran, Syria, and Libya seem unfazed—and even provoked—by Israel's missile defenses?" And "why is Russia determined to preserve its retaliatory strike capability against possible U.S. defenses? . . . The lesson from the Middle East and Russia is that missile defenses encourage proliferation."[20]

Nevertheless, any ongoing debate about the need for or feasibility of national missile defense takes place even as the corporations and the Pentagon quietly go about designing, contracting, and constructing most of the elements. There is no public discussion, no informed debate within or by the media, and the American public is being asked to foot the multibillion-dollar bill and take the catastrophic risks such developments entail. William Cohen, Clinton's secretary of defense, had enthusiastically endorsed NMD when he increased the missile defense budget in January 1999, referring to North Korea by saying, "We affirm that there is a threat and the threat is growing." Congress added to the pressure two months later by endorsing legislation introduced by Republican Senator Thad Cochran mandating national missile-defense deployment "as soon as is technically possible,"[21] and stating, "It is the policy of the United States to deploy a national missile defense."

Star Wars had been revived.

On October 2, 2001—21 days after September 11—the Senate unanimously passed a massive 345 billion dollar Defense Appropriations bill, which included George W. Bush's demands for flexibility on missile defense (which itself cost 8.3 billion dollars).[22]

COMPONENTS OF MISSILE DEFENSE

The categorization of Star Wars or missile defense systems is complex and intertwined, and the nomenclature is continually changing. During the nineties' revival of Reagan's Star Wars concept, less belligerent terminology was devised to make the whole concept seem more acceptable. *Missile defense* was the chosen lexicon, and, as noted previously, it had two components: theater missile defense (TMD) and national missile defense (NMD). TMD was to be used to hit in midair, low-flying short-range missiles—sometimes known as "tactical missiles"—like Scuds, which were used by Iraq in the Gulf confrontation. (The flight time of these missiles is minutes only.) NMD was conjured up to describe the interception of intercontinental ballistic missiles, usually nuclear armed. (The flight time of sea-launched ballistic missiles—sometimes known as "intermediate-range missiles"—is fifteen minutes; the flight time of land-based ballistic missiles—sometimes known as "strategic missiles"—is thirty minutes.)

Star Wars and each of the options that have succeeded it encompass plans to protect against the whole spectrum of weapons, from the most primitive to the most dangerous and sophisticated. Individual politicians, lobbyists, and others endorse more or less extensive versions of missile defense, ostensibly related to the level of threat they perceive (but clearly often driven by more mercenary factors):

LIMITED MISSILE DEFENSE

Some believe that America need only protect itself against "rogue" states or "states of concern" like North Korea, Iraq, Iran, Libya, etc. These countries possess conventional weapons but none possess missiles capable of hitting the U.S., and none currently possess nuclear weapons. Advocates of this approach favor antimissile missiles, based on land, on sea, and in the air.

EXTENSIVE MISSILE DEFENSE

Others argue that China must now be considered the new global threat, although it maintains only twenty primitive nuclear-armed ICBMs that are liquid-fueled and take days to prepare before they can be launched against the U.S. But the Pentagon is projecting that China will shortly be arming itself with ever more nuclear-armed ICBMs, and therefore argues for a more extensive missile defense than that currently planned for rogue states. Russia, on the other hand, retains a nuclear arsenal capable of destroying the U.S. and inducing nuclear winter. It is obvious that no antimissile system could ever protect the U.S. against some 5000 Russian nuclear weapons descending upon it from space. But the missile defense system makes sense in conjunction with the other components of the overall U.S. official policy to "fight and win" a nuclear war against Russia. In a surprise attack the U.S. will initiate a first strike, which means it will go first and win the nuclear war by taking out most of the Russian missiles before they are launched from their silos. Star Wars will then "mop up" the few missiles that have escaped destruction and have actually been launched into space, so there will be no more Russian missiles to hit the U.S. This scenario will create nuclear winter, of course.

SPACE-BASED DEFENSE

An even more aggressive contingent within the official U.S. establishment is pushing for a still more extensive, space-based system, both to provide a greater degree of missile defense and to protect America's *economic* interest in space. Beyond protecting America's current borders from missile attack, this contingent plans to exploit natural resources by "mining" the moon, the asteroids, and the planets for rare minerals. Naturally, if the U.S. invests billions of dollars in space research and development, it must be prepared to "protect" its investment. This logic led to the establishment of a new military entity—the U.S. space command, created by the Joint Chiefs of Staff in 1985 to help "institutionalize the use of space in U.S. deterrence."[23]

The U.S. space command explicitly states that the U.S. must "[dominate] the space dimension of military operations to protect U.S. interest and investment," domination that will be attained by the militarization of space with antisatellite weapons, antiballistic missile weapons, laser beam weapons, nuclear missiles, nuclear reactors, and possibly orbiting nuclear weapons. (So concerned is the rest of the world that on November 1, 1999, 138 nations voted at the United Nations for a resolution titled "Prevention of an Arms Race in Outer Space," which recognized "the common interest of all mankind in the exploration and uses of outer space for peaceful purposes" and "reaffirmed the will of all states that the exploration and uses of space shall be for peaceful purposes and shall be carried out for the benefit and in the interests of all countries. . . . Prevention of an arms race in outer space would avert a grave danger for international peace and security." Only the United States and Israel refused to support this resolution.[24]

THREE WAYS TO DESTROY AN INTERCONTINENTAL BALLISTIC MISSILE

A ballistic missile is like a bullet shot from a gun. It leaves its launchpad or silo on a predetermined trajectory, cannot be recalled, and will land where it is targeted. Missile defense systems are categorized based on the point in flight at which they intercept enemy missiles:

- *Boost-phase systems* hit "enemy" missiles immediately after they are launched, in their "boost" phase—the five minutes available after launch and before the missile leaves the atmosphere
- *Midcourse systems* hit missiles in space during their "transit" phases, as the bombs, or "passengers," separate from their missiles and coast through space at tremendous speeds
- *Terminal systems* hit missiles as they reenter the earth's atmosphere to land on and "kill" their target

Destruction of a ballistic missile at any stage—boost, transit, or terminal—carries grave medical implications.

BOOST PHASE

The boost phase is possibly the best time to destroy the missile, particularly if it is MIRV'ed (multiple independent reentry vehicles), for it carries numerous hydrogen bombs that are much harder to target once they have separated. If the missile is loaded with numerous submunitions of chemical or biological weapons, the only efficient time to destroy them is during the boost phase. During the boost phase, the missile itself is large and slow compared to tiny warheads barreling through space at many times the speed of sound. During its rapid ascent the missile pours forth great jets of fire, which are readily identifiable by infrared-tracking early-warning satellite, thus making them "easy" targets.

There are three disadvantages to boost-phase destruction. First, the missile must be detected within two minutes of launch, leaving no time for human decision or intervention either to detect or to attack the missile. This means that World War III could be computer initiated by error or by design, with software determining our future.

Second is a medical problem of grave import. If ten hydrogen bombs on one missile were destroyed in the atmosphere, approximately 100 pounds of carcinogenic plutonium would rain down upon the population, causing long-term havoc and mayhem. Prevailing winds would scatter the deadly, long-lived carcinogenic pollution hundreds to thousands of miles. The contaminated earth would be polluted forever. Likewise, if the missile were carrying biological or chemical weapons, lethal genetically modified viruses and bacteria, or highly toxic chemicals, would descend upon the underlying population.

The third disadvantage is that the intercepted nuclear weapons could accidentally explode when intercepted.

TRANSIT PHASE

As a MIRV'ed missile zooms through space, the launch rocket separates from the front end, or "bus," which contains its "passengers"—the ten hydrogen bombs.

This transit phase lasts about 25 minutes. It is very difficult to detect hydrogen bombs hurtling through space at very cold temperatures. But because the metal bombs originate in the earth's atmosphere, they retain their warmth relative to the subfreezing temperatures of space. Heat-sensing mechanisms on an antiballistic missile or "kill" vehicle are designed to detect the temperature differential and allow the missile to seek out its target.

However, it has long been recognized that it is relatively easy to fool an antiballistic missile system. Numerous decoys could accompany the bombs—such as mylar balloons inflated to bomb size and coated with the appropriate radar reflecting material to simulate the bomb, or pieces of aluminum to confuse the radar systems of the kill vehicle. Balloons can be made to be the same shape as the warhead, and if they contain a lightbulb and a battery, they maintain the same temperature as the warhead, thus confusing the interceptor sensors. Or the real bomb can be surrounded by a cooled balloon to make it resemble a decoy. The truth is that the Pentagon has never tested an interceptor system against a large array of decoys. Burton Richter, winner of the 1976 Nobel Prize in physics, compares the task to hitting a gnat with a gun that fires pins, with only one pin in each gun. Not surprisingly, most of the tests performed thus far by the Pentagon using a hit-to-kill missile have failed.

Richter and other eminent scientists suggest that the only way to effectively halt or intercept missiles and bombs in space is to deploy nuclear weapons in space. Decoys would then be irrelevant, because the nuclear explosion would destroy bombs and decoys over a wide area.[25] But even an effective space-based missile defense would create what are known as "exotic" effects, including electromagnetic pulse (EMP). In 1962, for example, the United States exploded a hydrogen bomb 248 miles high in space. In an unexpected turn of events, it was thus discovered that destructive electromagnetic radiation emitted from a nuclear blast in space travels vast distances.

It has since been calculated that a single bomb exploded 200 miles above the continental U.S. could paralyze North America, destroying most electronic systems, including long runs of cable, piping, or conduit; large antennae and their feed cables; guy wires and their support lines; overland power and telephone lines; long runs of electrical wiring; railroad tracks; aluminum aircraft bodies; computers; power supplies; alarm systems; intercoms; life-support control systems; transistorized receivers and transmitters; base radio stations; satellites; and some telephone equipment. Fewer than five explosions could blanket the U.S. with as much as 100,000 volts per square meter.[26]

Ted Taylor, one of the inventors of the miniaturized hydrogen bomb, estimates that there are approximately fifty exotic effects from a nuclear explosion, including many types of EMP, gamma radiation, X rays, and electron effects from bomb debris.

TERMINAL PHASE

As the hydrogen bombs reenter the earth's atmosphere, at 20 times the speed of sound, it is very difficult to destroy them. Even if some of them could be successfully hit, they would spread plutonium across the targeted country.

• • •

Despite all these drawbacks, missile defense systems seem destined for manufacture unless the American people, realizing that their lives are in great jeopardy, rise up to save themselves, their children, and all future generations.

While I have tried to give a neat overview of missile defense systems, as recently as August 2001 the Pentagon changed the terminology again, which will keep the public—conveniently for the Pentagon—confused. TMD and NMD are now intertwined, the differences between them unclear. This terminology shell game means that those who previously supported TMD only, including many Democratic politicians, may be forced to support the whole system, unless they have the courage to challenge the Pentagon.[27]

WEAPON SYSTEMS INVOLVED IN MISSILE DEFENSE[28]

I invite you to absorb the following with a skeptical eye, being ever aware of the innate dangers technology brings to the world. You need to understand how the U.S. government is spending your tax dollars, and how this spending spree is contributing to the destabilization of an armed world seething with ancient animosities between nations. Bear in mind that in determining numbers of weapons systems needed, the Pentagon's overall strategy has been to prepare the equipment to fight two conventional wars simultaneously (although before September 11, Defense Secretary Rumsfeld had planned to downscale to a single major war).

In each case, I have described the particular weapon system, given the cost to taxpayers, indicated who will benefit from the contract to build it, and evaluated the weapon's usefulness, track record, feasibility, etc., drawing on reports of the General Accounting Office and others who have analyzed each system in detail. I have also tried to indicate which systems are in violation of existing treaties, but because the Antiballistic Missile (ABM) treaty is not absolutely specific and does not cover theater missile defense, it is unclear whether some of the systems under development constitute violations or not. Some Americans would contend that theater defense does not violate the ABM, for example, but Russia is not so sure. Several of the systems with bilateral functions definitely do violate the ABM treaty, as they cross the line between the theater defense arena and NMD. It is deeply worrying that the U.S. military-industrial complex is already constructing many of these systems regardless of treaty violations.

Many Americans are under the impression that weapons developed under the rubric of "missile defense" do not count as new weapons or are permitted by current arms control treaties. This was the case with a man from the national guard in Alaska, who told me that he is involved in installing the foundations for the first 100 missiles near Fairbanks, the initial part of the exoatmospheric missile defense system initiated by Clinton. The man was very surprised by an anti–Star Wars speech I gave, saying that he had been under the impression that NMD was specifically for defense. The fact is that missiles used in missile defense violate all arms control treaties and will likely initiate a massive new nuclear arms race involving China, Russia, India, Pakistan, and others, despite the express purpose of the ABM and other international agreements.

LOWER-TIER DEFENSE (ENDOATMOSPHERIC)

The army and navy are in charge of these particular systems, designed to intercept missiles or bombs at low levels in the atmosphere. Components of the systems include the antimissile missiles themselves, and detection and tracking systems to locate and target enemy missiles for destruction.

Patriot PAC-3 Army System

This is a hit-to-kill warhead on a missile guided by aerodynamic fins. The current version is an upgraded model of the Patriot PAC-2 defense used against Iraqi Scud missiles during the Gulf War. The Pentagon, despite the dazzling TV propaganda at the time, has been forced to admit that not one of the Patriot missiles intercepted a single Scud,[29] a fact that does not bode well for the future development and upgrading of the Patriot. Although the missiles certainly seemed to be hitting the Scuds, these images that played and replayed clearly did not represent what was actually happening in "real time" during the Gulf conflict.

The new, upgraded version of the Patriot missile, PAC-3, will be 17 feet long and weigh 640 pounds with a 22-mile or 33-kilometer range. The warheads will be equipped with sensors to locate and home in on the target, with small rocket thrusters to maneuver the bomb onto a collision course. Destruction of the enemy missile will be accomplished by energy of the impact. Sixteen of these interceptor missiles are to be loaded onto a Patriot launcher.

COST: Original estimates for the upgraded Patriot came in at 5 million dollars for each interceptor, based on building 2200 PAC-3s to meet the two-war criteria. This figure is now reduced to 1200 PAC-3s at 2 million dollars each.

The total estimated cost of the PAC-3 system is 7.4 billion dollars. But according to the Government Accounting Office, this figure may be an underestimate because contractor costs could exceed current estimates, and twelve to fifteen additional flight tests may be conducted as well, meaning twelve to fifteen replacements.

BENEFICIARIES: Principle contractors are Lockheed Martin Missiles and Fire Control for the interceptors, and Raytheon Company for the launchers and the fire control vehicle with its small phase-array radar and the engagement control vehicle with computers and displays.

There are five subcontractors.

EVALUATION: There is no guarantee that these weapons will work if the performance of their predecessors is any indication. Note that the destruction of one missile will cost 2 million dollars just for one antimissile, and this amount does not include the infrastructure, plus the R and D necessary for its construction.

Navy Area Defense

The missiles in this system—called Block-4A—have a range of 62 to 124 miles, longer than that of the army's PAC-3, and are to be placed within vertical launch tubes on Aegis destroyer ships. These are an updated version of the Standard-2 anti-air missile, which is already deployed. They will be equipped with a hit-to-kill warhead for endo-atmospheric intercepts, an infrared seeker to supplement their radar seeker, and a radio-frequency adjunct sensor.

Development and operational testing are already complete; the system is in low-rate initial production.

COST: The total cost to American taxpayers is estimated at 8.98 billion dollars.

BENEFICIARIES: Raytheon is the main contractor with five subcontractors.

EVALUATION: The General Accounting Office warns: "The Navy plans to contract for the low-rate initial production of 185 Block-4A missiles, at an estimated cost of $568.2 million, prior to the completion of any realistic operational testing. . . . We are concerned that the Navy will make a premature commitment to production of unproven missiles."

However, the navy is convinced that their system is superior to the army's Patriot system because the army requires more than 126 C-5A airplane flights to Korea, for example, to rapidly deploy a single Patriot battalion (194 missiles) just to "protect" U.S. troops. The navy would need only three to four Aegis ships to "protect" most U.S. troops in Korea and Japan. (Nevertheless, the navy intends to build 1500 missiles to put on fifty-seven Aegis destroyers and twenty-two Aegis cruisers by the year 2011.)

Medium Extended Air Defense System (MEADS)

MEADS is designed to be a rapidly deployable, highly mobile theater missile defense system to be used in the battlefield to protect soldiers.

Traversing rough terrain and maneuvering with troops, it will provide a protection of 360 degrees.

There will be sixteen missiles per launcher and 100 launchers in a battery.

COST: Under pressure by the U.S. government, Germany and Italy have been persuaded to cofinance this particular antimissile system—the U.S. will fund 55 percent, Germany 28 percent, and Italy 17 percent. In 1996 MEADS was estimated to cost a total of 40 billion dollars, but new estimates are now predicted to be many times this amount.

BENEFICIARIES: Prime contractors are Lockheed Martin Missiles and Fire Control; Alenia Marconi Systems in Rome, Italy; and Daimler Chrysler Aerospace AG in Munich, Germany.

EVALUATION: The 1996 estimate for developing and producing 100 complete MEADS systems—sixty for the U.S. and forty for Europe, was estimated at 40 billion dollars over fifteen years, based on the PAC-3 missile costing 2 million dollars each. The subsequent increase to 3 million dollars per missile caused an uproar in the MEADS program.

Airborne Warming and Control System (AWACS)

The air force already has a fleet of thirty-four AWACS—a strange Boeing 707 aircraft with a saucer-shaped radar dish on the top of the plane—as do Britain and Saudi Arabia. NATO operates eighteen AWACS. South Korea, Turkey, and Italy are interested in buying. The AWAC planes are to be upgraded by Boeing to track missiles and provide target information specifically for Star Wars operations.

COST: Upgrades will cost 60 million dollars, and the infrared tracking system for each plane is to cost 8 to 15 million dollars.

BENEFICIARY: Boeing Defense and Space Group.

EVALUATION: This radar will be very useful for missile tracking and it has been modified to track elusive cruise missiles.

Joint Surveillance and Target Attack Radar System (J-STARS)

The J-STARS surveillance plane is designed to detect, track, classify, and support the attack on moving and stationary targets from a distance of 120 miles. A joint army and air force project, it will either pinpoint mobile missile batteries, destroying them before their missiles are launched, or it will provide early detection of missiles after launching.

COST: 11 billion dollars.

BENEFICIARY: Northrop Grumman Corp.

EVALUATION: These new planes were tested during the Bosnian war in 1995–96, and they were found to be unsuitable for their task. Despite this problem an undersecretary of defense approved full-scale production. The GAO blasted this move as being premature and raising the program's level of risk.

UPPER-TIER DEFENSE (EXOATMOSPHERIC)

In this area, once again, the army and navy are competing with each other. Upper-tier defense systems are designed to attack incoming missiles and bombs at high levels in the earth's atmosphere or just above the atmosphere in space.

Theater High Altitude Area Defense (THAAD)

THAAD is a ground-based launcher of upper-tier interceptors—i.e., missiles launched from the ground to intercept other missiles high in the atmosphere. Defending an area of 120 miles at heights of more than 90 miles, it is more extensive than the lower-tier systems.

Its missiles will have a range of 650 miles and will deploy a hit-to-kill interceptor destroying its target with collision energy, not explosive forces. However, THAAD cannot sit alone in the field because it is vulnerable to attack from cruise missiles or weapons launched from planes. So it must be protected with a Patriot or some other lower-tier defense system—protecting a missile with a missile so it can destroy a missile.

Each THAAD launcher is designed to hold ten interceptors. A total of nine to thirteen launchers compose a battery. A tactical operations center and an X-band TMD-GBR (theater missile defense ground-based radar) are needed.

COST: The current estimate for the acquisition of THAAD and its twenty years of operational life is 23 billion dollars.

BENEFICIARIES: Lockheed Martin Missiles and Space is the prime contractor. They are constructing a plant forty miles west of Huntsville, Alabama, specifically for THAAD work. On June 28, 2000, Lockheed Martin signed a 4-billion-dollar eight-year contract with the army for full-scale engineering, manufacturing, and development for configuration 1—the first stage of THAAD. This will include twenty-seven flight tests. The company hopes that sales to other countries could be in the range of several billion dollars, exceeding national Pentagon purchases. THAAD has twelve subcontractors, including Raytheon, Boeing, United Technologies, Northrop Grumman, Honeywell, and Westinghouse.

EVALUATION: The first two trial flights of the THAAD interceptors at White Sands Missile Range in New Mexico in April and July 1995, tested only the ability of THAAD to fly, maneuver, and separate from the warhead. One test worked, the other test failed. A third test in October was reported as successful. Subsequent flight tests for the missiles' infrared sensors had dismal results, six attempts and six failures spanning four years. During the parade of failures, the army kept justifying more tests in order to compete with the navy for the upper-tier interceptor that will eventually prevail.

The General Accounting Office is critical of THAAD. "A suitable target for testing the THAAD system against longer-range missiles does not exist, and funds have not been requested for target development and production. Without a longer-range test target to represent the more formidable higher-velocity missiles that THAAD could face, the system's operational effectiveness will remain in doubt, and DOD will not have reasonable assurance that it could rely on THAAD in an actual conflict."

When THAAD finally intercepted a target missile in 1999, the army optimistically decided that the program was so successful that final flight tests would be unnecessary. Phillip E. Coyle III, the director of operational test and evaluation for the Pentagon, was scathing in his criticism. He said the THAAD missiles used at the White Sands range were prototypes and not the correct configuration that will be used. He called the tests "highly scripted" and nowhere near the situation that would be encountered with actual hostile missiles.

Retired Air Force Lieutenant General Larry Welch called the extraordinary push to deploy THAAD and other hit-to-kill vehicles as a "rush to failure." An aid to a senior Democratic senator said, "The taxpayers have paid for something we still don't have." Bob Aldridge, (writer of "Son of Star Wars") who compiled much of this material, described the system as a corporate golden goose.

Naval Theater Wide (NTW) Missile Defense

An upper tier system to be deployed on Aegis ships, NTW will use a Standard-3 missile to carry a twenty-pound hit-to-kill lightweight exoatmospheric projectile (LEAP) as a warhead. With a range of 370 to 620 miles, it is designed to intercept missiles above the atmosphere, and as such is classified as exoatmospheric. NTW will require space-based and/or airborne early-warning sensors to detect and to help it hit the ballistic missiles. It is to be developed in two segments, Block-1 and Block-2.

Block-1 will have eighty interceptors carried on four ships. To be deployed by 2010, it will protect against rudimentary missiles like the North Korean Nodong-1 with ranges of 1000 kilometers. Block-2 is to be used against missiles with ranges of up to 3000 kilometers—missiles from China, and Russian ballistic missiles—and as such constitutes a clear violation of the ABM treaty.

Block-3 or Standard-3 is a four-stage missile. The first two stages launch the interceptor into space, the third stage boosts the interceptor farther, and the fourth stage is the LEAP kill vehicle which, using infrared sensors, is designed to detect and hit the target. The third stage of the rocket will take readings from NAVSTAR global positioning system (GPS) satellites for course correction.

COST: 1.9 billion dollars is earmarked to be spent on the naval theater wide missile defense system between 2000 and 2005.

BENEFICIARIES: Principle contractors are Lockheed Martin, Raytheon, and Boeing. The navy has established its own specific missile defense office to implement NTW. The Aegis-guided missile cruiser USS *Lake Erie,* home ported at Pearl Harbor, is to be dedicated to navy missile defense tests over the next two years.

Obviously the navy will need more Aegis ships (and crew) to compensate for those being used for NMD. New ships would cost 1 billion dollars to build and 20 million dollars a year to operate.[30]

EVALUATION: A report from the Council for a Livable World said that sea-based and boost-phase alternatives to NMD could cost between 30 and 36 billion dollars, would be detrimental to other naval operations, and would not be deployed until 2014. This estimate precludes hidden costs to the navy and does not include costs of space-based tracking sensors. The addition of seven more ships to cope with simultaneous geographical threats could raise the cost to 43 billion dollars, the report says.[31] The report also points out that it would be impossible to incorporate boost-phase interceptors with very high acceleration and high burnout velocity on Aegis ships in the present vertical-launch system modules, so new ones would have to be built. Despite the navy's enthusiasm, the General Accounting Office warned that the NTW has significant technical and schedule problems. It also questions the navy's ability to design a kill vehicle capable of discriminating between an actual bomb and decoys in the time allocated to testing.

On an even more frightening note, it is important to understand that if the missiles were to be used for boost-phase interception, the ships that carry them would need to be located near the enemy country, making them an easy target. Furthermore, the theater commander would have virtually no time to assess the threat of enemy missile launches, so the launch of antimissile missiles would be initiated by a computer, a process aptly described as the tyranny of reaction time.

Operational testing will not occur until 2010. Despite this time frame, more than 50 percent of the interceptors are to be deployed by 2008.

HIGH ENERGY LASER WEAPONS

A whole other category of laser-based weapons, appropriately called "killer lasers," is also planned as part of overall missile defense. These weapons directly violate the ABM treaty because they are to be used against intercontinental ballistic missiles. Under development since Reagan's Star Wars program began, they are now divided into three types.

Air Force Airborne Laser (ABL)

Carried aboard a Boeing 747 plane, this laser is designed to destroy an intercontinental missile in its boost phase. The 747s will be equipped with passive infrared sensors and megawatt-class chemical oxygen-iodine lasers (COILs), which will focus intense laser energy on "hostile" missiles at altitudes between 39,000 to 70,000 feet. The intensity of the focused laser beam will burst the motor casing of the missile. Each plane will carry chemicals for twenty to forty shots, and each shot will cost 1000 dollars. It is planned that two planes will circle constantly at 40,000 feet, ever-ready for an attack.

COST: 11 billion dollars.

BENEFICIARIES: Lockheed Martin, Boeing, and TRW.

EVALUATION: Serious technical obstacles face chemical laser weapons, including diffusion of the beam through the atmosphere, accurate target tracking during air turbulence, and miniaturization and packing of the equipment so that it will fit into a plane. David Collier, chief scientist for the army space and strategic defense command, said, "Laser geeks tend to overestimate their effectiveness. . . . There's a major disagreement on the effectiveness of almost any laser system." Finally, depending upon whether the missile is carrying hydrogen bombs or chemical or biological weapons, the country that launches the missiles and/or its neighbors will be contaminated either by plutonium, highly toxic chemicals, or genetically modified lethal bacteria or viruses.

Space-Based Laser (SBL)

A Reagan concept, conceived in 1977, the SBL has been resurrected to become the Pentagon's first space-based weapon for use in both the ballistic missile defense and theater missile defense programs, both overt violations of ABM. Jointly funded by the ballistic missile defense organization and the air force, and operated by the air force, SBL will employ twenty to twenty-five satellites, each equipped with a cylindrical hydrogen-fluoride chemical laser capable of destroying 100 missiles from a range of 2672 miles. The first SBL launch is scheduled for 2012.

COST: The total cost is estimated to be in the billions of dollars.

BENEFICIARIES: Lockheed Martin, Boeing, and TRW were awarded an initial contract of 125 million dollars in February 1999 to begin a space-based laser integrated flight experiment.

EVALUATION: A technology demonstration phase scheduled in autumn 2001 will culminate in a systems definition review. Each review and modification tends to increase the cost of the system.

Tactical High Energy Laser (THEL)

THEL is a ground-based laser incorporating command, control, communications, and intelligence systems, as well as a fire-control and target-acquisition radar, and a laser pointer/tracker. The laser can fire sixty shots without reloading, each shot costing 3000 dollars. THEL is to be used to defend Israel's northern border against the small Katyusha rockets fired by Hezbollah guerrillas from Lebanon. (Katyusha rockets are much cheaper, and the THEL system can readily be overwhelmed by more rockets). THEL is jointly funded by Israel and the U.S. and managed by the U.S. army, but it is not designed for American use.

COST: 201.8 million dollars has been spent on the program since 1996, with Israel's contribution at 67.5 million dollars.

BENEFICIARY: TRW Space and Electronics.

EVALUATION: Yiftah Shapir, from the Jaffee Center for Strategic Studies in Tel Aviv, said on May 26, 2000, that THEL is not cost-effective or practical. Each truck-mounted system can launch only forty of these 120-mm diameter rockets without reloading, but a Katyusha battery has six trucks that can ripple-fire 240 rockets. Major General Gaby Ashkenazi, commander of the Israel Defense Force's northern command, said, "It's like trying to protect the entire northern part of Israel from rain with a single umbrella."

BATTLE MANAGEMENT/COMMAND, CONTROL, AND COMMUNICATIONS (BM/C3)

This intricate computerized system will be the nerve center of all missile defense. It will receive information from myriad sensors and sources the U.S. has deployed on land, on sea, and in space around the world. The information will be instantaneously processed by a battle-management computer, designed to produce a detailed picture of the missile attack. Because missiles move so fast, there will be no time for human input; the computer will therefore be programmed to initiate its own antimissile attack (obviously the computer can never be tested under the realistic conditions of an attack).

The elements that must be in place for BM/C3 to function include rockets, radars, satellites, transmitters, and command centers as follows:

Ground-Based Interceptor (GBI)

The GBI is the NMD system which is ground-launched. It consists of a "booster stack" missile with an exoatmospheric kill vehicle (EKV) deployed atop this three-stage rocket. The GBI will travel at speeds of 25,000 miles per hour, firing the EKV into space to shatter the enemy missile by impact.

BOOSTER STACK

In July 1998, the department of defense selected a booster stack design deploying commercial off-the-shelf motor stages.

COST: Each booster stack is estimated to cost 3 million dollars.

BENEFICIARIES: Boeing is the main contractor; Alliant Tech Systems and United Technologies are subcontractors.

EVALUATION: The first test of a booster stack will not take place until August or September 2001 at the earliest. This means Clinton was pressured to make a decision to proceed with NMD before the rockets had been constructed, let alone tested.

EXOATMOSPHERIC KILL VEHICLE (EKV)

The following description of the EKV was provided by Raytheon, the prime contractor. The EKV "has its own [long wavelength infrared] seeker, [liquid bipropellant] propulsion, communications, guidance, and computers to support intercept targeting decisions and maneuvers." Cold gas thrusters are used to control the altitude (position) of the 55-inch long, 130-pound EKV and aim its seeker as it approaches the target at 4500 miles per hour.

The EKV will have six to eight minutes to home in on the target and destroy it with a combined impact velocity of 12,000 to 20,000 miles per hour, taking place at an altitude of 140 miles.

COST: A total of twenty-four integrated test flights are planned (six have already occurred). Each test costs about 100 million dollars, so the testing alone will cost about 2.6 billion dollars before actual deployment occurs.

BENEFICIARIES: Raytheon, and subcontractor Axsys Technologies.

EVALUATION: It was announced by the Clinton administration that two out of three flight tests of a prototype GBI-EKV must be successful before presidential approval would be given to develop NMD. The first qualifying test took place on October 2, 1999. The test was rigged to score a hit, as were some of its earlier predecessors. The hostile missile launched from Vandenberg Air Force Base in California carried a large balloon that traveled alongside the target bomb. Because there is no friction in space, the balloon traveled as fast as the bomb, but it was designed so that its infrared signal was constant and did not flicker like a normal signal from a tumbling bomb. Although the Pentagon claimed that the balloon was a decoy, it actually served as a marker buoy to lure the EKV close enough to site the target, because the EKV had failed to orient itself correctly with the stars and had drifted off course.[32]

Eventually it "saw" the balloon from the corner of its visual field, and, after homing in on the balloon, it was able to see the bomb's flickering signal and make a "kill." This strange sequence was described by Undersecretary of Defense Dr. Jacques Gansler:

> In this early test what we were trying to do was to pull it off and so used something that was even larger and much more obvious, and we figured that might pull the interceptor off to the target, and in fact, it did, in the flight. It found this decoy first because it was larger, did have more radiation, and it found it first, and it said, "Oh, there's the target," and started to go for it. . . . And its software said "That's the wrong target," and then it shifted to the target that had the characteristics it was supposed to have had . . .[33]

As reported by the *Washington Post*, both the interceptor and the target missile used the NAVSTAR global positioning system (GPS) to maneuver onto a collision course. Obviously a "hostile" missile would not be so obliging as to broadcast its position and trajectory, to signal its position and to send up a marker balloon for its bomb.

The next test was conducted on January 19, 2000. The EKV failed to intercept the target bomb because of a leak of liquid nitrogen utilized to cryogenically cool its infrared sensors. As in the previous test, a large balloon was also deployed, and the NAVSTAR GPS accurately positioned the missile and interceptor. Space-based sensors and the battle management/command, control, and communications system were also deployed and the field of view for the EKV was increased by 210 percent. Still it failed.

The last test before Clinton was to make his decision took place on July 8, 2000. It failed for three reasons: the balloon did not inflate, the interceptor missile veered off course, and the EKV did not separate from the surrogate booster rocket.

Apart from these problems, the tests in no way resemble the conditions that would exist in battle. Russian, North Korean, or Chinese missiles would fly from west to east, but the NMB test "offensive" missiles are launched from California, to be intercepted by "kill vehicles" launched from an atoll in the mid-Pacific. As of this writing, fourteen more test flights are scheduled, with all the artificial Band-Aids that the previous tests deployed. As one senior official was heard to say during a briefing, "I am trying to avoid defining, 'What means success?' " However, Secretary of Defense Cohen, after the last failed test, said, with what journalist Mary McGrory of the *Washington Post* called "striking sophistry" that "the test itself was a disappointment but it was one of those failures that was least expected. . . . That happens from time to time—that you have a failure of something that's fairly routine." [34]

Ted Postol, a professor at MIT who was a scientific advisor to the chief of naval operations in the eighties and helped develop the Trident-2 missile, said that the Pentagon had rigged missile tests to ensure success. After a 1997 test of the antimissile revealed that it couldn't effectively distinguish decoys from warheads, the Pentagon stopped using decoys that would seriously challenge the defensive weapon.[35] Nina Schwartz, a senior physicist who worked at TRW in 1995 and 1996, charged that the TRW corporation had falsified work in an effort to portray a "kill vehicle" as more capable than it actually was. She said that TRW certified to the government that interceptors using its computer programs would succeed more than 95 percent of the time in the identification of enemy warheads, but in fact they could do so only 5 to 15 percent of the time. Dr. Schwartz said that at some level the Pentagon and its contractors were in collusion. "It's not a defense of the United States, it's a conspiracy to allow them to milk the government. They are creating for themselves a job for life."[36] Schwartz said that TRW fired her when she protested about alleged efforts to fudge test data to hide flaws in the system's ability to distinguish warheads from decoys.

Postol alleges that the Pentagon colluded with TRW to collate fraudulent test documents. (The FBI is investigating these charges of fraud.)[37] Postol also accused the Pentagon of significantly reducing the difficulty of the next sixteen tests planned.[38] Postol and David Wright conducted a study of the efficacy of NMD and found that the defense would not work because it can be overwhelmed with simpler, cheaper technology—decoys.[39] Three major scientific groups supported Postol in his stand. The American Physical Society with 42,000 physicists, the Federation of American Scientists and the Union of Concerned Scientists, and fifty Nobel laureates called the planned system "premature, wasteful, and dangerous."

Theater Missile Defense Ground-Based Radar (TMD-GBR)

This particular radar is a small, ground-based portable sensor that can be transported by plane. It can search, track, and discriminate for specific missiles. Designed to receive and instantaneously process data from all relevant sensors (satellites, other radars) it can form a detailed picture of the attack. A commander will then theoretically be equipped with the necessary data to direct the TMD weapons to intercept a hostile missile attack—if he has the time.

COST: An estimated 5.4 billion dollars.

BENEFICIARY: Raytheon is the primary contractor.

EVALUATION: No evaluation available.

Ballistic Missile Early Warning System (BMEWS)

This is one of two early-warning radar systems that feed into the ground-based radar system. The radar at Fylingdale in Yorkshire,

England, has three faces and therefore operates over a 360-degree circle. (Other installations at Clear, Alaska, and Thule, Greenland, consist of two-faced phased-array radars that monitor 240 degrees of azimuth; each face monitors 120 degrees of azimuth—the arc of the heavens from horizon to zenith.)

COST: Not available.

BENEFICIARY: BMEWS radars are made by Raytheon.

EVALUATION: The Pentagon wishes to upgrade these facilities to become X-band radars, but neither Denmark nor Britain is willing to approve any new installations that do not comply with the ABM treaty. The U.S. is assessing alternative plans, including placing X-band radars on commercial ships in international waters.

Perimeter Acquisition of Vehicle Entry Phased-Array Warning System (PAVE PAWS)

ANOTHER RADAR REQUIRED FOR BM/C3

There are two of these two-faced phased-array radars in the United States, one at the Cape Cod Air Force Station in Massachusetts and one at Beale Air Force Base in California.

COST: Not available.

BENEFICIARY: Manufactured by Raytheon.

EVALUATION: PAVE PAWS has been in place for many years as an integral part of the early-warning system, but it is to be upgraded to a more sophisticated system for NMD.

SPACE-BASED INFRARED SYSTEM (SBIRS)

Radar systems must be supported and complemented by infrared tracking satellites that detect heat and flames emanating from the tail ends of missiles. The current system of infrared satellites is called the defense support program (DSP) and consists of three satellites deployed in geosynchronous orbit—they move at the same speed as the earth's rotation, and continuously overlook one area of the earth, namely the Indian, Pacific, and Atlantic Oceans. There may be more DSP satellites, but the exact number is classified. Three upgraded replacement satellites of the DSP system are about to be launched, the last scheduled for 2003.

Apart from DSP, the Pentagon is about to deploy another set of satellites specifically for Star Wars:

High Orbit Space-Based Infrared System (SBIRS-High)

Approved by the Pentagon since 1994, this system will consist of four satellites in geosynchronous orbit around the equator, plus another two satellites in highly elliptical polar orbits, providing effective coverage of the northern regions of the globe.

SBIRS-High will monitor the hot exhaust plumes of missile launches, and is due to replace the DSP system in 2004. This system will be better able to determine the exact launch and impact points of a missile, and its trajectory.

COST: 2 billion dollars for six geosynchronous-orbit satellites and infrared sensors that will ride piggyback on other satellites.

BENEFICIARIES: The main contractor is Lockheed Martin; there are six subcontractors.

EVALUATION: The comptroller's office has instructed the air force to delay the launches of the satellites 2 through 4 by one year so that money can go to other programs.

Low Orbit Space-Based Infrared System (SBIRS-Low)

Low orbit satellites will complement the high orbit satellites by tracking hostile missiles and hydrogen bombs through space (the midcourse phase) after their booster motors have died, thus providing better targeting and engagements for the kill-vehicles. SBIRS-

Low will consist of between eighteen and thirty-two small satellites in low orbit—about 250 miles high. They will have the ability to look through clouds and darkness; some will use electronic cameras. Data is to be relayed from one low orbit satellite to another by laser beam, reaching the relevant command center with the speed of light. The information will be rapidly relayed to the ground-based radars. In turn, they will send the trajectory information about the missiles to the kill interceptors.

COST: The air force plans to spend a total of 11.8 billion dollars on SBIRS-Low.

BENEFICIARIES: Eleven contractors are already working on this project. The prime contractor is to be Spectrum Astro, with Northrop Grumman Corp. as its main partner.

EVALUATION: In February 2001 the GAO warned, "the air force's current SBIRS-Low acquisition schedule is at high risk of not delivering the system on time or at a cost with expected performance." It identified three problem areas:

1. The current acquisition schedule does not provide for flight-test results or crucial satellite functions and capabilities until five years after production has started.
2. Five of the six critical technologies have been judged immature for the current state of the program.
3. Alternative terrestrial systems to the SBIRS-Low have not been investigated.

Single Integrated Air Picture (SIAP)

SIAP will provide a sophisticated common battlefield picture for aircraft, cruise missile, and ballistic missile defense. It will be designed to integrate huge quantities of information from sensors and intelligence information from the three services, and the results will be instantaneously available to every commander.

The navy already has such a system, called cooperative engagement capability (CEC), in place. Computers combine all the fleet's radar, sensor, and targeting systems into a single picture displayed on computer screens in ships and aircraft that determine which ship or aircraft should track the targets and which should engage them. By 2007 the navy hopes to have CEC equipment on all cruisers and destroyers with Aegis radars. The army wants CEC for its Patriot PAC-3 batteries, and the air force will also develop their own form of CEC for its AWACS.

COST: Tens of billions of dollars.

BENEFICIARIES: Lockheed Martin and Raytheon.

NMD INFRASTRUCTURE

Even a relatively simple missile defense system requires a massively complex interconnecting system of ground-based radars, sensors, detectors, satellites, command centers, computers, radio transmitters, and personnel. Let us now examine this infrastructure, remembering that it could be modified for a full-scale first-strike system.

Radar stations already exist in strategic locations around the world, as part of the U.S. early-warning system. These can also be used for the Star Wars systems. Coordinating their data collection with space-based infrared sensors on satellites, they will be able to detect launches of "hostile" missiles and to give an imprecise idea of the missile's location. Once the imprecise location is determined, newly constructed X-band radars, which would violate the ABM treaty, will take over and give the precise location and condition of the missile by tracking the target. The X-band radar will then provide the "kill assessment."

The construction of the first X-band radar is planned for Shemya Island, part of the Aleutian chain of islands in Alaska, the most western point of the United States—in direct line with any attack on the U.S. from North Korea, but also conveniently in direct line with Russia and China. Three other X-band radars are to be constructed in other strategic locations of the globe, including Fylingdale in Yorkshire, England, and in Vardo, Norway. There are also rumors that America is planning a total of nine X-band radars in places such as Pine Gap, Australia, and possibly in Japan and South Korea.

A multiweek exercise called integrated ground test (IGT-6) was conducted in February 2001 at the Integrated System Test Capability-2 facility, a new site located at the Army Space and Missile Defense Command's Advanced Research Center in Huntsville, Alabama. This IGT-6 operation involved the test of the next NMD intercept. The previous three have failed.

Officials assessed the operability of the NMD integration efforts by deploying "nodal" computers representing each element of the complex system, using the most advanced software and processors. The exercises were conducted in "real time"—meaning no delay—and, according to Pentagonese language, were designed to validate "the functionality" of element-to-element interface and to mitigate the risk to NMD intercept tests. These ground tests are crucial to the NMD program because they will provide, as the military says, the vast majority of information needed for "milestone" decisions along the way to a fully integrated and operational Star Wars system. IGT-6 was used to test engagement scenarios involving limited attacks from three geographical regions: North Korea, the Middle East, Libya, and from accidental unauthorized launches from Russia and China.

The Ballistic Missile Defense Organization (BMDO) already has operational IGT nodes for the antiballistic missile's battle management/command, control, and communication system, for the ground-based X-band, the upgraded early-warning radar, the in-flight interceptor communications system, the defense support program satellites, the space-based infrared system satellites, and the ground-based interceptor.[40]

This infrastructure will all feed into a battle management computer.

OVERALL EVALUATION OF BATTLE MANAGEMENT/ COMMAND, CONTROL, AND COMMUNICATIONS (BM/C3)

The crux of the Star Wars system—a battle-management computer designed to plan, coordinate, direct, and control the Star Wars weapons and its sensors—is essentially a computer system with millions or billions of lines of programming. No computer is perfect, even the simplest desktop computers fail because of software problems. According to software experts, the increase in difficulty of writing software is not linear but exponential. Moving from ten to twenty lines is not twice but 100 times as difficult. The difficulties inherent in a program of millions upon millions of lines of computer code are impossible to imagine. A bug in a desktop computer is a nuisance, but in a missile-defense computer it could mean nuclear winter.[41]

Under conditions of attack, there will be virtually no human input, except perhaps a split-second decision by a military operator. Certainly there will be no time for civilian or political input. John Pike, a space and military policy analyst, formerly of the Federation of American Scientists, says that by the time the missile-defense system is operational, the computer software that assesses the attack and analyzes response options "will be the culmination of many thousands of work-years of modeling and calculation and simulation and refinement and testing. The software is going to be in an infinitely better position to make a considered judgment about what should be done than the few human beings sitting in the room. There will be too much stuff going on too fast for any human operators to figure it all out. There just won't be any time for mere human meddling."[42]

In other words, the decision to go to war or to annihilation will be removed from the president in the oval office and given instead to a computer manned by a military officer sequestered in an underground command post. Computerized or fully automated war would definitely be necessary in a boost-phase counterattack, favored by George W. Bush, where there would be only a few tens of seconds to detect a launch and another few seconds to fire. Unfortunately, the battle-management computer can never be tested under operating conditions; the first actual test will occur when the U.S. is under attack.

Here is one scenario: North Korea fires a missile containing five chemical warheads. In response, the U.S. launches a dozen interceptor missiles, which appear on China's primitive early-warning radar screen. Believing it is under attack, China launches its nuclear missiles at the U.S. before they can be destroyed in their silos from a U.S. first strike. America, detecting this unexpected Chinese attack, immediately launches its hair-trigger missiles, initiating a full-scale nuclear war.[43]

Another scenario, postulated by former missileer Bruce Blair: "What if a country is just going to test a missile? Are we going to knock it out just because it has the range to reach our country? It could be a peaceful launch."

THE INNATE CHAOS OF COMPLEX COMPUTER SYSTEMS

Other insuperable problems plague the Star Wars systems. The most fundamental is an inherent aspect of rocket science. Called the "brittle" problem by students of complexity theory, it is simply this: Should one tiny part of a hugely complex interconnected system fail, the whole thing fails. Compounding the brittle factor is the "flub" factor. The more complex a system, the more likely it is that something unanticipated will fail.

With thirty minutes or less from the time a missile is launched until it reaches its target, there is no time to fix anything. As Gottfried J. Mayer, adjunct professor of kinesiology at Pennsylvania State University, memorably noted some years ago, "the booster fails to separate from the payload—and New York is history,"[44] a particularly chilling speculation in light of the September 11 attacks.

IS NMD JUST A FRONT FOR FIRST-STRIKE WINNABLE NUCLEAR WAR?

In 1977 and 1980 Jimmy Carter's Presidential Directives 18 and 59 clearly described the four components of first-strike capability:

1. *Antisatellite (ASAT):* Weapons to knock out the Soviet early-warning system
2. *Decapitation:* Destruction of the Soviet leadership with extremely accurate Pershing 11 missiles before they pressed their button

3. *Counterforce:* Destruction of most Soviet missiles in hardened silos, submarines, mobile launchers, and the strategic bomber fleet by MX and D5 missiles
4. *Strategic Defense Initiative (SDI):* A ballistic missile defense system to mop up any Soviet missiles that survived counterforce and had been launched[45]

No presidents have signed any significant treaties agreeing to back away from a stance that was adopted at the height of the cold war, and I would submit that first-strike winnable nuclear war is the real (secret?) agenda of Star Wars revitalization.

DOES NMD VIOLATE INTERNATIONAL TREATIES?

Almost all the plans for NMD and most involving TMD will violate the ABM treaty, the cornerstone of all other nuclear arms control treaties. The ABM treaty, for example, directs that America and the former Soviet Union—now specifically Russia—can operate only one regional interceptor defense system each. (The current systems are in North Dakota and Moscow, respectively, making the new Alaska-based system a clear violation.)

The treaty would also be violated by upgrading the present U.S. radar systems, by implementing a defense system covering all fifty states instead of the agreed-upon forty-eight, by installing a new satellite network, or by shifting the interceptor system to a new location—all of which are currently proposed as a part of George W. Bush's national missile-defense plan.

The ABM treaty states that because no country can protect itself against a nuclear attack, each side must therefore live in fear of mutually assured destruction. Logically, under these circumstances, no country would be foolish enough to launch a nuclear war. Thus, the ABM treaty has always been intended as a brake on unrestrained nuclear arms buildup, and has proven effective since its signing in 1972. Its violation by either party would be an unconscionable and extraordinarily destabilizing act in a world bristling with nuclear weapons.

Yet the U.S. openly plans to violate the ABM treaty. In justifying his plans, George W. Bush told an audience in Iowa in 1999, "When I was coming up, it was a dangerous world, and you knew exactly who they were. . . . It was us versus them, and it was clear who them was. Today, we are not so sure who they are, but we know they're there."[46]

Violation of the ABM would in turn jeopardize other international treaties. Currently, for example, the Russian Duma has ratified a new nuclear arms treaty, START II, calling for the bilateral reduction of strategic nuclear weapons to 3500. Should the ABM be violated, Russia has indicated that it may well cancel plans to reduce its nuclear arsenal and refuse to consider additional reductions under START III. Surprisingly, START II actually allows the U.S. to maintain 3500 deployed strategic weapons, as well as 950 operational tactical nuclear weapons, 2500 "hedge" strategic weapons, and 2500 in the "inactive reserve."[47] Furthermore, the START II treaty does not actively call for the elimination of the hydrogen bombs, only for destruction of the launch platforms, so that in the future the bombs could be hauled out of storage and redeployed.

START III, however, if agreed upon, would reduce Russia's and America's strategic arsenals to fewer than 2500 nuclear bombs each, and would, for the first time, include requirements for the actual destruction of nuclear bombs, with the plutonium and uranium disposed of in such a way that they will never be available for the future construction of nuclear weapons. (It is relatively easy to monitor these procedures technically, given the goodwill that currently exists between the countries concerned, but this may not continue to be the case under the Bush administration.)[48]

Furthermore, President Putin, wishing to discourage America's NMD developments and wanting to move rapidly toward nuclear disarmament, recently offered unilaterally to reduce Russia's nuclear arsenal to between 1500 and 1000 weapons, or even less—at least 1000 to 1500 fewer than the number demanded by START III. This offer comes with the proviso that America not proceed with national missile defense, abide by the ABM treaty, and that the Senate ratify the Comprehensive Test Ban Treaty.

However, at the Crawford ranch meeting in Texas between President George Bush and President Vladimir Putin during the second week of November 2001, Bush proposed a unilateral reduction of U.S. strategic weapons to between 2200 and 1700 to take place over a period of ten years, from the current level of more than 6000. This would obviate the START II treaty ban on Russian land-based missiles with multiple nuclear warheads, and would leave most of the U.S. deterrent on submarines invulnerable to surprise attacks. Putin left the meeting without a response, although he is expected to reciprocate in kind. The Bush move is intended to "soften up" the Russians for the U.S. intended violation of the ABM treaty.[49, 50]

But the U.S.'s attachment to NMD is so bizarre that the state department actively encouraged Russia to maintain "large, diversified, viable arsenals of strategic offensive weapons capable of delivering an annihilating counterattack," as long as Russia allows the U.S. to violate the ABM treaty and to proceed with national missile defense.[51, 52]

China, with its twenty intercontinental nuclear weapons, has already confirmed that it might well speed up deployment of a new generation of weapons systems if America goes ahead with NMD. Indeed, China will be encouraged to do so. In a speech in early November 2000, foreign minister spokesman Zhu Bangzoa said:

> The United States is a country with the largest and most sophisticated arsenals of both nuclear and conventional weapons in the world and now it is engaging itself to develop NMD and TMD (theater missile defense). Such an act is contrary to the trend of the times because it is not conducive to the international efforts of disarmament and arms control. It will also exert a lasting negative impact on world peace. The Chinese side expresses serious concern, and in particular if the U.S. is to develop TMD and to include Taiwan, this is something that will be by no means accepted by the Chinese side.[53]

(Ironically, the small NMD system for "rogue" states that Clinton advocated would actually be an adequate "defense" against China's twenty nuclear-armed intercontinental missiles that could reach the U.S.—as opposed to the multilayered missile defense planned by George W. Bush.)

Likewise, European allies are increasingly worried that violation of the ABM will initiate a new nuclear arms race and separate European security from that of the U.S. French President Jacques Chirac said in the *New York Times* on December 17, 1999, "If you look at world history, ever since men began waging war, you will see that there's a permanent race between sword and shield. The sword always wins. The more improvements that are made to the shield, the more improvements are made to the sword."[54]

WHAT THE WORLD THINKS OF NMD

Star Wars is designed to protect only the United States, but obviously should other countries be persuaded to host Star Wars facilities, they are not necessarily protected but become targets of a nuclear attack.

Citizens of certain countries due to participate in Star Wars are not happy about the prospect. England, for instance, has been deeply involved in the U.S. early-warning system for many years, hosting two American bases at Menwith Hill and at Fylingdale. And the level of British participation is increasing. Over the past year, almost 500 British military-scientific representatives visited the U.S. under the auspices of a 1958 mutual defense agreement, a twofold increase in visits from 1995. And the U.S. military establishment visited the British scientific military facility at AWE Aldermaston 110 times during the same period. Two Aldermaston staff were seconded to Los Alamos and one to Lawrence Livermore "to assist with the technical development of facilities of mutual interest."[55] Washington plans to upgrade the U.S. base at Menwith Hill in North Yorkshire, giving it a crucial role in America's plans for a space-based infrared missile-launch-detection system. Tony Blair has already granted approval for Fylingdale Moor to be upgraded, but the Parliament has not concurred. The U.S. also plans to construct a fifteen-story–sized radar building at some unknown location in the U.K.[56]

But strong opposition is mounting in England as U.S. plans expand. Aware that Bush is in favor of the full Star Wars system, a committee of twelve members of Parliament concluded after deliberation: "The government should articulate the very strong concerns that have been expressed about NMD within the U.K. We are not convinced that the U.S. plan to deploy NMD represents an appropriate response to the proliferation problems faced by the international community. We recommend that the government encourages the U.S. to seek other ways of reducing the threats it perceives."[57]

And Hugo Young, writing in the *Guardian,* says NMD is "born of an arrogance that Russia could not be expected to watch in silence, nor China, with its relatively small missile armory, to countenance without increasing its own nuclear force," adding that "for Europe, the project is all downside risk," because Iran and Iraq are closer to Europe than to North America.[58]

Similar opposition exists in Denmark about the upgrading of early-warning radars in Thule, Greenland, a Danish province. Strategically significant early-warning radars that require upgrading to X-band status include the facilities in Thule, Greenland; Grand Forks, North Dakota; and Clear, Alaska. According to Ted Postol, these upgrades are exactly what the U.S. will need for a national missile defense program aimed specifically at Russia and China.[59]

Thus, incredibly, the U.S. seems to have allowed the perceived threat by North Korea, Iran, and Iraq to justify a system actually aimed at China and Russia.

The most obvious clue about these intentions is the current deployment of the world's most sophisticated advanced tracking and imaging intelligence-gathering radar on the northern tip of Norway, forty miles from the Russian border. This new X-band radar, along with the one to be deployed at Eareckson Air Station at Shemya Island, 1500 miles southwest of Anchorage, will be used to collect data on Russia's long-range missiles tests, rendering Norway a prime Russian target.

Called Vardo, code-named HAVE STARE, this U.S.-owned, Norwegian-based radar could well present a formal violation of the ABM treaty. With a potential resolution of about 10 to 15 centimeters, it will provide extremely detailed images of Russian warheads and their missiles. (To date, the most sophisticated radars have resolutions of at best 5 to 10 meters.) The two radars in Norway and Shemya will be capable of monitoring the entire trajectory of Russian missile tests, including their powered flight, the "bus" maneuvers, deployment, and separation of warheads and decoys. Precise data will be collected on every phase of the missile and its bombs from launch to splashdown. The radars will be linked directly to the nerve center of the proposed NMD, buried deep inside Cheyenne Mountain in Colorado. This data will be entered into the NMD database, increasing enormously the discrimination capabilities of the NMD system against Russian intercontinental ballistic missiles.

As Ted Postol says, "If the purpose of a national missile defense system is to protect the United States from North Korean missiles, why is the world's most advanced tracking and imaging radar about to go online at the northern tip of Norway instead of northern Japan?" According to Postol, Russia and China will be constantly concerned "that the U.S. will eventually expand and modify their missile defense with nuclear armed interceptors instead of the pitiful hit-to-kill interceptors now planned for the system." [60] Postol points out that the U.S. should at least be honest about its intentions. Both Russia and China are under no illusions about the U.S. agenda, he argues, but America is lying to the rest of the world—including its own population—using North Korea as a camouflage to disguise its true intentions.

As noted, Shemya Island is to receive the next X-band radar. Part of the Aleutian Islands chain, Shemya is a remote, windswept place. The closest inhabited point is an Eskimo village 100 miles away. Shemya is therefore not the most convenient place for this facility. Because of its isolation, it is also an easy target for destruction, either from a missile or a small artillery piece mounted on a fishing trawler.

The U.S. claims that this particular site has been chosen because it is in line with a missile attack from North Korea.[61] But there is a political reason that Shemya was chosen as a site. Senator Ted Stevens, the powerful ex-head of the Senate appropriations committee, is from Alaska. And because Clinton needed his support, an attempt had to be made to protect Alaska from Russian attack, even though this radar was precluded under the ABM treaty.

The Rumsfeld report stated that "a number of countries with regional ambitions do not welcome the U.S. role as a stabilizing power in their regions and have not accepted it passively. Because of their ambitions they want to place restraints on the U.S. ability to project power or influence into their regions."

But perhaps the U.S. should begin by questioning its right to project its power into other regions of the world: 6.5 billion people inhabit this planet, not just 280 million Americans. Given the reality of past and present U.S. interference in the politics of numerous foreign, sovereign states, the U.S. missile shield signals to the world that America maintains a significantly hostile intent. A working nuclear shield above the United States would be the equivalent of giving a sniper a bulletproof bodysuit. Would he be more or less likely to shoot others if he himself were immune?[62]

Chapter Seven

SPACE: THE NEXT AMERICAN EMPIRE

It's politically sensitive, but it's going to happen. Some people don't want to hear this, and it sure isn't in vogue, but—absolutely—we're going to fight in space. We're going to fight from space and we're going to fight into space. That's why the U.S. has developed programs in directed energy and hit-to-kill mechanisms. We will engage terrestrial targets someday—ships, airplanes, land targets—from space. We will engage targets in space, from space.

—General Joseph Ashy, former commander in chief of the U.S. space command, 1996[1]

The threat, ladies and gentlemen, I believe is real. It's a threat to our economic well-being. This is why we must work together to find common ground between commercial imperatives and the president's tasking me for space control and protection.

—General Richard B. Meyers, former commander in chief of the U.S. space command, 1999, now the new chairman of the Joint Chiefs of Staff for President George W. Bush[2]

With regard to space dominance, we have it, we like it, and we're going to keep it.

—Keith Hall, the air force assistant secretary for space and director of the National Reconnaissance Office[3]

COMMISSIONED BY Congress, John Collins's 1989 book *Military Space Forces: The Next 50 Years,* was one of the earliest studies to explore in depth the notion of fighting a war from space and in space. Collins, a senior specialist in national defense at the Library of Congress, was funded by the air force association and the association of the U.S. army, which meant that his book had a particular point of view. Endorsed by prominent members of Congress, including John Glenn and John Kasich, the book described the possibilities and problems associated with space warfare. Other endorsees included Senator Sam Nunn, chairman of the Senate armed services committee, who said, "Space, a distinctive military medium, deserves a new school of thought. This book will be an indispensable starting point," and former Representative Les Aspin, later secretary of defense for President Bill Clinton, who said, "No other military space study puts all the pieces of the puzzle together."

Collins begins the book by paraphrasing Halford J. Mackinder's "Heartland statement":[4]

> Who rules circumterrestrial space commands Planet Earth;
> Who rules the moon commands circumterrestial space;
> Who rules L 4 and L 5* commands the Earth-Moon System.

Military Space Forces is a recipe for space-based warfare. It is simultaneously belligerent, nationalistic, provocative, well researched, and extremely scary. And it forms the basis for much official U.S. policy regarding the militarization of space.

Among other topics, Collins discusses the fact that the moon in particular is rich in many natural resources that could be mined and brought back to earth for economic returns. He says that parties "that hope to satisfy economic interests in space must maintain ready access to resources on the moon and beyond, despite opposition if necessary, and perhaps deny access to competitors who seek monopolies." He warns, however, that rival forces may lie in wait to hijack shipments on return from the moon. Obviously, if America invests huge capital in mining the moon, it must then defend its investments. Antisatellite warfare is analyzed.

Collins's thinking is dangerous, advocating "soft kill" weapons that penetrate target surfaces without impairing them, and that can selectively disorient, damage, or destroy human beings as well as

* areas in space where the respective gravitational forces of the moon and earth are in balance

damage sensitive equipment within satellites or space stations. He also suggests jamming communication systems, spray-painting satellite camera lenses, focusing blinding light onto laser reflectors, or the surreptitious introduction of foreign objects into booster fuel of enemy rockets, and he discusses the merits of laser-beam weapons, and of particle beam weapons consisting of highly energetic protons, neutrons, electrons, or hydrogen atoms.

He talks of the use of nuclear weapons in space and of the efficacy of various forms of nuclear radiation, which, he says, is unimpeded because there is no atmosphere in space, and could therefore cover much more space volume than if used in the atmosphere near the earth's surface. It would work especially well against targets in low space orbit. However, he concedes that nuclear radiation cannot distinguish friend from foe. Electromagnetic pulses from nuclear explosions could "wound" users as well as the intended victims.

Collins explores war on the moon, saying that strike forces there could use the full range of offensive maneuvers that are now used on earth. Space mines could be easily positioned. He describes how space-based "civilian" vehicles could be used surreptitiously for military activities. He says that lasers, sensors, and telecommunications devices can be concealed within satellites that appear perfectly harmless. Weapons could "piggyback" on satellites that are ostensibly for reconnaissance and surveillance.

He is particularly keen on biological and chemical warfare in space, saying that self-contained biospheres like a space station offer a "superlative" environment for these sort of attacks because they rely on a closed-circuit life-support system that continually recirculates air and water. Clandestine agents could dispense into space stations lethal or incapacitating chemical or biological agents, which—because they are colorless and odorless—are impossible to spot before symptoms appear.

He introduces the notion of fighting from space, targeting particular installations on earth, and quotes former astronaut Michael Collins, who said that space is an ideal place from which to attack surface combatants and aircraft carriers, because ships "stand out as clearly as billiard balls on green felt" when seen from space.

Collins advocates the use of psychological operations (psyops). These techniques of psychological warfare would be used to control elitist and popular opinion as nonlethal weapons systems, or to convince rivals that it would be useless to start or to continue military space operations. Collins says that these psyop maneuvers would "deprive opponents of freedom of action, while preserving it for oneself," and advocates using psyop propaganda to spread subversive ideas, including the futility of space for the achievement of military superiority, the perils to world peace by militarizing space, and the waste of global resources better spent on people than on a fruitless arms race. He says that U.S. superiority in space "could culminate in bloodless total victory, if lagging powers could neither cope nor catch up technologically."

This is not a pleasant scenario for 95 percent of the earth's population who do not happen to be American, and who rightly feel that the moon and the heavens belong to them, too.

U.S. PLANS FOR WAR IN SPACE[5]

During the sixties and seventies, the army, navy, and air force came to rely upon advanced and expanded space technologies in communications, meteorology, geodesy, navigation, and reconnaissance. The military use of space supported strategic deterrence by providing treaty verification, arms control, and early-warning systems of impending nuclear attack. In 1985 the Joint Chiefs of Staff officially institutionalized the military use of space by establishing a new unified command called the U.S. space command, whose motto is *Master of Space*. During Operation Desert Storm in the Persian Gulf in 1991, military space operations were used to produce what is called a "multiplier" effect, which considerably enhanced communications, navigation, and targeting.

The U.S. space command then took on more responsibilities. Composed of three active elements—the United States army space command, the fourteenth air force, and the naval space command—the U.S. command's mission statement calls for it to "integrate space forces into war-fighting capabilities across the full spectrum of conflict," in addition to "dominating the space dimension of military operations to protect U.S. interests and investment," as previously noted.

In 1996 the space command published a pamphlet called "Vision for 2020" in which it overtly enunciated its goals of war in space.[6] In 1998 the space command expanded the original 1996 plans in a comprehensive 100-page document, "The Long Range Plan" (LRP), written with the cooperation of seventy-five military corporations, including Boeing, Aerojet, Hughes Space, Lockheed Martin, Raytheon, Sparta Corp, TRW, and Vista Technologies. During the year 2000, a coalition of aerospace corporations engaged in a campaign called "declaration of space leadership," meant to persuade their congressional allies to introduce the idea of the militarization of space in the form of a House resolution. The declaration calls for funding of "defensive" systems and NASA at levels that "guarantee American leadership in the exploration of space."

The aerospace corporations produced rafts of propaganda designed specifically to convince American children that everything that happens in space is exciting and must be supported, while NASA—working closely with the U.S. space command—has designed a program to reach every science teacher in the U.S. with the efficacy of their space message. The aim is to program children to believe that a large portion of the U.S. national treasure should be spent on Mars exploration, and that war in space is inevitable.[7]

The long range plan opens by stating that the military must guard against allowing its dependency on space to become a vulnerability and thus must develop an ability to "deny" others (the enemy) the use of space. The way a nation makes wealth, it proclaims, is the way it makes war. According to the plan, the time has come for national policy-makers to understand that space is now the center of gravity for both the department of defense and for the nation—exactly the tack that the Bush administration is adopting.

The plan sets out five basic goals:

1. To assure the means to get to space and to operate once there
2. To surveil the region to achieve and to maintain situational understanding
3. To protect America's critical space systems from hostile action
4. To prevent unauthorized access to, and exploitation of U.S. and allied space systems
5. To negate hostile space systems that place U.S. and allied systems at risk

The LRP then discusses global engagement, which it says is "the combination of worldwide situational awareness and precise application of force from space." There must be "a seamlessly integrated force of theater land, sea, air, and space capabilities through a worldwide global defense information network."

U.S. space command will observe "high interest areas" on the earth from space so the military will have "complete awareness in peace, crisis, or war." The plan is to defend America against ballistic and cruise missile attacks from an enemy—aka, Star Wars. The space command will also "hold at risk" a finite number of "high value" earth targets with near-instantaneous force application—i.e., the ability to kill from space. The long term plan continues:

> One of the long acknowledged and commonly understood advantages of space-based platforms is no restriction or country clearances to overfly a nation from space. We expect this advantage to endure. . . . Achieving space superiority during conflicts will be critical to the U.S. success on the battlefield.

The LRP, however, does acknowledge that there could be problems: "At present, the notion of weapons in space is not consistent with U.S. national policy. Planning for this possibility is the purpose of this long range plan should our civilian leadership later decide that the application of force from space is in our national interest." (Is the Bush administration this civilian leadership?)

The long range plan envisions an end state: "By 2020, a robust and fully integrated suite of space and terrestrial capabilities will provide dominant battlespace awareness enabling on-demand targeting and engagement of all ballistic and cruise missiles; and if directed by the National Command Authority [the President] the ability to identify, track and hold at risk designated high value terrestrial targets." One of the space command members, retired General Ronald R. Fogleman, former chief of staff of the air force and a member of the Joint Chiefs of Staff, said, "I think that space, in and of itself, is going to be very quickly recognized as a fourth dimension of warfare."

The long range plan gives an indication of how the military elite in U.S. society view the world and their place in it:

- The United States will remain a global power and exert global leadership.
- It is unlikely that the United States will face a global military peer competitor through 2020.
- The United States won't always be able to forward base its forces (fight wars in other people's territory).
- Widespread communications will highlight disparities in resources and quality of life—contributing to unrest in developing countries.
- The global economy will continue to become more interdependent. Economic alliances, as well as the growth and influence of multinational corporations, will blur security agreements.
- The gap between the "have" and "have-not" nations will widen—creating regional unrest.
- The United States will remain the only nation able to project power globally.[8]

This last statement means that as the world becomes more and more divided economically, the U.S. can use its military and space superiority to maintain the imbalance between the rich and the poor. In this context, it is well to remember that the U.S. contains 5 percent of the world's population and uses 40 percent of the world's natural resources.

U.S. SPACE FORCE

At the start of the twenty-first century, for the first time since the air force was created in 1947, there is talk of creating a specific new service within the Pentagon (even though the established Pentagon services ruthlessly guard their domains and are fiercely resistant to change). First proposed by General Ronald Fogleman when he and his staff concluded that the air force should evolve into a space and air force, the service would be quite different from the space command, which is not an official arm of the Pentagon.

The idea gained ground after the Gulf conflict and the Kosovo war, in which use of space was critical. The Pentagon's GPS satellite constellation guided precision bombs to their targets in bad weather.

Spy satellites monitored Serbian troop movements and intercepted conversations among top officials. And satellites tracked the impact point of thousands of NATO bombs (though they did not count the number of people killed or injured). This kind of space-controlled war is easier for U.S. soldiers to handle psychologically because it means long-distance killing, eliminating the trauma of close-up death. In a statement issued on June 17, 1999, the space command proclaimed that "any questions about the role or effectiveness of the use of space for military operations have been answered by NATO's Operation Allied Force in Kosovo." [9]

Republican Senator Bob Smith of New Hampshire enthusiastically supports the concept of a space and air force service, contending that the air force, which controls most of the military's space assets under the space command, spends too much time on aircraft and not enough time on spacecraft. A thirteen-member congressional panel has been established to examine all aspects of how a space force would operate.[10]

The air force organization magazine reported on an air force association conference in February 2000, at which General Michael Ryan pronounced that the military implications of the increased use of space systems are immense. He supported the concepts of the space command, noting that the U.S. must be able to control space when need be, as it controls the atmosphere. Space and air are not separate domains for the air force; they are two parts of the same whole, as closely related as the oceans and seas, he said. "We should think of the aerospace domain as a seamless volume from which we provide military capabilities in support of national security," he continued. For instance, the Kosovo "effort" connected forty different locations in fifteen countries using a variety of military and civilian lines and satellites, and many new ones were established. "We worked over 44,000 spectrum requests, some terrestrial, some atmospheric, some for space systems, and, as you may know, these are very gnarly issues with our host countries," he told his audience. He added that partnerships with industry were very important. "We are on a journey, combining and evolving aerospace competencies into a full-spectrum aerospace force." [11] This cyberspace technology is being used just as effectively in the Afghanistan war, and here again the equipment fails to monitor the number and variety of civilian casualties, but was used only to locate "targets" and to guide the missiles, planes, and bombs.

CIVILIAN USES OF CYBERSPACE

The military is muscling into cyberspace territory that has become an essential ingredient for the daily lives of millions of people—cell phones, the internet, weather predictions, traffic control and monitoring, and accurate locating mechanisms for ships and terrestrial events via the GPS satellite systems. International currency and stability are dependent upon space. Trillions of dollars are transferred with a flick of the finger through cyberspace. Business and international globalization could not function without space.

What will happen, then, if America proceeds with its plans to militarize space? How will antisatellite warfare, space-based killer lasers, or nuclear explosions in space affect our daily lives? Does any country have the right to invade space for its own nationalistic purposes?

MERGING OF CIVILIAN AND MILITARY ACTIVITIES

Without a distinct separation between the military and civilian life, agendas become blurred, as was demonstrated recently by a project designed to use the space shuttle for a mission to map the earth's topology. On January 31, 2000, the space shuttle *Endeavor* took off from Cape Canaveral on a secret military mission: an eleven-day journey to obtain high resolution, three-dimensional maps for 80 percent of the earth's surface. The Pentagon gave NASA 200 million dollars for the shuttle flight, and most of these high-resolution maps will be classified, under military control, but the American people were not told that this was a military expedition. Instead, it was billed simply as a NASA earth topology mapping mission in the Pentagon-funded Global 3-D Mapping Mission.

While the maps may indeed provide better global mapping, they will also increase the ability of the Pentagon to identify and hit targets virtually anywhere on the planet using space technology. These pictures are designed to provide the military not only with the location, but the precise height of every tree, hill, and mountaintop, the depth of every ditch, valley, and canyon in the mapped area. As John Pike, former space policy chief at the Federation of American Scientists in Washington said, "Smart weapons need smart maps, and right now the military does not have smart maps."[12] Thus, under the guise of NASA exploration, the Pentagon has developed new technology that will enhance its ability to kill people or destroy property with extraordinary precision.

This detailed mapping by NASA has been enhanced by an experimental satellite launched in September 2000 from Kirtland Air Force Base in New Mexico. The satellite carries a hyperspectral imaging instrument that uses hundreds of very narrow wavelength bands to "see" reflected energy from objects on the ground. Military questions such as, *Is this field too muddy for a tank assault? Are breaking waves too high for an amphibious landing? What is the natural foliage? Am I looking at a distant parking lot or a grassy playground? Is this an armored personnel carrier or a school bus?* may now be satisfactorily answered.[13] Thus, although it was initially established in 1958 for "peaceful" space exploration, NASA is becoming progressively militarized.[14]

In another example of the militarization of the civilian sector, the air force decided to expand its space-lift partnership between commercial industry and the federal government. Because space launches are almost prohibitively expensive, a White House interagency working group initiated a report titled "Future Management and Use of U.S. Space Launch Bases and Ranges," to explore the cooperation of the department of defense and the civilian sector in space. Encouraging this partnership, Dr. Neal Lane, assistant to President Clinton for science and technology, said that "U.S. commercial launch rates have more than tripled since the early 1990s and now make up about 40 percent of the launch manifest at Vandenberg Air Force Base, California, and Cape Canaveral Air Force Station, Florida." Proceeding apace, the air force is putting mechanisms in place to benefit both the government and the private sector, in order to maximize the effectiveness of everyone's investment.[15] So once again, the lines are becoming blurred.

RECENT DEVELOPMENTS

The space command has recently conducted a range of exercises to demonstrate the supposed need to expand the scope of their program. On July 10, 2000, for example, an annual joint warrior interoperability demonstration (JWID) took place at Peterson Air Force Base in Colorado, during which industry and government joined forces to demonstrate that earth-bound war-fighters could be supported by integrating space forces and space-derived information with land, air, and sea forces. During this exercise, demonstrations were conducted at many locations around the world, including Cheyenne Mountain Operations Center near Colorado Springs; the U.S. Pacific Command at Camp Smith, Hawaii; and the U.S. Joint Forces Command in Norfolk, Virginia. Facilities in many NATO nations were included as well as U.S. bases in Australia and New Zealand.

As Air Force General Ralph E. Eberhart, commander in chief of the space command said, "It's clear this reliance on space will continue to grow. Traditionally we've talked about space as a combat multiplier in a combat support role. . . . However, now space has become much more basic and intrinsic than just a force multiplier. Space is a prerequisite. It's not a luxury any more; it's a requirement for conducting military operations. Space has proven itself vital to our national interests." [16]

Meanwhile, the air force announced on September 8, 2000, that their aerospace operations center (AOC) at Hurlburt Field in Florida had become an official weapons system. The AOC is essentially a forward-deployed war room described as "light, lean, and lethal." During an exercise on September 15, 2000, which assessed air force expeditionary forces using new technologies and capabilities in a simulated war-fighting environment, the AOC was the hub for all the information coming in from combined live-fly forces, models, simulations, and technology insertions at eleven different sites across the U.S. Information from space played a major role in this exercise.[17] According to Air Force Chief of Staff General Michael E. Ryan, the AOC will be the eyes, ears, hands, and legs of the commander during a real war operation.

And at Fort Bliss, Texas, a simulated military exercise called Roving Sands 2000 took place, again utilizing cyberspace for coordination. Using sophisticated computerized systems, military teams from different locations in the U.S. engaged in separate missions supporting an overall military objective. Not only was the battlefield a simulated target area, all the missile systems and other tools of engagement were also simulated so that smaller numbers of troops could command a greater range of territory.[18]

This was one of the first virtual cyberspace war exercises.

SPACE-BASED STAR WARS WEAPONS UNDER DEVELOPMENT

Space-based weapons are exotic imaginary systems that have never been tried or tested, but many are already under construction. These include space-based lasers, hypersonic military space planes, various forms of antisatellite weapons, electronic jamming satellites, and space-based nuclear weapons.

SWORDS INTO LASERS

At least two specific, space-based laser weapons are already under development, both of which involve a concept the magazine *Space Daily* calls "turning swords into lasers."

- *The Space-Based Laser Demonstrator*, the first step in space-based weaponry, is currently being developed by Lockheed Martin, TRW, Boeing, the U.S. Air Force, and the Ballistic Missile Defense Organization.
- *The Alpha High-Energy Laser* is the second space-based laser under development. Also constructed by TRW, it underwent its twenty-second successful test firing in April 2000. The success of this test was trumpeted by *Space Daily* as "a significant step forward in the nation's disciplined maturation of the technology required to deploy the Space-Based Laser Integrated Flight Experiment."[19, 20]

The military excitement over and the moral implications of these weapons are reflected in a quote from a 1996 air force board report:

> In the next two decades, new technologies will allow the fielding of space-based weapons of devastating effectiveness to be used to deliver energy and mass as force projection [read killing] in tactical and strategic conflict. These advances will enable lasers with reasonable mass and cost to affect very many kills. This can be done rapidly, continuously and with surgical precision, minimizing exposure of friendly forces. The technologies exist or can be developed in this time period.

The report continues, "Force application by kinetic kill weapons will enable pinpoint strikes on targets anywhere in the world. The equivalent of the Desert Storm strategic air campaign against Iraqi infrastructure would be possible to complete in minutes to hours essentially on immediate notice."[21]

(There is dissent. Mike Moore, the former editor of the *Bulletin of Atomic Scientists,* wrote in 1999: "The notion that the United States—or any country—might actually place weapons in space, as envisioned by the U.S. Space Command, is so repugnant that the United States ought to clearly repudiate it. Better yet, it should push to amend the Outer Space Treaty so as to definitively prohibit all weapons in space, not just weapons of mass destruction."[22] This attitude is reflected by the international community who repeatedly vote at the UN to endorse the Outer Space Treaty prohibiting the militarization of space. The U.S. consistently abstains.)

HYPERSONIC MILITARY SPACE PLANES

The air force is also in the process of developing a plane designed to perform reconnaissance, space control, and strike missions from orbit. Called an aerospace operations vehicle (AOV), it is a two-stage-to-orbit vehicle with a reusable booster. It has a "mission specific" upper stage, which is based upon Lockheed Martin's X-33 reusable launch vehicle technology demonstrator. Boeing is also involved in the development of the plane, and full-scale development is projected within three years.

The most contentious part of the plane is the upper stage, or common aero vehicle (CAV), a lifting-body-boost-glide vehicle that is designed for immediate attack on earth targets. So although the space plane is not technically an "in-orbit" weapon, and thus avoids Clinton's ban on these, it is a "strike" system that violates the belief—and indeed the UN Outer Space Convention—that space should be weapons-free.[23]

While the Clinton administration was reluctant to militarize space, the Bush team will probably endorse this new space-plane. This will allow the air force to maneuver outside the atmosphere and to place systems in orbit that can be recovered and reused.

ANTISATELLITE WARFARE

A whole other area of space-based weapons development involves building and protecting satellites, as well as potentially destroying those of other nations. (The Pentagon's term for satellite destruction is "Navigation Warfare" or "NavWar".) Because satellites have become essential to commercial, scientific, and national security services, the United States believes that it must control all satellite use. Satellites have no built-in protective mechanisms and are extremely vulnerable to attack, but until recently, no one thought to protect them. As Allen Thomson, a retired CIA analyst, said, attack on a satellite would be like an act of war.

Yet lasers can readily destroy satellites. So can something as simple as buckshot introduced into low-earth orbit where the satellites function. Computer hackers can interrupt signals sent between satellites and their ground operators. And commandos can attack ground stations that serve as control centers or relay points for data. NASA and the air force are also building a space maneuverable vehicle (SMV). Billed as giving the air force a new flexibility in space operations, the SMV has antisatellite applications as well. Other methods of satellite destruction—many of which rely on cyber technology—are in development. An order from the National Security Command Authority in 1999, backed by President Clinton and his secretary of defense, William Cohen, recently instructed the military to gear up to wage cyberwar. Cyberwar involves attacking satellites and infecting them with virus-like systems rendering them inoperable. To this end, Lieutenant General Edward Anderson, deputy commander in chief at the U.S. space command, was assigned the task of creating cyberwar strategies, including massive "denial-of-service" assaults that can be unleashed by launching crippling viruses called *trojan horses,* and jamming the enemy's computer systems with electronic radio-frequency interference.[24]

THREAT TO U.S. SATELLITE SYSTEMS

Because the Pentagon has been planning antisatellite warfare, it is intensely aware that its own satellites are at risk. Indeed, so vulnerable is America's satellite program that her present critical advantage in warfare could be destroyed if her GPS system was damaged. Private satellites now used for military communications are also vulnerable. For instance, the Iridium satellite constellation could be irreparably damaged if just one receiving building on the ground were destroyed. Signals from GPS satellites travel like radio waves and are available to anyone with a receiver. It is thought that China could develop antisatellite techniques within ten years, while a private Russian company has already developed a handheld GPS jammer with a range of 150 miles. In fact, "enemy" countries already use the American GPS system to enhance the accuracy of their weapons, including Scud missiles in North Korea, Iran, and Iraq.

Meanwhile, American satellites continue to become more and more sophisticated. The next generation of spy satellites was launched in 2000—smaller and more numerous than those in orbit—and is able to distinguish ground objects as small as 6 inches from a height of 500 miles. Canada is about to launch a satellite with these capabilities, with more to follow.

THE PHILOSOPHY OF ANTISATELLITE WARFARE

Antisatellite warfare is a tenuous proposition. How do you destroy other countries' satellites without endangering your own? How can you separate yourself from other countries when the communication systems are so interdependent? For instance, the army conducted a war game in 1998. The enemy was a fictitious country in the Middle East. During the exercise, China provided the "enemy" with satellite imagery of U.S. troop movements using the same satellites the U.S. uses to monitor its own troops. Should the U.S. destroy the satellites under these circumstances?

And how can we distinguish between peaceful and legitimate uses of satellite technology and those that are aspects of an overtly militarized "defense?" For example, it is now commonplace for the Pentagon to intersperse radomes for intelligence gathering with Star Wars radomes. Buckley Air Force Base, located east of Denver in Aurora, Colorado, the largest consolidated intelligence center in the western hemisphere—is jointly used by the National Reconnaissance Office (NRO) and the National Security Agency (NSA). Buckley boasts thirteen radomes—big white domes that envelope downloading stations for satellite data. Used for space-based intelligence gathering, they are also an integral component of the Star Wars system and will download information from the new high orbit space-based infrared system (SBIRS-High). A similar comingling of uses is happening at Pine Gap in Australia and at Menwith Hill in England. Because intelligence gathering is top secret, this technique of combined intelligence gathering and Star Wars planning can also be used to prevent local politicians from inspecting American Star Wars bases, vehemently opposed by the general public in those two countries.

Because the military is so dependent upon them, the space command stopped publishing information on the whereabouts of their twenty-seven GPS satellites, previously posted on the NASA web site. Most satellites, military or commercial, have no defenses against attack by laser beams or other objects targeted to destroy them. It is very expensive to add protective mechanisms to satellites because they add extra weight and launch costs become prohibitive. (It costs 10,000 dollars a pound to launch a payload into low earth orbit, and shielding mechanisms are heavy.)

Former Virginia Democratic Senator Charles Robb, a member of the Senate arms committee, said that the development of space weapons, including antisatellite capabilities, would be "a mistake of historic proportions" that would trigger an arms race in space. He noted that other nations would necessarily follow the U.S.'s example, and frantic generals, unable to know exactly who has put what in orbit—would plead for extravagant countermeasures.[25]

The increasing interdependency of the global economy and all military systems on satellite technology means that all destructive military thinking must cease and be replaced by an international resolution to preserve space for peaceful purposes only. In other words, the civilian lawmakers must exert control over their aberrant military.

MARS AND THE ASTEROIDS

While John Collins said that the moon contains valuable minerals and resources, he did not mention that the asteroids and other planets are also being examined for possible economic exploitation. The U.S. has plans to send manned and unmanned missions to Mars in the near future to explore and extract valuable minerals for earthly use.

Enthusiasm for the project was somewhat tempered in 1999, when NASA experienced two manmade catastrophes: the Mars Climate Orbiter and the Mars Polar Lander both mysteriously disappeared. The Climate Orbiter was lost after a navigational error sent it skimming too deeply into the Martian atmosphere, because engineers failed to convert English to metric units. The Polar Lander, which incorporated innovative lightweight materials, extraordinarily small microchips, and a low-cost laser-based navigational system, was scheduled to make a soft landing on September 23, 1999, at the Martian south pole. It would drop two probes, which, falling at high speed would penetrate a few feet into the Martian crust to explore for evidence of groundwater. NASA realized just prior to Lander's arrival that the mission was doomed because of a fatal design flaw. Lander probably blew up.[26]

But NASA scientists, undeterred, are planning future expeditions, including missions to recover rock samples from Mars and to do deep drilling to search for water, microbes, and minerals. Shell Oil and Los Alamos National Lab are among the outside groups assisting NASA in these investigations. The orbits of Earth and Mars offer favorable flight opportunities once every twenty-five months, when they are in such a position that the trip takes less than a year.[27] The current Mars schedule is as follows:

- In the spring of 2001, the Mars Odyssey Orbiter was launched, equipped with remote sensors to study surface minerals.
- In 2003, two small roving vehicles will be launched to land on

Mars in January 2004. These are 300-pound wheeled robots capable of traveling 300 feet a day while taking pictures, analyzing rocks, and investigating surface geology and possible subsurface water deposits.

- In 2005, NASA plans to send a Mars reconnaissance orbiter, which will be modeled on the now-successful Mars Global Surveyer still in orbit mapping Mars, for further mapping.
- In 2007, a "smart" landing craft will be launched, equipped with precision guidance and navigation, and hazard avoidance systems so that future missions will be able to land in the prescribed place all in one piece.
- Also in 2007 the first scout mission, deploying instrument-bearing balloons or a small airplane, will be launched.
- Again in 2007, NASA and the Italian space agency may team to place an orbiting satellite around Mars to help relay the increasingly heavy communications load from the Martian spacecraft. France may also participate.
- In 2009, NASA may team with the Italian space agency to deploy ground-penetrating radar to prospect for water while in orbit. These flights are being planned to search for water and traces of life, past or present.
- NASA's long-term plan is to launch a sample-return mission sometime during 2011 to 2014.[28]

Manned trips to Mars are on the drawing board. There is a possibility that some very primitive forms of life exist on the planet. The atmosphere probably contains traces of hydrogen peroxide, a strong oxidizing agent, and the planet is bathed in searingly high levels of ultraviolet light. Hence any trace of life would be found only at some depth from the surface.

Human habitation of Mars, a dream of many at NASA and other influential scientific organizations, will present huge physiological problems. An article written by Jerome Groopman, professor of medicine at Harvard Medical School, in the *New Yorker* in January 2000 summarizes this medical dilemma. Groopman questions whether human beings can survive weightlessness and deep-space radiation for prolonged periods. He worries about the possible psychological ramifications of isolation, stress, and confinement, and the problem of medical emergencies that could arise during the trip. Among other problems, it is virtually impossible for the human body, which evolved under the influence of gravity, to survive intact without it. Blood, which under the influence of gravity normally pools in the legs and lower body, rushes to the head, triggering severe pounding headaches. The fluid-controlling mechanisms are fooled by this redistribution, and dehydration rapidly develops as the kidneys excrete the "excess" fluid. The thickened blood then sends signals to the bone marrow to cease making red blood cells, inducing a mild anemia.

Muscles and bones almost melt in a weightless environment. Tendons and ligaments deteriorate, and minor stresses cause both ligaments and muscles to tear like tissue paper. Bone mass dissolves at a rate of 1.5 percent per month. Then there is the danger from radiation emanating from cosmic rays. These are essentially iron particles traveling at the speed of light that go right through the body, causing breakage of chromosomes and destruction of genes. Chromosomal and genetic damage increases the risk of developing cancer, and a recent review by the National Research Council found a 40 percent increased cancer risk from a trip to Mars, more than 10 times higher than the level deemed acceptable.

Surgery under any circumstances would be highly dangerous; if someone seriously injured a leg, the most appropriate treatment might well be amputation rather than an arduous repair. And a head injury would be almost impossible to treat. Neurosurgery at zero G could not be imagined.

Sleep deprivation, monotony, claustrophobia, anxiety, and depression will produce mental instability. It has been noted during missions in harsh, lonely environments that more than 10 percent of subjects develop serious problems of psychological adaptation and up to 3 percent develop psychiatric disorders, such as major depression. It has been recommended that older astronauts be chosen for a Mars trip because they would not live long enough to develop cancer from the cosmic radiation, or have fewer years to lose if they did. Also, younger men would be unable to have children because of radiation damage to their sperm.[29]

There are also grave concerns that the introduction of Martian material into the earth's biosphere may inject microorganisms that could unleash serious hazards. (Until the recent NASA Mars failures, plans to return Martian samples to earth were scheduled for 2008, but that date has been delayed until 2011.) Barry DiGregorio, who founded the International Committee Against Mars Sample Return, pointed out some pertinent lessons from history:

- In the early- to mid-1300s, one quarter of Europeans died when a flea from China carrying an unfamiliar microbe was introduced into a susceptible population.
- When the Spaniards explored the Americas, they introduced the smallpox virus that decimated tens of thousand of native inhabitants.
- European explorers infected the susceptible native inhabitants of the Polynesian and Hawaiian Islands with many different infectious diseases. Nearly half of these populations died.

At present NASA plans to return the Martian samples to earth in a passive Earth-entry capsule that will enter the atmosphere without a parachute and slam into the Utah desert, where it will sustain a 300–400 G force impact. Engineers say that the capsule will remain intact, but the potential ramifications of a mistake are difficult even to contemplate.[30] A report issued by the space studies board of the national research council (NRC), a research arm of the National Academy of Sciences, concluded that space samples will require very careful handling, and NASA must create a special facility to contain any material that might be contaminated with dangerous organisms. While they point out that the risk of bringing back something very dangerous is extremely low, it is not zero. NASA must err on the side of being prudent.[31]

John Rummel, NASA planetary protection officer, said that NASA will quarantine the Martian samples in a high-level containment facility similar to those used to harbor the world's deadliest viruses.[32] But DiGregorio said, "If we make one mistake it could mean the extinction—maybe for our species—or maybe another; for instance, bumblebees or photoplankton, which are a huge part of our ecology."

NASA's interest is not limited to Mars. A NASA mission scheduled for November 2003 will orbit Europa, a moon of Jupiter, which may have a deep, watery ocean. The next Europa mission may launch a "submarine" into this ocean to explore it, which exposes the probes to massive concentrations of damaging extraterrestrial radiation, similar to that experienced in post–nuclear war.[33]

The Colorado School of Mines, long involved in the concepts of space mining and minerals extraction, and in space-based market development and minerals economics, is the motivating force behind these extraordinarily ambitious mining plans. Engineering students and faculty are currently establishing an ongoing space utilization roundtable to calculate methods to retrieve useful products and services from space. Everything from tourism, to mining, solar power, water extraction, and manufacturing on the moon is under consideration. Space mining may be ten to twenty years away, but someone has to start thinking about these possibilities now, they say.[34]

INTERNATIONAL SPACE STATION

On October 31, 2000, a three-member Expedition One crew was launched from the Baikonur Cosmodrome on a Russian Soyuz rocket to dock at the International Space Station (ISS) two days later. This eighth mission marked the start of a permanent human presence in space, initiating a planned permanent occupancy of ten years. It is intended that the ISS will eventually be the launching pad for missions to other planets.[35] A total of sixteen countries are involved in this project: Russia, Germany, Belgium, Canada, Italy, Japan, the Netherlands, Denmark, Norway, France, Spain, Sweden, Switzerland, the U.S., the U.K., and Brazil. More than 900 researchers from these and other countries are developing experiments to be conducted in zero-gravity conditions in fields such as biotechnology, combustion science, fluid physics, materials science, life sciences, engineering and technology, and earth sciences.

The stated goals of the International Space Station are as follows (most are worthy, but some are troublesome):

- To find solutions to crucial problems in medicine, ecology, and other areas of science

- To lay the foundation for developing space-based commerce and enterprise
- To create great worldwide demand for space-related education at all levels by cultivating the excitement, wonder, and discovery that the ISS symbolizes
- To foster world peace through high-profile, long-term international cooperation in space[36]

It would appear that the internationalism of the ISS would mitigate against unilateral exploitation and control of space by a single nation. However, I do not trust the present Bush administration, and Congress has rarely acted in the best interests of the international community. The military and space corporations, along with other multinationals, paid billions of dollars for the last U.S. election, and have control over upcoming legislation. Furthermore, the Republican right-wing openly supports U.S. militarization and domination of space.

Is the function of the ISS just window-dressing for a more ominous future?

NUCLEAR DEVICES IN SPACE

The surface of Mars is bone-dry and covered with a fine dust of an average particle size of about two microns—the same dimensions as cigarette smoke. The dust is so fine and pervasive that it would gum up space suits, scratch helmet visors, induce electrical shorts, sandblast instruments, and clog motors. The corrosive hydrogen peroxide in the Martian atmosphere could also slowly wear away rubber seals.

Astronauts would need to maintain a dust-free environment because tiny particles of inhaled silicon dust induce a severe lung disease called *silicosis*. The particles will be electrically charged so the dust will cling to everything. But the dust means something else. Solar power necessary to fuel a mission would become almost impossible to generate, because Martian powder would accumulate on the solar panels. On the Mars Pathfinder mission, for instance, the electrical output from the solar panels fell 1 percent every three days as powder covered them.

Therefore, the preferred choice for power generation becomes nuclear, in the form of a 100-kilowatt nuclear reactor.[37] And this brings us to some of the worst of the Star Wars hazards that will threaten planet Earth: nuclear-powered rockets; orbiting nuclear reactors; nuclear reactors destined for asteroids, the moon, or Mars; and plutonium-fueled space probes to investigate other planets—all of which pose potentially severe risks to the earth's biological systems.

NASA consistently plays down these nuclear threats, which are an integral part of its space program, while emphasizing the glory of space research, and of extraterrestrial adventure. But the threats are very serious.

THE HISTORY OF NUCLEAR DEVICES IN SPACE

Over a period of decades, while Russia launched more than thirty nuclear space reactors, America has launched only one. Some of these Russian reactors have crashed to Earth, permanently polluting swathes of hundreds of miles with potent, long-lived, radioactive material. The most serious Russian nuclear space accident occurred in 1978 when a Cosmos 954 satellite carrying a nuclear reactor smashed into the Northwest Territories of Canada. Sizable amounts of radioactive debris were distributed over a 600-kilometer path from Slave Lake to Baker Lake. Fifty large radioactive fragments were recovered, along with other chunks, flakes, and slivers. But a wide area stretching southward from the Great Slave Lake was also affected by smaller, scattered particles from the reactor core. The total search covered 124,000 square kilometers of the Northwest Territories. These carcinogenic, radioactive particles posed a serious risk to the population, because they could be either inhaled or ingested through the food chain.

The most recent Russian accident happened in 1996 when its Mars space probe, carrying half a pound of plutonium 238 (not a nuclear reactor), fell from space. President Clinton urgently contacted the prime minister of Australia, offering help when it was thought that the probe would hit Australia. Instead, it fell into the less politically important countries of Bolivia and Chile, and international concern ceased. (Not a word was uttered again about the risk to biological systems or to human life.)

Russia is not alone in its nuclear space accidents. The most significant U.S. accident occurred in 1964 when a Transit 5BN-3 satellite with a SNAP plutonium power system crashed. Some 2.1 pounds of plutonium 238 were dispersed around the world. A report prepared in 1989 by the health and radiation agencies in Europe stated that, "a worldwide sampling program carried out in 1970 showed SNAP debris to be present at all continents and at all latitudes." (Small quantities of plutonium 238 are used to provide electricity to space probes, which is generated by the decay heat of the radioactive element. Plutonium 238 is used because it has a shorter half-life than plutonium 239 and therefore produces more heat.) Dr. John Gofman, professor emeritus of medical physics at the University of California–Berkeley, relates that accident to a subsequent worldwide increase in lung cancer.[38]

Between the U.S. and Russia, there has been a 15 percent accident rate in both countries' space programs.

NUCLEAR POWERED SPACE PROBES

Despite these disasters, NASA has continued for thirty years to use plutonium 238 for its space exploration power systems and has launched a total of twenty-five missions with radioactive power packs. Plutonium 238 is 280 times more carcinogenic than the more prevalent isotope, plutonium 239. Glenn Seaborg, plutonium 239's discoverer, called plutonium 238 the most dangerous material on Earth. And plutonium 239 is almost the most carcinogenic substance known to the human race—as previously stated, one pound, if adequately distributed, could induce lung cancer in every human being on the planet.

NASA is playing with the most deadly of materials with seeming impunity, evidently not caring if one of its rockets malfunctions and sprays plutonium 238 onto countries that happen to be located beneath. Previous plutonium 238–fueled NASA missions included the Apollo lunar scientific packages, and the Pioneer, Viking, Voyager, and Ulysses deep-space probes. More recent missions include the Mars Pathfinder mission, launched in 1996, and the Cassini mission, launched in 1997.

Future NASA plans include plutonium 238 power systems for the

Pluto-Kuiper Express mission scheduled for launch in 2004, the Europa Orbiter mission scheduled for 2006, and the solar probe mission for 2007. The Pluto-Kuiper Express mission will require about 16.3 pounds of plutonium 238, and the Europa Orbiter and solar probe missions each will require about 6.6 pounds.

Eight plutonium 238–fueled RHUs will also be required for each Mars Surveyor mission over the next decade. Approximately thirty will be launched. Each plutonium 238 capsule will weigh 0.7 pounds. Small amounts of curium 242, curium 244, and cobalt 57 will also be required for scientific instruments. Each of these radioactive elements is almost as toxic as plutonium. According to the General Accounting Office report, *Space Exploration: Power Sources for Deep Space Probes,* NASA is contemplating eight more nuclear-fueled electric generator space missions by 2015.

HEALTH CONSEQUENCES OF PLUTONIUM 238 PRODUCTION

By law, the department of energy is responsible for the supply of plutonium 238 for the space program. Historically, the military reactors and reprocessing plants at Savannah River, South Carolina, were used to manufacture this plutonium. However, these dangerously polluted facilities were closed down in 1996 when the end of the cold war determined that plutonium 239 for bombs was not needed (plutonium 238 and 239 were manufactured in parallel).[39]

Because the plutonium 238 supply of the U.S. was limited, in 1992 the DOE signed a five-year contract with Russia to supply it. In 1997 this contract was renewed for another five years. But because the long-term viability of Russian plutonium could be in jeopardy, and the inventory of plutonium 238 for space missions might be depleted by 2005, the DOE is considering restarting old military nuclear reactors or using civilian light-water reactors for its plutonium 238 production.[40]

Episodes of worker contamination are frequent. The plutonium 238 for the Cassini mission was manufactured at Los Alamos Lab. The total amount of radiation exposure increased during this production period at Los Alamos and the number of people contaminated with plutonium 238 rose from 139 to 244 (between 1993 and

1995). More recently, eight more Los Alamos workers were exposed to plutonium 238 at potentially dangerous levels in March 2000. These people received medical treatment, but in truth, there is no effective way to decontaminate workers once plutonium 238 has entered their bodies.[41]

Significantly, the European Space Agency has developed high-efficiency solar space cells to replace nuclear generators. In 2003 this agency will launch its Rosetta probe to travel beyond the orbit of Jupiter and to rendezvous with a comet named Wirtanen—the first such probe. Wirtanen is 675 million kilometers from the sun, where the sunlight is twenty times weaker than on earth.[42] If solar power is capable of supplying the very small amount of electricity needed for these missions, why does NASA persist in using plutonium 238? To ascertain the source of pressure for nuclear space probes, follow the money.

For many years, General Electric made the nuclear space systems. Now this lucrative business has been subsumed by Lockheed Martin. Over the years, both companies have lobbied long and hard for nuclear space systems. Los Alamos National Laboratory and Oak Ridge National Laboratory are also heavily invested in the development of nuclear space systems.

The militarization of the space program has had a significant effect upon NASA's nuclear commitment. One reason that NASA insists on using nuclear power instead of solar power is because the military is enthusiastic about nuclear weapons in space. One recent NASA plutonium 238 space launch was the Cassini Saturn probe, which flew atop a Lockheed Martin Titan-4 military rocket. Cassini carried 72.3 pounds of plutonium 238—more plutonium than had ever been launched into space. The Titan-4 rocket is an unreliable, dangerous old rocket with a one-in-ten record—one catastrophic accident in every ten launches. Not long after the Cassini launch, three Titan rockets blew up, either on the space pad or shortly after launching. NASA designed Cassini to circle Venus and then to return toward earth via a "gravity assist" slingshot in order to increase its momentum to Saturn. Cassini circled the earth above the atmosphere at 42,300 miles per hour, at an altitude of 700 miles on August 1999. Luckily, unlike Apollo 13, the vectors were accurate, and Cassini with its plutonium load did not enter the atmosphere to disintegrate and spread its deadly cargo across the planet.

In its final environmental-impact statement, NASA said that if the flyby did not go as planned, and Cassini made an inadvertent reentry into the atmosphere, the plutonium 238 would have been released and "approximately five billion of the . . . world population at the time . . . could receive 99 percent or more of the radiation exposure." NASA also acknowledged that if plutonium rained down on areas of natural vegetation, it might have to "relocate animals"; if it fell on agricultural land, it might need to "ban future agricultural land uses"; and if it rained down upon urban areas it would have to "demolish all or some structures" and "relocate affected population permanently." Dr. Gofman of the University of California–Berkeley, who is also the codiscoverer of uranium 235, predicted a death toll of 950,000 as a result of a Cassini accident.

The Outer Space Treaty specifically states that "states shall be liable for damage caused by their space objects." However, in 1991 NASA and the department of energy drew up a "space power agreement" to cover American nuclear space flights using the government-sponsored Price-Anderson Act as its basis. Price-Anderson allocates a domestic liability of 8.9 billion dollars in the event of a nuclear accident, but just 100 million dollars for damage incurred in all foreign nations.

NUCLEAR POWERED ROCKETS

At the thirty-sixth Joint Propulsion Conference in Huntsville, Alabama, in July 2000, at least a dozen papers were presented devoted to space propulsion using nuclear thermal rockets (NTR). (This particular project had been terminated in 1973 because of growing antinuclear feelings among the U.S. population, but it is now back on the drawing board.) Stanley Borowski, a nuclear engineer who manages the NTR studies at NASA's Glenn Research Center, enthusiastically sees NTR as a "three-fer," offering three mission types for the price of a single engine: "We could use it to fly missions to the moon, to Mars, and to near-Earth asteroids—all with the same vehicle," he said. (As one of NASA's spokemen, Borowski speaks to audiences ranging from kindergartens to retirees and receives a nearly uniform response. He must be a very persuasive speaker because the audiences are enthusiastic: "Why hasn't this country developed this option yet?" they ask.)[43]

Some add that the NTR could be used for defending space systems, for reboosting the international space station, and for the eventual colonization of Mars. Russia will participate in the NTR program because they developed robust fuel nuclear rods that could be used in the nuclear engine. It has been suggested that the air force invest a small part of its budget in development of the nuclear thermal rocket, which could be used to assist the North American Aerospace Defense Command in the tracking and defense of U.S. space systems. Borowski predicts that the rocket could be ready to fly in ten years. NASA and the department of energy have recently undertaken a major public relations campaign to sell the nuclear rocket to the public. A conventional rocket would take a year to get to Mars, they explain, but the nuclear option would cut travel time in half.

NASA's Marshall Space Flight Center in Huntsville, Alabama, will be coordinating work on the nuclear rocket with Los Alamos National Lab, NASA in Cleveland, and the University of Florida's nuclear engineering department. In January 2000, at the seventeenth annual Symposium on Space Power and Propulsion, 600 conferees from NASA, DOE, aerospace corporations, nuclear academia, and the air force met to discuss the expansion of nuclear power in space. NASA scientist Roger Lenard, who works at the Marshall Space Flight Center, said, "Want to go to Mars quickly? Detonate some nuclear warheads and months later you're there." He had another proposal: How about a nuclear-powered "space tug" capable of deflecting a comet or asteroid heading for impact with earth? Less exotic proposals focused on using nuclear power to fuel human exploration and colonization on the Moon, Mars, Jupiter, and Saturn.

NUCLEAR POWERED WEAPONS

Some of the weapons that are currently proposed in the Star Wars plans, including laser-beam weapons, particle-beam weapons, and others, will require orbiting nuclear reactors for their power sources.

The 1996 air force board report points out that because "power limitations impose restrictions" on space-based weapons systems, making them "relatively unfeasible . . . a natural technology to enable high power is nuclear power in space." The report's authors seem amazingly confident that their ideas will be viable. "Setting the emotional issues of nuclear power aside," they say, "this technology offers a viable alternative for large amounts of power in space."

OZONE DEPLETION AND THE SPACE PROGRAM

Quite apart from the obvious dangers of nuclear war, nuclear accidents, and the like, many of the efforts that make up America's space-based defense program presuppose ongoing and continuous launching of rockets into space, posing the imminent danger that the ozone layer will be seriously damaged.

Solid fuel used in U.S. rockets and in the space shuttle releases chlorine atoms into the stratosphere. The space shuttle, for example, releases 240 tons of concentrated hydrochloric acid (HCl) at each launch. Chlorine, which splits off from the HCl molecule, is the substance that combines with and destroys ozone molecules. Scientists in 1989 predicted that if NASA continued to launch solid-fuel rocket boosters at a rate of ten per year, this would induce a 10 percent depletion in the ozone by 2005.[44, 45, 46] Yet the number of civilian and military launches have increased alarmingly since that prediction was made. (For each 1 percent decrease in stratospheric ozone there will be a 4 to 6 percent increase in skin cancer. We are experiencing these effects in Australia, where we see a proliferation of skin-cancer clinics within our cities, and where the hole in the ozone layer of the southern hemisphere was larger in the year 2000 than ever before.)

INTERNATIONAL CONCERN

At the opening of the conference for disarmament in Geneva in January 2000, UN Secretary General Kofi Annan called for nations to join together to maintain space "as a weapons-free environment." China received wide support for a proposal to create "an international legal instrument banning the testing, deployment and use of any weapons, weapons systems and their components in outer space, with a view to preventing the weaponization of outer space." Nevertheless, the U.S. is attempting to block the proposal.

International concern about American plans is so great that in November 2000, 138 nations voted in the UN to reaffirm the Outer Space Treaty, stating specifically that space be set aside "for peaceful purposes." The motion was titled "Prevention of an Arms Race in Outer Space." As noted, only the United States and Israel abstained.[47] The Clinton administration quietly acquiesced to the pressure exerted by the military-industrial complex to militarize space.

With George W. Bush in the White House, and an administration staffed by major hawks enthusiastic about a full-blown Star Wars system, many of the proposals discussed above will become reality unless we rise up and use our democracy in an efficient and passionate way.

Chapter Eight

NUCLEAR WAR IN THE GULF AND KOSOVO

IN 1990, SHORTLY before he invaded Kuwait—which had been drilling oil beneath Iraq's border and selling it at a steep discount—President Saddam Hussein of Iraq approached the U.S. ambassador, April Glaspie, about his plan, and she indicated that the U.S. had no defense treaties or security commitments to Kuwait. In a subsequent face-to-face meeting with Glaspie, Hussein told her that Iraq was in dire economic straits, and the low oil price induced by Kuwait's and the United Arab Emirates' overproduction was hurting them badly. She told Hussein that Iraq had "a right to prosper"; and Glaspie continued, "I know you need funds. We understand that, and our opinion is that you should have the opportunity to rebuild your country. But we have no opinion on the Arab-Arab conflicts, like your border disagreement with Kuwait."[1] (Subsequently Glaspie lied about this conversation when she testified before the Senate Foreign Relations Committee: "I told him orally we would defend our vital interests, we would support our friends in the Gulf, we would defend their sovereignty and integrity.")

The U.S. response when Iraq invaded Kuwait belied Glaspie's reassurances. Contrary to Glaspie's "no opinion on the Arab-Arab conflicts," the U.S. staged a military operation on Kuwait's behalf that had been planned for months and amounted to a veritable arms bazaar for U.S. weapons manufacturers. Eighty-eight thousand, five hundred tons of bombs (the equivalent of more than seven Hiroshimas) were dropped on Iraq and Kuwait (fewer than 7 percent of the weapons used were "smart"; most were old fashioned "dumb" bombs), and 70 percent of these did not hit military targets, but fell on civilian areas. (Smart bombs have computer guidance systems and maps of the terrain to guide them accurately to their targets. This technology, however, often fails. Dumb bombs are dropped from planes and may or may not land where they are intended.)

Contrary to accepted norms of wartime behavior, the U.S. attacked columns of retreating Iraqi soldiers and civilians with carrier-based planes, using cluster bombs and napalm—the petroleum compound that adheres to the skin while burning. (Returning pilots spoke of partaking in a "duck or turkey shoot" and of "shooting fish in a barrel.") And, in an equally controversial move, U.S. forces failed to support Iraqi dissidents or the Kurdish or Shi'a uprising at the end of the war, preventing the Iraqi troops who were rebelling against Hussein in the south of the country from reaching captured arms depots, and circling in planes overhead as Hussein's helicopters slaughtered his own dissenting troops.[2] (Not one American or allied soldier was killed by Iraqi troops, though some died through "friendly fire.")

The U.S. response to Iraq's invasion of Kuwait also made history for another horrific reason: Operation Desert Storm was the first conflict in history to create a radioactive battlefield. America's deployment of radioactive-uranium weapons in the Gulf countries—used as a basic tool of combat for the first time—has permanently contaminated the area and will continue to affect citizens of the region for thousands of years after the war ended.

HISTORY OF URANIUM WEAPONS

During the fifties, the department of defense became interested in using uranium 238 to manufacture weapons for several reasons. Over 700,000 tons of the element were dispersed in various locations around the United States, a by-product of nuclear weapons and nuclear power production. It had no specific use, it was free, and it was dangerous. Several uses for the element were conceived:

- Uranium is 1.7 times more dense than lead and is therefore extremely effective as ammunition for penetrating metal armor. A 120-mm tank round, for example, contains about ten pounds of solid uranium, which at high speed can slice through tank armor like a hot knife through butter. (The Pentagon refers to uranium shells and bullets as "nuclear tipped." They are not: the shells are composed of solid uranium. The uranium is alloyed with other elements that may also be medically dangerous, but these materials are classified.)

- Uranium 238 can also be used as armor plating in tanks because its density prevents penetration by conventional weapons.
- Uranium is heavy, and thus works as ballast in cruise missiles and aircraft.

The U.S. began testing uranium weapons in 1954 at a secret place near the Los Alamos Lab. They continued researching and testing at various locations around the U.S. during the sixties and seventies, and the first usable ammunition was produced in 1978, though it was not used in battle until Operation Desert Storm in 1991.

COMPONENTS OF URANIUM WEAPONS

Natural uranium, found in the earth's crust, is composed primarily of two isotopes: Uranium 235, the most valuable, which is present in concentrations of only 0.7 percent, and uranium 238, which is virtually worthless and constitutes the remaining 99.3 percent.

Uranium 235 is the fissionable material, and is used as fuel for nuclear weapons and nuclear reactors. It must be enriched to concentrations of 3 percent for reactors and over 50 percent for nuclear weapons. Enrichment is a process that involves converting the uranium ore to a gas, which is then forced through minute pores in a large nickel shield, separating the two isotopes. Also called *gaseous diffusion,* this process is extraordinarily energy consuming. (The process was first used during the Manhattan Project in the early forties, and the Hiroshima bomb was a uranium-fueled weapon.) Uranium 238, the unfissionable isotope remaining after enrichment, is dubbed *depleted uranium,* or DU.

Over sixty years of uranium enrichment saw very few safeguards put in place, and regulations controlling the enrichment process were virtually nonexistent. Most of the enrichment was conducted at the

Paducah Gaseous Diffusion Plant in Kentucky. It involved not just the pure uranium that had been extracted from the ground, but reclamation of uranium from nuclear reactors dedicated to the manufacture of plutonium—at Savannah River, South Carolina; at Hanford, Washington; and at Oak Ridge, Tennessee.

Enrichment of reclaimed uranium poses special problems because a variety of other radioactive elements come into play during the process, "polluting" the uranium and posing additional health hazards. When uranium 235 is fissioned in a nuclear reactor, over 200 new radioactive elements are created, and the uranium, when mixed with its fission products, becomes 1 million times more radioactive than in its natural state. One of the most valuable by-products of the fission process is plutonium, which is created when a uranium 238 atom captures a neutron. Plutonium is not a fission product, but a transuranic element with an atomic weight greater than uranium. Plutonium is the most efficient fuel for nuclear weapons—ten pounds, a chunk the size of a grapefruit, is fuel for a hydrogen bomb. An enormous quantity of plutonium was created during the cold war, when the U.S. manufactured 70,203 nuclear weapons. Pure bomb-grade plutonium was obtained from the mess of fission products in the fuel rods by dissolving the rods in concentrated nitric acid, and removing the plutonium from the thermally hot, highly radioactively corrosive solution.

Along with plutonium, unfissioned uranium remaining in the fuel rods was also extracted for further use. This reclaimed uranium is a mixture of uranium 238 and uranium 235. The uranium 235 must then be reenriched to 3 percent for use again in nuclear reactors.

Consequently, uranium 238 again accumulates. But because it came from spent fuel rods, it is contaminated with plutonium and other dangerous elements such as neptunium (also a transuranic element), and possibly with fission products such as technetium, strontium, and cesium. Shipments of this polluted reclaimed uranium were sent to Paducah for more than twenty years. (Although Paducah was a department of energy plant, the private contractors responsible for its well-being were Lockheed Martin and Union Carbide. Recently, the department of energy admitted that the Paducah plant is surrounded by high concentrations of plutonium contamination. Pollution has been detected over a mile from the plant; the Ohio River, two miles from the plant, contains elevated levels of plutonium; and the element has contaminated streams, ponds, and groundwater.[3])

Uranium purified after extraction from the soil contains three isotopes: 234, 235, and 238. (*Purification* means the removal of soil together with daughter products such as radium, radon, polonium, and many other long-lived radioactive decay products.) Uranium 238 has a half-life of 4.5 billion years. In the depleted form after the enrichment process, it still contains small amounts of uranium 235 and uranium 234. All three uranium isotopes are alpha emitters and as such are potentially highly carcinogenic. In 1 gram of uranium 238, 12,400 atomic transformations occur each second, and each throws off an alpha particle consisting of two protons and two neutrons.

The depleted uranium 238 used for weapons has half the radioactivity of the original natural uranium (uranium 235 is 0.7 percent, and uranium 238 is 0.93 percent), because uranium 235 itself is very energetic. Nevertheless, the radiation emanating from 238 can be dangerous if it enters and resides within human or animal bodies. Uranium 238 weapons are made even more dangerous by the contaminant isotopes from Paducah plutonium 239, alpha emitter—half-life 24,400 years; and neptunium 237, alpha and gamma emitter—half-life 2 million years. (The U.S. military is fond of saying that depleted uranium is less radioactive than naturally occurring uranium. However, uranium 238 is 100 percent uranium, unlike the uranium ore in the ground, which is considerably diluted with soil. Thus, comparing DU with natural uranium ore is like comparing apples and oranges. It is simply not relevant.)

MEDICAL RISKS OF URANIUM PROCESSING

Uranium processing exposes hundreds of thousands of people to inhaled and ingested radiation throughout the nuclear-fuel cycle—which includes mining, milling, enriching, fuel fabrication, nuclear fission, reprocessing, and storage of radioactive waste.[4] Uranium miners are at significant risk for developing lung and other forms of cancers, as demonstrated in workers in Canada, Germany, Namibia, Czech Republic, France, Russia, and the United States.[5]

Workers at and neighbors of uranium milling and processing plants are also at risk for cancers. For example, the Feed Materials Production Center at Fernald, Ohio, which commenced operation in 1953, manufactured uranium pellets for plutonium production reactors at Hanford and Rocky Flats, and parts for nuclear weapons made at Rocky Flats and the Y12 plant at Oak Ridge, Tennessee. During its decades of operation it released 298,000 pounds of uranium dust into the air—167,000 pounds into the Great Miami River and 12.7 million pounds into unlined earthern pits. Large silos on the reservation contain 9700 tons or 1600 to 4600 curies, which continually emit high concentrations of carcinogenic gas. Local people have developed highly malignant bone sarcomas and other cancers secondary to uranium deposits in their bodies.[6]

There are radioactive facilities such as this all over the United States as well as in other countries—all integral components of the nuclear fuel cycle, producing uranium ammunition, uranium fuel rods for nuclear power plants, and plutonium for nuclear weapons. Up to eighty sites in America have been involved in the production, manufacture, development, testing, and storage of uranium 238.

Firing ranges for uranium 238 weapons in Madison, Indiana; Yuma, Arizona; and Aberdeen, Maryland may never be decontaminated. Uranium-polluted soil was discovered almost a mile away from a munitions production plant in Concord, Massachusetts, where 400,000 ponds of uranium wastes lie in an unlined pit. Groundwater and a nearby cranberry bog are contaminated.[7] (For a comprehensive list of uranium weapons–related sites, I refer you to the excellent book, *Metal of Dishonor*, pages 212 to 216.)[8]

As far back as 1943, scientists in the Manhattan Project postulated that uranium could be viewed as an air and terrain contaminant, saying that inhalation would cause "bronchial irritation coming on in a few hours to a few days." They also noted that the acute radiation effects could induce ulcers and perforations of the gut, followed by death.[9] On January 29, 2000, the U.S. department of energy finally acknowledged—after many years of denial—that employees of uranium-processing facilities experience significantly high rates of leukemia, Hodgkin's disease, and cancers of the prostate, kidney, liver, salivary glands, and lungs. In England, a study commissioned by British Nuclear Fuels and released in July 2000, found a link between radiation and lung cancer at the Springfield uranium-fuel fabrication plant near Preston in Lancashire.[10] And the highest incidence of childhood leukemia in the United Kingdom has been reported around a uranium firing range at Duindrennan, Scotland.[11] The National Academy of Sciences recently reported that of 144 highly contaminated nuclear sites around the U.S., 109 would remain radioactive in perpetuity, because it was virtually impossible to clean them up.[12]

MEDICAL IMPLICATIONS OF URANIUM WEAPON USE IN THE GULF WAR

During Operation Desert Storm, American M1A1, M1, and M60 tanks fired 14,000 depleted uranium (DU) anti-tank shells. Seven thousand rounds were used during training before Desert Storm, fired into sand berms in Saudi Arabia; 4000 were fired during combat; and 3000 more were lost in fires and other accidents. The air force A-10 "tank-killer" planes also fired approximately 940,000 30-mm DU rounds in combat, totaling 564,000 pounds of DU that either hit their targets or were scattered over the desert floor. (For those that hit their targets, it is important to note that uranium 238 is pyrophoric: when it hits a tank at high speed it burst into flame. Up to 70 percent of the shell is vaporized and converted to tiny particles of oxidized uranium 238. Sixty percent of the particles are tiny—less than 5 microns in diameter. Because these particles are light, they can be transported many miles on wind currents, and they are small enough to be inhaled into the terminal bronchi—the tiniest air passages of the lungs. They can reside in these terminal bronchi for many years, irradiating a small volume of surrounding cells with high doses of radiation. The larger particles can be wafted up to the throat carried by the mucous and cilial action of the airways and then swallowed.)

One third, or 654 of the 2054 American tanks used during Desert Storm, were equipped with uranium armor plating, providing them with a tactical advantage, because the conventional Iraqi weapons would have no chance of penetrating them. But by their use, the American tank crews were exposed to whole-body gamma radiation, similar to X rays emanating from the uranium armor.

At the end of the operation, between 300 and 800 tons of uranium 238 with a half-life of 4.5 billion years lay across the battlefield of Iraq, Kuwait, and Saudi Arabia, never to be retrieved, in spent rounds, in solid and powdered form, in various states of decay and dispersal.

External Dose

External gamma radiation emitted from uranium shells can be as high as 200 millirads per hour, more than the yearly dose received from natural background radiation. One DU penetrator found at the port of Dammam in Saudi Arabia measured 260 to 270 millirads per hour. If, for example, a person picked up a shell and kept it in her pocket for ten hours, she would absorb 2.7 rads of gamma radiation, a relatively high dose. Children have been found playing with the empty shells and people collect shell fragments to display in their houses. Soldiers took home the radioactive ammunition as souvenirs, unaware that it was dangerous.

Internal Dose

The water supplies in the affected areas are at risk. The dissolved uranium will concentrate in the food chain, thousands of times at each step, particularly in milk—including human breast milk. (As noted, it is not possible to taste, smell, or see radiation.) Children and babies are ten to twenty times more sensitive to the carcinogenic effects of radiation than adults.

The geographical areas in the Gulf that are now contaminated with uranium will remain radioactive for the rest of time, the inhabitants being at risk for cancers and congenital deformities forever more. Insoluble, tiny ceramic particles of uranium dioxide aerosol will be inhaled into the lungs of the surrounding population, be they soldiers, adult civilians, or children. And the radioactive water will cause pollution of the food supply.

Because the uranium, its daughter isotopes, and the contaminants named above emit both alpha and beta particles, the lung cells with which they are in contact will absorb high doses of radiation. It takes a single alpha or beta particle or gamma ray to damage a single regulatory gene in a single cell to kill the patient. Like a parasite, cancer uses up the nutrients of the body, and the patient wastes away and then dies.

Insoluble uranium is also transported from the lungs by macrophages (white blood cells that ingest insoluble or foreign bodies), to the lymph glands in the center of the thorax. The cells in the glands receive a radiation dose ten times that of the lung cells. The complications of irradiated lymph tissue are leukemia and lymphoma. Indeed, some of the NATO troops who were exposed to uranium weapons in Bosnia and Kosovo are now reporting an increase in leukemia, as are the civilians in Iraq. Uranium is solubilized in the lymph glands and transported to the liver, where it can cause liver cancer, and to the bone, where it can induce bone cancer or leukemia.

The biological half-life of uranium 238 in bone is 300 days.[13] This element can also be deposited in brain, kidney, muscle, spleen, and—most important—in the reproductive organs.[14] In 1997 uranium 238 was found in the semen of five out of twenty-two American veterans who had been carrying uranium fragments in their bodies since 1991.[15] This finding is significant because there have been reports of an increased incidence of congenital abnormalities in the offspring of veterans and also in the newborn babies in Iraq; the uranium is finding its way into testicles where it is mutating genes in the sperm cells. Uranium can also induce testicular cancer.

Uranium crosses the placenta, where, like the drug thalidomide, it can induce severe fetal abnormalities by killing cells that are imperative to normal fetal development. This is called *teratogenesis.*[16]

Uranium is also a heavy metal. As such, it can cause a particular form of nephritis or kidney disease. It is excreted through the kidney, so this organ is at particular risk. It is known that many Gulf War veterans are suffering from kidney disease. The kidney is also at risk because the heavy-metal uranium is also radioactive. As the kidney is the main organ of excretion for the uranium that is stored in the body, there is the risk of renal carcinoma. No epidemiological studies have been done by the Pentagon to determine the true incidence of renal disease amongst the veterans. Nor have there been any studies to determine whether malignancies have increased.

The Pentagon is also steadfastly refusing to conduct studies of the civilians living in the contaminated areas. What is their prognosis or life expectancy? What will happen to future generations? Instead, the Pentagon and the British ministry of defense are blocking efforts to study their troops for relevant diseases, disclaiming any association of the so-called Gulf War syndrome with uranium ammunition, even though a secret report issued by the United Kingdom atomic energy authority in April 1991—a month after the conclusion of Desert Storm—warned that only 40 tons of uranium debris left from the DU weapons could cause over 500,000 deaths.[17] (Actual debris amounts to not 40 tons but 300 to 800 tons.)

Aware of the radioactive dangers, Saudi Arabia demanded that the U.S. army collect all the tanks, vehicles, and instruments of war destroyed by uranium munitions on their territory. Because Saudi Arabia is a close American ally, the request was honored and the contaminated equipment taken back to the U.S. to be stored with extreme care.[18] To this end, the Pentagon has constructed a high-priced, high-security, high-tech cocoon at the Savannah River Nuclear Facility in Georgia to process radioactive materials from the contaminated equipment. This building, Building 101, has special walls and flooring to prevent air or dust from escaping to the outside world.

Kuwait and Iraq have not been so lucky. There is no U.S. commitment to decontaminate their radioactive land.

PRIOR KNOWLEDGE

It is clear that the Pentagon understood the medical hazards of uranium munitions well before Desert Storm. Numerous reports from the military acknowledged that uranium 238 can cause kidney damage, cancers of the lung and bone, nonmalignant lung disease, skin disorders, neurocognitive disorders, chromosomal damage, and birth defects.[19] In July 1990, an army contractor warned, "Aerosol DU exposures to soldiers on the battlefield could be significant with potential radiological and toxicological effects. Under combat conditions, the MEIs [most exposed individuals] are probably the ground troops that reenter a battlefield following the exchange of armor-piercing munitions, either on foot or motorized transport." However, no warnings about the dangers of uranium were given to the American or coalition forces deployed during Desert Storm, let alone to the surrounding civilian population.[20]

Finally, in their only statement of responsibility, the department of defense admitted in January 1998, "Our investigations into potential health hazards of depleted uranium point to serious deficiencies in what our troops understand about the health effects DU posed on the battlefield. . . . Combat troops or those carrying out support functions generally did not know that DU contaminated equipment, such as enemy vehicles struck by DU rounds, required special handling. . . . The failure to properly disseminate information to troops at all levels may have resulted in thousands of unnecessary exposures."

The military cover-up was partially explained in a statement made by Lieutenant Colonel M. V. Ziehmn of Los Alamos Lab in 1991: "There has been and continues to be a concern regarding the impact of DU on the environment. Therefore, if no one makes a case for the effectiveness of DU on the battlefield, DU rounds may become politically unacceptable and thus, be deleted from the arsenal. . . . I believe we should keep this sensitive issue at mind when after-action reports are written."[21] Because of the cover-up, support personnel were not told to check soldiers for uranium-contaminated shrapnel wounds, nor were they told to wear protective suits during their own contact with contaminated soldiers, equipment, or soil. In direct violation of the operative army and Nuclear Regulatory Commission regulations, there was no medical testing or follow-up of the soldiers who were either wounded by uranium or who may have inhaled or ingested uranium dust.

The symptoms of Gulf War syndrome are difficult to collate within a specific disease entity. Nevertheless, the complaints of the veterans are surprisingly similar in pattern to the various pathologies induced by uranium exposure as described by the U.S. military. Without definitive medical and epidemiological studies, it is at this stage impossible to know exactly what the future holds for the people exposed to uranium from the weapons used in the Gulf and the Balkans. Estimates must suffice. The president of the American Gulf

War Veterans estimates that 50,000 to 80,000 veterans are afflicted with Gulf War syndrome, 39,000 have already been dismissed from active service, and 2400 to 5000 have died. In Britain about 4000 returned servicemen have Gulf War syndrome and 160 have died.

What were the causes of death? Why the cover-up? Collation of the diagnoses would make plain the link between pathology and uranium.[22] If there is nothing to hide, why not publish the data?

And the intrigue continues.

The World Health Organization (WHO) has steadfastly resisted conducting studies on the health effects of exposure to uranium 238 following Desert Storm, Bosnia, and Kosovo. The reason for this refusal is an agreement forged in 1959 between the International Atomic Energy Agency (IAEA), which actively promotes nuclear power worldwide, and the WHO, stating that if one agency wishes to carry out a study that affects the work of the other, mutual agreement is required. The IAEA has never agreed to such studies.[23]

However, even Dr. Mike Repacholi, WHO's coordinator for occupational and environmental health, acknowledged that young children face a particular risk from depleted uranium: "Young children could receive greater depleted uranium exposure when playing within a conflict zone because of hand-to-mouth activity that could result in high depleted uranium ingestion from contaminated soil."[24] Medical reports from Iraq indicate that childhood malignancies have increased to seven times what they were and the incidence of congenital malformations has doubled in the areas where the bombing was the most intense.[25] International sanctions have worsened the medical situation. Pediatric physicians are unable to treat these patients because they have no access to chemotherapeutic agents, no antibiotics, and no radiotherapy.

CLEAN-UP

Back in the U.S. the concern about uranium has been so great that large, contaminated areas of soil were dredged, containerized, and removed during the clean-up of uranium 238 contamination at the Starmet plant in Concord, Massachusetts; at Sandia National Labs; and at Kirtland Air Force Base in New Mexico (where DU penetrators had been test fired). The army knows that it should have cleaned up its radioactive battlefield. In a report in July 1990, it warned, "Assuming U.S. regulatory standards and health physics practices are followed, it is likely that some form of remediable action will be required in a DU post-combat environment."[26] However, once the scale and cost of the clean-up were realized, the U.S. army Environmental Policy Institute informed U.S. policy makers that "no international law, treaty, regulation, or custom requires the United States to remediate the Persian Gulf War battlefields."[27] As Dan Fahey of the Military Toxics Project said, "The United States established a precedent during the Gulf War which permits an armed force to use depleted uranium weapons without warning civilian populations about contamination of the land."

PROLIFERATION OF URANIUM WEAPONS

The U.S. has either encouraged the construction of uranium weapons in, or exported uranium munitions to, sixteen other countries, including Australia, Britain, France, Greece, Turkey, Russia, Israel, Saudi Arabia, Kuwait, Bahrain, Egypt, Thailand, Taiwan, Pakistan, Japan, and New Zealand.[28] Other sources say that Iraq itself, Oman, Jordan, Abu Dhabi, and the United Arab Emirates may also have these weapons in their arsenals.

The UN subcommission on human rights has condemned uranium munitions as weapons of indiscriminate destruction. As such they fail:

- *The temporal test:* their effects continue after the war ends
- *The environmental test:* they pollute food, water, and soil
- *The humanness test:* they have effects beyond those necessary to achieve military objectives
- *The geographical test:* the particles can potentially travel to noncombatant countries

And the manufacture and testing of uranium weapons affects civilians, even if the weapons are not used.[29]

The navy has been testing their uranium munitions on a training range at Vieques, Puerto Rico. They admitted to firing 263 uranium bullets, of which they recovered only fifty-seven. (You may be sure these figures are underestimates.) The people in Vieques blame the navy for higher-than-normal cancer rates in that area. The navy denies that their activities have damaged anyone's health.[30]

Britain has been test firing uranium munitions in various locations, including Eskmeals Cumbria, Solway Firth, and Leelworth in Dorset. They were also test fired in Germany at Lower Saxony in the early seventies and at the upper Bavarian town of Schrobenhausen, where they were tested for seventeen years until 1996. And they were used by the U.S. in combat in Mogadishu in the early nineties, when a warning was issued to medics that they might encounter soldiers "who had unusually high levels of contact with depleted uranium."[31] Israel has almost certainly been using uranium armor plated tanks and uranium weapons against the Palestinians on the West Bank and in Gaza.[32]

BOSNIA AND KOSOVO

Two other "radioactive" wars have been fought in recent times, primarily by the United States and its NATO allies, in Bosnia and Kosovo.

As of this writing, an international furor is erupting, as soldiers and peacekeepers deployed in Kosovo are developing malignancies, including leukemia. Approximately 31,000 rounds of uranium ammunition were fired in Operation Allied Force—the seventy-eight day war in Kosovo in 1999—and over 10,800 uranium shells were fired in Bosnia in 1994–95, mainly around the city of Sarajevo,[33] where American A-10 Warthog planes fired uranium ammunition from its 30-mm Gatling guns at a rate of 3900 rounds per minute.

Initially, NATO officials were reluctant to give their member countries specific information about the use of uranium ammunitions in Kosovo or Bosnia, although in July 1999 NATO had warned those countries with armies and aid workers in the Balkans that there could be a "possible toxic threat" arising from the use of uranium weapons, and advised them to take preventive measures. (The head of the UN environment program criticized NATO for not being more forthcoming about where it had used the ammunition.)

Concern about uranium weapons began percolating among the NATO countries in December 2000, when Italy announced an investigation into thirty sick soldiers who had served in Bosnia in 1994–95 and Kosovo in 1999. Twelve have cancer and five to seven have died of leukemia. About 30,000 to 40,000 Italian soldiers served in the Balkans, and the Italian defense minister, Sergio Mattarella, said, "I must express my bitterness that the competent international organizations have waited until now to answer our request for information that is important to the Bosnian community and members of the military."

Spain will test all 32,000 of its soldiers stationed in the Balkans since 1992. Two confirmed cases of leukemia have been reported amongst the Spanish contingent. Apart from the leukemia deaths, an unknown number of soldiers who served as peacekeepers in the Balkans have an array of symptoms similar to the Gulf War syndrome, including hair loss and chronic fatigue.

Other countries concerned about the future health of their men include Kosovo, Denmark, France, Belgium, Portugal, and Holland. Ireland, Latvia, and Romania will also test their troops. Five Belgian soldiers have malignancies, as have two Portugese, two Finnish, and two Dutch soldiers. Portugal will send scientists to measure radiation levels in the affected areas. Russia is sending a team to check the zones where its people are deployed as international peacekeepers, and plans to test all military personnel before January 20, 2002.[34] Portugal and Italy have accused NATO of a cover-up.[35]

A former environment minister from Finland, Pekka Haavisto, who headed the UN inquiry into Kosovo, said after an inspection of the Kosovo battlefields, "We found some radiation in the middle of villages where children were playing. We were surprised to find this a year-and-a-half later [after the war]. People had collected ammunition shards as souvenirs and there were cows grazing in contaminated areas, which means the contaminated dust can get into the milk." Haavisto and his team discovered low-level beta radiation at eight of the eleven sites they sampled. They recommended that the contaminated areas be marked and fenced off, because, he said, the local people do not understand the material.

The eleven sites examined were chosen from 112 areas that NATO admitted it had targeted with radioactive munitions, although to

Haavisto's anger, NATO procrastinated, taking almost a year and a half before providing the necessary geographical data to the UN team. Haavisto also expressed concern that the use of controlled explosions to clear mines, unexploded munitions, and cluster bombs would scatter the radiation and toxic materials yet again.[36] After several weeks of European consternation and banner headlines in December 2000 and January 2001, NATO (which to a large degree is controlled by the U.S.) was finally forced to order a full investigation into the possible effects of depleted uranium. Apart from NATO, the fifteen-member European Union ordered its own inquiry.

After months of steadfast denial about the dangers, the British ministry of defense has asked for an independent study on the possible effects of uranium weapons. The House of Commons met on January 10, 2001, to decide whether to summon ministers to explain the government's policy.[37] Britain finally agreed that—along with the other NATO countries—it would conduct tests on its troops, 1400 of whom are said to be suffering from the Gulf War syndrome (469 of these have died; causes of death have yet to be made public).[38]

No doubt medical tests will benefit families and soldiers, but the doctors will be unable to ascertain whether or not these people have actually inhaled or ingested uranium particles. Blood tests will reveal only whether or not the patient has leukemia at the time of testing. X-ray scans of the body will determine whether there is an advanced cancer. Urine tests will reveal if the person is excreting uranium. If positive, the patient is at risk for developing a malignancy years later. Even if the urine shows no trace of uranium, it does not mean that uranium is not deposited in bone or in other organs. There is no way to determine whether or not there is uranium in the body, apart from placing the patient in a whole-body scanner, where a tiny specific spectrum of radiation can be detected, indicating the presence of uranium or its decay products. If the whole body scanner fails to detect traces of radioactivity, this still does not exclude damage. Uranium could have been in the body previously, mutated some regulatory genes, and then excreted. The patient could still go on to develop cancer.

Medically, one would not expect the symptoms of leukemia to arise for two to ten years following exposure. So the troops who were present at Operation Desert Storm and in the 1994–95 operation in Bosnia may well be developing leukemia, but it is early for soldiers exposed in 1999 to be manifesting malignancies. The incubation period for cancer may be shorter than we have been led to believe when exposed to internal uranium deposits. We have much yet to learn. Dr. Eric Wright, a British radiobiologist, said "I am not aware of any real radiobiology research in depleted uranium." [39]

That the soldiers and peacekeepers will be followed medically is appropriate. But there are tens of thousands—or indeed millions—of innocent civilians at risk in Saudi Arabia, Kuwait, Iraq, Bosnia, and Kosovo, as well as the other places around the globe where radioactive weapons have been aerosolized by testing.[40] These people must also be followed up and cared for. On January 17, 2001, the Swiss Federal Institute of Technology in Spiez also discovered traces of uranium 236 in the weapons used in Kosovo.[41] As Uranium 236 is made only in a nuclear reactor, these weapons are definitely contaminated with fission and transuranic products from nuclear fission. The U.S. military and department of energy must have known about this contamination. If there is uranium 236, almost certainly there will be plutonium, together with americium, neptunium, strontium 90, and cesium 137. This situation has extremely serious medical implications for the public health of the people who have been and will be contaminated.

Chapter Nine

THE LOCKHEED MARTIN PRESIDENCY AND THE STAR WARS ADMINISTRATION

We enter the twenty-first century locked in a mortal arms race with ourselves. Though the needs for more advanced weaponry are at best unclear, we proceed on the premise that "if we build it, they will come."

—M. W. Gruzy[1]

It's not right to have all those people in one building without a single watchdog. We're all in trouble . . . when the generals get that much power.

—Harry Truman on the Pentagon

GEORGE W. BUSH ASCENDED to the presidency propelled by a Republican-dominated Supreme Court. His cabinet is composed mostly of corporate executives. Among them are Dick Cheney, former CEO of Halliburton Oil; Andrew Card, chief of staff—General Motors vice president; Paul O'Neill, treasury secretary—chair of Alcoa; Don Evans, secretary of commerce—former CEO of Tom Brown Inc. Oil Company; Donald Rumsfeld, secretary of defense—former CEO of G. W. Searle and General Instrument; Condoleezza Rice, national security advisor—Chevron board of directors.[2]

Forty million dollars, the largest amount ever donated, paid for the festivities at the inauguration, including 100,000 dollars each by 168 corporations and individuals. More than forty-five corporations wrote five-digit checks for events that honored Texans. A news release said this will be "the only inaugural ball where guests can have their picture made with a 2500-pound Brahmin bull or sitting in the cockpit of a fighter jet."

The donating corporations included Ford, General Motors, major Washington law firms, Marriott Corporation, Enron, Conoco, Hunt Oil, Chevron, ExxonMobil, Southern Energy Company, American Airlines, major-league baseball companies, Coca-Cola, Pepsi, Philip Morris, U.S. Tobacco, Abbott Drug Laboratories, Bristol-Meyers Squibb, Pfizer, General Electric, AT&T, and Alcoa. The financial security and investment industry contributed over 2 million dollars.

Barron's Online wrote:

> The capital is filling up with pin-striped, Chamber of Commerce types, attracted by what promises to be the most pro-business, anti-regulatory administration since Ronald Reagan reigned. Bush has packed CEOs and industrial lobbyists on transition teams that are advising his new Cabinet secretaries and agency heads on pressing policy issues and new hires. The advisory team for nominee Gale Norton's Department of Interior is jammed with representatives of energy, mining and paper companies.[3]

As Steve Weiss from the Center for Responsive Politics observed, "The general public, which cannot give these large contributions, does not get access to the next president or his advisors. Money buys you access to the president and those who are shaping the policies."[4]

The world's most powerful corporation, one that literally controls the fate of the earth, is Lockheed Martin. As we have seen, this company, together with its smaller military corporate colleagues, is involved in the production of almost every single weapon and Star Wars system that we have examined. They are up to their necks in corporate donations to both presidential candidates, and congressional and senate candidates on both sides of politics. (Weapons-industry political action committees favored the Republicans to Democrats by a 2 to 1 margin in contributions. Since 1997, the four top missile contractors spent 4 million dollars in PAC contributions and 3 million dollars in soft-money contributions. They also spent 18 million dollars in lobbying—which is tax deductible.)[5]

Lockheed Martin was the top defense contractor for the year 2000, receiving 15.1 billion dollars of taxpayer funds. Boeing was next with 12 billion dollars, followed by Raytheon at 6.3 billion dollars.[6] As we know, Lockheed Martin employees sit on the boards of right-wing think tanks such as the Heritage Foundation and the Center for Policy Studies. But now that their man is ensconced in the White House, they are in the position to control domestic and international policies directly. These corporations are determined to build a multilayered Star Wars system, and to build every weapon they can conceive, whether America needs it or not.

If Bush proceeds with the full throttle, all systems green-and-go Star Wars, instead of the modest, modified 60-billion-dollar Clinton system, it could cost the nation 240 billion dollars over the years of construction. And while many of the expenditures would technically come under the rubric of "defense," as Bush noted in a speech in September 1999 before the Citadel military college in Charleston, South Carolina, when discussing "the need to bolster our unrivalled power," "I know the best defense can be a strong and swift offense," effectively offering a rubric for development of any weapon whatsoever.[7] We are heading rapidly toward a state of global disaster. A belligerent and ill-informed president sits in the White House (despite his perceived change of status since September 11, 2001), controlled by his corporate staff intent on extracting as much American tax money as they possibly can to build ever more exotic and dangerous weapons. Bush administration appointees are among the most hawkish and extreme in recent memory, and an alarming number of Bush's staff people have direct ties to Lockheed Martin.

The quartet of Vice President Cheney, Defense Secretary Rumsfeld, Secretary of State Colin Powell, and National Security Advisor Condoleezza Rice are now the most powerful people in the world. Believing as they do that America is the heart of the universe, that U.S. militarism must be used to protect American global business interests, that Russia is not to be trusted, and that China may need provoking into a new cold war arms race, they have embarked America upon a dangerous four-year journey.

Vice President Cheney, "a defacto leader of a somewhat ceremonial president," to quote the *Guardian* journalist Martin Kettle,[8] now occupies a position of great influence, orchestrating as he does the appointment of cabinet members, and directing the activities of the new president. As noted earlier, the vice president's wife, Lynn Cheney, is a former board member of Lockheed Martin.

Donald Rumsfeld, a former Republican congressman, former NATO ambassador, and former secretary of defense, maintains intimate ties to missile-defense advocates and anti–arms control proponents, and he is closely associated with Frank Gaffney's Center for Security Policy, the de-facto nerve center of the Star Wars lobby, as noted in Chapter Four. Rumsfeld also serves on the board of Empower America, which ran pro–Star Wars radio ads against an incumbent Nevada Democrat during the 1998 congressional elections.

His contrived Rumsfeld report of 1998 warned that America would be threatened by North Korean missiles within the next five years, although CIA estimates had placed that projected time frame at ten to fifteen years (this assuming that peacekeeping efforts to unite the Koreas and bring North Korea into the community of nations have failed),[9] and although, as U.S. intelligence analyst Robert Walpole said in testimony before Congress, the least likely way a foreign nation would deliver a nuclear weapon of mass destruction is a ballistic missile because it has a "return address." (On September 11, 2001, U.S. civilian planes were used as effective ballistic missiles.)

Shortly before his appointment as secretary of defense, Rumsfeld headed another Pentagon commission, that unveiled a report in January 2001 warning that America could face a "space Pearl Harbor." It advocated tighter security for American space systems and called for the appointment of an undersecretary of defense for space, intelligence, and information. It also called for increased military spending, estimating the cost to replace obsolete military satellites in the next decade at 50 billion dollars. Belligerent in tone, it said that the president should "have an option to deploy weapons in space to deter threats to, and, if necessary, defend against attacks on U.S. interests."[10]

At his Senate confirmation hearings Rumsfeld referred to the Antiballistic Missile treaty, the cornerstone of nuclear arms control, as "ancient history." He also questioned whether the U.S. could maintain its nuclear arsenal without nuclear testing. This testimony was supported by Senator Jesse Helms, head of the Senate foreign relations committee, when he said "The United States is no longer bound by the ABM treaty—that treaty expired when our treaty partner the Soviet Union ceased to exist." Helms went on to say "Personally, I do not think that a new kind of ABM treaty can be negotiated with Russia that would permit the kind of defenses that America needs and must have."[11] Helms had already antagonized Russia calling the country "an active proliferator" because of the transfer of sensitive technology to hostile states like Iran and North Korea. Russia's foreign ministry accused Rumsfeld and (deputy secretary of defense) Wolfowitz of behaving like cold war warriors who were trapped in a time warp.[12]

Rumsfeld is a forceful player who generally has his way against the most powerful opponents. As Gerald Ford's secretary of defense, he outmaneuvered Secretary of State Kissinger when Kissinger was in Moscow in a last-minute attempt to coax a SALT II arms-control agreement from the Soviets. Behind Kissinger's back, Rumsfeld convened a meeting of the national security council backed by the Joint Chiefs of Staff. After two hours of discussion, the Pentagon withdrew its support for SALT II. Rumsfeld was traveling and did not even attend the meeting. Ford was furious and SALT II became obsolete for that presidency. Kissinger calls him the most ruthless man he has ever known.

Rumsfeld's former colleagues describe him variously as a highly organized, highly political personality, and a master bureaucrat.[13] His outreach and influence is pervasive. Since 1992, he has been a member of the board of directors of the Tribune Company which, it boasts in its publicity statements, with "television, radio, newspapers and the internet, reaches nearly 80 percent of American households every day."[14]

Colin Powell, the new secretary of state, is an interesting enigma. Basically a company man, he worked his way up through the ranks of the bureaucracy, eventually becoming the first African American to be appointed chairman of the Joint Chiefs of Staff and subsequently the first African American secretary of state. However, he failed to protest the overt discrimination against blacks in Florida's vote-rigging, which gave Bush the presidency.

As an advisor in Vietnam during 1962 and 1963, unlike some others, he did not protest the destruction of villages and the killing of civilians. He had an early role in the investigation of the My Lai massacre, which he effectively covered up until it was exposed by other, more courageous men. He was involved in the Iran-Contra scandal while working with Defense Secretary Casper Weinberger.

Although a cautious person at heart, he was deeply involved in—and indeed responsible for—several military operations that flouted the international rule of law. In 1989, as chairman of the Joint Chiefs of Staff, he oversaw the invasion of Panama when an estimated 300 civilians were killed and buried by the U.S. military in secret graves. Three thousand more were seriously injured. America instigated this operation to capture Manuel Noriega, a man put into office by the CIA but who had ceased to please the American elite.

In his book, *Just Cause,* Powell enunciated his doctrine: "Use all the force necessary and do not apologize for going in big if that's what it takes."[15] Powell believes that American military force should only be used in overwhelming strength to achieve well-defined strategic interests, meaning that peacekeeping operations are not acceptable.[16]

He became a hero of Desert Storm when he warned the Iraqi army that "first we are going to cut it off, and then we are going to kill it."[17] Did he know that uranium weapons were used in that operation? If so, did he understand the medical implications of that operation, so clearly described in the military literature? If he did, he violated the fundamental principles of war. Innocent civilians are now threatened for the rest of time with malignancies and a damaged gene pool.

Powell describes Russia and China as countries that the U.S. would attempt to work with "not as potential enemies or adversaries, but not yet as strategic partners." By buying into this philosophy, he leaves the door open for more radical members of the administration to have their way.[18]

During his confirmation hearings, Powell said that the Bush administration would move full-speed ahead with a nationwide missile defense,[19] arguing that it was essential to build a "complete strategic framework" including defensive as well as offensive weapons. Taking the Rumsfeld line on the ABM treaty, he said "The framework that treaty was designed for was a framework that really isn't relevant now. We are moving forward with the capacity to develop a missile defense system, and the only way we can eventually move forward is to see the ABM treaty modified or eliminated or changed in some rather fundamental way."[20]

When Senators Joseph Biden and Lincoln Chafee said that the allies were skeptical about the NMD project, he brushed aside their concerns. "When people see something new come along they are terrified, but if it is the right thing to do, you do it anyway. . . . In the end of the day, it will benefit the world," he said.[21] Powell, however, says that if it was necessary to walk out of the ABM treaty, he would consult with the Russians and the allies. And in 1998 he joined the other Joint Chiefs of Staff by supporting ratification of the CTBT.[22]

Condoleezza Rice is at heart a right-wing ideologue who is dismissive of other countries. While having no direct Lockheed Martin connections, she fits in well with the White House ideology. She said that the trouble with Israel is that it is "so small," and that "Cuba is the road kill of history."[23] Strongly opposing the Comprehensive Test Ban Treaty, she wrote in *Foreign Affairs:*

> Since 1992, the United States has refrained unilaterally from testing nuclear weapons. It is an example to the rest of the world, yet does not tie its own hands "in perpetuity" if testing becomes necessary again. But in pursuit of a "norm" against the acquisition of nuclear weapons, the United States signed a treaty that was not verifiable, did not deal with the threat of the development of nuclear weapons by rogue states, and threatened the reliability of the nuclear stockpile. Legitimate congressional concerns about the substance of the treaty were ignored during negotiations.[24]

Other appointees mirror the corporate presidency:

As noted, Bruce Jackson, vice president of corporate strategy and development of Lockheed Martin, volunteered to be the overall chairman of the Bush foreign policy platform committee at the Republican convention, and it was he who wrote the Republican party's foreign policy platform.

Stephen J. Hadley, a partner in the Washington-based law firm Shea & Gardner, which represents Lockheed Martin, has been appointed deputy director of the National Security Council, working in the White House as Condoleezza Rice's chief deputy. An enthusiastic advocate of Star Wars, he is secretary of the committee to expand NATO and was also a member of the National Security Council staff of President Bush the first. Hadley also belongs to an eight-member foreign policy team formed during the Bush campaign, nicknamed the "Vulcans" after a statue representing the Roman god of fire and metalwork, commemorating the steel-making history in Birmingham, Alabama, Condoleezza Rice's hometown. Composed mostly of hawks, the group includes Rice and Hadley, and also Richard Armitage, Reagan's former assistant secretary of defense; Robert Blackwill, a member of Bush the first's National Security Council; Dov Zakheim, Reagan's former undersecretary of defense; Robert Zoellick, former undersecretary of defense for Bush; and Richard Perle, a man nicknamed "the prince of darkness" by his Pentagon colleagues during the Reagan administration when he was undersecretary of defense.[25, 26]

Another who is directing the Bush presidency toward a new cold war stance is Paul Wolfowitz, who headed the Paul Nitze Center for International Studies. Wolfowitz epitomizes the neoconservative wing of the Republican party cold war warriors. They still hate Russia, but were looking to China to fill the role of a new American threat on a global scale until terrorist activity recently took center stage.

Wolfowitz can take credit for the recent expansion of NATO; he authored a secret memorandum for the Pentagon, which leaked to the *New York Times* in 1992, warning that Yeltsin's Russia posed a grave potential threat to U.S. interests, and he advocated an all-out U.S.-led NATO war against Russia if it threatened the security of the newly independent Baltic republics. Although Russia did no such thing, Wolfowitz was installed as a neoconservative hero, and Clinton, ever compliant, expanded NATO into Czechoslovakia, Poland, and Hungary, much to Russia's discomfort and rage. (Now that the cold war is over, NATO has no tangible use, yet it continues to exist and is getting bigger. If Russia had been invited to become part of the NATO alliance, the act would have defused any cold war tensions that remained in Europe.) Wolfowitz and his accolytes believe that America must maintain its position as global superpower; no regional powers, such as China or Russia, must be allowed to develop, and American values and self-interests must reign supreme.

Richard Perle, who said on March 15, 1983, the fact that "nuclear winter that would wipe out all life on earth . . . is all the more reason to continue President Reagan's weapons buildup," is a friend of Wolfowitz. Perle is a hard-line ally of Israel, believing that there is no difference between the interests of the two countries. In 1996 he was simultaneously adviser to Dole's presidential bid and to Netanyahu's election campaign in Israel. During the Reagan days he often accused Secretary of State George Shultz of being too soft on Cuba, the Chinese, North Koreans, the Soviets, and Arabs.

Robert Zoellick, an ally of Wolfowitz and Perle, was White House deputy chief of staff to Bush the first. He supports NATO enlargement, uncritically supports Israel, and he regards Russia as an inherent adversary, not to be trusted or treated as a friend.[27]

John Bolton, undersecretary of state for arms control, nonproliferation, and international security is described by Senator Jesse Helms as "one of the best and wisest" nominations that Bush has made for a "senior foreign policy position." "Bolton is the kind of man with whom I would want to stand at Armageddon, for what the Bible describes as the final battle between good and evil in this world," Helms said at an American Enterprise Institute event. At Bolton's Senate confirmation hearing Helms said "John, I want you to take that ABM treaty and dump it in the same place we dumped our ABM cosigner, the Soviet Union—on the ash heap of history."

Bolton believes that the CTBT is dead, that Taiwan should have official diplomatic recognition separate from China, that the U.S. should stop paying dues to the United Nations, and that the U.S. should be indifferent to whether it ever has "normal" diplomatic relations with North Korea. With Bolton in control, not only will the ABM and CTB treaties be imperiled, but so will all the other arms control treaties, each of which took years to negotiate.[28]

Although he is currently enjoying record-breaking approval ratings in America, among the other 95 percent of the world's population there is a global fear of George W. Bush and his appointees:

> To describe Star Wars as criminally insane is to slander reputable psychopaths. It is inspired by the delusion that America can achieve absolute dominance, that she can fight without taking casualties, forget about deterrence and detonate nuclear weapons secure in the knowledge that her defensive missiles will shoot down any warheads launched in retaliation.
>
> —Nick Cohen, London *Observer*[29]

> The richer, stronger and more globally accountable America becomes, the more self-centered its politics grows. The end of the cold war should have brought great psychological dividends. Generous in global victory, free of paranoia and with wealth beyond imagining, here at last was its chance to become what it has always believed itself to be—the brave, the beautiful, the free and so on. . . . The high-flown rhetoric of the conventions is echoed in every high school valedictory speech, in every rotary and church, pledging allegiance to a constitution that has lost any vision of society beyond the pursuit of happiness. God's chosen people, uniquely blessed, nurture a self-image almost as deranged in its profound self-delusion as the old Soviet Union. The most advanced, knowledgeable, educated, psychoanalyzed, therapized nation on earth knows nothing of itself, irony-free and blind to the world around it.
>
> —Polly Toynbee, *The Guardian*[30]

Mikhail Gorbachev, the Soviet president who, more than any person on earth, helped to bring the cold war to an end, wrote a letter to

President Bush just after the Supreme Court made him president. He wrote:

> I hope, Mr. Bush, as the new American president, that you will give up any illusion that the twenty-first century can, or even should be the "American Century." Globalization is a given—but "American globalization" would be a mistake. . . . For ten years, U.S. foreign policy has been formulated as if it were the policy of a victor in war, the cold war. But at the highest reaches of U.S. policy making no one has grasped the fact that this could not be the basis for formulating post–cold war policy—from the standpoint of the old world, the post–cold war period ushered in hopes that are now fading. Over the past decade, the United States continued to operate along an ideological track identical to the one followed during the cold war . . . the expansion of NATO eastward, the handling of the Yugoslav crisis, the theory and practice of U.S. rearmament, including the utterly extravagant national missile defense system, which is based on the bizarre notion of "rogue states." . . . Isn't it amazing that disarmament moved further during the last phase of the cold war than during the period after its end?[31]

Russia is frightened of Star Wars. Because of the poor state of its weapons, Russia relies on a launch-on-warning policy. All 111 of Russia's operating satellites are on the brink of collapse, more than 70 percent are past their initial service lives, and 70 percent of them have military functions.[32] The deteriorating condition of the satellites and early-warning radars increases the possibility of false signals, and these conditions are compounded by the erosion of the Russian command and control system, possibly allowing a "rogue" commander to take control. We cannot assume that Russia has its weapons under strict control. The Bush people should realize that it is extremely unwise to threaten a wounded or inadequate nation, for they may respond in an unpredictable fashion.

In November 2000 Putin proposed a massive cut in the level of strategic weapons to 1000 or less, saying "there should be no pause in nuclear disarmament." He said a 1500 level could be reached by 2008, but only on the condition that the U.S. does not proceed with missile defense. Russia cannot afford its annual spending of 5.1 billion dollars on defense (compared with the U.S. expenditure of 310 billion dollars). To this end, Putin also approved a military reform program to cut his three million military personnel by 600,000.[33]

Because both sides recognized the inherent danger in the ongoing launch-on-warning posture, on December 16, 2000, Secretary of State Madeleine Albright and Russian Foreign Minister Igor Ivanov signed an agreement to strengthen cooperation on preventing accidental missile launches on both sides by expanding an early-warning center where both sides can exchange information.[34] However, the agreement—which still stands—will not cover missiles launched in combat, and either government can withhold advance information of certain space flights for national security reasons.[35]

Still, as a direct result of the U.S. election, Russia has changed its posture. Putin warned that the deployment of a national missile defense shield and NATO's continued expansion into Eastern Europe could "irreparably damage" global stability and the architecture of international relations.[36]

Thus, in January 2001, just after Bush was inaugurated, the Kremlin shelved its plans for radical cuts in its military structures. Soon thereafter Russia announced that it would double its defense spending over the next ten years if Washington decided to go ahead with its missile defense shield.[37]

During the same week, however, Putin wrote a letter to President Bush proposing broader Russian-American cooperation, and setting out the major issues on which he believes the two countries can cooperate. "When Russia and the U.S. act jointly or on parallel tracks, decisions meeting the interests of peace and international stability may be reached," he said, and affirmed that Russia wants warm relations with the United States. But Bush signaled that he will pay even less attention to Russian foreign policy concerns than did Clinton, who ignored Russia's protests about the expansion of NATO and the war against Yugoslavia.[38] However, at the November 2001 Crawford Ranch meeting in Texas between Bush and Putin, there was a post–September 11 magnanimity that pervaded the presidents' relationship, with Bush offering to reduce the U.S. strategic nuclear weapons arsenal down to between 1700 and 2200 within the next ten years. Putin did not give an immediate response.

Moscow analysts see Cheney, Rumsfeld, Powell, and Rice as hawks from a bygone era. "These are people who see themselves as victors of the cold war," according to Alexander Golts, a military commentator for the news magazine *Itogi*. "The Kremlin and the generals are flattered by that, because it reminds them of the days of the USSR when they were a great power. But the new American administration is making a very strong and negative impact on our military."[39]

Concerned about the missile shield, China and Russia hastily convened a meeting on January 13, 2001, at which they worked on a treaty to proclaim their friendship, while privately reassuring the U.S. that they still seek closer ties with them. Jonathon Pollack, chairman of the strategic research department at the Naval War College, says the treaty is a significant move in Sino-Russian ties and as such reflects Beijing's and Moscow's deep concerns about Bush and his people. James Mulvenon, a security expert at the Rand Corporation, echoed these sentiments: "The United States, through incompetence and ham-handed policy making, has effectively driven China and Russia together. . . . NMD is a perfect example. By not having a coordinated policy vis-à-vis the Europeans and the Russians, we let the Chinese play them off against us. There is an enormous resonance in both countries for blaming problems on American hegemony, and we have done nothing to drive a wedge between them.[40, 41]

The pact will almost certainly add fuel to the Wolfowitz clan stance. It will now be easy to convince the American people that China and Russia threaten the very existence of America with their newfound friendship and their combined nuclear arsenals. This dynamic will then reinforce exactly what the neoconservatives have been saying, and Star Wars will be legitimized.

CHINA AND THE BUSH ADMINISTRATION

What is China's response to Bush and Star Wars, apart from the Sino-Russian treaty, which at this stage is vague in its specific objectives?

China's view of America has taken a radical turn since 1998, when in its second white paper on national defense, it mentioned the United States ten times, each in a positive fashion. In September

2000, its third white paper mentions the U.S. thirteen times—all save two of the references are negative. China's attitude has been soured by events in recent years, including the expansion of NATO, the strengthening of the U.S.-Japan military relationship, a congressional report charging Chinese nationalists with two decades of espionage in the U.S., NMD, and the allied bombing of the Chinese embassy in Yugoslavia, which killed three of their journalists.[42] The bombing prompted serious internal debate about whether China should accelerate its military spending. However, the central committee decided to reaffirm their former emphasis on economic development.

American belligerence toward China is becoming uncomfortable. On a visit to Australia in July 2000, former secretary of defense William Cohen, having just left China, urged Australia to increase its military spending to ensure that its forces could support the U.S. if there were to be a war with China over Taiwan. Republican Tom DeLay, House majority whip, recently boasted of how he confronted the Chinese ambassador on *Meet the Press.* He grabbed the ambassador's hand as if to shake it, but instead squeezed it hard, yanked the ambassador close to him, and warned him not to underestimate the resolve of the American people. The ambassador, humiliated, left immediately.[43]

China is not a military threat to America. With a population of over 1.2 billion and a rapidly changing political arena moving from authoritarian communism to some form of free-enterprise capitalism, China's leaders have much to occupy their minds while providing food, education, and a decent standard of living for their people. The last thing that China needs is to divert money and attention to a new nuclear or conventional arms race in their region. But that is the dynamic that Bush is about to set up. If Congress approves the full Star Wars scenario, China will be forced to build more ballistic missiles to overcome America's missile defense. In fact, as noted previously, the U.S. intelligence agencies' report, "Foreign Responses to U.S. National Missile Defense Deployment," predicted just this.

But there is more at stake. The U.S. is about to deploy theater missile defense systems in Japan, South Korea, and possibly Taiwan, because TMD is legitimate under the ABM treaty. China will then be forced to build up her intermediate-range nuclear missile forces to "overload" the TMD system. Theoretically, these missiles could hit targets in India, an old enemy of China. The pro-nuclear regime in India will react badly to these developments and will be goaded into an ongoing nuclear arms race with China. Then what will nuclear Pakistan do? It will be pushed into an ongoing nuclear arms race against India, siding with its ally, China.[44]

However, since the American attack on Afghanistan, there is huge dissent in the streets of Pakistan amongst the Muslim fundamentalists who support the Taliban and Osama Bin Laden. These people also have a significant presence within the Pakistani military. There is a distinct prospect that if there were a civil war in Pakistan, they could gain the upper hand in the military and thereby control the twenty to thirty nuclear weapons that Pakistan has built over the past decade. This poses a terrifying prospect—arch enemies of a nuclear-armed India, themselves armed with nuclear weapons.

There is also Japan, a country with the third largest military in the world, with the world's most advanced technological base, a country with an aggressive past and huge stockpiles of pure plutonium, on the cusp of nuclearization. With a week's notice, Japan could construct nuclear weapons if it so decided. (Japan maintains the third largest military in the world because it can legally spend only 1 percent of its GNP on weapons, but it has a huge GNP.) China is well aware of these possibilities, and Japan is an old enemy of China. The nuclearization of Japan could then trigger a nuclear arms race between South Korea and Japan, two countries with deep enmities.

Taiwan is officially a part of China since Nixon's visit in the early seventies. However, animosity between China and Taiwan remains, and right-wing Republicans are enthusiastically adding fuel to this smoldering fire. In September 2000 the U.S. signed a 1.3 billion dollar arms deal with Taiwan, including the sale of 200 Amraam missiles, not to be made available unless China introduces a similar weapons system, an arrangement that is meant to signify America's pledge not to introduce new offensive military capacities into Asia.[45] But on April 1, 2001, an international incident induced a change in the Chinese-American relationship. A Chinese pilot collided with a U.S. spy plane off the coast of China, forcing the U.S. plane to land on Hainan, a Chinese island. The Chinese were furious that America was spying just off their coast and the U.S. was furious because the Chinese held the twenty-four-member crew for eleven days.

Despite the provocation and damage to U.S.-Chinese relations caused by this incident, the flights of the spy planes must continue, according to Secretary Rumsfeld.[46] This episode sharply increased tensions just before the Bush administration was to decide whether to send more military equipment to Taiwan. China was particularly concerned that Taiwan not obtain Aegis ships, which are an integral component of a theater missile defense system. Eventually, on April 24, 2001, the Bush administration announced that it would sell twelve P-3 Orion planes to enable Taiwan to patrol at sea and hunt for submarines, four Kidd-class destroyers that carry powerful sonar equipment to hunt for submarines and sub-hunting helicopters, and eight new diesel subs, to be made in Germany and the Netherlands. (However, these countries have announced their reluctance to assist the U.S. arming of Taiwan.) The Chinese find the submarines to be particularly provocative. For the moment, Bush has postponed the decision to equip Taiwan with Aegis ships and Patriot PAC-3 anti-missile batteries.

To make matters worse, two days after this decision was announced, President Bush declared that the United States would do "whatever it takes" to help Taiwan defend itself, including the use of military force. This statement was a distinct departure from the long-standing policy of American strategic ambiguity toward Taiwan—expressing a strong interest in that country's security while avoiding an outright promise to go to war in its defense.[47] Although Bush tried to backpedal in a subsequent interview, his statement was consistent with the hard-line Republican policy on China, whose platform states that "America will help Taiwan defend itself." Deputy Secretary of Defense Paul Wolfowitz and Deputy Secretary of State Richard Armitage have called for the strategic ambiguity to be abandoned completely.[48] Other nations were shocked and incensed about this change in strategy. Critical editorials abounded in the European and Australian press.

The Taiwanese themselves admit that they are close to China economically, with businesses on both sides involved in huge economic deals. China has evolved into Taiwan's second-largest market for trade and investment; 40 percent of Taiwan's foreign investment is in China. Students cross the Taiwanese straights to go to Chinese medical schools and universities. It is the Taiwan military, like the United States military, that is pushing for these weapons and influencing foreign policy.[49]

As Taiwan becomes more militarized, China may conclude that the U.S. is restoring a mutual defense pact with Taiwan, an agreement that fell by the wayside in 1979 when Washington normalized diplomatic relations with Beijing and adopted a "one-China" policy, recognizing the Chinese government as legitimate for Taiwan. With TMD systems deployed in Japan, South Korea, Taiwan, and possibly Australia, a compliant and peaceful U.S. ally, China will begin to feel encircled by military hostility. (As an aside, TMD systems do not pose as much of a threat to Russia as they do to China. Russia's ICBMs are located deep within their continental interior, so interceptor rockets launched from coastal waters, as currently proposed, will not achieve the velocity necessary to take out Russian missiles in their boost phase.)

China is the Pentagon's premier villain, according to a study conducted by the Naval War College in Newport, Rhode Island, called "Asia 2025." Since the fall of the Soviet Union, the major Pentagon war games increasingly take place in Asia. According to the report, the effort now is for the U.S. to "manage the rise of China as a great power," and the Pentagon is concentrating on expanding the naval, air, and space power in the Pacific region. They see China as "a force for instability and a constant competitor."

The Pentagon is concerned with the emergence of China as the greatest regional threat to U.S. interests, the lack of forward operating bases in Southeast Asia and South Asia if the U.S. is to remain a key player in these regions, the emerging strategic potential of India, and the need-at-all-costs to prevent a China-India alliance. They envision five possible scenarios where China could be a threat, including an "unstable China" scenario, a "strong China," a "new South Asian order," where India could either be an ally or opponent of

China, an "Asia realigns" scenario, or "the new Sino-Indian condominium" scenario.

There is a major conflict in the U.S. between engagement and containment of China. Instead of military confrontation, Clinton's policy was to engage China so that U.S. business interests could exploit the China market. He encouraged China's entry into the World Trade Organization so that it would end its protectionist trade policies, allowing U.S. corporations full access to Chinese resources. The Pentagon was unhappy with this approach, which strengthened China both economically and strategically. As Walden Bello says, the Asia 2025 study "speaks volumes about the Pentagon's grim determination to counter any significant threat to U.S. strategic hegemony in Asia.[50]

Another Pentagon study, "The 2001 Quadrennial Defense Review," also concentrates on China. While it continues to reiterate the U.S. policy of maintaining the ability to fight two conventional wars simultaneously, it states that the threat from Iraq and North Korea are fading (negating the Rumsfeld theory that legitimizes Star Wars). The review emphasizes the so-called China threat, stating that China should be the new focus of the U.S. military force structure, including its troop deployments, weapons procurement, research, and development. This policy ensures ever-increasing funding for the Pentagon's budget.

But China uses its Peoples Liberation Army not for international purposes, but to alleviate domestic problems such as floods and fires, to quell internal disputes, such as Xinjiang and Tibet, and for border disputes. Land forces are currently being reduced by hundreds of thousands. Even if Taiwan declares independence and America attempts to back Taiwan in its move, resulting in armed conflict, China has virtually no amphibious forces able to attack Taiwan.[51] It would prefer to spend its resources caring for the needs of its 1.3 billion people, and it has little interest in weapons construction. The risk of killing fellow Chinese and of provoking economic isolation and military failure would most likely result in China's peaceful wooing of Taiwan instead. As Dr. Nicholas Berry, senior analyst at the Center for Defense information, writes, "Americans who see China as the new imperialistic threat need to review the historical record. Unless history is meaningless as a predictor of events, China will not seek an empire. As long as China's periphery is secure and no country is prepared to attack it, the PLA will carry out its internal and defensive tasks, including putting pressure on Taiwan not to leave the fold."[52]

In warning the Bush administration not to include Taiwan in any missile defense system, China urged the U.S. to desist from any arms sales to that country. "If the United States is bent on its plan to include Taiwan in its TMD system, it will constitute a wanton interference and threat to Chinese sovereignty and security," it said, meaning that if forced to by U.S. policy, it will arm itself appropriately to fight a militarily aggressive Taiwan. This statement was issued only hours after Colin Powell opined that China should not now be regarded as a "strategic partner" as it had been during the Clinton administration.[53]

The air force is, at this moment, upgrading its bases in Guam and on Wake Island in the Pacific to handle more B-1 and B-2 bombers. They are repositioning cruise missiles in Guam, and American TMD is being widely promoted throughout the region. The navy is expected to nearly double its presence in the Pacific within the next few years. The U.S. has assigned over 230,000 military personnel, including the Pacific fleet, to the region.[54] Leaked internal documents dated January 29, 1998, show that the U.S. naval security group command entered into a host-nation partnership at the joint-defense facility at Pine Gap in Australia, where they are currently monitoring movements and telecommunications traffic of warships and naval vessels from Pakistan, India, Indonesia, China, and North Korea. China, the dominant country in the South China Sea, the Taiwan Strait, and the Sea of Japan, is obviously of most interest to the U.S. and intelligence officials.[55]

AMERICAN GLOBAL IMPERIALISM

Charmers Johnson, in a new book, *Blowback: The Costs and Consequences of the American Empire,* argues that instead of demobilizing at the end of the cold war, "the U.S. imprudently committed itself to maintaining a global empire." He believes that it is time to discuss how the cold war helped to conceal an American imperial project, and that America should by rights remove itself from South Korea and from its military bases in Japan, while unilaterally drastically cutting its nuclear forces and declaring a no-first-use policy.

American historian Paul Kennedy calls U.S. global dominance "imperial overreach" and says that the maps of major U.S. force deployments around the world "look extraordinarily similar to the chain of fleet bases and garrisons possessed by that former great power, Great Britain, at the end of its strategic overreach.[56]

The British today are in a pickle.

Tony Blair worked well with Clinton, but he will be under particular pressure to cooperate with his new-look American allies, even while knowing that if he allows the Fylingdale radar station on the North York Moors National Park to be expanded for Star Wars, he will have a civil uprising on his hands.

Fylingdale neighbors realize that they will become one of the targets of America's mad plans. As retired geologist Peter Woods said, "If this installation became a target for hostile action, it would be like William the Conqueror all over again, who starved to death half the local population a millenium ago," on the North York Moors.

"Imagine us going to you and asking to put up a radar station in the middle of Yosemite National Park to protect Britain," Woods added. "Do you think the United States would just say, okay?"[57]

If Blair permits the Fylingdale station upgrade, plus another at Menwith Hill, he will be at odds with his European colleagues, and many within his own party. Since the summer of 2000, two white globes have been installed at Fylingdale, supposedly for tracking satellites.[58]

Inevitably these stations will be aggressively picketed by the Campaign for Nuclear Disarmament, Greenpeace, and the North Yorkshire branch of the Women's Institute, who are deeply concerned about the despoilation of the countryside. It will be Greenham Common all over again.*

France is an open opponent of NMD. During Bush's inauguration,

* Thousands of women set up camp at Greenham Common and staged protests during the eighties against the deployment of American cruise missiles on the Common; they prevailed and the missiles were removed.

French Defense Minister Alain Richard flew to Moscow for talks about the proposed U.S. NMD plan which Bush said would "provide protection for America's allies." [59]

French analyst Camille Grand said the NMD could stand for "no more disarmament." And French Foreign Minister Hubert Vedrine said that it is "not very serious" to think that states such as North Korea, Iran, Libya, or Iraq could threaten the world's only superpower, calling these threats microscopic or theoretical.[60]

According to Hugo Young of the *Guardian,* "A quiet turmoil of alarm has gripped the Foreign Office and the Ministry of Defense for months," in Britain. "They now face a Washington being peopled by voices that make a different analysis: scornful of Russia, arrogant about China, intolerant of European sensitivities, overwhelmingly impressed by the case for defending U.S. territory—and confident that the practical failure of NMD so far, like the untested capabilities of the boost-phase project, are mere blips on the relentless American path toward technological mastery."

If Blair decides to support NMD, Young says, it will create the deepest rupture with continental Europe.[61]

Greenland, a Danish protectorate, where another radar station at Thule will need upgrading, has said that the unproven concept of NMD will sow the seeds of global instability and pitch the country unwillingly into the center of a new cold war. The Thule station is also presently part of the U.S. early-warning system.[62]

Almost all European countries are adamantly opposed to any form of Star Wars, and are deeply concerned about the direction in which this new president is taking the world.

Meanwhile, Europe is uncomfortable about the way NATO is structured. During the Kosovo war, the Europeans had little say about how that conflict was conducted—America had sole access to most of the space-based information flow, deciding how and when the seventy-eight day operation would proceed.

Pre-September 11 Europe was fed up with its sycophantic position in relation to the U.S., which regularly ignored the United Nations and which intervened unilaterally in the Sudan, Afghanistan, and

Iraq without consulting its closest allies. When it did intervene with other nations, it took a military stand that allowed for no American casualties, which made it more a hindrance than a help. As the *Guardian* editorial said, "*Saving Private Ryan* has become the leitmotif of the whole operation."[63]

September 11 changed many of these dynamics. The whole world was appalled by the attacks upon America and a new international spirit of cooperation brought most nations of the world together to support America in its tragedy and time of need. Furthermore, new alliances were quickly formed to support the war in Afghanistan, and although much of the war was fought from the air causing many thousands of civilian casualties, eventually American troops were brought in at the end for "mopping up" operations.

Consequently, in November 2001, Europe decided to set up its own military and peacekeeping force, pledging 60,000 troops and its own equipment by 2003. The first European military initiative since the end of the cold war, it will involve additional military spending and will give the Europeans the ability to operate without the United States.

The United States is nervous that this EU (European Union) peacekeeping force may surpass and ultimately become more important than NATO—a move that Washington would strongly oppose.[64] Former secretary of defense William Cohen warned, "There will be no EU caucus in NATO. . . . If . . . they try to or are desirous of a separate operational planning capability, separate and distinct from NATO itself, then that is going to weaken ties between the U.S. and NATO and NATO and the EU."[65]

The Pentagon is not easily going to forego its European footing. On December 1, 2000, it released the strategy report for Europe and NATO, titled "Strengthening Transatlantic Security," which states that the U.S. will continue its reliance on deterrence as a cornerstone of security while maintaining a commitment to American nuclear forces in Europe. It calls for NATO enlargement, saying that "the U.S. military presence in Europe plays a critical role in protecting our economic interests."

It also states that, "overall the United States has embarked on its largest sustained increase in defense spending in fifteen years" and that they are planning the "execution of joint and multinational military operations in NBC (nuclear, biological, and chemical) environments. . . ." Referring to Russia, the report adds, "The transatlantic community cannot be truly secure if its enormous nuclear-armed neighbor, with its rich human and natural resources, withdraws behind a new curtain of hostility and authoritarian rule or collapses economically." (This provocative statement seems to go counter to President Putin's numerous conciliatory overtures to the United States and his overtures to rapidly reduce bilaterally the strategic arsenals.)

BUSINESS ARE US

The world has gone backward since 1987, when Reagan and Gorbachev sat in an intimate sitting room in a house in Reykjavik, Iceland, and almost agreed to eliminate nuclear weapons between the superpowers, an agreement that failed when Reagan refused to forgo his Star Wars project.

General Henry Shelton, the chairman of the Joint Chiefs of Staff, told Congress in September 2000 that the services would need significant increases in spending in the coming years, suggesting that this could consume a large part of the current budget surplus.[66] He endorsed a study from the congressional budget office that called for an increase in spending on new weapons from 60 billion dollars to 90 billion dollars annually. Bush has already pledged to spend 45 billion dollars more on the military over the next ten years, plus at least another 70 billion dollars on Star Wars.[67]

However, since the September 11, 2001 attack, the Pentagon and military-industrial complex have cynically used these terrible events to capitalize upon the trauma and despair of the American people and the Congress. Within days, Congress appropriated a 60-billion-dollar emergency spending package for reconstruction and combating terrorism. The greatest beneficiaries will be weapons manufacturers such as Raytheon and Lockheed Martin. Interestingly, among the very few companies that showed increased stock prices the week the market reopened on September 17 were Raytheon, up 37 percent, Alliant Tech Systems, up 23.5 percent, and Northrop Gromman, up 21.2 percent.

Star Wars corporations used this opportunity to push their wares on Capitol Hill with homilies such as "just because you have insurance against theft doesn't mean you shouldn't buy fire insurance." The democrats backed off their fight against NMD tests or other actions that would violate the ABM treaty in the wake of September 11. So compliant has the Congress become that Christopher Hellman from the Center for Defense Information suggested that military spending for 2002 could reach 375 billion dollars, a 66-billion-dollar increase over 2001, and some right-wing analysts such as Loren Thompson of the Lexington Institute suggested Congress may now be willing to push the Pentagon budget to 400 billion dollars per year, or more. The NMD program stands to benefit the most, followed by the scandal-plagued V22 Osprey aircraft made in Republican Representative Kurt Weldon's district in Pennsylvania, Lockheed Martin's F22 pushed by the Texas and Georgia delegations, Northrop Grumman's B2 pushed by Democratic Representative Norm Dicks from Washington and Republican Representative Randy "Duke" Cunningham from California at more than 2 billion dollars per plane. In the wake of the September 11 attacks the Bush administration is to accelerate weapons sales in the Middle East and South Asia, including Lockheed Martin F-16s to Oman and the United Arab Emirates, and other weapons systems to Egypt and Pakistan.[68, 69]

Under the banner *Business Are Us,* the Pentagon hosts a paper on their web site proclaiming that they are America's largest company, the next being Exxon with a budget of 165 billion dollars. With 5.1 million employees, the Pentagon is the nation's largest employer. It maintains 600 fixed facilities nationwide, with more than 40,000 properties and 18 million acres of land. It stations employees in 130 countries out of a total 178 of the world.[70] Its global presence is ubiquitous.

America is a nation that spends only six cents out of every dollar on educating its children and four cents on health care for every fifty cents it spends on the military-industrial complex.[71] Overall, the Pentagon's 310 billion dollars per year dwarfs the 44.5 billion dollars for the education department and 20.3 billion dollars for the National Institutes of Health.

Globally, the annual military expenditure stands at 780 billion dollars. The total amount required to provide global health care, eliminate starvation and malnutrition, provide clean water and shelter for all, remove land mines, eliminate nuclear weapons, stop deforestation, prevent global warming, ozone depletion and acid rain, retire the paralyzing debt of developing nations, prevent soil erosion, produce safe, clean energy, stop overpopulation, and eliminate illiteracy is only one third that amount—237.5 billion dollars.[72]

In his farewell speech in January 1961, President Eisenhower warned, "In the councils of government, we must guard against the acquisition of unwarranted influence, whether sought or unsought, by the military-industrial complex. The potential for the disastrous rise of misplaced power exists and will persist. We must never let the weight of this combination endanger our liberties or democratic process."

This book illustrates in detail that these prophetic predictions have come to pass. We need to put aside our need for superiority over others, our need to be militarily powerful. America has excellent skills at conflict resolution. These must be deployed.

The Pentagon needs to be virtually dismantled. Amalgamating with the United Nations, its military expertise needs to be used quietly and efficiently for peacekeeping operations around the world. (Currently there are sixty-eight low-intensity wars in the world demanding attention.)[73] After the September 11 terrorist attack on the United States there was much discussion about what the response should be. I carefully advocated during my U.S. lecture tour over the next two weeks that the international community should work cooperatively together, including all the intelligence organizations—MI5, MI6, Mossad, the FBI, CIA, NSA—to identify, locate, and capture these international terrorists and bring them to trial before an international court of justice, as were their predecessors, the Nazis.

It is not necessary for America to proclaim itself the most powerful and the greatest nation on earth. It needs to *demonstrate* these qualities. As Edmund Burke said two centuries ago, "the only way evil flourishes is for good men to do nothing."

It is up to the women and men of the world to act. I would therefore like to address the men and women of America:

You belong to the most powerful nation on earth, an immensely wealthy country, populated by people who want to live their lives with compassion and integrity. You have a great and noble task ahead of you. Each of you can be as powerful as the most powerful person who ever lived. If you or your child were threatened with a lethal disease, you would do everything in your power to save that life. This is the analogy that you must now apply to the planet and in particular to your country.

America has the power and resources to reverse global warming, to save the ozone layer, to prevent chemical pollution, to stop deforestation, to curb the human overpopulation problem, and to prevent the rape of space. The money that America invests in killing must now be redirected urgently to the preservation of life. America must rise to its full moral and spiritual height to reach its intended destiny—the nation that saved the world.

In a similar vein, the people of Europe must resist the constant call from America to arm and re-arm. So too, the people of Canada, of Australia—and indeed all the people of the world. We cannot continue to behave as primitive animals killing for pleasure, killing for money, killing for religious imperatives, killing for greed and territorial imperative. Conflict resolution and peacekeeping must be our new priorities.

Even after the catastrophe of September 11, 2001, it is still inappropriate to rush off and kill thousands of innocent people for revenge. The only reaction by a civilized nation should be, as mentioned above, to work together with the international community to bring these criminals to justice. Never forget that thousands of nuclear weapons remain continuously on hair-trigger alert. Any disturbance of the international situation could trigger their launch and cast us all into the pall of conflagration and nuclear winter.

You cannot simultaneously prevent and prepare for war. The very prevention of war requires more faith, courage and resolution than are needed to prepare for war.

—Albert Einstein

APPENDIX A: MAJOR U.S. NUCLEAR-WEAPONS MAKERS

Five of the six companies below are among the top ten Pentagon contractors for 2002. All of these firms, plus the University of California, are heavily involved in many aspects of nuclear-weapons work, including the U.S. missile defense program.

Boeing, Lockheed Martin, TRW (now Northrop Grumman), and Raytheon, the four companies with the majority of missile defense contracts, spent over 40 million dollars on lobbying expenses and campaign contributions *from 1998 to 2001 alone*[1] to guarantee that mega-billion-dollar Pentagon contracts for Star Wars and other weapons systems will keep coming. Missile defense spending is expected to surpass 8 billion dollars in the 2003 fiscal year, with costs of deployment over the next decade projected at 200 billion dollars—a bonanza for Boeing, Lockheed Martin, Northrop Grumman, and Raytheon. Northrop Grumman acquired TRW in 2002 to reap TRW's lucrative Star Wars contracts. With firms like Boeing having a staff of 250,000 worldwide and Lockheed Martin operating plants in all fifty U.S. states, the weapons industry has tremendous political influence in Washington, D.C. The defense industry contributed over 15 million dollars in the 2002 election cycle alone. Median CEO salaries at the largest thirty-seven weapons contractors rose by a staggering 79% between 2001 and 2002, according to a study by United for a Fair Economy.

For another look at companies making nuclear and conventional weapons, see the Dirty Dozen list produced in 2001 by Reaching Critical Will, a disarmament project of the Women's International League for Peace and Freedom, at www.reachingcriticalwill.org/dd/ddindex.html.

The U.S. was by far the top global weapons seller in 2002, with 45% of the world market, according to a congressional report, "Conventional Arms Transfers to Developing Nations, 1995–2002." Earning 13.3 billion dollars in its 2002 arms deals, the U.S. was particularly dominant in sales to so-called "developing" nations. To read about the new campaign by Amnesty International and Oxfam against the world arms trade, visit www.controlarms.org. For data on companies selling weapons around the world, see the Federation of American Scientists Arms Sales Monitoring Project website: www.fas.org/asmp.

Lockheed Martin Corporation

2000–02 Pentagon contract awards: $47,156,000,000
2002 lobbying expenditures (inclusive of non-military products and services): $6,260,000
2000–02 campaign contributions: $4,165,682

Headquarters:
Lockheed Martin Corporation
6801 Rockledge Drive
Bethesda, MD 20817
(301) 897-6000
www.lockheedmartin.com

Primary locations for missile-defense work:
Space Systems, Missiles & Space Operations
1111 Lockheed Martin Way
Sunnyvale, CA 94089
(408) 742-7151

Space Systems, Astronautics Operations
12999 Deer Creek Canyon Road
Littleton, CO 80127-5146
(303) 977-3000

Also doing missile-defense work at Eagan, MN site.

Notes: Lockheed Martin is the world's biggest weapons maker. In 2002, the company received 17 billion dollars in Pentagon contracts and another 2 billion dollars from the department of energy for nuclear-weapons projects. Lockheed Martin and Boeing are by far the largest overseas arms dealers, with Lockheed's most profitable export the F-16 combat plane. Lockheed Martin develops many components for missile defense. In Sunnyvale, California, the company builds the Trident II Submarine-

Launched Ballistic missile, a multiple-warhead missile deployed on the Trident submarine, and the only long-range U.S. nuclear missile presently manufactured. The firm was awarded a 589-million-dollar contract in 1999 for twelve more D5 nuclear missiles for Trident submarines. The government previously bought 372 D5s at nearly 60 million dollars each. Each Trident submarine can destroy an entire continent with nuclear weapons.

Lockheed Martin designs and makes nuclear warheads as the prime contractor for Sandia National Laboratories. At the Nevada Test Site, Lockheed Martin conducts "subcritical testing" of new nuclear-weapons designs. Through its subsidiary Sandia Corporation, the company manages the Sandia National Laboratory in Livermore, California and Kirtland Air Force Base in New Mexico. Along with Bechtel Nevada and other smaller companies, Lockheed Martin administers the Nevada Test Site. Eight members of the Bush administration were once directly or indirectly part of Lockheed Martin, whose new slogan is "We Never Forget Who We're Working For." The company has produced depleted uranium munitions and landmines. Lockheed Martin's profits soared by 36% just prior to the 2003 Iraq war, including a 15% increase just in military aircraft. The firm's F-117 stealth attack aircraft bombed "leadership targets" in Baghdad. Lockheed Martin makes the Hellfire and Patriot (PAC-3) missiles and the Paveway II bombs, all used in Iraq, as well as "bunker buster" weapons. To read more on the company's contribution to the 2003 "Shock and Awe" bombing of Iraq, go to www.actagainstwar.org/article.php?id=165. In March 2003, Lockheed Martin won a 100-million-dollar contract to make 212 PAC-3 missiles for use in Iraq, with plans to build 20 PAC-3s a month by 2005. "Homeland security" work is a lucrative new arena for the company. Lockheed Martin makes depleted uranium munitions, used in Iraq in 1991 and 2003, and in Afghanistan and Kosovo, and also manufactures anti-personnel landmines. "The Pentagon and United Nations estimate that U.S. and British Forces used 1,100 to 2,200 tons of armor-piercing shells made of depleted uranium during attacks in Iraq in March and April [2003]—far more than the estimated 375 tons used in the 1991 Gulf War," writes Larry Johnson in the *Seattle Post-Intelligencer*, August 4, 2003.

In May 2003, Lockheed Martin Mission Systems, along with Northrop Grumman Mission Systems, was awarded a contract to start designing equipment for streamlined nuclear-war planning, and also for nuclear-wartime communication equipment, for what the military sees as a 10-fold increase in the number of target requests by 2007. This contract is part of a 200-million-dollar, eight-year Pentagon program to enlarge and upgrade U.S. computer and telephone gear intended to function, and survive, all through a protracted nuclear war, consistent with the Nuclear Posture Review's commitment to "defeat any aggressor." See links to more information on the Nuclear Posture Review, and on the updated nuclear war plans, near the end of Appendix B.

For Star Wars, Lockheed Martin designed the current booster system, including Payload Launch Vehicles, at sites in Sunnyvale, California; Dallas, Texas; and Orlando, Florida. The firm is the prime contractor for the Space-Based Infrared System (SBIRS), which provides the missile-defense system with early warning of missile launches against the U.S. (the first test is slated for 2012). The Airborne Laser program in Sunnyvale tests beams of laser energy to destroy theater ballistic missiles hundreds of miles away. Lasers will be placed on 747 aircraft to zap medium-range ballistic missiles in their boost or ascent phases.

Lockheed Martin is also the prime contractor for the Theater High Altitude Area Defense (THAAD) system—a ground-based system intended to destroy medium to long-range ballistic missiles. The company expects THAAD to be deployed in 2007. So far, the THAAD system has failed in 6 out of 8 tests, but in 2002 Lockheed Martin was awarded a contract extension of up to 4 billion dollars to continue research and development on THAAD.

Lockheed, along with Boeing, Northrop Grumman, and Raytheon, is heavily involved with the U.S. Space Command in building military space systems to dominate, and fight wars, from space.

In 2001, Lockheed Martin was awarded the biggest defense department contract in history—200 billion dollars—to develop the F-35 high-tech Joint Strike Fighter plane, expected to become the main attack plane for the Air Force, Navy, and Marines for decades to come. The contract could grow to 400 billion dollars when foreign sales are added. Versions of the JSF will be made for the Navy, Air Force, and Marines, as well as for the United Kingdom.

In 1999, Lockheed Martin won an Air Force contract valued at up to 1.5 billion dollars over fifteen years to modernize and integrate command systems of the North American Aerospace Defense Command (NORAD) in Colorado, as well as the command and control systems of the Colorado Springs, Colorado-based U.S. Space Command, the Air Force Space Command, and other sites in the United States and abroad. The upgrade will link some forty separate air, space, and missile-defense command and control systems into a network with new capabilities to handle space warfare, according to Lockheed Martin.

In addition, Lockheed Martin has a 47-million-dollar Air Force contract to upgrade the AN/FPS-117 radar that supports the Atmospheric Early Warning System. These long-range surveillance radar systems are located at thirty-three sites from the far reaches of Canada and Alaska, as well as Iceland, Hawaii, and Puerto Rico, supported by an engineering facility at Hill Air Force Base in Utah.

Lockheed Martin, along with Boeing, makes the F-16 as well as the F-22, which, at more than 200 million dollars each, is the most expensive fighter plane ever built. At its plant in Grand Prairie, Texas, Lockheed Martin is building the Patriot missile, which uses kinetic energy instead of a warhead to destroy enemy missiles. The U.S. Army may order over 1,000 Patriots, with foreign countries also expected to order them.

In the 1970s, Lockheed admitted to paying 22 million dollars in bribes to win overseas contracts.[2] In 2001, Lockheed Martin had to pay a 4.25-million-dollar settlement agreement between the U.S. government and the company's Naval Electronics and Surveillance Systems division. Lockheed Martin used Foreign Military Sales (FMS) funds illegally in a contract to modify sonar systems used by Egypt.[3] Former Lockheed Martin vice president Bruce Jackson chairs the Coalition for the Liberation of Iraq, a group that was one of the primary instigators of the 2003 bombing of Iraq. Watchdog group: www.stoplockheed.org.

Management:
Vance Coffman, Chairman and Chief Executive Officer
2002 salary, including stock gains, bonuses, etc.: $25,337,000
Total 2000–02: $47,734,000
Source: Business Week, *April 21, 2003*
G. Thomas Marsh, President and General Manager, Space Systems Company, Space & Strategic Missiles (Sunnyvale, California)
Albert E. Smith, Executive Vice President, Space Systems (Littleton, Colorado)

The Boeing Company

2000–02 Pentagon contract awards: $47,721,000,000
2002 lobbying expenditures (inclusive of non-military products and services): $8,260,000
2000–02 campaign contributions: $3,019,725

Headquarters:
Boeing World Headquarters
100 North Riverside Plaza
Chicago, IL 60606-1596
(312) 544-2000
www.boeing.com

Primary locations for missile defense work:
Boeing
1421 Jefferson Davis Highway
Arlington, VA 22202
(703) 472-4000

Boeing
499 Boeing Blvd.
Huntsville, AL 35806
(256) 461-2121

Boeing's other missile-defense facilities are located in Houston, Texas; St. Louis, Missouri; Wichita, Kansas; Anaheim and Canoga Park, California; Kent, Washington; Colorado Springs, Colorado; Tucson, Arizona; Bedford, Massachusetts; and Ogden, Utah.

Notes: Boeing obtained over 16 billion dollars in Pentagon contracts in 2002, an increase from 13 billion dollars in 2001 and 12 billion dollars in 2000. As the prime contractor for missile defense, Boeing is responsible for the development and integration of program components, including the Ground-Based Interceptor, X-Band Radar, Battle Management Command, Control and Communication (BMC3) systems, Upgraded Early Warning Radar, and interfaces to the Space-Based Infrared System Satellites. The firm employs 3,760 people in missile defense, and received 9.1 billion dollars for missile defense in the budget for the 2004 fiscal year. Seventy percent of U.S. missile defense testing is done at Boeing Huntsville. (Northrop Grumman's facility in Colorado Springs is another major test site.) The Redstone Arsenal, according to award-winning investigative reporter Karl Grossman, is "up to its neck in Star Wars work and sits alongside NASA's Marshall Space Flight Center, which is developing a nuclear-propelled rocket for military and civilian operations."

According to Boeing's website, the firm makes the following missile defense components: Airborne Laser and Advanced Tactical Laser (precise, directed-energy, laser weapons system intended to shoot down ballistic missiles in the boost phase); Ground-Based Midcourse Defense (designed to detect, track and destroy intercontinental ballistic missiles); Patriot Advanced Capability-3 Missile (intended to accurately defend against short- and medium-range threats); Arrow (joint American and Israel co-production of a ground-based ballistic missile defense system designed to protect against short- and medium-range missiles); Avenger (U.S. army's line-of-sight, short-range, shoot-on-the-move system); and Divert and Attitude Control System (intended to position the Theater High Altitude Area Defense System missile to intercept its target).

Boeing leads the Airborne Laser (ABL) program (collaborating with Lockheed Martin and Northrop Grumman). The ABL program is intended to put laser weapons on modified Boeing 747 freighter jets to detect and destroy theater ballistic missiles in their boost stages. Boeing provides the 747-400F aircraft and command-and-control computer system for this project.

In 2001, Boeing completed a 3-million-dollar missile-defense test silo at its airport plant in Huntsville, ninety feet underground. According to a company spokesperson, "A wide array of information is needed by Boeing. . . . Engineers need to know what amount of stress the silo's concrete structure can withstand, and how silo doors will behave in sub-zero conditions. . . . We are going to have a special shroud built around the top of the silo, and then lower the temperatures to at least 30 degrees below zero. That's just to test the doors." Boeing is also building test silos at Vandenburg Air Force Base in California and two at Meck Island in the South Pacific. Boeing's Rocketdyne division in Canoga Park does research for hit-to-kill warheads for missile defense.

Boeing, along with Lockheed Martin, Northrop Grumman, and Raytheon, is heavily involved with the U.S. Space Command in building military space systems to dominate, and fight wars, from space.

For the 2001 bombing of Afghanistan, Boeing made joint direct-attack munitions, B-52 bombers, and B-1B Lancer long-range bombers. Each Lancer carries up to eighty conventional bombs, thirty cluster bombs, and twenty-four guided "smart" bombs. B-52s also dropped 40% of the "smart bombs" and precision-guided weapons on Iraq during the 1991 Gulf War (which killed an estimated 250,000 Iraqi civilians).

Boeing and Lockheed are the largest U.S. arms exporters, with 60% of Boeing's sales made to other nations such as Israel, Saudi Arabia, Turkey, Egypt, South Korea, and Taiwan. They make F-16 planes for Israel, as well as the infamous V-22 Osprey aircraft, involved in accidents that have killed at least thirty U.S. military personnel.

Boeing manufactures the F-15 Eagle, which the firm calls "the world's most sophisticated fighter plane." They also produce Joint Direct Attack Munitions (JDAMs), the "smart bombs" used in the 2003 bombing of Iraq and in Afghanistan, where 7,200 JDAMs were dropped. Boeing provides guidance systems for the Peacekeeper and Minuteman missiles.

In 1994, Boeing paid 75 million dollars in order to avoid criminal prosecution, which, at that time, was the largest non-criminal Pentagon payback case in government statements. The payment included 52 million dollars for computer-related work, overcharging on non-domestic government work, and 9 million dollars for hazardous-waste disposal costs.[4] In 2001, the justice department sued Boeing for purportedly hiding a subcontractor's billing fraud of several million dollars.[5] In 2000, Boeing had to pay 15 million dollars to settle a racial discrimination lawsuit on behalf of 12,000 present and 7,000 former African-American employees.[6] Despite this record, the Pentagon still designated Boeing the prime missile-defense contractor. The firm was awarded 38 billion dollars in "homeland defense" contracts in the 2003 fiscal year. Presidential advisor Karl Rove has owned up to 250,000 dollars in Boeing stock, based on his disclosure documents. Boeing funds the right-wing think tank Center for Security Policy, a major proponent of the need for missile defense and new nuclear weapons. Boeing's slogan is "Forever New Frontiers."

Management:
Philip M. Condit, Chairman and Chief Executive Officer
2002 salary, including stock gains, bonuses, etc: $4,145,000
Total 2000–02: $27,794,000
Source: Business Week, *April 21, 2003*
James W. Evatt, Senior Vice President and General Manager, Boeing Missile Defense Systems

Northrop Grumman Corporation

(incorporated weapons giants Litton Industries in 2001, and TRW in 2002)

2000–02 Pentagon contract awards: $24,264,000,000
2002 lobbying expenditures (inclusive of non-military products and services): $11,770,618
2000–02 campaign contributions: $1,668,550

Headquarters:
Northrop Grumman Corporation
1840 Century Park East
Los Angeles, CA 90067-2199
(310) 553-6262
www.northgrum.com

Primary location for missile defense work:
Northrop Grumman Space Technology
One Space Park
Redondo Beach, CA
(310) 812-4321

Notes: With its 2002 acquisition of TRW, Northrop Grumman is now a major missile defense contractor. The company makes a central component of missile defense: the Battle Management Command, Control, and Communications (BMC3) system, which links the computer systems that are supposed to differentiate between nuclear warheads and Mylar decoy balloons. Northrop Grumman is also making spacecraft, Tactical High-Energy Lasers, Airborne Lasers, Space-Based Lasers, and target launch vehicles, and doing Theater Missile Defense work.

Northrop Grumman operates the Joint National Test Facility, a major missile-defense test site in Colorado Springs, Colorado, that carries out realistic national and theater missile-defense simulations (war games). The company is collaborating with Raytheon on the Space-Based Infrared System (SBIRS) missile early warning system. Northrop Grumman's site in Capistrano, California, is building the megawatt-class Scud-killing laser. The firm is collaborating on the Space-Based Infrared System (SBIRS), designed to track missiles and relay data to destroy them before impact, with Lockheed Martin, Boeing, Litton TASC, Analex Corporation, and the Space Dynamics Laboratory of Utah State University. Northrop Grumman is also involved in the 7-billion-dollar Airborne Laser program. Seven members of the Bush administration are former officials, shareholders, or consultants of Northrop Grumman, whose company slogan is "Defining the Future."

Northrop Grumman, along with Lockheed Martin, Boeing, and Raytheon, is heavily involved with the U.S. Space Command in building military space systems to dominate, and fight wars, from space.

According to a 2003 company press release, Northrop Grumman will be manufacturing a "smart bomb rack assembly for the B-2 stealth bomber, allowing the B-2 to carry as many as 80 independently targeted, GPS-guided weapons, compared with its current capacity of 16. The B-2 is America's most advanced strategic conventional and nuclear long-range heavy bomber. The primary mission of the B-2 is to 'enable any theater commander to hold at risk and, if necessary, attack an enemy's warmaking potential, especially those time-critical targets which, if not destroyed in the first hours or days of a conflict, would allow unacceptable damage to be inflicted.' The B-2 is the only aircraft in history to combine intercontinental range, large payload, precision weapons and stealth technology—a combination that is revolutionizing air warfare. 'We can fly missions with impunity anywhere in the world from the heartland of America and return the same day' (Lt. Col. Jay De Frank). Northrop Grumman is the prime contractor with Boeing, Raytheon and General Electric as principal team members. Total value of the work, scheduled to run through the first quarter of 2006, is 31.7 million dollars."

Since 1997, Northrop Grumman's Mission Systems, based in Reston, Virginia, has been the chief manager of the nation's Intercontinental Ballistic Missile (ICBM) force, intended to ensure the effectiveness of the U.S. "nuclear deterrent force" through 2020. The contract's total value is 6 billion dollars. Subcontractors are Lockheed Martin and Boeing. For over 40 years prior to this position, Northrop Grumman provided engineering and technical assistance to the Air Force to help it manage the ICBM force. The company is involved in updating Minuteman II launch facilities and missile alert facilities through its Clearfield, Utah, facility, including the propulsion, guidance, and launch command systems. According to a company press release, "The Nuclear Posture Review, released by the Department of Defense last year [2002] as required by Congress, presents the direction for American nuclear forces over the next 10 years and reaffirmed the need for the Minuteman III through 2020. Since keeping missiles on alert is so essential, Northrop Grumman initiated processes for weapons assessment and risk management to anticipate and resolve potential problems before resulting in unacceptable system performance."

Los Angeles Times defense writer William Arkin reported in July 2003 that Northrop Grumman Mission Systems and Lockheed Martin Mission Systems are contractors for a 200-million-dollar Pentagon program to make indestructible equipment for planning nuclear war, and for communication during a nuclear war, consistent with the Nuclear Posture Review. See more information under "Lockheed Martin" above.

In addition to its nuclear-weapons work, Northrop Grumman is a major supplier of the weapons that were used to bomb Iraq, Yugoslavia, and Afghanistan. They make the infamous B-2 Stealth bomber or "B-2 Spirit," which cost 2.2 billion dollars each. Northrop Grumman has built 21 B-2s so far. Politicians like Senator Norm Dicks (D-Washington) and Senator Randy "Duke" Cunningham (R-California) have been attempting to renew the Stealth program by requesting funding for up to forty more planes.

Management:
Ronald D. Sugar, chief executive officer and president
2002 salary, including stock gains, bonuses, etc.: $5,278,000
Total 2000–01 [Kent Kresa, former CEO]: $14,705,000
Source: Forbes, *May 12, 2003;* Business Week, *April 21, 2003*
Wesley G. Bush, Corporate Vice President and President, Northrop Grumman Space Technology

Raytheon Company

2000–02 Pentagon contract awards: $19,537,000,000
2002 lobbying expenditures (inclusive of non-military products and services): $3,440,000
2000–02 campaign contributions: $1,755,432

Headquarters:
Raytheon Company
141 Spring Street
Lexington, MA 02421
(781) 862-6600
www.raytheon.com

Primary location for missile defense work:
Raytheon Missile Systems
1151 East Herman Road, Building 80707
P.O. Box 11337
Tucson, AZ 85706
(520) 794-3000

Notes: Raytheon is a major missile-defense provider. They are the prime contractor for the Exoatmospheric Kill Vehicle (EKV), the intercept element of the Ground-Based Interceptor, intended to find and destroy its target with kinetic energy, or hit-to-kill technology. Along with Boeing, Raytheon will continue to construct and try out the EKV for possible use in Star Wars. They build the missile-defense program's X-Band Radar and Upgraded Early Warning Radar, and make the radar sensor for the Theater High Area Altitude Defense (THAAD) system. Raytheon produces missiles for the Navy Theater-Wide program, and manufactures missiles for Navy Aegis destroyers to intercept long-range ballistic missiles fired from North Korea.

Raytheon, along with Lockheed Martin, Boeing and Northrop Grumman, is heavily involved with the U.S. Space Command in building military space systems to dominate, and fight wars, from space.

Raytheon's new CEO, William Swanson, along with former CEO Daniel Burnham, supplied the U.S. government with arms for illegal bombings of known civilian targets in Iraq, Kosovo, Serbia, and Afghanistan, according to the Massachusetts Anti-Corporate Clearinghouse. Raytheon makes Patriot air defense missiles. They manufacture Tomahawk cruise missiles, launched from Navy ships and submarines and used in bombing Iraq, Bosnia, Kosovo, and Afghanistan. Raytheon constructs the HARM missile that exploded and killed sixty-two civilians in a Baghdad market in the 2003 Iraq war. In conjunction with Lockheed Martin, Raytheon makes the Paveway II bomb, guided by sensors, also used in the 2003 Iraq war. Other Raytheon products include the "bunker buster" GBU-28 weapons, each 5,000 pounds, plus the Javelin, Maverick, and TOW missiles—all used in the 2003 bombing. The name "Raytheon" means "light from the gods." The firm is actively working on more than 4,000 weapons programs, according to its literature, in primary areas of missiles, defense electronics, and information systems.

Raytheon paid 4 million dollars in 1994 to settle a government charge that the firm inflated a 71.5-million-dollar antimissile radar defense contract.[7] In 1999, according to Reuters, Raytheon was forced to pay 3 million dollars to competitor AGES group and buy up 13-million-dollars worth of AGES aircraft parts to resolve the claim that Raytheon had hired a security company to spy on AGES and steal confidential documents, after the AGES Group was awarded a government contract formerly granted to Raytheon.[8] There have been allegations that Raytheon's lobbyists may have paid off a senator in 1995 to secure a 1.4-billion-dollar radar contract with Brazil.[9] Deputy Secretary of State Richard Armitage is a former Raytheon board member. Raytheon's slogan is "Customer Success is Our Mission."

Management:
William H. Swanson, president and chief executive officer (as of July 2003)
2002 salary [of former CEO Daniel Burnham], including stock gains, bonuses, etc.: $8,922,000
Total 2000–02 [Burnham]: $19,591,000
Source: Business Week, *April 21, 2003*
Louise L. Francesconi, vice president and general manager, Missile Systems

General Dynamics Corporation

2000–02 Pentagon contract awards: $17,583,000,000
2002 lobbying expenditures (inclusive of non-military products and services): 5,250,933
2000–02 campaign contributions: $2,521,115

Headquarters:
General Dynamics
3190 Fairview Park Drive
Falls Church, Virginia 22042-4523

(703) 876-3000
www.generaldynamics.com
www.gdeb.com/about (Trident information)
www.gdbiw.com (Bath Iron Works)
www.gdds.com (other weapons)

Five major weapons-development sites:
General Dynamics Electric Boat (builds Trident submarines)
75 Eastern Point Road
Groton, CT 06340-4989
(860) 433-3000

Bangor Trident Site
General Dynamics Electric Boat
P.O. Box 6519
Silverdale, WA 98315-6519
(360) 598-5100

Kings Bay Trident Site
General Dynamics Electric Boat
1040 USS Georgia Avenue
Kings Bay, GA 31547
(912) 882-6551

General Dynamics
Bath Iron Works
700 Washington Street
Bath, ME 04530
(207) 443-3311

General Dynamics Defense Systems
100 Plastics Avenue
Pittsfield, MA 01201
(413) 494-1110

Notes: At its large Electric Boat Division in Groton, Connecticut, General Dynamics produces the U.S. Navy's Trident and Seawolf nuclear submarines. One Trident is capable of incinerating an area the size of Russia. Owned by General Dynamics, Bath Iron Works makes the Aegis destroyer, a guided-missile warship, each bearing 56 nuclear-capable Tomahawk Cruise missiles, each of which can carry a 200-kiloton nuclear warhead. One Tomahawk cruise missile can carry the equivalent of 15 Hiroshima bombs, with each destroyer representing the bombing force of 840 Hiroshimas. Each Aegis costs 900 million dollars to 1 billion dollars, and over 38 have been built so far. The Aegis also holds 20mm Vulcan cannons, which can fire depleted uranium munitions. General Dynamics's company slogan is "Strength on Your Side." For the missile defense system, they are working on sea-based systems for the Navy's Aegis cruisers. General Dynamics makes traditional F-16 jets and Abrams tanks. According to the company's website, "major products include the Virginia-class nuclear-powered submarine, Arleigh Burke-class Aegis destroyer, Abrams M1A2 digitized main battle tank, the Stryker wheeled assault vehicle, medium-caliber munitions and gun systems, tactical battlefield communications systems. . . . In our test facilities are 21st century platforms and systems like the Marine Corps Advanced Amphibious Assault Vehicle (AAAV), Navy SSGN guided missile submarines and next-generation communication systems for the military and select commercial customers." General Dynamics makes surface-to-air and surface-to-surface missiles, part of the inventory on more than 100 Navy ships. The company sells many of its products overseas, including tanks to Egypt, Kuwait, Greece, Morocco, Oman, Thailand, and Taiwan. A former vice president of General Dynamics, Gordon England, is now Secretary of the Navy.

Management:
Nicholas D. Chabraja, chairman of the board and chief executive officer
2002 salary, including stock gains, bonuses, etc.: $15,245,000
Total 2000–02: $31,367,000
Source: Business Week, *April 21, 2003*
Michael W. Toner, executive vice president and group executive, Marine Systems; and president, Electric Boat Division

Bechtel Group, Inc.

2002 Pentagon contract awards: $1,300,000,000
2002 lobbying expenditures (inclusive of non-military products and services): $520,000
1999–2002 campaign contributions: $1,300,000

Headquarters:
Bechtel Group, Inc.
50 Beale Street
San Francisco, CA 94105-1895
(415) 768-1234
www.bechtel.com

Notes: Bechtel, the world's largest engineering firm, has been involved with nuclear weapons since the Manhattan Project. Bechtel Nevada (in conjunction with Lockheed Martin) is in charge of advanced nuclear-weapons assembly, testing, and diagnostics facilities at the Nevada Test Site as part of a $1.9 billion contract for the National Nuclear Security Administration. The Test Site is now carrying out subcritical nuclear tests, in opposition to the Comprehensive Test Ban Treaty. Bechtel Nevada also has contracts with NASA, the Defense Threat Reduction Agency, the Nuclear Regulatory Commission, and the U.S. Air Force, Army, and Navy. Bechtel Nevada works on the Stockpile Stewardship program to "upgrade" the U.S. nuclear-weapons stockpile.

The new Kwajalein ballistic missile defense test site in the Marshall Islands is managed by Bechtel and Lockheed Martin. With Boeing, Bechtel is working on design and construction for the Ground-based Midcourse Defense system. Bechtel designs facilities and systems for the Yucca Mountain nuclear waste dump in Nevada. The company developed the first atomic power plant, and is now the largest nuclear power company in the world, having built forty-five plants in the U.S. alone. Bechtel manages the Bettis Atomic Power Laboratory.

Bechtel National (BNI) and Jacobs Engineering have a five-year, 2.5-billion-dollar management and operations contract to manage the Oak Ridge Y-12 nuclear weapons plant (see more on Oak Ridge below). BNI has also managed other nuclear-weapons sites, such as the Idaho National Engineering and Environmental Laboratory, the Savannah River Site, the Mound Site, and Hanford (radioactive waste cleanup contract). In 2002, a Bechtel division secured a 202-million-dollar contract to build naval nuclear-propulsion components.

In 2003, Bechtel won a controversial 680-million-dollar contract to rebuild Iraq after the 2003 U.S. bombing of the country. The company has come under increasing fire for privatizing the water supply in Bolivia's largest city, Chochabumba, and raising the rates poor citizens pay for water by 50%. According to San Francisco-based Direct Action to Stop the War, "Bechtel stood by while the government of Bolivia killed people in the streets who protested Bechtel's water hikes. After the people prevailed and kicked Bechtel out, Bechtel is now suing Bolivia for 25 million dollars. One can only imagine what the people of Iraq will have in store for them."

A report by Dena Montague of the Arms Trade Resource Center states that "Bechtel built the first Indian nuclear plant at Tarapur, the largest nuclear facility in Asia. The construction of the nuclear plant allowed for the detonation of India's first atomic bomb using plutonium produced by the Tarapur reactor. Not only did Bechtel's activities help foster a nuclear arms race in South Asia that has had global implications, the plant also experienced major leaks, causing severe radiation exposure in the area. This toxic phenomenon affected many nuclear power stations built by Bechtel. In fact, by the 1970s the entire generation of reactor plants Bechtel began building in the late 1950s were not in compliance with minimum Atomic Energy Commission safety requirements."

Management:
Riley P. Bechtel, chairman of the board and chief executive officer
2002 salary, including stock gains, bonuses, etc.: not available
2002 estimated worth: $3.2 billion
Source: Forbes.com
Adrian Zaccaria, president, chief operating officer, director

Sources: The Center for Responsive Politics; Frida Berrigan, William Hartung, Michelle Ciarrocca and Dena Montague, Arms Trade Resource Center/World Policy Institute; Reaching Critical Will; MotherJones.com; SpaceDaily.com; U.S. Arms Sales page; Direct Action to Stop the War; Bruce Gagnon/Global Network Against Weapons and Nuclear Power in Space; Multinational Monitor; Steven Saples; Pratap Chatterjee; "The Real Rogues Behind Star Wars," by Rachel Ries, Rachel Glick, Tim Nafziger, Mark Swier, and Kevin Martin; Center for Defense Information; CorpWatch; Public Citizen; Global Exchange; United for a Fair Economy; War Profiteers.com; Bulletin of the Atomic Scientists; Stephen Schwartz; Jack and Fay Bussell/Maine Veterans for Peace

OTHER U.S. COMPANIES WORKING ON NUCLEAR WEAPONS (A PARTIAL LIST)

Alliant Techsystems, Alliant Missile Products, British Aerospace Electronics (BAE Systems), British Nuclear Fuels (BNFL), BWX Technologies, Computer Sciences Corporation, Dyncorp, Fluor Corp., General Atomics, General Electric, GenCorp (Aerojet Missile and Space Propulsion Unit), Honeywell Inc. (1.8-billion-dollar contract in 2000 to make components to maintain existing nuclear weapons), IBM, ITT L-3 Communications Holding, Logicon Software, Mason & Hanger-Silas Mason Company, Inc. (refurbishes stockpiled nuclear weapons and dismantles old warheads at the Pantex plant, in Texas), Mitsubishi, Science Applications International Corporation,* SI International, Siemens, Textron, United Defense (makes the Bradley fighting vehicles that fire depleted uranium shells), United Technologies, and Westinghouse Electric Company (warhead assembly).

* Number seven of the top 10 Pentagon contractors in 2002 (awarded 2.1 billion dollars), San Diego-based Science Applications International Corporation (SAIC) has many highly classified CIA and military contracts. Nuclear-weapons projects for the DOD and DOE include several missile defense initiatives as well as radioactive waste management at Yucca Mountain, NV (in collaboration with Bechtel). SAIC is also heavily involved in biological warfare work. Homeland Security is another specialty of SAIC. The firm conducts "AIDS vaccine research" at the U.S. Army base in Ft. Dietrick, MD. Because of SAIC's top-secret work, company employees joke that SAIC is CIA(S) spelled backwards. In 2003, SAIC joined Diebold, ES&S, and Sequoia as one of the companies designated by the Bush administration (and given billions of dollars) to computerize U.S. voting machines before the 2004 election. Each company has strong ties to the Bush administration. SAIC runs the Iraqi Reconstruction and Development Council, established in February 2003, and profits from redevelopment work post-U.S. bombing. The firm manages the Iraqi Media Network, whose commitment is to be "a new information ministry, complete with television, radio and a newspaper, and the content that would make all three attractive to average Iraqis." *(Sources: Washington Post, St. Petersburg Times, Progressive Review, Guerilla News.)*

U.S. NUCLEAR-WEAPONS LABORATORIES

Lawrence Livermore National Laboratory (LLNL)
7000 East Avenue
Livermore, CA 94550-9234
(925) 422-1100
www.llnl.gov
llnlweb@llnl.gov

Contractor: University of California Board of Regents for the U.S. department of energy. Major nuclear-weapons work such as the massive Stockpile Stewardship and Management Program, including the National Ignition Facility which may design fusion weapons. According to watchdog group Tri Valley CARES, LLNL designs four nuclear-weapons systems for the current U.S. stockpile: W87 and W62 intercontinental ballistic missile warheads, the B83 gravity bomb, and the W84 cruise-missile warhead. LLNL and Los Alamos National Laboratory (LANL) are the weapons development component of a "new strategic triad" for up to 15,000 "offensive" and "defensive" nuclear- and non-nuclear-weapons systems allowed under the Nuclear Posture Review. The Lab is planning to take over the testing of plutonium bomb cores for the U.S. arsenal; is seeking a permit from the California department of toxic substances control for a new 32-million-dollar radioactive waste treatment facility without an Environmental Impact Report; has begun work on a "Robust Nuclear Earth Penetrator" (explosive force of 75 kilotons, five times more than Hiroshima) and "mini nukes" (under-5-kiloton bombs); and may soon build a biological weapons facility. Regarding LLNL and LANL, Dan Stober in the *San Jose Mercury* (October 10, 2002) writes: "The 'design contest' between the two labs is intended to generate enthusiasm among their workers, who have engaged in a spirited nuclear competition for five decades." According to Michael I. Niman of *The Humanist* (March/April 2003), major media outlets in Europe obtained complete copies of the Iraqi weapons declaration in 2002, much of which was censored in the U.S. media after the Bush administration deleted 8,000 pages of the 11,800-page report. The missing material describes how between 1983 and 1990, Lawrence Livermore, Sandia, and Los Alamos Laboratories, as well as weapons contractors Bechtel, Hewlett-Packard, and Honeywell, among others, helped supply Saddam Hussein with weapons materials such as the makings of nuclear weapons (and instructions on how to use the components), botulinum toxins, West Nile fever virus, anthrax, and gas gangrene bacteria.
Director: Michael R. Anastasio

Sandia National Laboratories
1515 Eubank SE
Albuquerque, NM 87123 (main facility)
(505) 845-0011

7011 East Avenue
Livermore, CA 94550
(925) 294-3000
www.sandia.gov
gperri@sandia.gov (public affairs office)

Contractor: Sandia Corporation, a wholly owned subsidiary of Lockheed Martin Corporation, for the U.S. department of energy. Headquarters in Albuquerque with a smaller laboratory in Livermore. According to their website, "designs all non-nuclear components for the nation's nuclear weapons."
Director: C. Paul Robinson

Los Alamos National Laboratory
1663 Central Avenue, MS A117
Los Alamos, NM 87545
(800) 508-4400; (505) 665-4400
www.lanl.gov
cro@lanl.gov (public affairs office)

Contractor: University of California (UC) Board of Regents for the National Nuclear Security Administration. All nuclear weapons in the U.S. arsenal were designed by a UC employee at Lawrence Livermore or Los Alamos National Laboratory. "[T]he Laboratory continues to ensure the safety and reliability of the U.S. nuclear weapons stockpile" according to their website. Along with Lawrence Livermore, now working on 6 billion dollar a year of nuclear-weapons research, testing and production (not including delivery systems), including the B61 bomb and W80 cruise-missile warhead.
Director: George (Pete) Nanos

Oak Ridge National Laboratory
One Bethel Valley Road
Oak Ridge, TN 37831
(865) 574-4163
www.ornl.gov
mclaughlinmz@ornl.gov (public affairs office)

Contractors: Lockheed Martin, Bechtel National, Westinghouse Electric, and others. Produces nuclear-weapon components to support the design laboratories and the Nevada Test Site. See additional information below regarding the planned National Security Complex.
Director: Jeffrey Wadsworth

Nevada Test Site
c/o U.S. Department of Energy
Nevada Operations Office
Office of Public Affairs and Information
P.O. Box 98518
Las Vegas, NV 89193-8518
(702) 295-0944
www.nv.doe.gov
carter@nv.doe.gov (public affairs office)

Contractors: Lockheed Martin, Bechtel National, and others. The Nevada Test Site, where nuclear weapons have been tested since the 1960s, is located about sixty-five miles northwest of the city of Las Vegas, and is surrounded on three sides by the Nellis Air Force Range.
Manager: Kathleen Carlson
Source: Brookings Institution, Tri Valley CARES

For more information on the laboratories and who is managing the U.S. department of energy nuclear weapons complex, see the Brookings Institution website www.brook.edu/fp/projects/nucwcost/sites.htm. Also see a map and description of weapons facilities at www.stopthebombs.org/nuke/map.html.

HUGE NEW NUCLEAR-WEAPONS COMPLEX IN THE WORKS

Still grounded in a Cold War mentality, the U.S. department of energy in late 1998 announced plans for a new, patriotically titled "National Security Complex" in Oak Ridge, Tennessee. Oak Ridge is presently home to the Y-12 Plant, the last remaining full-scale operating nuclear-weapons factory in the U.S., and the Oak Ridge National Laboratory, which designs nuclear-weapons parts. Three Tennessee Valley Authority commercial nuclear reactors—Watts Bar Unit 1 (near Spring City, Tennessee) and Sequoyah Units 1 and 2 (at Soddy Daisy, Tennessee) —have been chosen as the "preferred" sites to manufacture tritium for U.S. nuclear weapons. The decision breaches the longstanding policy of not producing bomb material in civilian nuclear power plants. According to Robert Tiller of Physicians for Social Responsibility, "Our leaders are upset that Iraq might use civilian facilities to produce components for weapons of mass destruction, but the United States is now committed to do that very thing—turning a civilian reactor into a bomb facility." As the Oak Ridge Environmental Peace Alliance website states, "the U.S. nuclear arsenal is being rebuilt, one warhead at a time, at the Y-12 plant in Oak Ridge, Tennessee. Our bombs are being refurbished to last for 120 years, a violation of the Nuclear Nonproliferation Treaty."

The DOE Environmental Impact Statement for Oak Ridge describes the first step in building a new 4-billion-dollar bomb plant, allowing the U.S. government to do ten times more nuclear-weapons work than current levels and to start production of new nuclear weapons. Nearly 7 billion dollars for nuclear bomb production, an increase of nearly 9% over the previous year, has been included in the Bush administration's 2004 fiscal year budget.

Sources: William Hartung, Brookings Institution; Stephen Schwartz, Charles D. Ferguson, Bulletin of the Atomic Scientists*; Oak Ridge Environmental Peace Alliance; Ralph Nader; Associated Press*

NEW PLUTONIUM TRIGGER PLANT

As of 2003, the department of energy plans to build a new facility to make plutonium cores or triggers, called "pits," for the stockpile of U.S. nuclear weapons. The Modern Pit Facility would cost up to 5 billion dollars to construct and 300 million dollars a year to operate. According to the Alliance for Nuclear Accountability, the facility would "waste billions of taxpayer dollars, threaten global nuclear nonproliferation efforts, and create further environmental contamination and health risks for workers and community members." Supporters of the facility in Congress and the Bush administration say that a provision needs to be made to replace aging pits, while the DOE's own analysis shows no aging in pits similar to those in the current arsenal, and thus no need for designing new plutonium pits. Potential locations for the plant are Los Alamos National Lab, New Mexico; Nevada Test Site; Carlsbad Site, New Mexico; Savannah River Site, South Carolina; Pantex, Texas.

Sources: Alliance for Nuclear Accountability, Environmental News Service

APPENDIX B: U.S. NUCLEAR-WEAPONS CONTROL CENTERS, GOVERNMENT AUTHORITIES, AND NUCLEAR WAR PLANS

CHEYENNE MOUNTAIN OPERATIONS CENTER (CMOC)
Cheyenne Mountain Air Force Station
1 NORAD Road, Suite 101-213
Cheyenne Mountain AFS, CO 80914-6066
Located on the south side of Colorado Springs, CO
(719) 474-2238; (719) 474-2240
www.cheyennemountain.af.mil/cmoc

The computer surveillance center for nuclear war, headquarters of the early warning system. According to their web site, "ACMOC serves as the command center for both North American Aerospace Defense (NORAD) and United States Space Command (USSPACECOM). NORAD is the central collection and coordination center for a worldwide system of satellites, radars, and sensors that provide unambiguous, timely, and accurate air, space, missile, and nuclear detonation warning and attack assessments." In addition, according to the *Washington Times* (3/29/01), "The U.S. Space Command recently became the military unit in charge of preparing for cyber-battle, or what the Pentagon calls 'computer network defense' and its offensive counterpart, 'computer network attack.'" CMOC is the expected command center of any future U.S. missile defense system.

Director: General Ralph E. Eberhart, United States Air Force, Commander in Chief, North American Aerospace Defense Command

UNITED STATES STRATEGIC COMMAND (STRATCOM)
U.S. Air Force's Strategic Air Command (SAC)
Offutt Air Force Base, Nebraska
Next to the city of Bellevue and just south of Omaha
www.stratcom.af.mil
(402) 294-5961 (Public Affairs Office)

The command and control center for all U.S. nuclear warheads. According to STRATCOM's website, the Command's mission is "to deter military attack on the United States and its allies, and should deterrence fail, employ forces so as to achieve national objectives. The Command has responsibility for all U.S. Air Force and U.S. Navy strategic nuclear forces supporting the national security objective of strategic deterrence." STRATCOM provides "intelligence on countries and other entities possessing or seeking weapons of mass destruction" and develops "a Single Integrated Operational Plan that fully satisfies national guidance." In August 2003, Defense Department officials and U.S. government scientists met at STRATCOM (with the public and Congressional staff kept out) to discuss modernizing the U.S. nuclear arsenal to include smaller nuclear weapons for a variety of purposes, raising the risk of increased nuclear-weapons proliferation. See "Dr. Strangeloves Meet to Plan New Nuclear Era" (August 7, 2003) by Julian Borger of *The Guardian* at http://www.guardian.co.uk/usa/story/0,12271,1013690,00.html. The sessions coincidentally began and ended on the anniversaries of the August 6 and 9 bombings of Hiroshima and Nagasaki by the United States.

Director: Admiral Richard W. Mies, Commander in Chief, United States Strategic Command

PROJECT ELF
Clam Lake, WI 54517
No listed number; see directions to site below

Relatively unknown to the general public, Project ELF (Extremely Low Frequency Communication System) controls the U.S. Navy's Trident submarine first-strike communication system for nuclear war.

According to Nukewatch, "The Project ELF center is an essential part of the Navy's offensive nuclear-war plan, a one-way communications trigger for its nuclear-armed Trident and Fast-Attack submarines. It is designed to coordinate a massive coordinated multi-submarine attack by submarine-launched ballistic nuclear missiles. Each sub carries twenty-four extremely accurate 'Trident II' missiles with up to 192 thermonuclear warheads. Combined, the Tridents threaten the equivalent of over 80,000 Hiroshima-sized bomb blasts. About half the Tridents subs are at sea at any one time, with their warheads continually on 'alert' launch status.

"The Trident submarine fleet and its ELF activation constitute the costliest and deadliest weapon system in history. Total long-term costs for the Trident fleet are estimated at 155 billion dollars, with each of eighteen subs costing 1.9 billion dollars."

Project ELF location: From WI Hwy 77, go south 4 miles on County GG. Turn right on fire road 173 and go 2.9 miles. Then turn right again on fire road 176 and go .2 mile. The Project ELF front gate is on the right.

Source: Nukewatch

Two watchdog groups for more information: Nukewatch / Coalition to Stop Project ELF and Loaves & Fishes Catholic Worker. (See the antinuclear group list.)

JOINT DEFENSE SPACE RESEARCH FACILITY (PINE GAP)
Near Alice Springs, Australia

A controversial Central Intelligence Agency (CIA) satellite-tracking station, Pine Gap is heavily involved in U.S. nuclear war-fighting readiness. The southern hemisphere adjunct to NORAD in

Colorado, Pine Gap's space-based missile early warning and monitoring system is designed to confirm an attack on the U.S. and launch nuclear war.

Two of its ground antennae are part of the U.S. Defense Satellite Communications System. These antennae connect to geostationary satellites which detect tactical and intermediate range missiles, as well as intercontinental ballistic missiles. The data is relayed immediately to NORAD.

Employing nearly 1,000 people, mainly from the CIA and the National Reconnaissance Office, Pine Gap is one of the world's largest satellite ground control stations, with spy satellites that circle the globe. What little data is released to the public suggests that Pine Gap conducts massive espionage with these electronic eavesdropping satellites, intercepting telephone, radio, data links, and other communications. The Australian government's 1994 Defense White Paper reaffirms support both for U.S. nuclear weapons and Pine Gap's part in policing Asia and the Pacific to secure U.S. and Australian strategic and economic interests.

Pine Gap may also be used as a frontline base for a planned U.S. National Missile Defense tracking program, called SBIRS (Space-Based Infra-Red System) designed to be operational by 2004. *Flight International* magazine has disclosed that the U.S. and Australia plan not only to jointly run this aspect of the missile-defense system, but to construct a new test range in Western Australia. North of Broome, the range would allow the U.S. Navy to test ship-based antimissile systems. Simulated ballistic missiles would be launched from Australia, and—if the tests succeeded—quickly be shot down by the U.S. Navy.

Popular Australian Prime Minister Gough Whitlam, it is widely believed, was deposed in 1975 because of his plans to announce in Parliament that Pine Gap was run by the CIA and the CIA were extremely reluctant to have this information released.

Pine Gap and about thirty other sites make up the joint U.S.-Australia facilities. During a May 1992 visit, U.S. Defense Secretary (now Vice President) Dick Cheney confirmed that the U.S. bases in Australia had been used in the Gulf War. In 1991, U.S. newspapers reported that Pine Gap was instrumental in the tracking of guidance and trajectory of U.S. Patriot missiles

The U.S. is developing a combination of satellite and laser technologies that goes far beyond what was unleashed against Iraq in 1991. Plans to militarize and control space are outlined in a document called "Vision for 2020." The plan would require the development of ground-based antisatellite weapons (ASATs), space-based ASATs, and space-based earth strike weapons. These systems are controlled and coordinated by ground bases such as those in Pine Gap, Australia, the Marshall Islands and other countries.

THE PENTAGON
700 Army Navy Drive (visitor entrance)
Arlington, VA 22202
(703) 545-6700
To visit:
Director, Pentagon Tours
Room 1E776, 1400 Defense Pentagon

Washington, DC 20301-1400
(703) 695-1776
www.defenselink.mil/pubs/pentagon and www.dtic.mil/ref/html/welcome/wlcm.htm
tourschd.pa@sd.mil

The headquarters of the U.S. Department of Defense
Sources: John Pike, Federation of American Scientists Intelligence Resource Program; Jennifer Thompson; Ross Dowe; Duncan Campbell; Zohl de Ishtar; Andrew Clark, The Sunday Age

PRESIDENT GEORGE W. BUSH
President of the United States of America and Commander in Chief of the U.S. Armed Forces
The White House
1600 Pennsylvania Avenue
Washington, DC 20500
(202) 456-1414
fax: (202) 456-2561
president@whitehouse.gov

As Commander in Chief, he is in charge of nuclear weapons and nuclear war. In the book *Bush at War* by Bob Woodward, the president is quoted as saying his administration will "rid the world of evil" and will "export death and violence to the four corners of the earth in defense of this great nation." *Counterpunch* writer Michael Ortiz Hill reveals that Bush became friends with and was influenced by Dr. Tony Evans, pastor of a church in Dallas who is said to believe in the "End Time" (Armageddon). To read psychologist Oliver James's analysis of George W. Bush's behavior as president, go to www.guardian.co.uk/usa/story/0,12271,1033904,00.html.

VICE PRESIDENT RICHARD B. CHENEY
Vice President of the United States of America
The White House
1600 Pennsylvania Avenue
Washington, DC 20500
(202) 456-1414
fax: (202) 456-2561
vice.president@whitehouse.gov

Considered by many to be the senior authority in the White House along with Donald Rumsfeld, Cheney was secretary of defense under George Bush, Sr., and former president of the Halliburton Company, a major provider of goods and services to the oil industry. Halliburton, which continues to compensate Cheney, is profiting enormously from the 2003 Iraq war and its aftermath. Inter Agency Press Service stories by Jim Lobe in August 2003 reveal that Cheney, along with the Office of Special Plans under U.S. Undersecretary of Defense Douglas Feith, mobilized a network of neo conservative political appointees to push the nation to war, violating the inter-agency chain of command. Retired Lt. Col. Karen Kwiatkowski, who worked under Feith, calls the activity she observed "a subversion of constitutional limits on executive power and a co-optation through deceit of a large segment of the Congress." Cheney advocates preemptive use of nuclear weapons by the U.S. against "rogue nations," as expressed in the Nuclear Posture Review exposed in 2002. "The arrangement [for] the twenty-first century is most assuredly being shaped right now . . . the United States will continue to be the dominant political, economic, and military power in the world," Cheney informed *The New Yorker* in spring 2001.

DONALD H. RUMSFELD
Secretary of Defense
1000 Defense Pentagon
Washington, DC 20301-1000
(703) 692-7100
DOD comment line: (703) 697-5737
website to send an e-mail:
www.defenselink.mil/faq/comment.html#Form

Like vice president Cheney, an ardent proponent of preemptive use of nuclear weapons (Rumsfeld plotted numerous nuclear targets for the 2003 Iraq war "Theater Nuclear Planning Document," according to Daniel Ellsberg), missile defense and war in space. Supports the Hitleresque new U.S. policy of "full spectrum dominance". The Nuclear Posture Review, submitted to Congress on December 31, 2001 and co-authored by Rumsfeld states: "Nuclear weapons . . . provide credible military options to deter a wide range of threats. . . . Greater flexibility is needed with respect to nuclear forces and planning than was the case during the Cold War. . . . Nuclear-attack options that vary in scale, scope and purpose will complement other military capabilities." Key figure among the neoconservatives determining U.S. foreign policy. Rumsfeld told the Senate Foreign Relations Committee in July 2002 that "1,700 to 2,000 operationally deployed warheads . . . remain an important part of our deterrence strategy" to "dissuade the emergence of potential or would-be peer competitors by underscoring the futility of trying to reach parity with us." An October 27, 2002 *Los Angeles Times* story by William Arkin described an expansive group of secret Pentagon armies Rumsfeld recommends be installed around the world, the Proactive, Preemptive Operations Group (the P2OG or "Pee-Twos"). Arkin examined a classified document written by Rumsfeld about the objectives of the Pee-Twos to deliberately incite violence. "Among other things, this body would launch secret operations aimed at 'stimulating reactions' among terrorists and states possessing weapons of mass destruction—that is, for instance, prodding terrorist cells into action and exposing themselves to 'quick-response' attacks by U.S. forces," writes Arkin. Read *Counterpunch* writer Chris Floyd's piece on Rumsfeld's P2OG strategy to achieve U.S. political aims: www.counterpunch.org/floyd1101.html.

PAUL WOLFOWITZ
Deputy Secretary of Defense
1010 Defense Pentagon
Washington, DC 20301-1010
(703) 692-7150
DOD comment line: (703) 697-5737
web site to send an e-mail: www.defenselink.mil/faq/comment.html#Form

Another major influence on Bush administration foreign policy. A leading proponent of bombing Iraq. Favors nuclear weapons, pre-emptive war, and U.S. world domination. Paul Wolfowitz's once-shocking 1992 "Defense Planning Guidance" draft stated that the primary mission of the U.S. is to remain the only superpower in the world. The essence of this document is now embraced by the George W. Bush administration. "If there is a war, anywhere at any time, that Paul Wolfowitz has opposed: if there is a single concession he ever endorsed, even one instance where he speculated that any degree of mutual disarmament or easing of tensions ought to take precedence over military action and preparations for war, then it has gone unrecorded," writes columnist Justin Raimondo for antiwar.com.

RICHARD PERLE
American Enterprise Institute
1150 Seventeenth Street, N.W.
Washington, DC 20036
(202) 862-5849
Assistant: (202) 862-5855
Fax: (202) 862-7177
rperle@aei.org

Member (former Chairman) of the Defense Policy Board (civilian advisory group to the Pentagon). Key advisor to Defense Secretary Donald Rumsfeld. Also a key proponent of preemptive war on Iraq and other nations. Dubbed the "Prince of Darkness," and a hawkish believer in nuclear weapons. Assistant Secretary of Defense under President Reagan, 1981–1987. Known to have persuaded Reagan not to sign a comprehensive U.S./Russian nuclear disarmament treaty with Mikhail Gorbachev in 1986, in order for the U.S. to pursue its plans for a missile defense system.

JOHN BOLTON
Undersecretary of State for Arms Control and International Security
Office of the Undersecretary of State for Arms Control and International Security and Senior Advisor to the President and the Secretary of State for Arms Control, Nonproliferation, and Disarmament
Department of State
2201 C Street NW, Room 7208
Washington, DC 20520
(202) 647-1522

A key advisor for the president's nuclear-weapons policy. John Bolton's extreme right-wing views and opposition to nuclear disarmament inspired the *Boston Globe* to label Bolton, before his confirmation, "the Armageddon Nominee." There is concern that his outlook on nuclear-weapons policy and foreign relations could increase the likelihood of nuclear war.

COLIN POWELL
Secretary of State
Harry Truman Building
2201 C Street, NW
Washington, D.C. 20520
(202) 647-9572
website to send an e-mail:
http://contact-us.state.gov/index.html

As the powerful Chairman (1989–1993) of the Joint Chiefs of Staff under President George Bush, Sr., Powell was in command during the 1991 Gulf War, which killed an estimated 250,000 Iraqi civilians and exposed thousands of Iraqis and U.S. soldiers to depleted uranium. When questioned about how many Iraqis were killed in the U.S. air and ground attack, he said, " It's really not a number I'm terribly interested in." (*New York Times*, 3/23/1991) Recommended that Bush, Sr. invade Panama, a military action which resulted in between 1,000 and 4,000 deaths. Under fire with the George W. Bush administration for allegations of presenting false information to justify the 2003 Iraq bombing. According to investigative journalist John Pilger's report for British TV in fall 2003, Powell, speaking in Cairo in February 24, 2001 was captured on video saying "He [Saddam Hussein] has not developed any significant capability with respect to weapons of mass destruction. He is unable to project conventional power against his neighbors." Powell bragged in this footage that America's containment policy and sanctions had successfully disarmed the Iraqi leader. Considered more rational than other members of the Bush White House.

KARL ROVE
Senior White House Advisor
The White House
1600 Pennsylvania Avenue
Second Floor, West Wing
Washington, DC 20500
(202) 456-2369
president@whitehouse.gov

The authors of *Bush's Brain: How Karl Rove Made George W. Bush Presidential*, James Moore and Wayne Slater, say Karl Rove is the most powerful person in the U.S. Bush admiringly calls Rove "the man with the plan." An insider quoted in *Bush's Brain* says Rove is hell-bent on using the 2003 Iraq war to increase Bush's power: "It has to be the most evil political calculation in American history." Columnist David Podvin reported on a deal made before the 2000 election, whereby political advisor Karl Rove phoned Jack Welch, then chairman of General Electric (which owns NBC), to guarantee that the Bush administration, if elected, would scrap regulations on communications conglomerates, if in turn major media such as NBC would slant media coverage to favor, and help elect, George W. Bush. In 2003, the FCC, under Michael Powell (son of Colin) attempted to dismantle laws on media ownership so large monopolies could increase their holdings. Rove works to craft a favorable image of George W. Bush, including staging the 2003 photo session with Bush in a flight suit on an aircraft carrier after the bombing of Iraq. Representative John Conyers, Jr. called for Rove's resignation in 2003, Rove being the most likely suspect in the White House identity leak of Ambassador Joseph Wilson. Rove was a key behind-the-scenes player in the gubernatorial recall election which replaced Gray Davis with Arnold Schwarzenegger. Articles investigating Rove's influence on the California election:

www.commondreams.org/views03/1006–08.htm
www.commondreams.org/views03/0813–08.htm
www.buzzflash.com/analysis/03/08/08_recall.html

CONDOLEEZZA RICE
Assistant to the President for National Security Affairs
The White House
1600 Pennsylvania Avenue
First Floor, West Wing
Washington, DC 20500
President@whitehouse.gov
(202) 456-9491

A product of the conservative Hoover Institution, Rice formerly worked on nuclear strategic planning for the Joint Chiefs of Staff under a Council on Foreign Relations fellowship. She is another influential pro-war voice for the Bush administration. Australian journalist John Pilger's television report for British television in fall 2003 presented evidence that Condoleezza Rice knew Iraqi leader Saddam Hussein did not have weapons of mass destruction and was no threat, delegitimizing the 2003 bombing of Iraq. Pilger says that after the September 11, 2001 terrorist attacks, Rice stated the U.S. "must move to take advantage of these new opportunities" to bomb Iraq and control its oil. According to Pilger, in April 2001, Rice said of Hussein that "we are able to keep his arms from him. His military forces have not been rebuilt."

SPENCER ABRAHAM
Energy Secretary
U.S. Department of Energy
1000 Independence Ave., SW
Room 7A-257
Washington, DC 20585
(202) 586 6210; (800) dial-DOE
www.energy.gov
the.secretary@doe.gov

Manages the U.S. department of energy, which controls nuclear-weapons development. Abraham actively supports missile defense. A former Michigan Senator, he voted to eliminate up to 90 percent of the toxic chemicals industry must report, undermining a community's right to know. He also consistently voted for the "Mobile Chernobyl" bill to transport irradiated reactor fuel to Yucca Mountain, 65 miles from Las Vegas.

PROJECT FOR THE NEW AMERICAN CENTURY
1150 17th Street NW
Suite 510
Washington, D.C.
(202) 293-4983
www.newamericancentury.org

Highly influential right-wing think tank started in 1997 with members Dick Cheney, Donald Rumsfeld, and Paul Wolfowitz, advocating U.S. global domination by military force, among other core values. Their seminal warmongering document, "Rebuilding America's Defenses," can be viewed under "Defense and National Security" on the Project's website. The report, written in 2000, states that the U.S. needs a tragedy—"a new Pearl Harbor" as the writers describe it—to jump-start the right-wing strategy for U.S. military and economic world domination. See "The Widening Crusade" by Sydney Schanberg: www.villagevoice.com/issues/0342/schanberg.php. Watchdog group: www.pnac.info.

SINGLE INTEGRATED OPERATIONAL PLAN (SIOP): THE U.S. NUCLEAR WAR PLAN

A June 2001 report from the Natural Resources Defense Council provides an independent analysis of the U.S. nuclear war plan known as SIOP, or Single Integrated Operational Plan, which still guides U.S. first-strike, "winnable" nuclear war plans even after the Cold War. To read this report, go to http://www.nrdc.org/nuclear/warplan/index.asp.

NUCLEAR POSTURE REVIEW/STREAMLINED NUCLEAR WAR PLANNING

Revealed in early 2002 by *Los Angeles Times* defense writer William Arkin, the Pentagon's new Nuclear Posture Review drastically lowers the threshold for the use of nuclear weapons by the U.S. in a broad array of circumstances, such as whenever conventional weapons are considered insufficient for the administration's purposes. Seven countries are targeted in the Review, including Russia, China, Iraq, Iran, North Korea, Syria and Libya. The military is also streamlining nuclear war planning and making communication equipment that can operate during nuclear war, as part of a 200 million dollar project under the Nuclear Posture Review. Read Arkin's March 10, 2002 *Los Angeles Times* article exposing the Posture Review at http://www.latimes.com/news/opinion/la-op-arkinmar10.story. Highlights of the Review, as well as multiple reports and resources on the dangers of the Review, can be found at http://www.wslfweb.org/nukes/npr.htm. Read more on findings of the NPR at http://www.mapw.org.au/nuclear/usnuclearposture/us-npr-2002.pdf. Read a July 2003 *LA Times* story by Arkin about the "assured, survivable and enduring" nuclear war communications network at http://www.cndyorks.gn.apc.org/news/articles/newnuclearage.htm.

JOINT VISION 2020 AND "FULL SPECTRUM DOMINANCE"

The Pentagon published "Joint Vision 2020" in June 2000, designed to illustrate how the U.S. can retain its position as the dominant military power in the world. The document, describing strategies for "full spectrum dominance" (e.g., the capability to crush any enemy and dominate any condition using some form of military force) can be read as a Power Point presentation at http://www.dtic.mil/jointvision/baseline.htm

PROJECT FORCE APPLICATION AND LAUNCH FROM THE CONTINENTAL UNITED STATES (FALCON)

A July 2003 story in *The Guardian* (Manchester, U.K.) by Julian Borger described the Pentagon's plans for "a new generation of weapons, including huge hypersonic drones and bombs dropped from space, that will allow the U.S. to strike its enemies at lightning speed from its own territory. Over the next 25 years, the new technology would free the U.S. from dependence on forward bases and the cooperation of regional allies, part of the drive towards self-sufficiency spurred by the difficulties of gaining international cooperation for the invasion of Iraq. The new weapons are being developed under a program code-named FALCON (Force Application and Launch from the Continental U.S.)." Defense Research Advanced Projects Agency (DARPA) has released the contract for this new technology, which according to the Center for Defense Information "would theoretically allow the U.S. military to strike anywhere in the world without leaving American territory. . . . FALCON's ultimate goal is to develop 'a reusable hypersonic cruise vehicle (HCV) capable of taking off from a conventional military runway and striking targets 9,000 nautical miles distant in less than two hours,' according to DARPA's website." Components of FALCON may be tested as early as 2006, with possible full deployment by 2025. To read the contract for FALCON, go to http://www.darpa.mil/body/NewsItems/pdf/FALCONSolicitationDraftRev1.pdf.

Sources: Western States Legal Foundation, Center for Defense Information, Natural Resources Defense Council, No War Collective, Ken Coates

APPENDIX C: LOCATIONS OF THE MAJORITY OF USABLE U.S. NUCLEAR WEAPONS

The mainstay of the U.S. nuclear-weapons arsenal is found at the locations below, including weapons for both strategic and tactical systems. For more information on the balance of U.S. nuclear forces (including Tomahawks, B-52 bombers, and non-strategic nuclear weapons), see the analysis published in June 2003 by the Bulletin of the Atomic Scientists at http://www.thebulletin.org/issues/nukenotes/mj03nukenote.html.

1. NAVAL WEAPONS

Naval Base, Kings Bay, Georgia

Naval Base, Bangor, Washington

(Kings Bay and Bangor together house the sixteen Ohio-class nuclear-powered ballistic missile submarines that carry the Trident I C-4 and the Trident II D-5 missiles, now with a renewed service life of up to 44 years. These submarines carry 384 missiles with up to 2,880 operational warheads, altogether comprising about half of U.S. nuclear weapons.)

2. AIR FORCE WEAPONS

Nellis Air Force Base (AFB), Las Vegas, Nevada

Whiteman AFB, Knob Knoster, Missouri

Barksdale AFB, Shreveport, Louisiana

Minot AFB, Minot , North Dakota (has 150 Minuteman III missiles (up to three warheads) in silo field)

Malstrom AFB, Great Falls, Montana (has 200 Minuteman III missiles (max. three warheads) in silo field as well as storing old ICBMs)

F. E. Warren AFB, Cheyenne, Wyoming (has approximately 200 missiles—150 Minuteman III's (one warhead each) and 50 MX—in silo field shared with Colorado and Nebraska. All MX missiles will be deactivated in stages by 2005, but will be kept for redeployment or for space launch vehicles, and their silos will be retained.)

Kirtland AFB, Albuquerque, New Mexico

Notes: 107 missiles of the missiles noted above are kept as spares, and for testing and replacement. Minuteman IIIs are being upgraded as part of a 6-billion-dollar program to prolong their service beyond 2020. Minuteman IVs may be developed starting in 2004.

3. U.S. NUCLEAR WARHEADS OVERSEAS

There are approximately 150 B61 U.S. tactical nuclear bombs on nine NATO bases in Europe.

More information on locations of U.S. nuclear weapons can be found at the following web links:

"The U.S. Nuclear Weapons Production and Naval Nuclear Propulsion Complex," at www.brook.edu/fp/projects/nucwcost/sites.htm (updated August 2002) and "Bombs in the Backyard: Bases and Facilities with Significant U.S. Nuclear Weapons or Naval Nuclear Propulsion Missions," at www.brook.edu/fp/projects/nucwcost/basesize.htm (updated August 2002).

4. GLOBAL NUCLEAR WEAPONS

The locations of all nuclear weapons worldwide (as of 2002), including Russian, Chinese, British, French, Indian, and Pakistani weapons, can be viewed at www.nrdc.org/nuclear/nudb/datainx.asp.

Sources: Center for Defense Information; Nukewatch; Stephen Schwartz, Bulletin of the Atomic Scientists*; Natural Resources Defense Council; Quicksilver, the Brookings Institution and Bill Sulzman*

5. STORAGE SITES FOR NUCLEAR-WEAPONS MATERIALS

Pantex Plant
P.O. Box 30020
Amarillo, TX
(806) 477-3000
www.pantex.com
Storage location for a large amount of material recovered from weapons disassembled since 1992 in the form of so-called nuclear pits (triggers).

Department of Energy
Westinghouse Savannah River Company Site
Aiken, South Carolina
(803) 725-6211; (803) 725-3011
http://sro.srs.gov
Storage location for disassembled secondaries for thermonuclear weapons. Has produced nuclear materials since 1951.

Source: Center for Defense Information

6. KEY MISSILE DEFENSE TESTING AND RESEARCH SITES

Redstone Arsenal
U.S. Army Strategic Space and Missile Defense Command
106 Wynn Drive
Huntsville, AL 35807
(256) 955-5369; (256) 876-2151
www.redstone.army.mil
See more information under "Boeing" in the nuclear-weapons-company list.

Joint National Test Facility
730 Irwin Avenue
Schriever AFB, CO 80912-7300
(719) 567-9202
http://www.jntf.osd.mil/
jntf.info@jntf.osd.mil
Along with Redstone, a major missile defense test facility. According to their web site, "The primary project currently hosted by the JNTF-DC is Wargame 2000, a real-time, interactive, discrete event, command-and-

control missile defense simulation. Wargame 2000 is intended to provide a simulated combat environment that will allow war-fighting commanders, their staffs, and the acquisition community to examine missile and air defense concepts of operation (CONOPS)." Operated by TRW in collaboration with Boeing.

Vandenberg Air Force Base
Visitor Center, Building Number 1796
Vandenberg AFB, CA 93437
On Highway 1, 55 miles north of Santa Barbara, CA
(805) 606-7662
www.vafb.af.mil
A "launch site" for missile defense tests. See http://mocc.vafb.af.mil/launchsched.asp for the nuclear-weapons test schedule. Its website boldly proclaims that ruling space, "the ultimate high ground," will allow the U.S. to dominate all battlegrounds.

Space Command Headquarters
Peterson Air Force Base
Directorate of Public Affairs
Headquarters, U.S. Space Command
250 S. Peterson Blvd, Suite 116
Peterson AFB, CO 80914-3190
(719) 554-6889
www.cheyennemountain.af.mi
See more information in the nuclear weapons control center list.

Patrick Air Force Base/Cape Canaveral
Public Affairs
45 SW/PA
1201 Edward H. White II Street
Patrick AFB, FL 32925
(321) 494-1110
Located south of Cocoa Beach, Florida
The Cape physically tests the missiles and Patrick administers/directs them.

Los Angeles Air Force Base
The Space and Missile Systems Center
Office of Public Affairs
2420 Vela Way Suite 1467
El Segundo, CA 90245
(310) 363-0030
www.losangeles.af.mil
Directs the space-based laser program.

Kirtland Air Force Base
Public Affairs
1680 Texas Street SE
Kirtland AFB, NM 87117
(505) 846-0011 (operator)
(505) 846-5500 (Defense Threat Reduction Agency)
www.kirtland.af.mil
Home to the Defense Nuclear Weapons School and The Nuclear Weapons Product Support Center.

Missile Test Center
NASA Stennis Space Center
Stennis Space Center, MI 39529
(800) 237-1821
www.ssc.nasa.gov
Testing for missile defense conducted by Lockheed.
Note: Fort Greely and Kodiak Island in Alaska are slated to be part of a vast Pacific "test bed" meant to allow for more realistic intercept tests. At present, the only integrated tests of interceptors designed to shoot down long-range missiles are launched from a U.S. test range in the Kwajalein Atoll of the Republic of the Marshall Islands (the Reagan Test Site). Thule, Greenland is the site of a radar station that will be retrofitted if the missile defense program goes

ahead. (Denmark, which controls Greenland, will have to permit the upgrade.) Shemya Island in the Alaskan Aleutians is the location for a proposed missile-defense battle-management radar station and 100 interceptors. Radar in the U.S. (including at Cape Cod, Massachusetts and Beale Air Force Base, California) and Great Britain are scheduled for Star Wars upgrades. The Pine Gap CIA base in Australia may become a key site for missile-defense activity.

Source: Global Network Against Weapons and Nuclear Power in Space

APPENDIX D: MAJOR ANTINUCLEAR ORGANIZATIONS IN THE UNITED STATES, EUROPE, RUSSIA, JAPAN, AND SOUTH ASIA

What follows is by no means an exhaustive list. There are many local groups and general-focus organizations that are also committed to nuclear disarmament.

On the internet, two comprehensive lists of U.S. and international antinuclear groups can be found at http://prop1.org/prop1/azantink.htm and www.reachingcriticalwill.org/ngocontacts/contactsindex.html. For organizations working to end the missile defense program, see www.space4peace.org (click on "Links & Music"). A compilation of U.S., U.K., and international antiwar groups can be found at www.guardian.co.uk/antiwar/subsection/0,12809,884056,00.html.

Abolition 2000
c/o Pax Christi USA
532 West 8th Street
Erie, PA 16502 USA
(814) 453-4955
www.abolition2000.org
admin@abolition2000.org
A network of over 200 organizations in more than 90 countries working for a global treaty to eliminate nuclear weapons.

Alliance for Nuclear Accountability
322 4th Street, NE
Washington, DC 20002
(202) 544-0217
and
1914 N. 34th St, Suite 407
Seattle, WA 98103
(206) 547-3175
www.ananuclear.org
ananuclear@earthlink.net
Active national network of organizations working on issues of nuclear weapons production and waste cleanup. In April 2003, after meeting with Bush administration officials, exposed the existence of two secret Pentagon documents stating the "military requirement" for nuclear bunker busters and providing an "implementation plan" for the Nuclear Posture Review.

Antiwar.com
520 S. Murphy Avenue, #202
Sunnyvale, CA 94086
www.antiwar.com
egarris@antiwar.com
Web site updated daily with extensive international news coverage culled

from major and alternative media. Devoted to noninterventionism.

ARC Ecology
833 Market Street, Suite 1104
San Francisco, CA 94103
(415) 495-1786
www.arcecology.org
Focuses on the connection between military activities and pollution. Among many issues ARC brings to the forefront is that today the U.S. military produces more hazardous waste annually than the five largest international chemical companies combined. Other issues: environmental restoration and community building.

British American Security Information Council (BASIC)
110 Maryland Ave, NE, Suite 205
Washington, DC 20002
(202) 546-8055
and
The Grayston Centre
2nd Floor, 28 Charles Street
London, N1 6HT ENGLAND
+44 020 7324 4680
www.basicint.org
basicus@basicint.org;
basicuk@basicint.org
BASIC is an independent research organization that analyzes government policies and promotes public awareness of defense, disarmament, military strategy and nuclear policies in order to foster informed debate.

Bulletin of the Atomic Scientists
(Educational Foundation for Nuclear Science)
6042 S. Kimbark Avenue
Chicago, IL 60637
(773) 702-2555
www.thebulletin.org
bulletin@thebulletin.org
Covers international security and nuclear policy issues in an authoritative, thoughtful, and non-technical style that is easily accessible. Known worldwide as the keeper of the minutes-to-midnight "Doomsday Clock."

Campaign for Nuclear Disarmament (U.K.)
162 Holloway Road
London N7 8DQ
England
020 7700 2393
www.cnduk.org
enquiries@cnduk.org
Campaigns non-violently to rid the world of nuclear weapons and other weapons of mass destruction, including changing government policies to eliminate British nuclear weapons. Several chapters in the United Kingdom and Ireland. Largest U.K. peace group.

CampusActivism.org
http://campusactivism.org
Facilitates networking among progressive student/youth activists in the US and Canada. Linked with over 140 groups. Active in opposing the 2003 war on Iraq. Affiliate group National Youth and Student Peace Coalition (www.nyspc.net) organized student walkouts on 500 campuses nationally. Links to student groups at http://campusactivism.org/listgroups.php.

Center for Defense Information
1779 Massachusetts Avenue, N.W.
Washington, DC 20036-2109
(202) 332-0600
www.cdi.org
info@cdi.org

Retired military officers and experienced civilians working together to analyze military spending, policies, and weapons systems, and inform the public with unbiased facts and valid alternatives. Publishes *The Defense Monitor*. No weapons contractor funding.

Center for Economic Conversion
222 View Street
Mountain View, CA 94041
(650) 968-8798
www.conversion.org
cec@igc.org
Committed to helping build an economy that meets social needs and works in harmony with the environment.

Citizens Against Weapons of Mass Destruction
P.O. Box 45088
Omaha, Nebraska 68145-0088
Fax: 402-625-2923
www.SOS2003.com
info@sos2003.com
Organized August 2003 protest at STRATCOM, the U.S. nuclear command and control center, as senior Pentagon officials met (the Public and Congressional staff were excluded) to plan a new generation of nuclear weapons, including "low-yield" and earth-penetrating nuclear weapons (EPW), aka "bunker busters." To read more on the meeting, read the August 3, 2003 *New York Times* article at http://home.earthlink.net/~platter/articles/030803-broad.html.

Council for a Livable World
332 4th Street, NE
Washington, DC 20002
(202) 543-4100
www.clw.org
clw@clw.org
The Council for a Livable World, the Council for a Livable World Education Fund and PeacePAC are arms control groups committed to ridding the world of weapons of mass destruction and eliminating wasteful military spending. The Council and PeacePAC are also political lobbies which endorse political candidates

Earth Island Institute
300 Broadway, Suite 28
San Francisco, CA 94133
(415) 788-3666
www.earthisland.org
www.the-edge.org
earthisland@earthisland.org
Founded by veteran environmentalist David Brower, EII is involved in over 30 environmental projects worldwide to preserve and restore the natural world. *Earth Island Journal* (the first magazine on tree-free paper) and the new on-line newsmagazine *The Edge* often report on nuclear weapons issues. Do a search for "nuclear" on *The Edge* homepage to access all recent nuclear weapons stories.

ECODEFENSE!
Russia, 23600, postbox 1477
7-0112-437286
www.ecodefense.ru
Active Russian environmental and antinuclear groups. Click "Eng" on website for English homepage.

Environmentalists Against the War
P.O. Box 27
Berkeley, CA 94701
www.envirosagainstwar.org
Concerned about the disastrous human and environmental implications of the U.S. government war agenda, in Iraq and beyond. Website reports.

Federation of American Scientists
307 Massachusetts Avenue, NE
Washington, DC 20002
(202) 546-3300
www.fas.org
fas@fas.org
Monitors nuclear weapons, radioactive waste and arms sales.

Fourth Freedom Forum
803 North Main Street
Elkhart, IN 46514
800-233-6786 (main office)
and
11 Dupont Circle, Ninth Floor
Washington, D.C. 20036
(202) 393-5201 (D.C. office)
www.fourthfreedom.org
info@fourthfreedom.org
Encourages sanctions and economic incentives, coupled with the force of law, to eliminate nuclear and other weapons. Research, education, and public advocacy on nonviolent conflict resolution. Issue areas: tactical nuclear weapons (mini nukes), U.S./Russian disarmament, South Asian nuclear weapons. Newsletter several times a year.

Friends Committee on National Legislation
245 Second Street, NE
Washington, DC, 20002-5795
(202) 547-6000
In the U.S. (800) 630-1330
www.fcnl.org
fcnl@fcnl.org
A Quaker lobby in the public interest, committed to a world free of war and the threat of war.

Global Network Against Weapons and Nuclear Power in Space
P.O. Box 652
Brunswick, ME 04011
(207) 729-0517
www.space4peace.org
globalnet@mindspring.com
A major group coordinating efforts to stop the missile defense and space war programs. Working to keep space free of weapons and nuclear power. Sponsors conferences and actions at test sites. Coordinates activities with many U.S. and international groups. Web site is updated frequently and has many links and protest calendars.

Global Resource Action Center for the Environment (GRACE)/Nuclear Abolition Project
215 Lexington Avenue
Suite 1001
New York, NY 10016
(212) 726-9161
www.gracelinks.org/nuke/
grace@gracelinks.org
Addressing the toxic legacy of the nuclear age, GRACE works with Abolition 2000 to ban the bomb, and supports UN disarmament initiatives and new solutions for the health and environmental consequences of nuclear waste. Action alert email bulletin.

Global Security Institute
300 Broadway, Suite 26
San Francisco, CA 94133
(415) 397-6760
www.gsinstitute.org
info@gsinstitute.org
Works with politicians and the public to eliminate nuclear weapons. Founded by Sen. Alan Cranston (1914–2000).

Grandmothers for Peace International
P.O. Box 580788
Elk Grove, CA 95758

(916) 685-1130
www.grandmothersforpeace.org
lorraine@grandmothersforpeace.org
Activist group of women who realize that if things did not change, their grandchildren could be part of the last generation on earth. Members visit elected officials, circulate petitions, march, protest, give speeches, publish an international newsletter, and do civil disobedience (including being arrested). Over 20 chapters nationwide.

Greenpeace
702 H Street, NW
Washington, DC 20001
(800) 326-0959
www.greenpeace.org
greenpeace.usa@wdc.greenpeace.org
Worldwide environmental and peace group with offices on most continents. Greenpeace's campaign for a nuclear-free future includes educational programs and protest actions (highlighted on web site). Actively working to stop missile defense, new generations of nuclear weapons and nuclear power. On the website, click on "Campaigns" and then "Nuclear."

Green Party of the United States
P.O. Box 57065
Washington, D.C. 20037
(866) 41-green
www.gp.org/
info@greenpartyus.org
Political party and movement with many state chapters and local affiliates. Included in their platform and values is the abolition of nuclear weapons and non-violent conflict resolution, environmentalism and social justice. Website links to state parties and Greens throughout the world.

Hiroshima Peace Institute (HPI)
Hiroshima Mitsui Bldg.
12Fl. 2-7-10 Ote-machi
Naka-ku, Hiroshima 730-0051 Japan
81-82-544-7570
http://serv.peace.hiroshima-cu.ac.jp/English/index.html
office-peace@peace.hiroshima-cu.ac.jp
Engages in a variety of research activities relating to peace, inspired by the city's being the first city in the world to experience devastation by a nuclear weapon. Committed to complete disarmament of nuclear weapons and peaceful conflict resolution.

Institute for Energy and Environmental Research
6935 Laurel Ave., Suite 204
Takoma Park, Maryland, 20912 USA
(301) 270-5500
www.ieer.org
ieer@ieer.org
Focus: environmental and security aspects of nuclear weapons production and nuclear technology, ozone layer depletion and energy-related climate issues. Many reports on website.

International Depleted Uranium Study Team (IDUST)
PO Box 345
Saguache, CO 81149
www.idust.net
info@idust.net
Disseminates information and coordinates advocacy efforts worldwide to bring about a total ban on depleted uranium weapons. On homepage, under "Documents," reports numbers 4 and 5 contain numerous papers by Iraqi medical doctors and scientists who have documented the alarming human and environmental impact on Iraq of U.S.

depleted uranium bombs (also see reports on researcher Alaf Durakovis's Uranium Medical Research Center site, www.umrc.net). Links to other DU websites.

Indian Scientists Against Nuclear Weapons
www.isanw.org
contact@isanw.org
Working to halt and roll-back nuclear weaponization in South Asia. Initiated after Indian scientists signed a statement opposing Indian nuclear tests. Website has links, fact sheets.

Indigenous Environmental Network
P.O.Box 485
Bemidji, MN 56601
(218) 751-4967
www.ienearth.org/hotspots.html (nuclear campaign)
ien@igc.org
"An alliance of grassroots indigenous peoples working to protect the sacredness of Mother Earth from contamination and exploitation by strengthening, maintaining and respecting traditional teachings and natural laws."

Institute for Defense & Disarmament Studies
675 Massachusetts Avenue
Cambridge MA 02139
(617) 354-4337
www.idds.org
info@idds.org
Think tank focused on reducing the risk of war, minimizing military spending, and fostering democratic institutions. IDDS staff members study global policies needed to make organized armed violence rare and brief. Coordinates UrgentCall.org: For a Better Path to Security, a coalition-based effort to educate the public on security options in the wake of 9/11. Director Randall Forsberg (with Helen Caldicott, M.D. a leader of the 1980's nuclear-freeze movement), edits the *Arms Control Reporter*, a monthly reference work, and the annually updated IDDS Database: *World Arms Holdings, Production, and Trade.*

International A.N.S.W.E.R. (Act Now to Stop War & End Racism)
39 W. 14 Street, #206
New York, NY 10011
(212) 633-6646
and
2489 Mission Street., #28
San Francisco, CA 94110
(415) 821-6545
www.internationalanswer.org
info@internationalanswer.org (NY)
answer@internationalanswer.org (SF)
Coordinates actions to build an active global antiwar movement. A leading organizer of opposition (including massive protests in New York, Washington, and San Francisco) against U.S. military bombing of Iraq in 1991 and 2003, and in Kosovo and Afghanistan. Links militarism and corporate greed with struggles against racism and oppression throughout the world. Organization grew from the International Action Center, founded by former U.S. attorney general Ramsey Clark. Web site has calendar of worldwide events.

International Network of Engineer and Scientists for Global Responsibility (INES)
Gutenbergstrasse 31

44139 Dortmund
Germany
+49 30 44010498
www.inesglobal.com/
Hellmich.INES@web.de
Focuses on nuclear disarmament and international peace. Affiliated with the United Nations and with UNESCO as a Non-Governmental Organization (NGO). Network of over 90 member organizations in 40 countries. Affiliated groups: International Engineers and Scientists for Global Responsibility, www.inesap.org/news.htm; and International Network of Engineers and Scientists Against Proliferation, www.inesglobal.com.

International Physicians for the Prevention of Nuclear War (IPPNW)
727 Massachusetts Avenue
Cambridge, MA 02139
(617) 868-5050
www.ippnw.org
ippnwbos@ippnw.org
A non-partisan global federation of medical organizations dedicated to research, education, and advocacy relevant to the prevention of nuclear war. 1985 Nobel Peace Prize winner. Initiated from the work of Physicians for Social Responsibility under the leadership of Dr. Helen Caldicott.

Japan Council against A & H Bombs (GENSUIKYO)
2-4-4 Yushima, Bunkyo-ku
Tokyo 113-8464
03-5842-6034
www10.plala.or.jp/antiatom/html/e/e.htm
antiatom@topaz.plala.or.jp
Since its founding in 1955, has worked for the prevention of nuclear war, elimination of nuclear weapons, and relief and solidarity with A and H Bomb victims in Japan and the world. Organizes annual World Conference Against A and H bombs, which attracts hundreds of delegates.

Lawyers' Committee on Nuclear Policy (LCNP)
211 East 43rd Street
New York, NY 10017
(212) 818-1861
www.lcnp.org
lcnp@aol.com
Works on many global initiatives to rid the world of nuclear weapons.

Los Alamos Study Group
2901 Summit Place NE
Albuquerque,NM 87106-2028
505-265-1200
www.lasg.org
gmello@lasg.org
Focuses attention on the plans of the Los Alamos National Laboratory and other components of the nuclear establishment. Issue areas include mini nukes, Stockpile Stewardship, nuclear waste and radiation contamination. Obtained a Pentagon document, confirmed in 2003 by the National Nuclear Security Administration, outlining government plans for new mini nukes and "bunker buster" nuclear weapons.

Military Toxics Project
P.O. Box 558
Lewiston, ME 04243
1-877-783-5091 toll free
www.miltoxproj.org
www.miltoxproj.org/staff/staff.htm

Committed to uniting activists, organizations, and communities to clean up military pollution and prevent toxic and radioactive pollution caused by military activities, including depleted uranium.

Mothers Alert
c/o Citizens Energy Council
P.O. Box U
Hewitt, NJ 07421
www.mothersalert.org
mothersalert@yahoo.com
Dedicated to providing information on the links between increased radiation in the environment and health. Active in many campaigns to stop nuclear power, including the Tooth Fairy project, showing very high levels of strontium 90 in baby teeth.

Movement in India for Nuclear Disarmament
www.angelfire.com/mi/MIND123/
mind123@angelfire.com
Committed to universal disarmament, the end of Indian and Pakistani nuclear testing, and no production and deployment of nuclear weapons in South Asia. Website has articles on South Asian nuclear issues. Website has links to other South Asian antinuclear groups.

MoveOn.org
www.moveon.org
Internet-based organization working to bring ordinary people back into politics. Catalyzes growing grassroots network of more than 2,000,000 online activists on many issues, including opposition to the Iraq war, demanding government accountability for the war, and in gauging support for presidential candidates (Gov. Howard Dean, M.D. "won" their on-line poll and become a prime contender). Sends action alert petitions on a regular basis to its email subscribers.

National Gulf War Resource Center, Inc.
8605 Cameron Street, Suite 400
Silver Spring, MD 20910
800-882-1316 x 162
www.ngwrc.org/
hq@ngwrc.org
International coalition of advocates and organizations providing a resource for information, support, and referrals for all those concerned with the complexities of Persian Gulf War issues, including Gulf War illnesses and their possible link to depleted uranium.

National Network To End The War Against Iraq
http://endthewar.org
Nation-wide coalition of over 140 organizations against the bombing and subsequent illegal occupation of Iraq by the U.S. Active toward bringing the Bush administration to justice for the illegal and unjustified 2003 war. Website has many actions, and includes a moving counter (Cost of the War in Iraq).

Natural Resources Defense Council (NRDC)/Nuclear Program
40 West 20th Street
New York, NY 10011
(212) 727-2700
www.nrdc.org/nuclear/default.asp
For more than 25 years, NRDC has played a major role in the formation of U.S. nuclear nonproliferation, arms control, energy, and environmental policies. Committed to applying envi-

ronmental laws to U.S. nuclear and national security programs, and to the reduction and elimination of nuclear weapons and power.

Nevada Desert Experience
P.O. Box 46645
Las Vegas, NV 89114-6645
(702) 646-4814
www.nevadadesertexperience.org
nde@igc.org; sallight1@earthlink.net
Calls for ending the destruction and for repairing the damage caused by U.S. and U.K. nuclear testing on Western Shoshone land at the Nevada Test Site. Sponsors gatherings. Also working to stop shipments of radioactive waste to the Site, 60 miles from Las Vegas.

A Non-Nuclear South Asia
http://members.tripod.com/~no_nukes_sa/
southasia_peace@yahoo.com
Web page devoted to establishing a South Asia (India, Pakistan, Sri Lanka, Nepal, Bangladesh and Bhutan) free of nuclear weapons or energy.

Not In Our Name
www.notinourname.net
Helped coordinate national protests during 2003 Iraq war. Holds that "if we're going to be able to STOP what's happening and have a chance at another future, we need a movement of resistance that dares to alter the course of history. We need a resistance movement powerful enough to send a message to the people of the world that we stand with them against . . . unlimited war." Email updates.

Nuclear Age Peace Foundation / Abolition 2000
PMB 121, 1187 Coast Village Road, Suite 1
Santa Barbara, California 93108-2794
(805) 965-3443
www.wagingpeace.org; www.abolition2000.org
wagingpeace@napf.org; admin@abolition2000.org
Committed to the abolition of all nuclear weapons and other weapons of mass destruction, and to promoting peaceful conflict resolution.

Nuclear Control Institute
1000 Connecticut Avenue NW, Suite 410
Washington, DC, 20036
(202) 822-8444
www.nci.org
nci@nci.org
Monitors nuclear activities worldwide and pursues strategies to halt nuclear arms, particularly eliminating atom-bomb materials—plutonium and uranium—from nuclear power and research programs.

Nuclear Information Resource Service
1424 16th Street NW, # 404
Washington, DC 20036
(202) 328-0002
www.nirs.org
nirsnet@nirs.org
Conducts many campaigns against nuclear power and radioactivity.

Nuclear Policy Research Institute (NPRI)
1925 K Street NW, Suite 210
Washington, DC 20006
(202) 822.9800
www.nuclearpolicy.org
info@nuclearpolicy.org
Educates the American public through

the mass media about the medical, environmental, political and moral consequences of nuclear weapons, power and waste. Places experts from the military, science, politics, journalism and academia on television and radio, and into print and on-line media. NPRI exposure in 2002–2003 included Fox News, *Washington Post, Larry King Live, Washington Journal, Wolf Blitzer Reports,* NPR, Pacifica Radio, *Oprah, New York Times, Los Angeles Times,* and Associated Press. Convened first-ever conference on the medical effects of depleted uranium in 2003. In January 2004, presented prominent international experts in Washington, D.C. for "The Impending Nuclear War," a three-day symposium exploring the implications of U.S. and Russian nuclear warheads still on hair-trigger computer alert, risking a global holocaust, as well as dangers of nuclear conflict among other nations. Website is updated daily with nuclear news, offers weekly nuclear news email bulletin, and includes reports from prior conferences. Founder and president is Helen Caldicott, M.D., also founding president (1978–83) of Physicians for Social Responsibility (PSR). Executive director is Charles-Sheehan Miles, Gulf War veteran, founder of the National Gulf War Resource Center.

The Nuclear Threat Reduction Campaign (An Initiative of the Vietnam Veterans of America Foundation and The Justice Project)
1725 Eye St., NW, Fourth Floor
Washington, DC 20006-2412
http://justice.policy.net/ntrc/
(202) 483-9222
ntrc@vi.org
Works on eliminating threats by nuclear, biological and chemical weapons in the hands of other nations, as well as pursuing reductions in the U.S. nuclear arsenal. Supports taking nuclear weapons off U.S. and Russian weapons off hair-trigger alert.

Peace Action
1100 Wayne Ave., Suite 1020
Silver Spring, MD 20910
(301) 565-4050
www.peace-action.org
kmartin@peace-action.org
Large grassroots peace and disarmament organization in the U.S., committed to the abolition of nuclear weapons and redirection of excessive Pentagon spending to domestic investment. 27 state chapters.

Physicians for Social Responsibility
1875 Connecticut Ave, NW
Suite 1012, Washington, DC 20009
(202) 667.4260
www.psr.org
psrnatl@psr.org
Works to create a world free of nuclear weapons, global environmental pollution, and gun violence. Over 30 chapters in the U.S. Under the direction of past president Dr. Helen Caldicott, PSR membership expanded to over 20,000.

Project On Government Oversight
666 11th Street NW, Suite 500
Washington, DC 20001
(202) 347-1122
www.pogo.org
pogo@pogo.org
Exposes weapons contractor ripoffs and inadequacies in weapons systems, among other issues. Came to promi-

nence in the early 1980's when the group questioned wasteful military expenditures such as 7,000 dollar coffee pots. Works with and helps protect corporate whistleblowers who come forward with incriminating data.

Proposition One Committee
P.O. Box 27217
Washington, DC 20038
(202) 462-0757
www.prop1.org
prop1@prop1.org
A grassroots voter initiative movement for disarmament of nuclear weapons and the conversion of the arms industries to human and environmental needs.

Reaching Critical Will
c/o WILPF UN
6th Floor, 777 UN Plaza
New York, New York 10017
(212) 682-1265
www.reachingcriticalwill.org
info@reachingcriticalwill.org
Works to centralize and disseminate information about intergovernmental meetings that discuss nuclear weapons and their elimination, and coordinates efforts with non-governmental organizations to promote nuclear disarmament, nonproliferation, and the Comprehensive Test Ban. Believes nuclear disarmament is inevitable, and reflects majority opinion. Extensive fact sheets (including nuclear weapons contractor profiles) and atomic bomb history chronologies on website.

Shundahai Network
1350 E. Flamingo, Box 255
Las Vegas, NV 89119
(702) 369-2730
www.shundahai.org
shundahai@shundahai.org
Formed at the Nevada Test Site in 1994 by long-term nuclear disarmament activists, at the request of Corbin Harney, a Western Shoshone spiritual leader. International network of activists and organizations integrating the environmental, peace and justice, and indigenous land rights communities. Affinity groups: Western Shoshone Defense Project, (702) 468-0230, and Western Shoshone National Council, (702) 879-5203.

South Asians Against Nukes
www.mnet.fr/aiindex/NoNukes.html
aiindex@mnet.fr
Active website raising awareness of nuclearization in India and Pakistan. Indian and Pakistani activists who "challenge the nuclear jingoism and war hysteria constantly launched by both our governments." News on Indian and Pakistani nuclear weapons and nuclear power issues updated frequently. Links to other South Asian antinuclear groups.

Tri-Valley CAREs (Communities Against a Radioactive Environment)
2582 Old First Street
Livermore, CA 94550
(925) 443-7148
www.trivalleycares.org/
marylia@earthlink.net
Founded in 1983 by local citizens concerned that nuclear weapons work at the Lawrence Livermore and Sandia Livermore Laboratories was poisoning their communities. Website offers extensive reports and fact sheets on current nuclear programs. Working to stop Stockpile Stewardship, mini nukes, nu-

clear testing and a biological weapons facility at the Livermore facility. Monthly newsletter and action alerts. Coordinates Livermore Lab protest events.

TUC Radio
P.O. Box 410009
San Francisco, CA 94141
(415) 861-6962
www.tucradio.org
tuc@tucradio.org
Produces weekly national radio program on planetary well-being and the impact of globalization heard on over 100 stations. Archive of over 400 programs—many feature environmental and antinuclear themes (including speeches by Dr. Helen Caldicott, missile defense expert Bruce Gagnon, and nuclear laboratory authority Jacqueline Cabasso).

Union of Concerned Scientists
2 Brattle Square
Cambridge, MA 02238
617-547-5552
www.ucsusa.org/global_security
www.thebulletin.org
ucs@ucsusa.org
Working toward changes in U.S. policy to allow deep cuts in nuclear forces and to reduce the alert status of nuclear missiles. Also has global food, environment and clean energy programs. Publishes *Bulletin of the Atomic Scientists.*

United For Peace And Justice
(212) 603-3700
www.unitedforpeace.org
www.unitedforpeace.org/contactus.php
Coalition of more than 650 local and national groups throughout the United States opposing the U.S. government's policy of permanent warfare and "empire-building." Co-coordinated U.S. protests during the 2003 Iraq war, including 500,000 people at the United Nations. Active website and email alert bulletin. Organizing major protests at the Republican Convention in New York and worldwide on August 29, 2004, "The World Says No to Bush" (see www.unitedforpeace.org/article.php?id=1810.)

United Nations Institute for Disarmament Research (UNIDIR)
Palais des Nations
1211 Geneva 10
Switzerland
+41 (0)22 917 31 86
www.unidir.org
unidir@unog.ch
Inter-governmental organization within the UN founded on the belief that peace and security for all peoples will only be possible through disarmament. Conducts research to assist the international community in their and security thinking. Based in Geneva, home of the Conference on Disarmament.

Veterans for Common Sense
www.veteransforcommonsense.org
sethrpollack@veteransforcommonsense.org
Provides balance in debate over war and national security dominated by public servants who have never served in uniform by providing perspective of war veterans. Website has daily news items re: effects of war on troops, realities of U.S. policies overseas.

Veterans for Peace
World Community Center
438 N. Skinker
St. Louis, MO 63130
(314) 725-6005
www.veteransforpeace.org
vfp@igc.org
Non-profit 501(c)(3) educational and humanitarian organization dedicated to the abolishment of war. Founded in 1985 by ex-service members committed to sharing the horrors they experienced.

The Video Project
P.O. Box 77188
San Francisco, CA 94107
1-800-4-PLANET (1-800-475-2638)
www.videoproject.org
video@videoproject.net
Distributes the largest collection of nuclear disarmament-oriented videos to schools, groups, individuals. Also offers many environmental videos. Run by Act Now Productions.

VoteToImpeach.org
www.votetoimpeach.org
www.impeachbush.org
Coordinating activity to impeach President Bush for illegal and unjustified 2003 Iraq war. Through national ad campaigns and on-line petition signed by over 300,000 people, has given significance to the impeachment issue. Started by former U.S. attorney general Ramsey Clark, who drafted the articles of impeachment (which can be read on-line). Affiliated with International ANSWER (see above).

Washington Peace Center
1801 Columbia Rd., NW, Suite 104
Washington, DC 20009
(202) 234-2000
www.washingtonpeacecenter.org
wpc@igc.org
Has played a significant role in the antinuclear movements of the 1970s and was a key player in the Central America and Middle East solidarity movements of the 1980s. Today, the Peace Center plays a critical role in organizing opposition to U.S. militarism in Iraq, Afghanistan, and elsewhere. Also addresses organizing for economic and social justice (nationally and internationally) toward establishing structures and relationships that are nonviolent, non-hierarchical, humane and just.

Western States Legal Foundation
1504 Franklin Street, Suite 202
Oakland, CA 94612
(510) 839-5877
www.wslfweb.orgwslf
webmaster@wslfweb.org
A non-profit, public interest organization which monitors, analyzes, and challenges nuclear weapons programs at the Livermore, Los Alamos, and Sandia National Laboratories and the Nevada Test Site. Missile defense, new weapons facilities, "mini nukes" and nuclear testing are among many issue areas.

Women Against Military Madness (WAMM)
310 East 38th Street, Suite 225
Minneapolis, MN 55409
(612) 827-5364
www.worldwidewamm.org
wamm@mtn.org
A nonviolent feminist organization working to dismantle systems of militarism and global oppression.

Women's Action for New Directions
691 Massachusetts Avenue
Arlington, MA 02476
(781) 643-6740
www.wand.org
info@wand.org
Mission: To empower women to act politically to reduce militarism and violence and to redirect excessive military spending to human and environmental needs. Weekly e-mail nuclear political action alert bulletin to members, as well as a quarterly newsletter. Supports women political candidates who support WAND objectives. Over 30 U.S. chapters. Founded by Dr. Helen Caldicott. Working to stop the U.S. from developing low-yield nuclear weapons and building a nuclear version of the bunker-buster weapon, as well as opposing missile defense.

Women's International League for Peace and Freedom (WILPF)
1213 Race Street
Philadelphia, PA 19107
(215) 563-7110
www.wilpf.org/disarm/disarmnew.htm
wilpf@wilpf.org
Working to achieve through peaceful means world disarmament, full rights for women, racial and economic justice, and an end to all forms of violence. Dismantling the War Economy Campaign helps to expose the military-industrial complex. Weekly disarmament and military budget email action alerts.

World Policy Institute / Arms Trade Resource Center (ATRC)
New School University
66 Fifth Avenue, 9th Fl.
New York, NY 10011
(212) 229-5808
www.worldpolicy.org/projects/arms/
berrigaf@newschool.edu
ATRC does original research, public education, and policy advocacy on the problem of conventional arms proliferation. Many projects focused on nuclear weapons, global arms sales, stopping terrorism, etc.

A FOUNDATION THAT DONATES TO ANTINUCLEAR CAUSES

Ploughshares Fund
Fort Mason Center
Bldg. B, Suite 330
San Francisco, CA 94123
(415) 775-2244
www.ploughshares.org
ploughshares@ploughshares.org
A public grantmaking foundation that supports initiatives for stopping the spread of weapons of war, from nuclear arms to land mines. Funds over 130 programs, many of them focused on reducing the nuclear threat.

VOTER FRAUD RESOURCES

The following websites offer information on the dangers of computerized voting machines which leave no paper trail. Some of these sites raise concerns about the validity of the 2003 California recall election results. The Bush administration is heavily involved in the computerization of U.S. voting systems before the 2004 election.
www.blackboxvoting.org
(or under www.talion.com/blackboxvoting.org.htm)

www.ecotalk.org/votingsecurity.htm
www.markcrispinmiller.blogspot.com/
www.notablesoftware.com
www.votescam.com
http://scoop.co.nz/mason/features/?s=usacoup
www.gregpalast.com (click "Theft of Presidency")
www.votefraud.org
www.commondreams.org/headlines03/1013-01.htm (article)

WEBSITES MONITORING THE RELIGIOUS RIGHT

A December 2001 *Washington Post* article by Dana Milbank illuminated the Christian Right's role in the George W. Bush White House: www.commondreams.org/headlines01/1224-02.htm. See also www.democraticunderground.com/articles/02/04/03_policy.html. These websites monitor the political influence of the radical religious right, many of whom believe in Armageddon:

www.againstbombing.com/ArmageddonUpdates.htm
www.theocracywatch.org (click on "Middle East")
www.angelfire.com/ny5/dvera/CoEvan/ReligRight.html

Articles on Armageddon preacher/nuclear proponent Pat Robertson's financial dealings:

www.theperspective.org/patrobertson_taylor.html
www.gregpalast.com/detail.cfm?artid=49&row=1

ANTINUCLEAR RESISTANCE GROUPS UNITED STATES AND GREAT BRITIAN

In the nonviolent tradition of Martin Luther King, Jr., Mahatma Gandhi and Rosa Parks, these groups work to end the nuclear threat by incorporating civil resistance to bear witness or consciously disrupt the nuclear war machine. Defending their actions under international law, many activists risk arrest and jail sentences to prevent the crime against all humanity that is a nuclear holocaust. General antinuclear groups also engage in civil resistance as the circumstances merit. Gandhi looked into the future after the U.S. bombed Hiroshima, and anticipated the U.S. might someday face nuclear terror akin to the destruction it has unleashed: "A slave holder cannot hold a slave without putting himself or his deputy in the cage holding the slave," he said.

Members of many religious faiths, including indigenous peoples, Christians, Muslims, Jews and Buddhists, have come together to oppose nuclear weapons and work for their elimination.

Many Catholic Worker group houses in the U.S. support local and national resistance to nuclear weapons in addition to their tradition of hospitality to the poor.

The work of Rosalie Bertell, Roman Catholic nun, scientist and internationally recognized expert on low-level radiation, has documented how more than 1.3 billion people have been killed, sickened or maimed by nuclearism over the past 60 years, and how pollution released from nuclear weapons operations has drastically changed the global environment and endangers all life forms.

Plowshares (or Ploughshares) groups are faith-based activists who, in the spirit of Bible passage, *Isaiah* 2:4, are willing to hammer on launch computers and pour their blood on missile silos and pray until arrested, and be sent to prison, in some cases for long periods of time. Rev. Phillip Berrigan (1923–2002), who started the Plowshares movement, spent the last three and a half decades of his life focused on passionate opposition to nuclear weapons, "the taproot," he said, of the violence in America. He predicted that "the people of Iraq, Yugoslavia [and] Afghanistan . . . will be battling cancer, mostly from depleted uranium, for decades." Among Berrigan's last words were: "I die with the conviction . . . that nuclear weapons are the scourge of the earth; to mine for them, manufacture them, deploy them, use them, is a curse against God, the human family and the earth itself." For information about Plowshares groups and their actions, see www.plowsharesactions.org.

[Katya Komisaruk; Jack Cohen-Joppa, *The Nuclear Resister;* Bonnie Urfer; Bruce Gagnon, Global Network Against Weapons and Nuclear Power in Space; Ground Zero Center for Nonviolent Action and many other groups helped compile this list].

Aldermaston Women's Peace Camp
07904 450 307
http://aldermastonwpc.gn.apc.org
info@aldermaston.net
Conducts a monthly peace-camp at AWE Aldermaston in Berkshire, England. A women-only campaign, committed to stop the production of Britain's nuclear weapons at AWE Aldermaston, and to see the site shut down and safely decommissioned.

Alliant Action
(651) 698-9352; (651) 698-2810
www.circlevision.org/alliantaction.html
alliantaction@circlevision.org
Focus: Weekly vigils at Minnesota's

largest military contractor and war merchant Alliant Techsystems (affiliated with Lockheed Martin), doing missile defense work in Eagan, MN. Alliant makes depleted uranium munitions widely used in Iraq and its CEO earned $16,800,000 in the last year.

Brandywine Peace Community
P.O. Box 81
Swarthmore, PA 19081
(610) 544-1818
www.geocities.com/brandywinepeace/index.htm
brandywine@juno.com
Focus: Lockheed Martin, the world's largest weapons corporation and the major U.S. nuclear weapons contractor.

Buddhist Peace Fellowship
P.O. Box 4650
Berkeley, CA 94704
(510) 655-6169
www.bpf.org
bpf@bpf.org
Many Dharma centers and local practice groups campaign against nuclear weapons and nuclear waste, including actions at weapons locations and the Nevada Test Site.

Campaign for the Accountability of American Bases (CAAB)
8 Park Row
Otley, West Yorkshire
LS21 1HQ, England, U.K.
+44 (0)1943 466405
www.caab.org.uk
anniandlindis@caab.org.uk or caab@btclick.com
A campaign opposed to weapons of mass destruction in general and nuclear weapons in particular the U.S. missile defense system. Focus: American bases in the U.K. and abroad.

Catholic Worker Movement, The
www.catholicworker.org
Catholic Worker communities in Duluth, Norfolk, Des Moines, Los Angeles, Sacramento, Tacoma, Washington, D.C., Milwaukee, Chicago, New York, Raleigh, and many other cities are very involved in opposing nuclear weapons, including participating in nonviolent resistance (see website chapter directory). Founded by pacifist Dorothy Day, who was arrested "with others [who] refused to take shelter during civil defense drills that simulated a nuclear attack on New York City," according to their website, while "she and a group of women fasted for ten days in 1963 in Rome, at Vatican Council II, wanting the bishops to condemn all war. They did condemn nuclear war."

Christian Campaign for Nuclear Disarmament
162 Holloway Rd
London, N7 8DQ
England
(+44) 207 700 4200
http://ccnd.gn.apc.org/
ccnd@gn.apc.org
Provides a focus for Christians who want to witness on the basis of their faith against nuclear weapons and other weapons of mass destruction, while also positively campaigning for peace.

Citizen Weapons Inspections
www.motherearth.org/nuke/inspection.php
www.nonviolence.org/nukeresister/nr112/citizeninspections.html
Perspective: Without a recognized

means to enforce international law against weapons of mass destruction, individuals are responsible for identifying the sites and elements of weapons that represent crimes against humanity. Website includes coalition contact information.

Citizens for Peace in Space
P.O. Box 915
Colorado Springs, CO 80901
(719) 389-0644
Focus: U.S. Space Command (Colorado Springs, CO). Very active in stopping missile defense.

Direct Action to Stop the War
(415) 820-9649
www.actagainstwar.org
dasw@riseup.net
Leads protests and supports San Francisco Bay area resistance actions at corporate war profiteers, such as Bechtel, Lockheed Martin, the Carlyle Group, Citigroup and ChevronTexaco. Provides nonviolent resistance trainings. Website has corporate fact sheets, up-to-date event information, and a direct action handbook.

Earth First!
P.O. Box 3023
Tucson, AZ 85702
(520) 620-6900
www.earthfirstjournal.org
collective@earthfirstjournal.org
Billing itself as the "radical environmental journal," this bimonthly printed magazine features articles on the "no-compromise environmental movement," people who put themselves on the line for old-growth forests, for endangered species, against genetically modified foods, opposing corporate "free trade" treaties and against nuclear weapons, among many issues of concern. Perspective: "Today is the most critical moment in the . . . history of life on Earth. Never before has there been such an intense period of extinction as we are now witnessing, such a drastic reduction in the biological diversity of this planet. . . . We believe in using all the tools in the tool box, ranging from grassroots organizing and involvement in the legal process to civil disobedience and monkeywrenching."

Fellowship of Reconciliation
P.O.B. 271
Nyack, NY 10960
(914) 358-4601
www.forusa.org
Conducts nonviolence training. Works to urge nuclear disarmament and action for justice on many issues. Website has many resources. Peacemaker Training Institute helps young people become more effective peace and justice activists; trainings held across the country.

Global Network Against Weapons and Nuclear Power in Space
[see earlier group list]
Helps coordinate many protest actions, particularly related to missile defense and war in space.

Ground Zero Center for Nonviolent Action
16159 Clear Creek Road NW
Poulsbo, WA 98370
(360) 779-4672; (360) 377-2586
www.gzcenter.org
info@gzcenter.org
Focus: Bangor Submarine Base, the Pacific home for Trident submarines, and

witnessing to and resisting all nuclear weapons.

Healing Global Wounds
P.O. Box 420
Tecopa, CA 92389
(760) 852-4175
hgw@scruznet.com
Focus: Nuclear weapons testing and its impact on Native Americans

Jonah House
Baltimore, MD
(410) 233-6238
disarmnow@erols.com
Focus: Plowshares activism against nuclear weapons.

Livermore Conversion Project
POB 31835, Oakland, CA 94604
(510) 663-8065
Focus: Lawrence Livermore Laboratory

National War Tax Resistance Coordinating Committee
P.O. Box 150553
Brooklyn, NY 11215
(800) 269-7464
nwtrcc@nwtrcc.org

National Trident Resistance Network
(203) 777-3849
skobasa@snet.net
Focus: Trident missiles on submarines.

The Nuclear Resister (magazine)
P.O. Box 43383
Tucson AZ 85733
(520) 323-8697
www.nonviolence.org/nukeresister
email: nukeresister@igc.org
Information about and support for imprisoned antinuclear and antiwar activists.

Nukewatch/Coalition to Stop Project ELF
P.O. Box 649
Luck, WI 54853
(715) 472-4185
www.nukewatch.com
nukewatch@lakeland.ws
Focus: Project ELF, the launching system for Trident nuclear submarines. Collaboration of several antinuclear groups. Offers workshops and training in nonviolence and civil resistance.

Oak Ridge Environmental Peace Alliance (OREPA)
P.O. Box 5743
Oak Ridge, TN 37831
(865) 483-8202
www.stopthebombs.org
orep@earthlink.net
Focus: Oak RidgeY-12 nuclear weapons plant

Peace Action New Mexico
226 Fiesta Street Suite F
Santa Fe, NM 87501
(505) 989-4812
lanlaction@igc.org
Focus: Los Alamos National Laboratory

Peace Park Antinuclear Vigil
http://prop1.org [click on "Peace Park"]
Outside the White House 24 hours a day since June 3, 1981.

Raytheon Peacemakers
c/o Martha Gagliardi & Hattie Nestel
P.O. Box 248
Athol, MA 01331
(978) 249-9400
mgagliardi@arrsd.mec.edu
P.O. Box 43383
Tucson, AZ 85733

(520) 323-8697
nukeresister@igc.org
Focus: Weapons giant Raytheon

South Bay Mobilization
480 North First St,
Suite 205
San Jose, CA 95112
(408) 998-8504
www.southbaymobilization.org
sbm@southbaymobilization.org
Coalition of groups opposing U.S. war policies and attacks on civil liberties. Website offers many resources and event listings, as well collection of reports on global warming. Joined local affinity groups to protest Lockheed-Martin's Sunnyvale Trident missile facility (where over 50 people were arrested during the 2003 Iraq war). Affiliated website: www.stoplockheed.org.

Trident Ploughshares 2000 (United Kingdom)
42-46 Bethel Street
Norwich NR2 1NR
United Kingdom
01324 880744
www.tridentploughshares.org
tp@gn.apc.org
Focus: Trident submarines in the U.K.

War Resisters League
339 Lafayette Street
New York, NY 10012
(212) 228-0450
www.warresisters.org
wrl@igc.apc.org
Advocates Gandhian nonviolence to create a democratic society free of war and oppression. Publishes *The Nonviolent Activist* (readable on-line). Over 40 local chapters. Organizes yearly Day Without The Pentagon nationwide to educate about the impact of a weapons economy. YouthPeace campaign counters militarism and the culture of violence it perpetuates.

APPENDIX E: MEDIA

1. Finding Nuclear News

For daily nuclear news, see the website of the Nuclear Policy Research Institute (NPRI), www.nuclearpolicy.org. NPRI also offers a free weekly nuclear news bulletin. The bimonthly magazine *Bulletin of the Atomic Scientists,* (www.thebulletin.org; subscriptions are available for on-line and print editions; back issues can be read on-line for no charge) features important nuclear weapons stories. The Center for Defense Information home page (www.cdi.org) has numerous military and nuclear-weapons articles (updated several times a week). A daily collection of international news and editorials on war and weapons can be found at www.antiwar.com. Women's Action for New Directions (www.wand.org) offers a free wide-ranging biweekly nuclear/political alert email bulletin.

Environmental publications that often feature nuclear topics include *The Edge* (on-line, www.earthislandjournal.org/the-edge), *E/The Environmental Magazine* (print and on-line, www.emagazine.com), *Earth Island Journal* (print and on-line, www.earthisland.org/eijournal), and *Earth First!* (print and on-line, www.earthfirstjournal.org).

To locate and read all major U.S. and international mainstream and alternative media on-line, see the comprehensive links to newspapers, magazines and news websites on the homepage of www.commondreams.org, which also gathers "breaking news and views for the progressive community," including important but overlooked nuclear news items.

FAIR, a media watchdog group, released a study showing that during the 2003 Iraq war, "official voices . . . dominated U.S. network newscasts, while opponents of the war [were] notably underrepresented." To read the study, go to www.fair.org/extra/0305/

warstudy.html. To read how the corporate-owned mainstream media and the Bush campaign collaborated to influence reporting on the 2000 election, see www.makethemaccountable.com/podvin/media/030629_kickback.htm and www.makethemaccountable.com/podvin/media/020131_payoff.htm.

"Fact-Free News" by Harold Meyerson, *Washington Post*, October 15, 2003 (www.washingtonpost.com/wp-dyn/articles/A27061-2003Oct14.html); reports on a study by the Program on International Policy Attitudes, "Misperceptions, The Media and The Iraq War" showing that Americans had major misconceptions about the rationale for the 2003 war on Iraq. Read the report at www.pipa.org. Those respondents who received their information from Fox News were the most misled/least informed.

See an analysis of how the Pentagon controls war-time reporting: "Information Warriors—Pentagon's Ministry of Truth shapes war coverage" by Danny Schechter at www.media-alliance.org/mediafile/22-1/schecter.html. Read how Vice President Cheney and the American Enterprise Institute manipulated polling data for TV's *Meet the Press* to build public support for the Iraq war at www.commondreams.org/views03/1022–12.htm.

2. Major Television News Analysis/Public Affairs Programs

(From "Talking Heads" by Chris Bushnell, *The Wave* magazine, March 27, 2003. See email information for many of these programs, as well as for other public affairs and news shows, in the following section, National Media Contact List.)

The Beltway Boys
Hosts: Fred Barnes and Mort Kondracke
Fox News / weekends
Viewers: 480,000
Bias: Moderate to conservative
Show times, topics, feedback: www.foxnews.com/beltwayboys

Buchanan and Press
Hosts: Pat Buchanan and Bill Press
MSNBC / weekdays
Viewers: 220,000
Bias: Liberal to conservative
Show times, topics, feedback: www.msnbc.com/news/buchananpress_front.asp

The Capital Gang
Host: Mark Shields
CNN / Saturdays
Viewers: 375,000
Bias: Moderate to conservative
Show times, topics, feedback:
www.cnn.com/CNN/programs/capital.gang

Charlie Rose
PBX / weeknights
Viewers: 3 million
Bias: Liberal to conservative
Show times, topics, feedback:
www.charlierose.com

Crossfire
Hosts: James Carville, Paul Begala ("moderates"),
Tucker Carlson, Bob Novak ("conservatives")
CNN / weekdays
Viewers: 625,000
Bias: Moderate to conservative
Show times, topics, feedback:
www.cnn.com/CNN/programs/crossfire

The Daily Show with Jon Stewart
Comedy Central / weeknights
Viewers: 2 million
Bias: Liberal to conservative
Show times, topics, feedback:
www.comedycentral.com/tv_shows/thedailyshowwithjonstewart

Face the Nation
Host: Bob Schieffer
CBS / Sundays
Viewers: 3.4 million
Bias: Liberal to conservative
Show times, topics, feedback:
www.cbsnews.com/sections/ftn/main3460.shtml

Hannity & Colmes*
Hosts: Sean Hannity and Alan Colmes
Fox News / weeknights*
Viewers: 2.2 million
Bias: Moderate to conservative
Show times, topics, feedback:
www.foxnews.com/hannityandcolmes
*Also on radio as of 2003, though the "left-leaning" Alan Colmes is starting his own program (see www.alan.com).

Hardball with Chris Matthews
MSNBC / weeknights
Viewers: 530,000
Bias: Moderate to conservative
Show times, topics, feedback:
www.msnbc.com/news/hardball_front.asp

Inside Washington
Host: Gordon Peterson
PBS / Sundays
Viewers: 750,000
Bias: Liberal to conservative
Show times, topics, feedback:
www.wusatv9.com/insidewashington/default.asp

The McLaughlin Group
Host: John McLaughlin
PBS and other / Fridays
Viewers: 1.5 million
Bias: Conservative
Show times, topics, feedback:
www.mclaughlin.com

Meet the Press
Host: Tim Russert*
NBC / Sundays
Viewers: 5.7 million
Bias: Moderate to conservative
Show times, topics, feedback:

www.msnbc.com/news/meetpress_front.asp
*Called "king of Sunday morning shows," and highly influential (read "Ganging Up on Dean," www.alternet.org/story.html?StoryID=16570)

Newshour with Jim Lehrer
PBS / weekdays
Viewers: 3 million
Bias: Liberal to conservative
Show times, topics, feedback:
www.pbs.org/newshour

On the Record with Greta Van Susteren
Fox News / weeknights
Viewers: 1 million
Bias: Moderate to conservative
Show times, topics, feedback:
www.foxnews.com/ontherecord

The O'Reilly Factor
Host: Bill O'Reilly
Fox News / weeknights
Viewers: 2.7 million
Bias: Conservative
Show times, topics, feedback:
www.foxnews.com/oreilly

Real Time with Bill Maher
HBO / Fridays
Viewers: 1.8 million
Bias: Liberal to moderate
Show times, topics, feedback:
www.hbo.com/billmaher

Scarborough Country
Host: Joe Scarborough
MSNBC / M–F, 10 pm ET
Viewers: [not available]
Bias: Conservative
Show times, topics, feedback:
www.msnbc.com/news/scarborough country_front.asp?ta=y

This Week with George Stephanopoulos
ABC / Sundays
Viewers: 2.9 million
Bias: Moderate to conservative
Show times, topics, feedback:
http://abcnews.go.com/sections/ThisWeek

Washington Journal
Host: Varies
C-Span / Daily, 7–10 am ET
Viewers. 20 million (per 6-month C-Span study)
Bias: Liberal to conservative
Show times, topics, feedback:
www.c-span.org (click "Washington Journal")

3. National Media Contact List

(All material from Fairness and Accuracy in Reporting, www.fair.org, except portions of National Radio section)

A. Network/Cable Television

ABC News
77 W. 66 Street
New York, NY 10023
212-456-7777
General email: netaudr@abc.com
Email forms for all ABC news programs:

http://abcnews.go.com/service/help/abccontact.html
Nightline: nightline@abcnews.com
20/20: 2020@abc.com

CBS News
524 W. 57 St.
New York, NY 10019
212-975-4321
Fax: 212-975-1893
Email forms for all CBS news programs:
www.cbsnews.com/htdocs/feedback/fb_news_form.shtml
CBS Evening News with Dan Rather: evening@cbsnews.com
The Early Show: earlyshow@cbs.com
60 Minutes II: 60II@cbsnews.com
48 Hours: 48hours@cbsnews.com
Face The Nation: ftn@cbsnews.com

CNBC
2200 Fletcher Avenue
Fort Lee, NJ 07024
201-585-2622
Fax: 201-583-5453
info@cnbc.com
List of email addresses for all CNBC news programs:
http://moneycentral.msn.com/Content/CNBCTV/TV_Info/email.asp

CNN
One CNN Center, Box 105366
Atlanta, GA 30303-5366
404-827-1500
Fax: 404-827-1906
Email forms for all CNN news programs: www.cnn.com/feedback/

Fox News Channel
1211 Avenue of the Americas
New York, NY 10036
212-301-3000
Fax: 212-301-4229
comments@foxnews.com
List of email addresses for all Fox News Channel programs:
www.foxnews.com/story/0,2933,77538,00.html
Special Report with Brit Hume: special@foxnews.com
FOX Report with Shepard Smith: foxreport@foxnews.com
The O'Reilly Factor: oreilly@foxnews.com
Hannity & Colmes: hannity@foxnews.com, colmes@foxnews.com
On the Record with Greta: ontherecord@foxnews.com

MSNBC
One MSNBC Plaza
Secaucus, NJ 07094
201-583-5000
Fax: 201-583-5453
world@msnbc.com
List of email addresses for all MSNBC news programs:
www.msnbc.com/news/435157.asp?obb=-m1#nbc
Hardball with Chris Matthews: hardball@msnbc.com
MSNBC Reports with Joe Scarborough: msnbcreports@msnbc.com

NBC
30 Rockefeller Plaza
New York, NY 10112
212-664-4444
Fax: 212-664-4426
List of email addresses for all NBC news programs:
www.msnbc.com/news/435157.asp?obb=-m1#nbc

NBC Nightly News with Tom Brokaw: nightly@nbc.com
NBC News' Today: today@nbc.com
Dateline NBC: dateline@nbc.com

PBS
1320 Braddock Place
Alexandria, VA 22314
703-739-5000
Fax: 703-739-8458
Feedback to PBS:
www.pbs.org/aboutsite/feedback.html
The NewsHour with Jim Lehrer: newshour@pbs.org

B. National Radio

Alternative Radio
P.O. Box 551
Boulder, Colorado 80306
800-444-1977
www.alternativeradio.org
info@alternativeradio.org
According to their website, "Alternative Radio is a weekly one-hour public affairs program offered free to all public radio stations in the U.S., Canada, Europe, South Africa, Australia, and on short-wave on Radio for Peace International, [which] provides information, analyses and views that are frequently ignored or distorted in other media." Variety of speakers. Reaches over 125 radio stations "and millions of listeners." Frequently discusses U.S. foreign policy/war agenda. Occasionally covers nuclear issues.

Counterspin
Hosts: Janine Jackson, Steve Rendall and Peter Hart
c/o FAIR
112 W. 27th Street
New York, NY 10001
www.fair.org/counterspin
jjackson@fair.org
Providing "the news behind the headlines" as the weekly hour-long program of Fairness and Accuracy in Reporting (FAIR). Emphasis on analysis of major news coverage, exposing the biases and flawed reporting in mainstream media. Often discusses how television and newspaper reporters parrot Bush administration views and promote war without sufficient analysis of the issues involved. Occasionally covers nuclear issues. Can be heard on 125 stations (see list on website) and on-line.

Democracy Now!
Hosts: Amy Goodman and Juan Gonzalez
P.O. Box 693
New York, NY 10013
212-431-9090 (main number)
800-881-2359 (tape orders)
www.democracynow.org
mail@democracynow.org
Weekday morning radio and television program (two one-hour segments) on over 125 stations, hosted by award-winning journalists. See website for stations, or to listen on-line. Cutting-edge investigative reports and interviews that often break important new stories. Issues of war and peace, including nuclear weapons, given thorough coverage.

Making Contact
National Radio Project
1904 Franklin St., Suite 415
Oakland, California 94612
510-251-1332
www.radioproject.org
makingcontact@radioproject.org

A "weekly international 29-minute radio program committed to investigative journalism and in-depth critical analysis which goes beyond the breaking news." Various speakers/segments. Occasionally features nuclear stories.

Mike Malloy
American Radio Network
P.O. Box 238
Decatur, GA 30031
800-825-5937 (on-air line)
http://mikemalloy.pmachine hosting.com
mikedmalloy@aol.com
Weeknight three-hour program. According to *Salon* magazine: "For nearly 20 years, Mike Malloy has been making talk radio like this: caustic, abrasive, inventive, confrontational and resolutely left of center. It has won him admirers and awards . . . At a time when the very genre of talk radio is widely seen as synonymous with strident conservatism, his career both ratifies and belies that premise." Covers nuclear issues, and mentions protests (such as the August 2003 gathering at STRATCOM during meetings to plan a new generation of nuclear weapons). Many programs on threats to democracy, U.S. foreign policy, and the "Bush Crime Family." Click "Listen" to hear the show on-line or find a local affiliate.

National Public Radio (NPR)
635 Massachusetts Avenue NW
Washington, DC 20001-3753
202-513-2000
www.npri.org
Jeffrey Dvorkin, Ombudsman: ombudsman@npr.org
All Things Considered: atc@npr.org
Morning Edition: morning@npr.org
Talk Of The Nation: totn@npr.org
List of email addresses for all NPR news programs:
www.npr.org/contact/index.html#email
Moderate to conservative and increasingly corporate-sponsor-influenced news, public affairs and cultural programming. Website has station directory (numerous affiliates play NPR programs).

Pacifica Radio
www.pacificaradio.org
Over the past 50 years, this listener-sponsored "free speech" radio network, founded by pacifists, has built a listenership in the millions. Stations in New York, Los Angeles, Berkeley, Houston, and Washington, D.C. present 24-hour progressive news, public affairs and cultural programming. See Pacifica homepage for links to each station's website to hear programs on-line. Network has discussed the dangers of nuclear weapons since 1949. Pacifica Radio Archives, www.pacificaradioarchives.org, sells numerous nuclear-related programs, including presentations by Helen Caldicott, M.D. and many other speakers.

The Rush Limbaugh Show
1270 Avenue of the Americas
New York, NY 10020
800-282-2882
www.rushlimbaugh.com
rush@eibnet.com
Right-wing radio and TV host with a strong opinion on everything. Influential program with audience in the mil-

lions. Website has station directory and on-line listening options.

Working Assets Radio
Host: Laura Flanders
101 Market Street, 7th Floor
San Francisco, CA 94105
415-841-4121 (host station KALW)
Listener line: 866-798-TALK
www.workingassetsradio.com
radio@workingassets.com
Weekday, one-hour show on public radio and the Internet with "timely discussions about pressing political issues and current cultural trends." Occasionally focuses on nuclear subjects. Visit website to listen online.

Time of Useful Consciousness (TUC) Radio
P.O. Box 410009
San Francisco, CA 94141
800-TUCTAPE
www.tucradio.org
info@tucradio.org
Weekly half-hour radio series featuring "the untold story—the impact of big corporations on society." Different speakers. Catalog of over 400 programs on environmental, political, and nuclear issues, including several speeches by Helen Caldicott, M.D. and other experts. Nuclear topics including depleted uranium, the threat of nuclear war, and missile defense. TUC produced a six-part fall 2003 special, "Weapons in Space: The Hidden Agenda Behind Star Wars." First radio series to discuss the impact of global trade agreements. Programs play on over 50 independent radio stations (see website for information on how your local station can offer TUC programs).

C. National Newspapers

Los Angeles Times
202 West First Street
Los Angeles, CA 90012
800-528-4637 or 213-237-5000
Fax: 213-237-4712
Letters to the Editor:
letters@latimes.com
Readers' Representative:
readers.rep@latimes.com
LA Times contact information by department:
www.latimes.com/services/site/la-contactus.htmlstory

New York Times
229 W. 43rd Street
New York, NY 10036
212-556-1234
Fax: 212-556-3690
D.C. Bureau phone: 202-862-0300
Letters to the Editor (for publication):
letters@nytimes.com
Write to the news editors:
nytnews@nytimes.com
NY Times contact information by department:
www.nytimes.com/ref/membercenter/help/infoservdirectory.html
How to contact NY Times reporters and editors:
www.nytimes.com/ref/membercenter/help/contactpaper.html

USA Today
7950 Jones Branch Drive
McLean, VA 22108
800-872-0001 or 703-854-3400
Fax: 703-854-2165
Letters to the Editor:
editor@usatoday.com
Give feedback to USA Today:

http://contact.usatoday.com/feedback/print/feedback-form.asp

Wall Street Journal
200 Liberty Street
New York, NY 10281
212-416-2000
Fax: 212-416-2658
Letters to the Editor: wsj.ltrs@wsj.com
Comment on news articles: wsjcontact@dowjones.com

Washington Post
1150 15th St., NW
Washington, DC 20071
Phone: 202-334-6000
Fax: 202-334-5269
Letters to the Editor: letters@washpost.com
Ombudsman: ombudsman@washpost.com
Contact Washington Post writers and editors:
www.washingtonpost.com/wp-srv/interact/longterm/stfbio/wpemail.htm

D. Magazines

Newsweek
251 W 57th Street
New York, NY 10019
212-445-4000
Fax: 212-445-5068
Letters to the Editor: letters@newsweek.com

Time Magazine
Time & Life Building
Rockefeller Center
New York, NY 10020
212-522-1212
Fax: 212-522-0323
Letters to the Editor: letters@time.com

U.S. News & World Report
1050 Thomas Jefferson Street
Washington, DC 20007
202-955-2000
Fax: 202-955-2049
Letters to the Editor: letters@usnews.com

E. News Services / Wires

Associated Press
50 Rockefeller Plaza
New York, NY 10020
212-621-1500
Fax: 212-621-7523
General questions and comments: info@ap.org
Partial contact information for the Associated Press by department and bureau:
www.ap.org/pages/aptoday/ap_contacts1.html

Reuters
Three Times Square
New York, NY 10036
646-223-4000
Reuters Editorial Feedback:
http://aboutreuters.custhelp.com/cgi-bin/aboutreuters.cfg/php/enduser/site_fdbck.php

United Press International
1510 H Street, NW
Washington, DC 20005
202-898-8000
Fax: 202-898-8057
Comment and Tips: tips@upi.com

4. Weapons Industry News Websites

Jane's Defense Weekly
www.janes.com

Space News (Weekly Aerospace Industry Publication)
www.spacenews.com

Space Daily
www.spacedaily.com/index.html

ABM Daily
www.spacewar.com

Spacewar.com
www.spacewar.com/abmdaily.html

Space.com
www.space.com

Aviation Week & Space Technology
www.aviationweek.com

5. Contacting Local Media

An effective way for citizens to "talk back" about nuclear issues coverage is first through their local media outlets. In local media, their response may even be mentioned on air, or their letter or opinion piece may be printed. For example, if there is enough of a response to a local ABC station about a national ABC story, it (a) becomes a local story unto itself, and (b) will have a greater impact on the national producers/decision-makers (i.e., there's a huge response to locate affiliates in Omaha, Des Moines, or Tampa, versus a limited number of calls to the media outlet's New York main offices).

To locate contact information for most local media across the U.S., check these comprehensive websites (courtesy of FAIR): www.newslink. org or www.congress.org/congressorg/dbq/media or www.newsdirectory.com; see also the Media Access tool kit at www.mediachannel.org/getinvolved/access.shtml. (sources: FAIR, Christine Haenn, MediaChannel.org)

6. Becoming a Media Activist

See FAIR's resources to become a media activist and identify and challenge biased media coverage, at www.fair.org/activism/activismkit.html.

7. Media Watchdog and Analysis Websites:

Fairness and Accuracy in Reporting, www.fair.org
www.MediaChannel.org
Institute for Public Accuracy, www.ipa.org
www.MediaReform.net
www.Media-Alliance.org
www.ProjectCensored.org

8. Books Analyzing Right-Wing Media

Big Lies: The Right-Wing Propaganda Machine and How It Distorts the Truth by Joe Conason
Target Iraq: What the News Media Didn't Tell You by Norman Solomon
Embedded—Weapons of Mass Deception: How the Media Failed to Cover the War in Iraq by Danny Schechter
Weapons of Mass Deception: The Uses of Propaganda in Bush's War on Iraq by Sheldon Rampton, John C. Stauber
The Habits of Highly Deceptive Media: Decoding Spin and Lies in Mainstream News by Norman Solomon
The Oh Really? Factor: Unspinning Fox News Channel's Bill O'Reilly by Peter Hart, Robert McChesney
What Liberal Media? The Truth About Bias and the News by Eric Alterman
The Best Democracy Money Can Buy by Greg Palast
Lies and the Lying Liars Who Tell Them by Al Franken
Rush Limbaugh Is a Big Fat Idiot: And Other Observations by Al Franken

9. Media Ownership/Consolidation

See "Who Owns the Media" at www.takebackthemedia.com/owners.html. Also see the extensive reports from the Center for Public Integrity at www.openairwaves.org/telecom/report.aspx?aid=16 and www.publicintegrity.org/download/wellconnected5.pdf (the latter in Adobe Acrobat). Another resource: "Who Owns What" page on Columbia Journalism Review site, www.cjr.org/tools/owners

NOTES

Preface

1. Situation Reports, STATFOR.com (September 11, 2001)
2. "Pentagon Recommends the use of Nuclear Weapons," *Japan Today* (September 19, 2001)
3. Jeffrey St. Clair, "Trigger Happy, Bush Administration Hawks Want to Deploy 'Mini-nukes' Against Osama Bin Laden," www.inthesetimes.com/issue/25/26/news2.shtm
4. Dana Milbank, "U.S. Pressed on Nuclear Response, A Policy of Less Ambiguity, More Pointed Threat Is Urged," *The Washington Post* (October 5, 2001)
5. Wes Vernon, "Father of Neutron Bomb: Use it on Osama," www.af.mil/vision (September 25, 2001)
6. James Carroll, "Bombing with Blindfolds On" *The Boston Globe* (November 11, 2001)
7. Nigel Chamberlain and Dave Andrews, "Thermobaric Warfare," www.cnduk.org/briefing/thermo.htm (January 11, 2001)
8. Andrew Maykuth and Jonathan S. Landay, "US Intensfies Attacks with BLU-82s," Knight Ridder Newspapers (November 6, 2001)
9. "Backgrounder on Russian Fuel Air Explosives (Vacuum Bombs)," Human Rights Watch, www.hrw.org/press/2000/02/chech0215b (February 2000)
10. Tim Weiner, "U.S. Bombs Strike 3 Villages and Reportedly Kill Scores," *The New York Times* (December 1, 2001)
11. "Protocol 1, Relating to the Protection of Victims of International Armed Conflicts, Article 51"
12. Geov Parrish, "Where the Bodies Are," www.workingforchange.com (October 22, 2001)
13. "Unexploded Cluster Bombs Pose Threat to Civilians, Dawn, Pakistan," Centre for Research on Globilisation, www.globalresearch.ca/articles/DAW111B (November 15, 2001)
14. Amy Waldman, "Food Drops Go Awry, Damaging Houses," *The New York Times* (November 21, 2001)
15. "Unexploded Cluster Bombs Pose Threat to Civilians"
16. USAF, www.aviationzone.com/facts/ac130
17. "International Action Center Factsheet: The Truth About the U.S. War in Afghanistan," [www.iacenter.org] *Toronto Globe and Mail* (November 3, 2001)
18. Michael R. Gordon, "U.S. Hope to Break the Taliban with Pounding From the Air," *The New York Times* (October 17, 2001)
19. Thom Shanker and Stephen Lee Myers, "U.S. Sends in Special Plane with Heavy Guns," *The New York Times* (October 16, 2001)

20. "Bunker Busters Brought Into Use," *The Daily Camera*, Camera Wire Services; and Raymond Whitaker, "Attack on Afghanistan: Washington's Fearsome Arsenal," *The Independent* (November 4, 2001)
21. Dr. Helen Caldicott, *Missile Envy* (New York: William Morrow, 1984)
22. "Afghan War Will Shape Future U.S. Military Structure," www.stratfor.com (November 23, 2001)
23. Dr. Farrukh Saleem, "Stop the Bombing Please," *JANG*, Pakistan, www.jang.com.pk/thenews/index (November 4, 2001)
24. Professor Marc Herold, "A Dossier on Civilian Victims of United States' Aerial Bombing of Afghanistan," www.cursor.org/stories/civilian_deaths.htm (December 6, 2001)
25. Bill Nichols and Peter Eisler, "The Threat of Nuclear Terror Is Slim But Real," *USA Today* (November 28, 2001)
26. Ibid.
27. Louis Charbonneau, "Experts Warn of Low Grade Nuclear Terror Attack," *Reuters* (November 2, 2001)
28. Matthew Wald, "Reactors and Their Fuel are Among the Flanks U.S. Needs to Shore Up," *The New York Times* (November 4, 2001)
29. Dr Helen Caldicott, *Nuclear Madness* (New York: W.W. Norton, 1994)
30. Michael Grunwald and Peter Behr, "Are Nuclear Plants Secure?" *The Washington Post* (November 3, 2001)
31. Matthew Wald, "Agency Weighs Buying Drug to Protect Against Radiation-Induced Ailments," *The New York Times* (November 29, 2001)
32. Efward Luttwak, "New Fears, New Alliance," *The New York Times* (October 2, 2001)
33. Barbara Slavin, "Pentagon Builds Case to Bomb Iraq," *USA Today* (November 11, 2001)
34. "Iraq Says to Consider Return of Weapons Monitoring," *Reuters* (November 21, 2001)
35. Elaine Scolino and Alison Mitchell, "Calls for New Push into Iraq Gain Power in Washington," *The New York Times* (December 3, 2001)
36. Anton La Guardia, "Iraq 'Not Linked to September 11,' " *The Telegraph* (November 11, 2001)
37. Barbara Slavin, "Pentagon Builds Case to Bomb Iraq," *USA Today* (November 19, 2001)
38. Jason Vest, "Beyond Osama: The Pentagon's Battle with Powell Heats Up," *The Village Voice* (November 20, 2001)
39. Sandra Sobieraj, "U.S. to Pursue Missile Test Plans," The Associated Press (November 16, 2001)
40. Jim Wurst, "U.S. Supports Weapons Cut While Opposing International Agreements," *News World Communications Inc.* (November 14, 2001)
41. "N-Testing to Resume?" Opinion/Editorial, www.downwinders.org
42. Jim Wurst, "A Call to Arms Control," *The Washington Times* (November 12, 2001)
43. "Action on Threat Reduction," andrew@californianpeaceaction.org (November 9, 2001)
44. Ibid.
45. William D. Hartung, "Bush's War on Terrorism: Who Will Pay and Who Will Benefit?" www.motherjones.com (September 27, 2001)

46. William D. Hartung, "The War Dividend," www.motherjones.com (September 28, 2001)
47. John Pilger, "The Truths They Never Tell Us," *The New Statesman* (November 26, 2001)
48. James Dao, "U.S. is Expecting to Spend $1 Billion a Month on War," *The New York Times* (November 12, 2001)
49. Frida Berrigan, "The War Profiteers: How Are Weapons Manufacturers Faring in the War," World Policy Institute (December 17, 2001)
50. "The Military Budget Up, Up, and Away," Arms Trade Resource (December 20, 2001)
51. Michael R. Gordon, "U.S. Arsenal: Treaties vs. Nontreaties," *The New York Times* (November 14, 2001)
52. Simon Tisdall, "How the Future was Shanghaied," *The Guardian* (October 21, 2001)

Introduction to the 2004 Edition

1. Michael Dobbs, "For Wolfowitz, a Vision May be Realized," *New York Times* (April 7, 2003)
2. Joseph Cirincione, "Origins of Regime Change in Iraq," Proliferation brief, Volume 6, Number 5, Carnegie Endowment for International Peace (March 19, 2003)
3. Sam Tanenhaus, "Bush's Brain Trust," *Vanity Fair*, July 2003; and Bernard Weiner, "A PNAC Primer: How We Got into This Mess," www.antiwar.com/orig/weiner6.html (June 2, 2003)
4. Cirincione, "Origins of Regime Change in Iraq"
5. William Rivers Pitt, "Blood Money," truthout.org (February 28, 2003)
6. PNAC also strongly recommends the use of nuclear weapons on non-nuclear nations (www.newamericancentury.org), a recommendation implemented by the U.S. Strategic Air Command in 1997 [see "The Weird Men Behind George Bush's War," which, in keeping with PNAC's recommendations, now maintains a nuclear target list not just for Russia, China, and North Korea, but also for Iran, Libya, Syria, Sudan, and Algeria according to Bruce Blair, President of the Center for Defense Information; see also "U.S. Nukes Can be Adapted for Use Against Enemy: Bush," *Pakistan Tribune* (May 26, 2003)]
7. "The Weird Men Behind George Bush's War"
8. Dobbs
9. "The Weird Men Behind George Bush's War"
10. Ibid.
11. "Advisers of influence: Nine Members of the Defense Policy Board Have Ties to Defense Contractors," Andre Verloy and Daniel Politi, Center for Public Integrity, publicintegrity.org. (April 23, 2003)
12. Ibid.
13. Weiner
14. Dobbs
15. Spencer Ackerman and John B Judis, "The First Casualty," *The New Republic* (June 30, 2003)
16. Seymour Hersh, "Selective Intelligence," *The New Yorker* (May 12, 2003)
17. In the months leading up to the invasion, PNAC also established a Committee for the Liberation of Iraq, staffed entirely by PNAC members, while it catalyzed the chan-

neling of millions of taxpayer dollars to the Iraqi National Congress, a self-proclaimed Iraqi government-in-exile, and to Ahmed Chalabi, the Iraqi exile who was a colleague of Wolfowitz's at the University of Chicago in the late 1960s and who had been selected by PNAC to replace Hussein (despite Chalabi's having been sentenced to twenty-two years in jail by a Jordanian court on thirty-one counts of bank fraud [Pitt, "Blood Money"]). See "My Alma mater is a moral cesspool," by Francis Boyle, Professor of Law, University of Illinois School of Law (August 2, 2003)

18. Ackerman and Judis
19. Ibid.
20. "Sam Tanenhaus," Bush's Brain Trust, *Vanity Fair* (July 2003)
21. Ibid.
22. Ackerman and Judis
23. "The Secret History of the Aqaba Pipeline," Guerrilla News Network War On Terrorism, www.guerrillanews.com
24. Jim Vallette, Steve Kretzmann, Daphne Wysham, "Crude Vision: How Oil Interests Obscured U.S. Government Focus on Chemical Weapons Use by Saddam Hussein," Institute for Policy Studies (2003)
25. Ibid.
26. Ibid.
27. Ibid.
28. Patrick Tyler, "In First Step, New Iraqi Council Abolishes Hussein's Holidays," *New York Times* (July 14, 2003)
29. Richard Sale, UPI intelligence correspondent, "Exclusive: Saddam Key in Early CIA Plot," United Press International (April 10, 2003)
30. Eric Schmitt, "Rumsfeld Says that Iraq May Need a Larger Force," *The New York Times* (July 14, 2003)
31. "The Secret History of the Aqaba Pipeline"
32. Ahmad Faruqui, "The CIA in Iran: The Oil Business of Regime Change," *Counterpunch* (March 28, 2003)
33. Ibid.
34. Bob Herbert, "Ultimate Insiders," *The New York Times* (April 14, 2003)
35. Laton McCartney, *Friends in High Places, the Bechtel Story: The most secret corporation and how it engineered the world* (New York: Simon and Schuster, 1988)
36. "The Secret History of the Aqaba Pipeline"
37. Jim Crogan, "Made in the U.S.A.: A Guide to Iraq's Weapons of Mass Destruction," *LA Weekly* (March 21-27, 2003)
38. Ibid.
39. Ibid.
40. Ibid.
41. Ibid.
42. Paul Rockwell, "Iraq's US Arsenal: Complicity of firms in Saddam's crimes against humanity now well-documented," http://www.metroactive.com/papers/metro/02.20.03/iraq-0308.html (February 20-26, 2003)
43. Ibid.
44. "The Secret History of the Aqaba Pipeline"
45. The invasion of Kuwait came six days after U.S. Ambassador April Glaspie assured Iraq that the U.S. had no opinion on Arab-Arab conflicts. Some of the medical consequences of this episode are described in Chapter 8: Nuclear War in the Gulf and Kosovo.

46. Fred Kaplan, "The Iraqi War Wasn't as Modern as it Looked," *MSN Slate* (May 27, 2003)
47. Rockwell
48. Thalif Deen, "There's No Business Like War Business," *Common Dreams News Center* (April 8, 2003)
49. Edward Wong, "Paris Air Show: Where are the Americans?" *International Herald Tribune* (June 17, 2003)
50. Eric Schmitt, "Rumsfeld Says Iraq May Need a Larger Force"
51. Dan Morgan and Walter Pincus, "High Cost of Defense Plan Gets Little Discussion," The Washington Post, May 26, 2003
52. The Iraqi Time Bomb, Jeff Madrick, (April 6, 2003) *New York Times*
53. "Military Waste Under Fire: $1 Trillion Missing-Bush Plans to Target Pentagon Spending," SFGate.com (May 18, 2003)
54. Morgan and Pincus
55. Ibid.
56. Frida Berrigan, Arms Trade Resource Center, "Lockheed Martin: Mega-Merchant of Death," www.worldpolicy.org/projects/arms/updates (May 16, 2003)
57. Ibid.
58. Ibid.
59. Ibid.
60. Andre Verloy, Daniel Politi, and Aron Pilhofer, "Advisors of Influence: Nine members of the defense advisory board have ties to defense contractors," Center for Public Integrity (March 29, 2003)
61. Ibid.
62. Ibid.
63. Ibid.
64. Ibid.
65. Ibid.
66. Interestingly, Donald Rumsfeld is a member of the CFIUS.
67. Interestingly Perle, along with Jean Kirkpatrick and Newt Gingrich is also a resident fellow of the influential right-wing think tank called the American Enterprise Institute.
68. Frida Berrigan, "Richard Perle: It Pays to be the Prince of Darkness," *In These Times* (March 21, 2003)
69. David Corn, "Capital Games," *The Nation* (April 4, 2003)
70. "Woolsey's Role Crucial to Impact of Occupation," Jim Lobe, www.fpif.org, www.ForeignPolicy-inFocus.org (April 8, 2003)
71. Ibid.
72. Jim Lobe, "Woolsey's role crucial to impact of occupation," Foreign Policy in Focus, www.fpif.org (April 8, 2003)
73. Verloy, Politi, and Pilhofer. Other influential members of the Defense Policy Review Board include: *Thomas S. Foley,* Speaker of the House of Representatives from 1989 to 1994, Japanese Ambassador from 1997 to 2001, and a registered lobbyist. He has no military clients. *Kenneth Adelman,* the Reagan Director of the Arms Control and Disarmament Agency from 1983 to 1987, who opposed nuclear arms control. *Richard Allen,* who worked for Nixon and Reagan, and is a senior fellow at the conservative Hoover Institute and a member of the National Security Advisory Group, which advises the Senate Majority Leader and the Speaker of the House. *Newt Gingrich,* Speaker of the House of Representatives from 1995 to 1999.

He is CEO of the consulting firm The Gingrich Group, a senior fellow at the conservative American Enterprise Institute, a visiting fellow at the Hoover Institute, and an analyst on the Fox news channel. *Henry Kissinger,* Secretary of state under Nixon from 1973 to 1977. Chairman of Kissinger Associates, an international consulting firm, he was awarded the Nobel Peace Prize in 1973. *Dan Quayle,* vice president of the United States from 1989 to 1993, a consultant, public speaker and author.

Attempts by weapons manufacturers to influence policy do not stop with the Defense Policy Board. Many of the leading arms companies place former government officials on their own staffs and boards, contribute cash to political candidates, and pay well-placed lobbyists to steer business their way. Since 1996, for instance, Raytheon has contributed more than 3.3 million dollars in soft money and Political Action Committee donations. At Boeing, John M. Shalikashvili, retired chairman of the Joint Chiefs of Staff, sits on the board, and former Deputy Secretary of Defense Rudy de Leon runs the Boeing Washington office. Boeing also assiduously cultivates ties to members of Congress and the Pentagon using well-placed political contributions and sophisticated lobbyists. It provides financial contributions, for example, to Frank Gaffney's right-wing think tank, the Center for Security Policy—the de facto nerve center of the Washington lobby for Star Wars—and Andrew Ellis, Vice President for Government Relations at Boeing, sits on the Center's board (not coincidentally, Boeing is the country's second largest contractor for Star Wars) [Frida Berrigan, "RAYTHEON: We own the kill chain," Arms Trade Resource Center (March 24, 2003)].

74. Elizabeth Becker, "Two Democrats Call for Scrutiny of Bidding to Reconstruct Iraq," *The New York Times* (April 9, 2003)
75. Simon English, "Cheney Had Iraq in Sight Two Years Ago," *The Telegraph On-line Edition* (UK) (July 22, 2003)
76. Naomi Klein, "Privatization in Disguise," *The Nation* (April 18, 2003)
77. Ibid.
78. Ibid.
79. Ibid.
80. Ibid.
81. Elizabether Becker, "Companies from All Over Seek a Piece of the Action Rebuilding Iraq," *The New York Times* (May 21 2003); and Diana B. Henriques, "Which companies will put Iraq back together?" *The New York Times* (March 23, 2003)
82. Henriques
83. "Rebuilding Iraq—The contractors," The Center for Responsive Politics, www.opensectrets.org/news/rebuilding_iraq (April 7, 2003)
84. Klein
85. Elizabeth Becker, "Two Democrats Call for Scrutiny of Bidding to Reconstruct Iraq," *The New York Times* (April 9, 2003)
86. Ibid
87. "Congress Must Investigate War Profiteering by Halliburton, Other Bush Connected Companies," Duran SC, August 20, 2003, rania@southern studies.org
88. Becker, "Companies from All Over Seek a Piece of the Action Rebuilding Iraq"
89. Jane Mayer, "The Contractors," *The New Yorker* (May 5, 2003)
90. "Bechtel: Profiting from Destruction," CorpWatch, Global Exchange, Public Citizen, www.globalexchange.org (June 2003)

91. Chana R. Schoenberger, "Gambling on Iraq's Reconstruction," Forbes.com (April 4, 2003)
92. Ibid.
93. Mark Fineman, "More Flak on the Halliburton Deal," *Los Angeles Times* (April 11, 2003)
94. Pitt
95. Dan Baum, "Nation Builder for Hire," *The New York Times Magazine* (June 22, 2003)
96. Ibid.
97. P. W. Singer, "Have Guns, Will Travel," *The New York Times* (July 21, 2003)
98. Ibid.
99. Ibid, and "Crony Capitalism Goes to War," www.ariannaonline.com (April 23, 2003)
100. Cheney decided not to receive the amount in a lump sum but have it paid over a period of five years. See Baum; and Pratap Chatterjee, "Halliburton makes a killing on Iraq war," Corpwatch.org (March 20, 2003)
101. Huffington
102. Baum
103. Maureen Dowd, "Who's Losing Iraq," *The New York Times* (September 1, 2003)
104. Baum
105. Pratap Chatterjee, "Dyncorp Rent-a-Cops May Head to Post-Saddam Iraq," Corpwatch.org (April 9, 2003)
106. Antony Barnett, "Scandal-hit firm Wins Key Contracts," *The Observer* (London) (April 13, 2003)
107. William D. Hartung, "Imperial Power or Global Partner: the Right Way to Rebuild Iraq," www.tompaine.com/feature.fm (April 9, 2003)
108. Baum
109. Neela Banerjee, "Candidate for Production Job is a Retired Shell Executive," *The New York Times* (April 2, 2003)
110. Mark Fineman, "Oil Overseer Says He'll Keep it Honest," *The Sydney Morning Herald* (May 17-18)
111. Survey Group Head's Link to Arms Industry, Glen Rangwala, *The Independent* (London) (October 5, 2003)
112. David E. Sanger, "Bush Declares 'One Victory in a War on Terror' " *The New York Times* (May 2, 2003)
113. Robert Fisk, "Children Killed and Maimed in Bomb Attack on Town," *The Independent* (London) (April 2, 2003)
114. Paul McGeough, "In the Ruins, All that's Left is Death and Fear," *Sydney Morning Herald* (April, 4, 2003)
115. Ibid.
116. Charles Hanley, "Hospitals Buckle as Casualties Escalate," *Sydney Morning Herald* (April 7, 2003)
117. Paul McGeough, "Descent into a Charnel House Hospital Hell," *Sydney Morning Herald* (April 10, 2003)
118. Bob Graham, "U.S. Troops Shoot Civilians," *Evening Standard* (London) (June 19, 2003)
119. Erik Baard, "New Science Raises the Specter of a World Without Regret," *The Village Voice* (January 22-28, 2003)

120. Ibid.
121. Ibid.
122. John M Broder, "Iraqi Army Toll is a Mystery Because No Count is Kept," *International Herald Tribune* (April 2, 2003)
123. Peter Ford, "Surveys Point to High Civilian Death Toll in Iraq: Preliminary suveys suggest casualties well above the Gulf War," *Christian Science Monitor* (May 22, 2003)
124. "Counting the Bodies," James Ridgway, *The Village Voice* (September 3-9, 2003). This would correspond only to the period since war was officially declared; beginning in June, 2002, nine months before the official invasion, the U.S. began attacking the fiber-optic cable system used to transmit Iraqi military communications as well as key command centers, radars, and other significant military assets. From June 2002 to the beginning of the invasion, America and England flew 21,736 sorties over Iraq and attacked (usually without warning) 349 targets. The number of civilians killed in the pre-war war is not part of any calculation
125. John M Broder, "No Neat Categories for the Casualties of War," *The New York Times* (April 9, 2003)
126. Ford
127. "Millions of People in Iraq at Risk as Water and Sewage Systems Crumble," www.care.org (May 21, 2003)
128. "Nuclear Nightmare in Iraq," www.janes.com/security/international_security/news (May 29, 2003)
129. Patrick E Tyler, "Barrels Looted at Nuclear Site Raise Fears for Iraqi Villagers," (June 8, 2003); John Hendren. "Dangerous Loot South of Baghdad," *Los Angeles Times* (May 22, 2003); Anna Badkhen, "Many Have Symptoms Tied to Material Looted from Nearby Facility," *The San Francisco Chronicle* (May 26, 2003); and Mehru Jaffer, "IAEA to Send Inspectors to Nuclear Plant," Inter Press Service (May 28, 2003)
130. Jaffer

Chapter One: The Tragedy of Wasted Opportunities

1. Robert S. Norris and William M. Arkin, "Global Nuclear Stockpiles, 1945–2000" *Bulletin of the Atomic Scientists* (March/April 2000)
2. William D. Hartung, "Quick on the Trigger," *The Progressive Report* (November 2000)
3. Janne E. Nolan, *An Elusive Consensus: Nuclear Weapons and American Security After the Cold War* (Washington, DC: The Brookings Institution Press, 1999)
4. Robert S. Norris and William M. Arkin, "U.S. Nuclear Forces, 2000," *Bulletin of the Atomic Scientists* (May/June 2000)
5. Robert S. Norris and William M. Arkin, "Russian Nuclear Forces, 2000," *Bulletin of the Atomic Scientists* (July/August, 2000)
6. Personal communication with Admiral Eugene Carroll, Center for Defense Information, Washington, D.C.
7. *Peace Action: People for Nuclear Disarmament*, Australia (August/September 2000)
8. Bruce Blair, "U.S. Expanding Nuclear Targets," *The Guardian* (June 16, 2000)
9. Ibid.

10. Andrew Lichterman and Jacqueline Cabasso, *Faustian Bargain 2000—why "stockpile stewardship" is fundamentally incompatible with the process of nuclear disarmament,* Western States Legal Foundation (5108395387)
11. Jacqueline Cabasso, "The Role of National Legislations and International Legal Instruments," *Proceedings of the International Symposium, Science, Ethique & Society, Federation Mondiale Des Travailleurs Scientifiques* (Case 404-93514 Montreuil, Cedex)
12. William D. Hartung and Frida Berrigan, "Lockheed Martin and the GOP: Profiteering and Pork Barrel Politics with a Purpose," www.worldpolicy.org/projects/arms
13. William D. Hartung, "Stop Throwing Money at the Arms Trade Resource Center," (October 12, 2000)

Chapter Two: The Reality of Nuclear War

1. "1MT Surface Blast: Pressure Damage," *The American Experience,* WGBH/PBS Online
2. Dr. Helen Caldicott, *Missile Envy, Revised Edition* (New York: Bantam Books, 1986)
3. Stephen A. Fetter and Kosta Tsipis, "Catastrophic Releases of Radioactivity," *Scientific American*, vol. 244, no. 4 (April 1981)
4. Caldicott
5. R. P. Turco, A. B. Toon, T. P. Ackerman, J. B. Pollack, C. Sagan, "The Climatic Effects of Nuclear War," *Scientific American* (August 1984)
6. Dean Babst, "Nuclear Winter," www.geocities.com/mothersalert/nuclearwinter.html
7. Ibid.
8. Bruce G. Blair, Harold A. Feiveson, and Frank N. von Hippel, "Taking Nuclear Weapons off Hair Trigger Alert," *Scientific American* (November 1999)
9. Ibid.
10. Ibid.
11. James Risen, "Computer Ills Meant U.S. Couldn't Read Its Spy Photos," *The New York Times* (April 12, 2000)

Chapter Three: It's a Mad, Mad World: Nuclear Scientists and the Pentagon Play with Deadly Gadgets

1. David Pasztor, "Building a Better Bomb," *San Francisco Weekly* (May 27, 1998)
2. Normon Solomon, "Los Alamos Spin," *San Francisco Bay Guardian* (June 28, 2000)
3. Ibid.
4. R. P. Turco, A. B. Toon, T. P. Ackerman, J. B. Pollack, C. Sagan, "The Climatic Effects of Nuclear War," *Scientific American* (August 1984)
5. David Beers, "The Bomb Tribe," *Mother Jones* (March/April 1995)
6. Dr. Andreas Toupadakis, "Personal Responsibility for World Peace," University of Notre Dame Conference on Averting Nuclear Anarchy: The Current Crisis in Arms Control (March 31, 2000)
7. Raphael Aron, *Cults Too Good to Be True* (New York: HarperCollins, 1999)

8. Ibid.
9. Beers
10. Hugh Gusterson, *Nuclear Rites: A Weapons Laboratory at the End of the Cold War* (Berkeley, CA: University of California Press, 1996)
11. Ibid.
12. Ibid.
13. Ibid.
14. Ibid.
15. Ibid.
16. Ibid.
17. William M. Arkin, "The Last Word," *The Bulletin of the Atomic Scientists* (September/October 2000)
18. Gusterson
19. Ibid.
20. Ibid.
21. Much of the material for this section was obtained from a study conducted by Janne E. Nolan in the book *An Elusive Consensus: Nuclear Weapons and American Security After the Cold War* (Washington, DC: Brookings Institution Press, 1999)
22. Ibid.
23. Ibid.
24. Ibid.
25. Ibid.
26. Ibid.
27. Ibid.
28. Ibid.
29. Ibid.
30. Ibid.
31. Ibid.
32. Ibid.
33. Ibid.
34. Ibid.
35. Ibid.
36. Ibid.
37. Ibid.
38. Ibid.
39. Ibid.
40. Ibid.
41. Ibid.
42. Ibid.
43. Ibid.
44. Ibid.
45. Ibid.
46. Ibid.

Chapter Four: Corporate Madness and the Death Merchants

1. Dr. Helen Caldicott, *If You Love This Planet* (New York: W.W. Norton, 1992)
2. Ibid.
3. Ibid.
4. William Greider, "Waking Up the Global Elite," *The Nation* (October 2, 2000)
5. The Heritage Foundation 1999 Annual Report, 214 Massachusetts Avenue, NE, Washington, DC, 20002
6. Caldicott
7. William D. Hartung, World Policy Institute, "The Military-Industrial Complex Revisited: How Weapons Makers Are Shaping U.S. Foreign and Military Policies," *The Progressive Response,* Vol. 3, No. 23 (July 2, 1999)
8. The CATO Institute 1998 Annual Report, 1000 Massachusetts Avenue, NW, Washington, DC, 20001
9. Leslie Wayne, "After High-Pressure Years, Contractors Tone Down Missile Defense Lobbying," *The New York Times* (June 13, 2000)
10. Ibid.
11. Hartung
12. Ibid.
13. Ibid.
14. Ibid.
15. Steven Lee Meyers, "Pentagon Says North Korea Is Still a Dangerous Military Threat," *The New York Times* (September 22, 2000)
16. Bill Mesler, "Why the Pentagon Hates Peace in Korea," *The Progressive Response* (September 2000)
17. Hartung
18. Howard French, "Seoul Fears U.S. Is Chilly About Détente with North," *The New York Times* (March 23, 2001)
19. Hartung
20. Ibid.
21. Frida Berrigan, Michelle Ciarrocca, and William Hartung, "Lockheed Martin: All-Purpose Merchant of Death," *ATRC Update,* Part III, Arms Trade and Resource Center, (212) 229-5808, ext. 106, (June 26, 2000)
22. "Smart Shopping by the Pentagon," *The New York Times* (October 31, 2001)
23. William D. Hartung, "Saint Augustine's Rules—Norman Augustine and the Future of the American Defense Industry," *World Policy,* Volume XIII, Number 2, (Summer 1996)
24. Ibid.
25. Ibid.
26. Ibid.
27. Ibid.
28. Ibid.
29. Norman Kempster, "New Anti-terror Cabinet Agency Urged; Defense; The Plan Calls for an Overhaul of the Government's Approach to Security and Predicts an Attack on American Soil Within 25 Years," *Los Angeles Times* (February 1, 2001)
30. Ibid.
31. Berrigan, et al.

32. Ibid.
33. Hartung
34. Ibid.
35. Hartung, "The Military-Industrial Complex Revisited"
36. Ibid.
37. William D. Hartung and Frida Berrigan, "Lott and Lockheed: Partners in Influence Peddling," hartung@newschool.edu (July 31, 2000); Alice Slater, "The Big Guns Behind the Global War Machine," *The WTO and the Global War System,* International Network on Disarmament and Globalization (November 28, 1999)
38. Ibid.
39. William D. Hartung, "Lawmakers, Guns and Money," World Policy Institute (September 23, 2000)
40. Dana Milbank, "On the Outside Looking In as Tom DeLay Whips Up Some Fundraisers," *The Washington Post* (August 2, 2000)
41. Charles Lewis, " 'Reformer With Results'? Don't Count on It," an investigative report for the Center for Public Integrity (August 8, 2000)
42. Hartung and Berrigan, "Lott and Lockheed: Partners in Influence Peddling"
43. Ibid.
44. Lewis
45. William D. Hartung, "Moderate or Militant: Will the Real Dick Cheney Please Stand Up?" World Policy Institute and Arms Trade Resource Center, hartung@newschool.edu
46. Personal communication with Admiral Eugene Carroll, Center for Defense Information
47. Lowell Bergman, Diana B. Henriques, Richard A. Oppel, Jr., and Michael Moss, "Mixed Reviews for Cheney in Chief Executive Role at Halliburton," *The New York Times* (August 24, 2000)
48. Gretchen Morgenson, "The Stock Option and the Stump, Cheney's Retirement Package, Some Uncharted Territory," *The New York Times* (August 18, 2000)
49. William D. Hartung, "Blue Dogs, Pork and 'Morality': The Arms Industry's Buyout of the Democratic Party," Arms Trade Resource Center, hartung@newschool.edu (August 11, 2000)
50. John Isaacs "Senator Lieberman: On the Right of the Democratic Party on National Security Issues," Council for a Livable World, jdi@clw.org (August 7, 2000)
51. Hartung, "Blue Dogs, Pork and 'Morality' "
52. "Lockheed Martin: All-Purpose Merchant of Death," World Policy Institute Issue Brief (July 2000)
53. Alice Slater, "Star Wars and the Global War System," www.gracelinks.org/nuke/index.html
54. Ibid.
55. Aaron Rothenburger, "Arms Makers' Cozy Relationship with the Government" in "Action Atlas on U.S. Arms," *Mother Jones,* motherjones.com (1999)
56. Geov Parrish, "General Electric, U.S. Arms Exporters," *Mother Jones,* Mojowire
57. Ibid.
58. Slater
59. Pamina Firchow and Tamar Gabelnick, "Uncle Sam: Arms Merchant to the World," *San Francisco Examiner* (September 8, 2000)

60. Firchow, et al.
61. Geov Parrish, "Lockheed Martin, U.S. Arms Exporters," *Mother Jones,* Mojowire

Chapter Five: Manhattan II

1. Nuclear Non-Proliferation Treaty, 1995
2. "Stockpile Stewardship and Management Program," Department of Energy, Defense Programs (February 29, 1996)
3. Ibid.
4. Dr. Robert Civiak, "Managing the U.S. Nuclear Weapons Stockpile," Tri-Valley CAREs (July 2000)
5. David Pasztor, "Building a Better Bomb," *San Francisco Weekly* (May 27, 1998)
6. Ibid.
7. Pasztor
8. Ibid.
9. Civiak
10. Senior Airman Adam Stump, 354th Fighter Wing Public Affairs, "B-2 Successfully Drops Improved Bunker Buster Bomb," *Air Force News Service* (March 26, 1998)
11. Andrew Lichterman and Jacqueline Cabasso, "Faustian Bargain 2000: Why 'Stockpile Stewardship' Is Fundamentally Incompatible with the Process of Nuclear Disarmament," Western States Legal Foundation, 1440 Broadway, Suite 500, Oakland, CA 94612 (May 2000)
12. Ibid.
13. Ibid.
14. Ibid.
15. Steve Goldstein, "Bill Would Give Push to 'Mini-Nuke,' " *The Philadelphia Inquirer* (October 16, 2000)
16. Dana Milbank, "U.S. Pressed on Nuclear Response," *The Washington Post* (October 5, 2001)
17. Ibid.
18. Wes Vernon, "Father of Neutron Bomb: Use It on Osama," www.af.mil/vision (September 25, 2001)
19. Civiak
20. Lichterman and Cabasso
21. Christopher E. Paine and Dr. Matthew McKinzie, "When Peer Review Fails: The Roots of the National Ignition Facility (NIF) Debate," Natural Resources and Defense Council (www.nrdc.org/nuclear/nif2/findings.asp)
22. James Glanz, "Laser Project Is Delayed and Over Budget," *The New York Times* (August 19, 2000)
23. "National Ignition Facility Amendment," susangordon@earthlink.net (June 24, 2000)
24. Richard Boone, " 'Stockpile Stewardship' of Nuclear Weapons: the Deal to Subsidize Nuclear Weaponeers," *Facing Reality,* Project for Participatory Democracy (March 1998)
25. Greg Mello, "Subcritical Tests," Western States Legal Foundation (February 10, 2000)
26. Civiak
27. Walter Pincus, "Virtual Nuclear Arms Tests," *The Washington Post* (July 22, 2000)

28. Boone
29. M. G. McKinzie, T. B. Cochran, C. E. Paine, "Explosive Alliances: Nuclear Weapons Simulation Research at American Universities," NRDC Nuclear Program (January 1998)
30. William Broad, "Los Alamos Scientist's Book Creates a New Controversy," *The New York Times* (August 5, 2001)
31. McKinzie, et al., "Explosive Alliances"
32. Ibid.
33. Ibid.
34. Ibid.
35. Ibid.
36. Ibid.
37. Boone
38. Matthew L. Wald, "Nuclear Sites May Be Toxic in Perpetuity, Report Finds," *The New York Times* (August 8, 2000)
39. H. Joseph Hebert, "Nuke Sites May Not Be Rid of Contaminants," AP (August 8, 2000)
40. Ibid.
41. "Study: Levels of Waste Unknown," AP (October 27, 2000)
42. Matthew L. Wald, "U.S. Raises Estimate of Plutonium Spilled Making Arms," *The New York Times* (October 21, 2000)
43. Ibid.
44. Mary Manning, "Nuclear Tests Released More Harmful Elements Than Admitted Before," *Las Vegas Sun* (October 23, 2000)
45. Robert Alveraz, "Nuclear Wildfires," *The Nation* (September 18/25, 2001, Vol. 271, No. 8, p 30, 2000)
46. Personal communication with Robert Alveraz
47. Judith Graham, "U.S. Hot to Fireproof Nuclear Sites, Western Fires Spark Fear of Catastrophe," *Chicago Tribune* (October 25, 2000)
48. "Gap Questions Government Assurances on Hanford Fire," Government Accountability Project, www.whistleblower.org/www/hanfire.htm (July 20, 2000)
49. Graham
50. Alveraz
51. Judith Graham, "U.S. Hot to Fireproof Nuclear Sites, Western Fires Spark Fear of Catastrophe," *Chicago Tribune* (October 25, 2000)
52. Alveraz

Chapter Six: Star Wars: The Story of National Missile Defense Systems

1. "National Missile Defense," Union of Concerned Scientists Fact Sheet, "The Safeguard Experience" (February 1999)
2. Francis Fitzgerald, *Way Out There in the Blue* (New York: Simon and Schuster, 2000)
3. Ibid.
4. Ibid.
5. Ibid.

6. Ibid.
7. Robert Aldridge, "Son of Star Wars: A Background Paper on National Missile Defense," Pacific Life Research Center (August 15, 2000)
8. Ibid.
9. Ibid.
10. Theodore Postol, "The Target Is Russia," *The Bulletin of the Atomic Scientists* (March/April 2000)
11. Ibid.
12. Andrew Marshall, "U.S. Spies Inflate Risk from 'Rogue' States," *Independent Digital (UK) LTD* (June 11, 2000)
13. Ibid.
14. Fitzgerald
15. Aldridge
16. John Isaacs, "A Political Decision," *The Bulletin of the Atomic Scientists* (March/April 2000)
17. Steven Lee Myers, "U.S. Missile Plan Could Reportedly Provoke China," *The New York Times* (August 10, 2000)
18. President Bush's speech on missile defense, CNN.com (May 1, 2001)
19. Jack Spencer and Michael Scardaville, "In Defense of Development of Missiles," *The Miami Herald* (October 17, 2000)
20. Steve LaMontagne, "Missile Defense Encourages Proliferation," *Washington Times* (October 22, 2000)
21. John Isaac, "A Political Decision," *The Bulletin of the Atomic Scientists* (March/April, 2000)
22. AFP, "Senate Overwhelmingly Passes U.S. Defense Authorization Bill" (October 2, 2001)
23. Karl Grossman, *Weapons in Space* (New York: Seven Stories Press, 2001)
24. Karl Grossman, "Master of Space," *The Progressive Report* (January 2000)
25. Burton Richter, "It Doesn't Take Rocket Science," *The Washington Post* (July 23, 2000)
26. Dr. Helen Caldicott, *Missile Envy* (New York: Bantam, 1986)
27. Bruce Gagnon, "New Names for Star Wars Systems," globalnet@mindspring.com (August 16, 2001)
28. Much of this section is derived from the excellent work by Bob Aldridge, who became one of my mentors in the early 1980s after I read his book *Counterforce Syndrome.*
29. "Theater Missile Defense," Union of Concerned Scientists, Appendix 2, from the UCS Fact Sheet
30. Charles Pena, "From the Sea: National Missile Defense Is Neither Cheap Nor Easy," CATO Institute (September 6, 2000)
31. Rodney Jones, "Taking National Missile Defense to Sea: A Critique of Sea-based and Boost Phase Proposals," Council for a Livable World (October 2000)
32. Aldridge
33. Ibid.
34. Mary McGrory, "Star Wars: Calling a Bomb a Bomb," *The Washington Post* (July 13, 2000)
35. William Broad, "Ex-Employee Says Contractor Faked Results of Missile Tests," *The New York Times* (March 7, 2000)

36. Ibid.
37. Jim Wolf, "FBI Probing TRW for Missile Defense Related Fraud," Reuters (September 11, 2000)
38. David Abel, "Tiff Between White House, MIT Professor Gets Personal," *The Boston Globe* (September 8, 2000)
39. David Wright and Theodore Postol, "Missile Defense System Won't Work," *The Boston Globe* (May 11, 2000)
40. "BMDO Plans Next NMD Integrated Ground Test in Early 2001," *Inside Missile Defense* (September 20, 2000)
41. Stan Crock, "The Dodgy Science of Missile Defense," *Business Week* (August 17, 2000)
42. David Wood, "Missile Defense Would Take President—and Maybe Humans—Out of the Loop," *The Seattle Times* (July 19, 2000)
43. Ibid.
44. Crock
45. David Morgan, "Ballistic Missile Defense: A Submission to the Standing Committee on National Defense and Veterans Affairs," House of Commons, Ottawa, Canada (April 5, 2000)
46. Nick Cohen, "Protection Racket. It Matters Not Whether It's Bush or Gore. We'll Still Have Son of Star Wars Foisted on U.S.," *The Observer* (November 12, 2000)
47. Robert Alveraz, "Nuclear Wildfires," *The Nation* (September 18/25, 2001)
48. "Warhead Elimination," Union of Concerned Scientists Briefing (July 11, 2000)
49. Michael R. Gordon, "U.S. Arsenal: Treaties vs. Nontreaties," *The New York Times* (November 14, 2001)
50. David E. Sanger, "Before and After Bush and Putin's Banter: No Agreement on Missile Defense," *The New York Times* (November 16, 2001)
51. "Warhead Elimination"
52. "ABM Talking Points," *Bulletin of the Atomic Scientists* (January 20, 2000)
53. "China Warns Future U.S. President Over Missile Shield," AFP (November 2, 2000)
54. John Isaacs, "A Political Decision," *Bulletin of the Atomic Scientists* (March/April, 2000)
55. Nigel Chamberlain, "CND's Response to Paul Brown" *The Guardian* (April 5, 2000)
56. Richard Norton-Taylor, "Son of Star Wars British Ministers Are Going Along Meekly with Washington's Grandiose and Dangerous Plans," *The Guardian* (April 15, 2000)
57. Christopher Lockwood, "Westminster Backlash Over 'Son of Star Wars,' " *Telegraph* (August 3, 2000)
58. Hugo Young, "The Planned American Missile Shield May Not Even Work Properly," *The Guardian* (February 1, 2000)
59. Theodore Postol, "The Target Is Russia," *Bulletin of the Atomic Scientists* (March/April, 2000)
60. Ibid.
61. Robert Suro, "Key Missile Defense Radar Planned for Remote Island," *The Washington Post* (May 7, 2000)
62. Srdja Trifkovic, "The Coming National Missile Defense Scandal," The Rockford Institute (June 21, 2000)

Chapter Seven: Space: The Next American Empire

1. William B. Scott, "USSC Prepares for Future Combat Missions in Space," *Aviation Week & Space Technology* (August 5, 1996)
2. "Implementing Our Vision for Space Control," Speech by General Richard B. Meyers, United States Space Foundation, Colorado Springs (April 7, 1999)
3. Keith Hall, speech to National Space Club (September 15, 1997)
4. Halford J. Mackinder, "The Geographical Pivot of History," *Geographical Journal* (1904)
5. Karl Grossman, *Weapons in Space* (New York: Seven Stories Press, 2001)
6. "Vision for 2020," U.S. Space Command, Director of Plans (February 1997)
7. Bruce Gagnon, "Space Domination: Pyramid to the Heavens," www.globenet.free-online.co.uk (July 16, 2000)
8. Grossman
9. Gagnon
10. "Space Force Is an Idea Whose Time May Have Come," editorial, *Florida Today* (March 14, 2000)
11. "The Investment in Space," *Air Force Association Organization Magazine* (February 2000)
12. Paul Hoversten, "The Best Defense May Be a Better Map," *The Washington Post* (February 19, 2000)
13. "The Warfighters Edge: First Hyperspectral Images from Space," *Spacewar*, Kirtland Air Force Base (September 8, 2000)
14. Bruce Gagnon, "Pentagon Funds Global 3-D Mapping Mission," www.spacedaily.com/spacecast/news/milspace-00c.html (January 31, 2000)
15. "White House Supports Air Force Vision on Spacelift Partnership," Air Force press release (February 9, 2000)
16. Bruce Gagnon, "Global Network Against Weapons & Nuclear Power in Space"
17. Tech. Sgt. Stefan Alford, "AOC Declared Official Weapons System," www.af.mil/news/Sept2000 (September 12, 2000)
18. Army Captain Deanna Bague, "Joint Services Conduct Modern Day War Games," *Air Force News* (June 21, 2000)
19. "Megawatt Laser Test Brings Space Based Lasers One Step Closer," *Space Daily* (April 26, 2000)
20. Grossman
21. U.S. Air Force Advisory Board, "New World Vistas: Air and Space Power for the 21st Century," *Space Technology Volume* (1996)
22. Mike Moore, "Unintended Consequences," *Bulletin of the Atomic Scientists* (January/February 2000)
23. Bill Sweetman, "Securing Space for the Military," *Jane's Defense Weekly*
24. Ellen Messmer, "US Army Kick-Starts Cyberwar Machine," *CNN-Technology* (November 22, 2000)
25. Richard J. Newman, "The New Space Race," *US News and World Report* (November 8, 1999)
26. James Oberg, "NASA Knew Mars Polar Lander Doomed," UPI (March 21, 2000)
27. John Noble Wilford, "NASA Sending 2 Rovers to Mars in Twin Trips Landing in 2004," *The New York Times* (August 11, 2000)

28. John Noble Wilford, "Shaken NASA Offers New Plan for Mars Exploration Missions," *The New York Times* (October 27, 2000)
29. Jerome Groopman, "Medicine on Mars: How Sick Can You Get During Three Years in Deep Space?" *The New Yorker* (February 14, 2000)
30. Barry E. DiGregorio, "Rethinking Mars Sample Return," *Space News* (1997)
31. Leonard David, "NASA Urged to Create Facility for Mars Samples," *Space News* (March 31–April 6, 1997)
32. Brian Berger, "NASA Considers Building Mars-Sample Quarantine Facility," *Space News* (April 12, 1999)
33. Keay Davidson, "NASA, Slightly Humbled, Dreams On," *San Francisco Examiner* (January 23, 2000)
34. Leonard David, "Business Sees Cash Among the Constellations," *Space.com* (January 9, 2000)
35. Jackie Alan Giuliano, *Healing Our World: Weekly Comment,* "The Migration Begins: The International Space Station,", 2000 Lycos, Inc., registered trademark of Carnegie Mellon University (September 2000)
36. "International Space Station: Missions Accomplished and Continued Assembly, and Background," www.boeing.com (November 7, 2000)
37. George Musser and Mark Alpert, "How to go to Mars," *Scientific American* (March 2000)
38. Karl Grossman, "U.S. Plans to Wage War in Space," presentation in Toronto, Canada (October 2000)
39. Paul Hoversten, "Nuclear-powered Probes in the Plans for Mars," *Space.com*
40. "DRAFT Programmatic Environmental Impact Statement for Accomplishing Expanded Civilian Nuclear Energy Research and Development and Isotope Production Missions in the United States, Including the Role of the Fast Flux Test Facility," Summary, United States Department of Energy, Office of Nuclear Energy, Science and Technology, Washington DC (July 2000)
41. AP, "Lab Contamination rises," *The Denver Post* (July 30, 1996); Reuters, "Workers exposed to plutonium at U.S. Lab" (March 17, 2000)
42. Grossman
43. Dave Dooling, "Nuclear Power: The Future of Space Flight," *Space.com* (July 22, 2000)
44. "U.S. Launch Vehicles Claimed Harmful to Ozone Layer," *Moscow Aviatsiya Rosmonavtika* (December 6, 1989)
45. William J. Broad, "NASA Moves to End Longtime Reliance on Big Spacecraft," *The New York Times* (September 16, 1991)
46. Sharon Ebner, "Solid Fuel Critics Say Ozone Is in Danger," Mississippi *Sun Herald* (March 17, 1990)
47. Karl Grossman, "The Pentagon Prepares to 'Master Space,' " *Network* (July/August 2000)

Chapter Eight: Nuclear War in the Gulf and Kosovo

1. Nicholas Arons, "A Few Vignettes from Iraq," *The Guardian, Iraq Notebook* (Volume 7, 2000)
2. John Pilger, "War Against the Children," *The Guardian, Iraq Notebook* (Volume 7, 2000)

3. Joby Warrick, "Maps Reveal Scattering of Ky. Plutonium," *The Washington Post* (October 1, 2000)
4. Dr. Helen Caldicott, *Nuclear Madness* (New York: W. W. Norton, 1994)
5. Dr. Asaf Durakovic, "Medical Consequences of Internal Contamination with Depleted Uranium," *Metal of Dishonor*, International Action Center, NY (1999)
6. Caldicott
7. Dolores Lymburner, "Another Human Experiment," *Metal of Dishonor*, International Action Center, NY (1999)
8. Ibid.
9. "Former Head of Pentagon's Depleted Uranium Project Condemns Environmental Contamination of Vieques, Puerto Rico, an Island Close to 10,000 U.S. Citizens," www.viequeslibre.org (June 14, 2000)
10. Rob Edwards, "Dangerous Work," *New Scientist* (July 8, 2000)
11. Thomas Williams, "Depleted Uranium in NATO Bases Raises Health Issues," *Hartford Courant* (May 20, 1999)
12. Matthew L. Wald, "Nuclear Sites May Be Toxic in Perpetuity," *The New York Times* (August 8, 2000)
13. Personal communication with Dr. Hari Sharma
14. Federally Sponsored Research on Persian Gulf Veterans' Illnesses, Annual Report to the Congress of the Research Working Group of the Persian Gulf Veterans Coordinating Board (April 1997)
15. Dr. Melissa McDiarmid, Transcript of March 25, 1998 VA.DoD teleconference on the D.U. Program
16. Cat Euler, "The Consequences of Depleted Uranium Ammunitions," Campaign for Depleted Uranium (July 6, 2000)
17. Sara Flounders, "The Struggle for an Independent Inquiry," *Metal of Dishonor*, International Action Center, NY (1999)
18. Siegwart-Horst Gunther, "How Depleted Uranium Shell Residues Poison Iraq, Kuwait and Saudi Arabia," *Metal of Dishonor*, International Action Center, NY (1999)
19. Dan Fahey, "Depleted Uranium Weapons: Lessons from the 1991 Gulf War, A Postwar Disaster for Environment and Health," Laka Foundation (May 1999)
20. Ibid.
21. Ibid.
22. Gunther
23. Euler
24. Environmental News Service, "Children Most at Risk from Depleted Uranium" (April 26, 2001)
25. Cherry Norton, "Health Danger that Divides Medical Opinion," *Independent News* (October 4, 1999)
26. Fahey
27. Ibid.
28. Ibid.
29. Cat Euler, "Depleted Uranium Exposures to Civilians and Military Personnel," Paper presented at the 14th Low Level Radiation and Health Conference in Reading (July 14, 2000)
30. Lilliam Irizarry, "Puerto Rico Wants Uranium Probe," AP (January 11, 2001)
31. Max Sinclair and Jared Israel, "DU Used—in Somalia and Germany," *Der Spiegel* (January 23, 2001)

32. John Catalinotto and Sarah Flounders, "Is the Israeli Military Using Depleted-Uranium Weapons Against the Palestinians?" International Action Center, NY (November 27, 2000)
33. "Depleted Uranium Weapons," Issue Brief, Physicians for Social Responsibility (July 1999)
34. "European Countries Announce Balkans Syndrome Tests for Military Personnel," SGT (January 10, 2001)
35. "Radiation Fears Widen in Balkan Peace Force," *London Telegraph* (December 31, 2000)
36. Marlise Simons, "Radiation from Bombing Alarms Europe," *The New York Times* (January 7, 2001)
37. Burt Herman, "Uranium Use in Kosovo War Suspected as Veterans Fall Ill," *The Sydney Morning Herald* (January 9, 2001)
38. Kim Sengupta, "MoD 'Monitoring' Health Checks on Kosovo Soldiers," news@antic.org (December 28, 2000)
39. Patricia Reaney, "Scientists Doubt Uranium Weapons Cancer Link," *The New York Times* (January 9, 2001)
40. BBC News, "Depleted Uranium Threatens Balkan Cancer Epidemic" (July 30, 1999)
41. The Committee for National Solidarity, UNEP, Geneva (January 16, 2001)

Chapter Nine: The Lockheed Martin Presidency and the Star Wars Administration

1. M. W. Gruzy, "Viewpoints: Fighting Fictional Foes," *St. Louis Post-Dispatch* (January 17, 2001)
2. Russell Mokhiber and Robert Weissman, "Corporate Conservative, Corporate President," *Focus on the Corporation* (January 11–18, 2001)
3. Diedre Griswold, "As Economic Storm Gathers, CEOs & Bush Meet in Secret," *Workers World Newspaper* (January 18, 2000)
4. Jerry White and Paul Scherrer, "Washington Inaugural Celebrations: Corporate America Welcomes Bush," *WSWS: News and Analysis: North America: U.S. Politics* (January 20, 2001)
5. William D. Hartung and Michelle Ciarrocca, "Reviving Star Wars," *The Baltimore Sun* (January 21, 2001)
6. United States Department of Defense press advisory (January 24, 2001)
7. Sean Gonsalves, "Star Wars: The Sequel," *The Cape Cod Times* (December 26, 2000)
8. Martin Kettle, "Bush Team Is Back with a Vengeance," *The Guardian Weekly* (January 4–10, 2001)
9. William D. Hartung, "Rumsfeld: An Ideologue on Missile Defense," World Policy Institute, www.foreignpolicy-infocus.org/papers/rumsfeld
10. Jean-Michel Stoullig, "Rumsfeld Commission Warns against 'Space Pearl Harbor,' " AFP (January 11, 2001)
11. Tabassum Zakaria, "Helms Says U.S. not Bound by ABM Treaty" *globalnet@mindspring.com* (January 11, 2000)
12. "Rumsfeld in Cold War Time Warp, Says Angry Moscow," Reuters (March 20, 2001)

13. Elaine Sciolino and Eric Schmitt, "In Defense Post, Infighter Known for Working the Means to his End," *The New York Times* (January 8, 2001)
14. Karl Grossman, globalnet@mindspring.com
15. David Corn, "Questions for Powell," *The Nation* (January 8, 2001)
16. Jane Perlez, "A Soldier Statesman Who Has Advocated a Blend of Strength and Caution," *The New York Times* (December 17, 2000)
17. Robert Parry, "From Vietnem to Florida's Disenfranchisement of Black Voters: Unheroic Moments in Secretary of State Nominee Colin Powell's Career," *Between the Lines* (December 25, 2000)
18. Ian Brodie, "Powell Insists Defense Rests on 'Star Wars,' " *London Times* (December 18, 2000)
19. Barry Schweid, "Powell Pushes for Missile Defense," AP (January 17, 2001)
20. David Storey, "Powell Endorses U.S. Missile Defense," Reuters (January 17, 2001)
21. Schweid
22. Ibid.
23. Kettle
24. Daryl Kimball, "N-Testing Update," dkimball@clw.org (December 19, 2000)
25. Karl Grossman, "Aerospace Executives on Bush Star Wars Team," globalnet@mindspring.com (December 24, 2000)
26. Serge Trifkovic, "President Bush's Foreign Affairs," www.rockfordinstitute.org/NewsST121500 (December 15, 2000)
27. Ibid.
28. "The Armageddon Nominee," *The Boston Globe* (April 2, 2001)
29. Nick Cohen, "Protection Racket," *The Observer* (November 12, 2000)
30. Polly Toynbee, "Special Report: The U.S. Elections," *The Guardian* (August 22, 2000)
31. Mikhail Gorbachev, "Mr. Bush, the World Doesn't Want to Be American," *International Herald Tribune* (December 30, 2000)
32. Simon Saradzhyan, "Russian Strategic Missile Force Stripped of Oversight for Two Space Forces," *Space News* (January 25, 2001)
33. Vladimir Isachenkov, "Putin Proposes Deeper Nuclear Cuts," AP (November 13, 2000)
34. "U.S., Russia Sign Missile Agreement," AP (December 16, 2000)
35. Space Wire, "Former Military Commanders Oppose U.S.-Russian Launch Notification Agreement," AFP (December 12, 2000)
36. AFP, "Putin Warns U.S. Against Missile Defense Buildup, Enlarging NATO" (January 26, 2001)
37. "Russia Threatens to Take Arms Race to Space," *London Times* (January 25, 2001)
38. Michael Wines "In Letter to Bush, Putin Urges Wider U.S.-Russian Cooperation," *The New York Times* (January 25, 2001)
39. Ian Traynor, "Russia Halts Military Cuts as Hawks Take over in U.S.," *The Guardian* (January 18, 2001)
40. Erik Eckholm, "Power of U.S. Draws China and Russia to Amity Pact" *The New York Times* (January 14, 2001)
41. John Pomfret, "Beijing and Moscow to Sign Pact, Stronger Ties Sought to Check U.S. Influence" *The Washington Post* (January 13, 2001)
42. John Pomfret, "U.S. Now a 'Threat' in China's Eyes," *The Washington Post* (November 15, 2000)

43. Bruce Gagnon, globalnet@mindspring.com
44. Achin Vanaik, "How Much of a Reprieve?" *The Hindu* (September 27, 2000)
45. "Missile Sale to Taiwan Has Unusual Clause," AP (September 30, 2000)
46. Robert Burns, "U.S. Military Chiefs Recommend Plan to Resume Surveillance Flights," AP (April 17, 2001)
47. Michael O'Hanlon, "A Need for Ambiguity" *The New York Times* (April 27, 2001)
48. Gay Alcorn, "Bush Backpedals on Taiwan" *The Sydney Morning Herald* (April 27, 2001)
49. William Foreman, "U.S. Weapons Would Be Little Help if China Gets Serious," *The Sydney Morning Herald* (April 27, 2001)
50. Walden Bello, "Asia 2025: The Pentagon Prepares for Asian Wars," www.focusweb.org (October 17, 2000)
51. Jon Basil Utley, "20 Facts About China (Rarely Reported to Conservatives)," www.againstbombing.com/chinapoints.html
52. Dr. Nicholas Berry, "Is China an Aggressive Power?" *The Defense Monitor* (2000)
53. AFP, "China Warns U.S. to Keep Taiwan out of Any Missile Defense Plans" (January 18, 2001)
54. Bruce Gagnon, globalnet@mindspring.com
55. "U.S. Secretly Monitors Asian Navies from Australia," AP (January 27, 2001)
56. Paul Monk, "Dragon's Tail," *The Australian's Review of Books* (November 2000)
57. Ellen Hale, "Radar Picks up 'Star Wars;' Rumor in England, Uneasiness at Key Site," *USA Today* (January 24, 2001)
58. Andy Beckett "Special Report: George Bush's America," *The Guardian* (April 20, 2001)
59. Julie Hyland, "Bush Commitment to U.S. National Defense Causes International Protests," www.wsws.org (January 24, 2001)
60. "Allies Ponder Response to Bush on Missile Defense," Reuters (January 25, 2001)
61. Hugo Young, "A Special Relationship Under Fire from Missile Defense," *The Guardian* (December 21)
62. "Bush Upsets Danish Opposition Over Missile Defense Station," AFP (January 24, 2001)
63. "Leader," *The Guardian* (January 4, 2001)
64. Michael Gordon, "EU to Go It Alone with New Army," *The New York Times* and *The Sydney Morning Herald* (November 22, 2001)
65. Ian Blach, "U.S. Warns Europe Against Building Own Defense Force," *The Guardian* and *The Sydney Morning Herald* (December 6, 2001)
66. Steven Lee Myers, "A Call to Put the Budget Surplus to Use for the Military," *The New York Times* (September 28, 2000)
67. Simon Tisdall, "Bush Plan for Fortress America Hawks Say Threats Justify Defense Boost," *The Guardian* (January 13, 2001)
68. William D. Hartung, "The War Dividend," *motherjones.com* (September 28, 2001)
69. William D. Hartung, "Bush's War on Terrorism: Who Will Pay and Who Will Benefit?" *motherjones.com* (September 27, 2001)
70. www.defenselink.mil/pubs/dod101/largest/html
71. Gustav Niebuhr, "A Mission to Redirect Money Used for Defense," *The New York Times* (October 3, 2000)
72. "What the World Wants," The World Game Institute, wgi@worldgame.org
73. "Bush's Defense Advisors Faced by 68 Conflicts Worldwide: Report," AFP (January 2, 2001)

Appendix A: Major U.S. Nuclear-Weapons Makers

1. Kevin Martin, Rachel Glick, Rachel Ries, Tim Nafziger, and Mark Swier, "The Real Rogues Behind Star Wars," *Z magazine,* www.thirdworldtraveler.com/Corporations/Real_Rogues.html (September 2000)
2. Ibid.
3. Ibid.
4. Ibid.
5. Ibid.
6. Ibid.
7. Ibid.
8. Ibid.
9. Ibid.

INDEX

Aberdeen (Maryland), 150
ABL (Air Force Airborn Laser), 94–95
ABM treaty
  and X-band radars, 104, 112
  and BMEWS, 101
  Colin Powell and, 168
  and Congress post-September 11th, 185
  Donald Rumsfeld and, 165–166
  and Heritage Foundation, 78
  John Bolton and, 170–171
  and laser weapons, 94
  and NMD, 108–109
  and political implications of George W. Bush administration behavior, xvi
  and SBL program, 95
  and TMD programs, 73, 86
Abrams, Elliott, xxii, xxiii
Abu Dhabi, 157
Academic Strategic Alliances Program (ASAP), 58–62
Accelerated Strategic Computer Initiative (ASCI), 55–56, 61, 62
ACDA (Arms Control and Disarmament Agency), 21
Acid Canyon, 66
administration behavior, xvi–xvii
Advanced hydrotest facility (AHF), 51
Aegis program, 73, 93
Aerojet, 119
aerospace corporations, 119
Aerospace Industries Association, 40
Aerospace operations center (AOC), 125
Aerospace operations vehicle (AOV), 127
Afghanistan, ix, x–xiii, xix, xxxiii, 28, 49, 122–123, 183
aging of nuclear weapons, 46
Agriculture Department, U.S., xxvii–xxviii
AHF (advanced hydrotest facility), 51
Aikin, Michael, 61
AIM-9 Sidewinder air-to-air missile, xxxiii
AIM-65 Maverick air-to-surface missile, xxxiii
AIM-120 Advanced Medium Range air-to-air missile, xxxiii
Air Force Airborn Laser (ABL), 94–95
Air Force One, xlv
Air Force, U.S., xxxvi
Airborne Warning and Control System (AWACS), 89–90
airplanes, xix, 3, 127–128
  see also type of airplane
Al Hillah hospital (Iraq), xlvii
al Qaeda, xiv, xvii, xxi, xxiv, xxv, xxxvii
  see also bin Laden, Osama
Al-Tuwaitha nuclear complex (Iraq), xlix, l
Albright, Madeleine, 173
Alcoa, 162
Alcolac International Inc., xxviii
Aldridge, Bob, 74, 92
Alenia, 37
Alenia Marconi Systems, 89
Alexander, Lamar, 31
Algarotti, Robert, xxxiii
Alliant Tech Systems, 97, 185
Allied Signal, 40
Alpha High-Energy Laser, 126
aluminum tubes, xxiv
American Conservative Union, 35
American Enterprise Institute, 35

American Friends of the Czech Republic, 38
American Gulf War Veterans, 155–156
American Physical Society, 100
American Type Culture Collection (ATCC), xxviii
Americans for Democratic Action, 35
Americium, 65
Anderson, Edward, 128–129
Annan, Kofi, 143
anthrax, xxviii, xxxvii
Antiballistic Missile Treaty, *see* ABM treaty
antisatellite (ASAT) weapons, 107
antisatellite warfare, xx, 128–131
antisatellite warfare philosophy, 129–131
  and cyberspace, 123
  hypersonic military space planes, 127–128
  international concerns about, 143–144
  and International Space Station, 135–136
  laser weapons, 126–127
  Mars and the asteroids, 131–137
  merging of civilian/military activities, 123–124
  nuclear devices in space, 136–144
  nuclear powered weapons in, 142–143
  recent developments in, 125–126
  threat to U.S. satellite systems, 129
  U.S. plans for, 118–121
  U.S. Space Force, 121–123
  weapons under development, 126–127
AOC (aerospace operations center), 125
AOV (aerospace operations vehicle), 127
Apache helicopters, xxx
APEC, 26
Appaloosa (subcritical test), 55
Aqaba, Jordan, xxvii
Arabs/Arab nations, xvi, xvii
  see also specific nation
armament industry, xxxi
Armitage, Richard, xxii, xxx, 169, 177
Arms Control and Disarmament Agency (ACDA), 21
Army Corps of Engineers, xlii–xliii
Army Space and Missile Defense Command, 105
ASAP, *see* Academic Strategic Alliances Program
ASAT (antisatellite) weapons, 108
ASCI, *see* Accelerated Strategic Computer Initiative
Ashkenazi, Gaby, 96
Ashy, Joseph, 115
Asia 2025 (Naval War College), 178, 179
asphyxiation, 8
Aspin, Les
  and BMDO, 72, 73
  and corporate mergers, 29, 30
  and nuclear posture review, 20–21
  and space warfare, 116
asteroids, 131–137
AT&T, 34
Augustine, Norman, 29, 31–32, 38
Australia, xx, xlvii, 105, 130, 157, 180
Autonomy Corporation, xxxv
AWACS (Airborne Warning and Control System), 89–90
AWE Aldermaston, 111
Axsys Technologies, 98

B-1, xii
B-2, xii
B52, xii, xxxii
B53, 47
B61, 48
B61–11, 47
Baath Party, xxv, xxvi, xxxvii
bacteriological cultures, xxviii
Baghdad Nuclear Research Facility, l
Baghdad Pact, xxv
Bahrain, 157
Balkan conflict, *see* Bosnian war; Kosovo war
Balkans, and economics of reconstruction, xliv
Ballistic Missile Defense Organization (BMDO), 72–73, 105, 126
Ballistic Missile Early Warning System (BMEWS), 101
balloons, 84, 98, 99
Banca Nazionale del Lavoro, xxviii
Barron' s Online, 163
Bassoon (subcritical test), 54

Battle Management/Command, Control, and Communications (BM/C3), 96–101, 105–111
Baum, Dan, xliii
Beale Air Force Base (California), 101
Bechtel, xxvii, xxviii, xxix–xxx, xxxvi, xxxix, xl–xlii, 26, 37, 54, 68
Belgium, 135, 159
Bellow, Walden, 179
below-ground nuclear testing, xviii
Berry, Nicholas, 179–180
beryllium, 56, 69
Bhagavad Gita, 16
bidding process, xxxix, xl
Biden, Joseph, 168
Big Dig (Boston, Massachusetts), xl, xli–xlii
bin Laden, Osama, xi, xiii, xxiii, xxxiii, xxxvii
bin Laden family, xli
biological agents/weapons, xviii, xxiv, xxv, xxviii
BIOS (bomb impact optimization system), 48
Blackwill, Robert, 169
Blair, Bruce, 107
Blair, Tony, 111, 181
blindness, 8
Block-4A, 88
Blowback: The Costs and Consequences of the American Empire (Charmers Johnson), 180
Blue Mountain computer, 56
Blue Pacific computer, 56
BM/C3, *see* Battle Management/Command, Control, and Communications
BMDO, *see* Ballistic Missile Defense Organization
BMEWS (Ballistic Missile Early Warning System), 101
Boeing 747 (aircraft), 94
Boeing
  and AOV, 127
  as contractor for booster stack, 97
  as contractor for high energy laser weapons, 94, 95
  as contractor for NTW, 93
  and economics of war, xxx, xxxii–xxxiii, xxxv
  and foreign arms sales, 39, 40
  laser weapons developed by, 126
  and Long Range Plan, 119
  merger with McDonnell Douglas, 30
  political clout of, 34, 37
  and political implications of George W. Bush administration behavior, xix
  as second-highest defense contractor, 164
  and THAAD, 91
  think tanks funded by, 27
Boeing Defense and Space Group, 89
Bofors cannons, xii
Bolton, John, xxii, xxiii, 170
bomb impact optimization system (BIOS), 48
boost phase systems, 82–83
booster stack, 97
Booz Allen Hamilton, xxxvi
Borowski, Stanley, 141–142
Bosnian war
  and cancer risks in troops, 153
  and economics of reconstruction, xlv–xlvi
  J-STARS tested in, 90
  police force in, xlv–xlvi
  uranium weapons used in, 158, 161
Boston, Massachusetts, Big Dig in, xl, xli–xlii
Bradley Infantry Fighting Vehicles, xxx
Brazil, 135
Bremmer, L. Paul, III, xlvi
Britain. *See* United Kingdom
British Nuclear Fuels, 151
British oil companies, and Iran, xxvi
British Petroleum, xxv
Britism media, xlvii
Brittle problem, 107
Brown, Harold, xvii, xxxvii
Buckley Air Force Base (Colorado), 130
budget deficit, xxxi
buildings, 8
bunker busters, x, xii, xxxiii, 47
Burke, Edmund, 186
Burns, 8

Bush, George H.W., xxiii
see also Bush administration (1989–1993)
Bush, George W., xvi, xix-xx, xxiv, xxv, xl, xlvii, 33, 35, 164
See also Bush administration (2001–)
Bush administration (1989–1993)
and end of cold war, 18–20
and Iraqi nuclear program, xxviii
and NATO, 37–38
and Operation Desert Storm, xxix
and planning for Iraq war, xxi
Bush administration (2001–), 162–184
and ABM treaty, 108–109
and Britain, 181
and China, 174–180
and computer control of BM/C3, 106
and defense spending, ix
destablizing plans of, xvi–xix
and economics of reconstruction, xl
and economics of war, xxx–xxxviii
and France, 182
international concerns about, 171–184
international ramifications of behavior of, xiii
and Korea, 29
and national missile defense program, 4, 71, 72, 77, 79
and NATO expansion, 39
and nuclear alert codes, ix
personnel of, 162–171
political implications of behavior of, xvi–xix
and Russia, 172–174
and space militarization, 128
and stockpile reductions, 5–6
and the war Americans didn't see, xlvii–l
See also Operation Iraqi Freedom; *specific person*
Byrd, Robert, xxii, xxxi

C-17s, xxxiii
C-130s, xii
California Institute of Technology (Caltech), 59–60
Cambodia, xii
Cambone, Stephen, x
Campaign for Nuclear Disarmament, 181
Canada, xiv, 135, 137
cancer
Balkan War veterans rates of, 158–161
and depleted uranium weapons, 152–154
and environmental hazards, 62, 68
and Operation Desert Storm, xxix
Puerto Rico residents rates of, 158
and uranium processing, 149–151
Cape Cod Air Force Station (Massachusetts), 101
Card, Andrew, 49, 162
carpet bombing, xii
Carroll, Eugene, 17
Carroll, Philip J., xlvi
Carter, Ashton, 21–23
Carter, Jimmy, xxvii
Carter administration, 40, 107–108
Casey, William, xlii
Cassini Saturn probe, 139–141
CAV (common aero vehicle), 127
CDMA cell-phone system, xxxix
CEC (cooperative engagement capability), 104
Center for Defense Information, 185
Center for Disease Control and Prevention, xxviii
Center for Policy Studies, 164
Center for Security Policy (CSP), 26–27, 165
cesium, xiv, xlix, l, 62, 67, 148
Chafee, Lincoln, 168
chemical facilities, 56
chemical oxygen-iodine lasers (COILs), 94
chemical weapons, xxiv, xxv, xxviii
chemistry and metallurgy research (CMR), 56–57
Cheney, Lynne, 35, 165
Cheney, Richard "Dick"
corporate connections of, xliv–xlv, 35
and economics of reconstruction, xxxviii, xliv
and economics of war, xxx
energy task force organized by, xxxviii
and Lockheed Martin, 164–165

Cheney, Richard "Dick" (*cont.*)
and planning for Iraq war, xxi–xxii, xxiii
and PNAC, xxiii
and political implications of George W. Bush administration behavior, xix
and proposed Congressional investigation of George W. Bush administration claims, xxv
review of SIOP by, 18–20
role in George W. Bush administration of, 162
and selling of Iraq war to American people, xxiv
Chevron, 162
Cheyenne Mountain (Colorado), 11, 113
children, xxix, xlix, 156
China
Bechtel in, xxvii
in BM/C3 scenario, 107
Bolton and, 170
and George W. Bush administration, 174–180
and Clinton administration, 179, 180
and economics of war, xxxv
and IGT-6 program, 105
and India, 176, 178–179
and international ramifications of U.S. behavior, xiii
and Iraqi oil, xxvii
liquid-fueled weapons of, 7
and new arms race, 86
and NMD, 110
nuclear facilities in, xxvii
nuclear testing in, xviii
nuclear weapons of, xiii, 46
and nuclear weapons treaties, 44
and PNAC, xxi
and political implications of George W. Bush administration behavior, xvi, xviii
as potential threat, 5, 28, 75, 77, 80–81
and Russia, 174
and space disarmament, 143–144
strategic weapons of, 4
and Taiwan, 170, 176–180
and war against terrorism, xvi
Chirac, Jacques, 111
Chowkar-Karez, Afghanistan, xii
Christopher, Warren, 21, 40
CIA (Central Intelligence Agency), xvii, xxiv, xxv–xxvi, 12
Cirincione, Joseph, xviii, 75
Citizen s Petition to Protect America Now (Heritage Foundation), 77–78
civilians
deaths of Afghanistani, xiii
and "near nuclear" weapons, xi, xii–xiii
as wounded/casualties, xlvii, xlix
clean-up, xli, 156–157
Clear (Alaska), 101, 112
Clinton, Bill, xxii, xxv
see also Clinton administration
Clinton administration
and X-band radars, 113
and China, 179, 180
and EKV testing, 98–100
and exo-atmospheric missile defense, 86
and foreign arms sales, 39–40
and national missile defense program, 71–74, 76, 77
and NATO expansion, 37–38, 173
and Outer Space Treaty, 144
and Pentagon, 20–23
presidential vacuum of, 2–3, 5–6
and space militarization, 128
wasted opportunities of, 2–3
cluster bombs, xi, xxvi
CMR (chemistry and metallurgy research), 56–57
CNN, xii
coalition, for war against terrorism, xvi
Coalition for the Liberation of Iraq, xxxii
Coalition to Protect Americans Now, 27
cobalt, xiv, xlix, l
Cochran, Thad, 35, 79
Coffman, Vance, 32
Cohen, Nick, 171
Cohen, Samuel, x, 49
Cohen, William
and China, 175
and cyberwar, 128
and EKV tests, 99
and European Union, 183

and foreign arms sales, 41
and national missile defense program, 76, 79
and North Korea, 28
COILs (chemical oxygen-iodine lasers), 94
collateral damage, 48
Collier, David, 95
Collins, John, 115–118
Collins, Michael, 117
collusion, 99–100
Colombia, xlvi
Commerce Department, xxvii, xxviii
Committee on Foreign Investment in the United States (CFIUS), xxxv
Committee for the Liberation of Iraq, xlii
Committee to Expand NATO, 38
common aero vehicle (CAV), 127
compensation, government, 68–70
Complete Test-Ban Treaty, 45, 168
Comprehensive Test-Ban Treaty (CTBT), xvii–xviii, 44, 54, 168, 170–171
computer simulations, 58–62
computers, 55–62
in BM/C3, 96, 106–111
and satellite viruses, 128–129
Concord (Massachusetts), 150, 156
Contract with America (Newt Gingrich), 73
cooperative denuclearization, 21
cooperative engagement capability (CEC), 104
Coors Beer, 26
corporations, 24–42, 162–171
aerospace, 119
George W. Bush administration ties to, 162–171
mergers and nuclear policy, 29–30
and NATO expansion, 37–39
and political donations, 33–36
and political favor through employment, 32–33
and post-September 11th Pentagon budget, 184–185
and think tanks, 24–25
see also specific corporation
Cosmos 954 satellite, 137
cost(s)
of Afghanistan war, xix
of AWACS program, 89
of Block-4A missiles, 88
of booster stack, 97
of COILS program, 94
of EKV, 97–98
of J-STARS program, 90
of MEAD program, 89
of NTW project, 93
of Patriot missiles, 87
of SBIRS-High, 102
of SBIRS-Low, 102
of SBL program, 95
of SIAP, 104
of THAAD program, 91
of THEL program, 96
of TMD-GBR, 100
Council for a Livable World, 93
Counterforce, 108
Coyle, Phillip E., III, 92
craters, bomb, 8
Cray, 56
CSP, *see* Center for Security Policy
CTBT, *see* Comprehensive Test-Ban Treaty
Cuba, 5
Cunningham, Randy Duke, 185
cyberspace, 122, 123
cyberwar, 128–129

DaimlerChrysler, 37
DaimlerChrysler Aerospace AG, 89
"Daisy Cutters" (fuel air explosives), x–xi
Dammam (Saudi Arabia), 152
DARHT, *see* dual-axis radiographic hydrodynamic test facility
Davy Crocketts, 49
death, 9
decapitation, 108
decoys, 83–84, 100
defects in nuclear weapons, 46–47
Defense Advanced Research Project, xxxiv
defense contractors, 163–164
See also corporations; *specific contractor*
Defense Department, U.S, *see* Pentagon

Defense Export Loan Guarantee (DELG), 41
defense industry, xxx
Defense Intelligence Agency (DIA), xxvi, xxxiv
Defense Policy Advisory Committee on Trade, 31
Defense Policy Board, xvi–xvii, xxiii, xxiv
Defense Policy Board Advisory Committee, xxxiii–xxxviii
Defense Policy Guidance, xxi–xxii
defense programs (DP) laboratories, 44
Defense Science Board (DSB), 31
defense support program (DSP), 102
degradation of nuclear weapons, 46–47
DeLay, Tom, 34, 175
DELG (Defense Export Loan Guarantee), 41
delivery platforms, 49
Denmark, 101, 112, 135, 159
Department of Energy (DOE)
  and economics of reconstruction, xli
  and environmental hazards, 62–65
  and justification for SS &, M, 46
  and Nuclear Nonproliferation Treaty, 43
  and nuclear testing, 54–55
  and nuclear weapon upgrades, 49–50
  and Paducah plant contamination, 148–149
  and risks to uranium-processing workers, 150–151
  and Russian plutonium, 139
  and support for Iraq, xxviii
depleted uranium (DU), xiii, 149
  definition of, 147
  and Desert Storm, 154–155
Desert Storm, *see* Operation Desert Storm
design of nuclear weapons, 44–50
  Congressional authorization for, 47–48
  new weapons, 47–50
  U.S. spending on, 45
Deutch, John, 21–23, 30
deuterium, 46, 52, 53
development of nuclear weapons, 47–50
development, weapons, 126–127
Dicks, Norm, 185
DigitalNet, xxxvi
DiGregorio, Barry, 134
Dingell, John D., xl
dirty bombs, l
dirty nuclear devices, xiv
disease, 10
DOE, *see* Department of Energy
Dole, Bob, 33
Dow Chemical, xxviii
DP Canyon, 66
DP (defense programs) laboratories, 44
DSB (Defense Science Board), 31
DSP (defense support program), 102
DTAG (Defense Trade Advisory Group), 40
DU, *see* depleted uranium
dual-axis radiographic hydrodynamic test (DARHT) facility, 51, 65
Duindrennan (Scotland), 151
"dumb" bombs, xxxii, 145–146
DuPont, xxix–xxx
DynCorp, xliv, xlv

Eareckson Air Station, 112
early-warning systems, xx, 7, 11–12, 101, 111
Eastern Bloc countries, 37–39
Eastman Kodak, xxix–xxx
Eberhart, Ralph E., 125
economic rationalism, 25
economics of reconstruction, xxxviii–xlvi
economics of war, xxx–xxxviii
Egypt, xxxii, 157, 185
Einstein, Albert, 187
Eisenhower, Dwight D., xxx, 186
EKV (exoatmospheric kill vehicle), 97–100
el-Adeli, Nazem, xlvii
elections of 2000, xxii–xxiii
electricity supply, and nuclear meltdowns, xv
electromagnetic pulse (EMP), 84
Electronic Industries Association, 40
An Elusive Consensus (Janne Nolan), 19
EMP (electromagnetic pulse), 84
Empower America, 165
Endoatmospheric defense, *see* lower-tier defense

England, *see* United Kingdom
enriched uranium, xiv, xviii, xxiv, xlix–l, 48–49
environmental hazards
  in Gulf conflict, 157
  with ICBM destruction, 83
  and ozone depletion, 143
  with SS, -M, 62–70
  and uranium clean-up, 156–157
Eskmeals Cumbria (England), 158
EU (European Union), 183
Europe, xvi, xxxii, 78, 110–111, 182–183
  see also specific nation
European Space Agency, 140
European Union (EU), 183
Evans, Don, 162
exoatmospheric defense, *see* upper-tier defense
exoatmospheric kill vehicle (EKV), 97–100
exotic effects, 84
extensive missile defense, 80–81
Exxon, xxv, 185

F-22s, xix
F-117s, xxxii
F/A-18E/F planes, xix
FAA, xv
facilities, nuclear, 50, 52–57
  and economics of reconstruction, xli
  fusion experiments at, 52–54
  hydrodynamic and high-explosive test, 51
  manufacturing, 57
  meltdowns of, xiv–xvi
  military-related, xv
  number of, xiv
  R&D at, 56–57
  for testing, xli, 54–55
  upgrading, 55–57
  see also specific nation
Fahey, Dan, 157
failure rate of nuclear weapons, 46
fallout shelters, 10
FBI, xxxv, 100
Federation of American Scientists, 100
Feed Materials Production Center (Fernald, Ohio), 150
Feith, Douglas, xxi, xxii, xxiii, xxxiv
Fetter, Steve, 22
"fight and win" policy, xx
Finland, 159
fires, 65–68
firestorms, 10
firing ranges, 150
first-strike capability, 107–108
Fisk, Robert, xlvii
flash floods, 67
flight-test facilities, 56
floods, flash, 67
flub factor, 107
Fluor Corporation, xxxix, xlvi
Fogleman, Ronald R., xxxvi, 120, 121
food contamination, 10
food parcels, dropping of, xi
Foreign Affairs, 168
foreign arms sales, 37–42
  loan-guarantee programs for, 36
  by Lockheed Martin, 41–42
  post-September 11th, 185
  to Latin American countries, 39–40
  to NATO countries, 37–39
Foreign Military Studies Office (Fort Leavenworth, Kansas), x
Foreign Responses to U.S. National Missile Defense Deployment, 77, 175
"Foreign Suitors for Iraqi Oilfield Contracts" document, xxxviii
Fort Bliss (Texas), 125–126
France
  and cancer in Balkan War veterans, 159
  and economics of war, xxxii
  and George W. Bush administration, 182
  and Iraqi oil, xxvii
  as nuclear weapons nation, 44
  nuclear weapons tests in, 46
  and Operation Iraqi Freedom, xxxi, xxxii
  proliferation of uranium weapons in, 157
  subcritical tests in, 55
Franks, Tommy, xlix
Freddie Mac, 34
Freedenberg, Paul, xxviii

Friedman, Thomas, 1
FTAA, 26
fuel air explosives (FAEs), x-xi
fusion, nuclear
  experiments with, 52–54
  facilities for, 50
  in nuclear weapons, 46
Fylingdales (England), 101, 105, 111, 181

Gaffney, Frank, 26–27, 73, 165
gamma rays, 45, 152
Gansler, Jacques, 98
GAO, *see* General Accounting Office
Garner, Jay, xlvi
gas gun, 52
gastrointestinal symptoms, 9
GATT, *see* General Agreement on Tariffs and Trade
Gattling guns, xii
GBI (Ground-Based Interceptor), 97
General Accounting Office (GAO), xxxi, xl, xliv, 87, 88, 90–93, 102, 139
General Agreement on Tariffs and Trade (GATT), 25, 41
General Dynamics, 27, 40
General Electric, 140
General Instrument, 162
General Motors, 162
Geneva Protocol, xi
germ warfare, xxviii
Germany, xxxii, 8, 89, 135, 158
Getronics Government Solutions, xxxvi
Gingrich, Newt, xvii, 33, 73
Glaspie, April, 145
Glenn,, John, 116
Global Crossing Ltd., xxxv
global positioning system (GPS)
  and BM/C3, 98, 99
  civilian/military uses of, 123
  and Kosovo war, 121
  and "near nuclear" weapons, xii
  vulnerability of, 129–130
"go-it-alone" attitude, xxii
Goering, Hermann, xxi
Gofman, John, 138, 141
Goldman Sachs, xxxv
Golts, Alexander, 174
Gorbachev, Mikhail, 18, 37, 172, 184
Gore, Al, 35
Government Accounting Office, *see* General Accounting Office
GPS, *see* global positioning system
Graham, Bob, xlviii
Grand, Camille, 182
Grand Forks (North Dakota), 112
Greece, 157
Greenland, 101, 112, 182
Greenpeace, 181
Groopman, Jerome, 132
Ground-Based Interceptor (GBI), 97
Grumman, xix
Guam, 180
Guantanamo Bay, xliii
Gulf conflict, 121, 145–146
  space force advanced by, 121
  and uranium clean-up, 157
  uranium weapons in, 151–156
Gulf War syndrome, 154–156, 159, 160
gun assembly mechanism, 48
gun ships, xii
Gusterson, Hugh, 16
G.W. Searle, 162

Haavisto, Pekka, 159–160
Hadley, Stephen J., x, 169
Hainan (China), 177
Hall, Keith, 115
Halliburton Oil, xxx, xxxix, xlii–xlv, 35, 162
Hamburg (Germany), 8
Hanely, Charles, xlvii–xlviii
Hanford Nuclear Reservation, 67
Hanford (Washington), 64, 65
hard targets, 48
Harshaw Chemical Company, 70
Hartung, William, 34, 36
HAVE STARE (radar), 112
hazards
  of Academic Strategic Alliances Program, 58–62
  computer, 57–58
  environmental, *see* environmental hazards
  fire, 65–68
  and government compensation, 68–70

of plutonium 238 production, 139–141
of SS, -M, 57–70
health concerns, *see* medical concerns
Hellfire missiles, xii
Hellman, Christopher, 185
Helms, Jesse, 166, 170
Heritage Foundation, 26, 27, 77–79, 164
Hertz Rent-A-Car, 26
Hewlett-Packard, xxix–xxx
Hezbollah, 96
high energy laser weapons, 94–96
High Orbit Space-Based Infrared System (SBIRS-High), 102
high-explosive facilities, 56
high-explosive test facilities, 51
Hiroshima, 8, 36, 46, 48, 145, 147
Holiday Inns, 26
Holog (subcritical test), 54
Homeland Security Department, U.S., xxxv
Honeywell, xxix–xxx, 91
Howitzer cannons, xii
Hughes, 40
Hughes Aircraft, 30
Hughes Space, 119
Human Rights Watch, xi
Huntsville (Alabama), 105, 142
Hurlburt Field (Florida), 125
Hussein, Saddam. *See* Iraq
hydrodynamic measuring facilities, 51
hydrogen bombs, 3, 46
hydrogen cyanide, xxviii
hypersonic military space planes, 127–128

IAEA, *see* International Atomic Energy Agency
IBM, 56
ICBMs, *see* Intercontinental ballistic missiles
Iceland, 184
ICF (Inertial Confinement Fusion), 52
Idaho National Engineering and Environmental Laboratory, 64, 65, 67–68
igniters, 50
ignition facility, 53
IGT (integrated ground test), 105
IMF (International Monetary Fund), 25
Import-Export Bank, xlv
The Independent, xlvii
India, 7
and arms race, 77, 78, 86
and China, 176, 178–179
and international ramifications of U.S. behavior, xiii
nuclear program in, xiii, xxvii, 44, 46
and political implications of George W. Bush administration behavior, xviii
Inertial Confinement Fusion (ICF), 52
infinity rooms, 63
Inhofe, James, 74
insects, 10
Institute for Energy and Environmental Research, 64
integrated ground test (IGT), 105
Integrated System Test Capability-2 facility, 105
Intel Corporation, 56
intelligence agencies, U.S., xxiii, xxiv, xxxvii
intercontinental ballistic missiles (ICBMs), 82–85
intercontinental land-based hydrogen bombs, 3
intercontinentl nuclear ballistic missiles, ix
International Atomic Energy Agency (IAEA), xlix–l, 10, 156
International Atomic Energy Commission, xxiv
international community
and Academic Strategic Alliances Program, 58–62
and Arms Race, 81–82
and George W. Bush administration, xiii, 171–184
and nuclear weapons treaties, 44
and space warfare, 127, 143–144
and Star Wars, 111–114
treaty concerns of, 110–111
and uranium weapons, 158–161
International Computer Systems, xxix–xxx
International Monetary Fund (IMF), 25
International Resources Group, xlv

International Space Station (ISS), 135–136
internet, design for dirty nuclear devices on, xiv
iodine, radioactive, 62
Iran, xxvi, xxxiv, xxxvii, xxxix, 4, 5, 75, 79, 80
Iran hostage affair, xxvi
Iran-Iraq war, xxvi–xxvii, xxviii, xxix
Iran/Contra, xxiii
Iraq, 4, 5
  and al Qaeda, xxiv, xxv
  Baath Party in, xxv, xxvi, xxxvii
  bombing of, xxix, xxx–xxxi
  and Britain, xxv, xxvi
  and cancer risks in civilians, xxix, 153
  children exposed to depleted uranium in, 156
  and China, xxvii
  and CIA, xxv
  depleted uranium used in, 152, 156
  and economics of reconstruction, xlix
  and economics of war, xxx–xxxviii
  and France, xxvii
  Halliburton sales to, xliv–xlv
  Hussein takes control in, xxvi
  infrastructure of, xxix, xxx–xxxi, xlix
  and Iran-Iraq war, xxvi, xxvii
  Kuwait invasion by, xxix
  mass killings in, xxvi
  nuclear scientists in, xxviii
  nuclear sites in, xlix
  nuclear weapons program in, xxiv, xxv, xxviii
  oil in, xxv, xxvi, xxvii, xxx, xxxviii, xxxix
  and Operation Desert Storm, xxix
  proliferation of uranium weapons in, 157
  public health system in, xlvii–l
  purchase of uranium from Niger by, xxiv
  radioactive contamination in, 154
  reconstruction of, xxxvi, xxxviii–xlvi
  as rogue state, 80
  Rumsfeld's meetings with Hussein in, xxvii
  and Russia/Soviet Union, xxv, xxvii
  U.N. sanctions against, xxix
  U.S. exports to, xxvii–xxviii
  U.S. loans to, xxviii, xlii
  U.S. plans for overthrow of, xvii
  and U.S. policy on Kuwait, 145
  U.S. sanctions on, xliv–xlv
  U.S. support for, xxvi-xxviii, xxix–xxx
  as U.S. target, xvi–xvii, 75
  weapons of mass destruction in, xxix–xxx
  and World Trade Center, xxxvii
  See also Operation Desert Storm; Operation Iraqi Freedom; *specific person*
Iraq Liberation Act, xxxvii
Iraq Survey Group, xlvi
Iraqi defectors/exiles, xxiv, xxxix
Iraqi military, xxvi
Iraqi National Congress (INC), xxiv, xxxvii
Iraqi National Guard, xxvi
Iraqi Petroleum Company, xxv
Iraqi police force, xlv
Ireland, 159
Israel
  as nuclear weapons nation, 44
  as potential target, 78
  Project for a New American Century support for, xxi
  proliferation of uranium weapons in, 157
  as purchaser of U.S. weapons, xxxii
  Richard Perle and, 170
  and THEL program, 96
  and U.N. Arms Race resolution, 82
  uranium weapons use in, 158
  weapons tests in, 79
ISS, *see* International Space Station
Issa, Darrell, xxxix
Italian space agency, 132
Italy, 89, 135, 159
Ivanov, Igor, 173

J-STARS (Joint Surveillance and Target Attack Radar System), 90
Jackson, Bruce, xxiii, xxxii, 33, 38, 168–169

Jalabad, Afghanistan, bombing of mosque in, xi
Jane's Defense Weekly, 74
Japan
X-band radars in, 105
and Aegis ships, 88
and International Space Station, 135
and Little Boy (Hiroshima bomb), 48
as military power, 176
and North Korean threat, 74–75
proliferation of uranium weapons in, 157
JASONS, 46
JASPER (Joint Actinide Shock Physics Experimental Research), 52
Javelin missile command launch units, xxxi, xxxiii
Jeremiah, David, xxxvi
Jewish Institute for National Security Affairs, xlvi
Johnson, Charmers, 180–181
Johnson, Lyndon, 72
Joint Actinide Shock Physics Experimental Research (JASPER), 52
Joint Direct Attack Munitions (JDAM), xxxii, xxxiii
Joint Strategic Planning Service, 19
Joint Strike fighter, xix
Joint Surveillance and Target Attack Radar System (J-STARS), 90
joint warrior interoperability demonstration (JWID), 125
Jordan, 157
JP Morgan Chase, xlii
Just Cause (Colin Powell), 167
JWID (joint warrior interoperability demonstration), 125

Kansas City plant (KCP), 50, 57
Karzai, Hamid, xlv
Kasich, John, 116
Katyusha rockets, 96
Kay, David, xlvi
KBR (Kellogg, Brown and Root), xlii–xlv
KCP (Kansas City plant), 50, 57
Kellogg, Brown and Root (KBR), xlii–xlv
Kennedy, Paul, 181
Kettle, Martin, 165
Keyworth, George, 27
Khomeini, Ayatollah, xxvi
kidney disease, 153–154
Kim Chong-il, 28
Kim Dae Jung, 28, 29
Kirtland Air Force Base (New Mexico), 124, 156–157
Kissinger, Henry, xii, xvii, 166
Klein, Naomi, xxxviii, xxxix
Korea, *see* North Korea; South Korea
Kosovo war
and cancer risks in troops, 153
uranium weapons used in, 158–161
and U.S. space force, 121–122
Kristol, William, xxi
Kucinich, Dennis, xxviii
Kurds, xxviii
Kuwait, xxix, xxxii, xxxix, 145, 152, 154, 157
Kyl, John, 27

Labaton, Stephen, xxxv
Lake, Anthony, 21
LaMontagne, Steve, 79
Lancashire (England), 151
Lane, Neal, 124
LANL, *see* Los Alamos National Laboratory
laser beams, 52, 53–54
laser guided bunker busters, xii
laser weapons, 94–96, 126–127
laser-powered fusion, 50
Lasswell, Harold, 25
lateral proliferation, 45
Latin America, 39–40
Latvia, 159
Lawrence Livermore National Laboratory (LLNL)
ASCI Blue Pacific computer at, 56
British cooperation with, 111
defense program at, 44
Iraq support by, xxviii
JASPER at, 52
Manhattan II project at, 4, 43
NIF at, 53
nuclear facilities at, 50
nuclear weapons lab at, 14–15

Lawrence Livermore National Laboratory (LLNL) (*cont.*)
personnel policies at, 14–15
TeraOPS computer at, 56
university alliances with, 59, 61
LEAP (lightweight exoatmospheric projectile), 92, 93
Lebanon, 96
Lee, Wen Ho, 59
Leelworth (England), 158
Lehman Brothers, xxxvii–xxxviii
Lenard, Roger, 142
Leprosy Letter, 40
Lexington Institute, 185
Libby, I. Lewis, xxiii
Libya, 5, 78, 79, 80, 105
Lieberman, Joseph, 35–36
lightweight exoatmospheric projectile (LEAP), 92, 93
limited missile defense, 80
Lincoln, Abraham, 24
lithium, 46
Little Boy (Hiroshima bomb), 48
Litton Industries, 40
LLNL, *see* Lawrence Livermore National Laboratory
Lockheed Martin, 29–42, 163–164
and AOV, 127
Augustine and, 31–32
George W. Bush and, 164
Cheney and, 164–165
as contractor at Paducah, 148
as contractor for COILS program, 94
as contractor for MEADS project, 89
as contractor for NTW project, 93
as contractor for Patriot project, xxxii, 87
as contractor for SBIRS-High, 102
as contractor for SBL program, 95
as contractor for SIAP, 104
as contractor for THAAD project, 91
and economics of war, xxx
and foreign arms sales, 39–42
Gingrich and, 33
government contracts of, xix, xxxii, 36–37
Hadley and, 169
Jackson and, 168–169
laser weapons developed by, 126
and Long Range Plan, 119
merger of Martin Marietta with, 29–30
"near nuclear" weapons developed by, xii
and Nevada Test Site, 54
and nuclear space systems, 140
Operation Iraqui Freedom weapons supplied by, xxxii
political clout of, 33–37, 39
and post-September 11th Pentagon budget, xix, 184, 185
think tanks funded by, 26, 27
as war lobby, xxxiii
Logistics Civil Augmentation Program "Logcap," xliii, xliv
London Evening Standard, xlviii
"The Long Range Plan" (LRP), 119–121
Loral Space Systems, 40
Los Alamos Canyon, 66
Los Alamos National Laboratory (LANL)
30-TeraOPS computer at, 56
ASCI Blue Mountain computer at, 56
British cooperation with, 111
chemistry and metallurgy research at, 56–57
DARHT at, 51
defense program at, 44
environmental hazards at, 64
fires at, 65–67
Iraq support by, xxviii
Manhattan II project at, 4, 43
manufacturing facilities at, 57
and Mars exploration, 131
new pit manufacturing at, 48
nuclear facilities at, 50
and nuclear powered rockets, 142
nuclear weapons lab at, 13–14
radiation exposure at, 139–140
subcritical tests at, 55
university alliances with, 59, 61
uranium testing at, 147
Lott, Trent, xxiii, 33, 34, 35
Louis Berger Group, Inc., xxxix
Low Orbit Space-Based Infrared System (SBIRS-Low), 102
Lower Saxony (Germany), 158

lower-tier defense (endoatmospheric), 86–90
LRP, *see* The Long Range Plan
Luti, William, xxiv

McCaffrey, Barry, xliii, 21
McCain, John, 33
McDonnell Douglas, 30, 38
McGeough, Paul, xlvii, xlviii
McGrory, Mary, 99
Mackay, Leo, 22
Mackinder, Halford J., 116
Madison (Indiana), 150
Madrick, Jeff, xxxi
Mandate for Leadership Policy Management in a Conservative Administration (Heritage Foundation), 26
Manhattan II Project, 4. *See also* stockpile stewardship and management program
Manhattan Project, xli, 13, 150
manufacturing facilities, 57
mapping mission, 123–124
Mark 5 missile, 48
Mars, 131–137, 142
Marsh & McLennan, xlvi
Marshall Plan, xxxix
Marshall Space Flight Center (Huntsville, Alabama), 142
Martin Marietta, 29–30
Mattarella, Sergio, 159
Maverick missiles, xxxiii
Mayer, Gottfried J., 107
MC-130s, x
MEADS (Medium Extended Air Defense System), 88–89
medical concerns, 62, *See also* cancer
  of ICBM destruction, 83
  about Mars exploration, 132–134, 136
  Pentagon s prior knowledge of, 154–156
  about plutonium, 138, 238
  of plutonium 238 production, 139–141
  about uranium processing, 149–151
  about uranium weapons, 151–156
Medium Extended Air Defense System (MEADS), 88–89
Meet the Press (NBC), xxiv
MEIs (most exposed individuals), 154–155
Mello, Greg, 55
Menwith Hill (England), 111, 130, 181
mergers, corporate, 29–30
Merritt, Jack, 17
MESA (microsystems and engineering sciences), 57
Metal of Dishonor, 150
Mexico, xiv, 66
Meyers, Richard B., 115
MI6 (British secret intelligence service), xxvi
microsystems and engineering sciences (MESA), 57
Middle East, 105
  century of oil and war in, xxv–xxx
military corporations, xxxiv
Military Space Forces: The Next 50 Years (John Collins), 115–116
Military, U.S., *see* U.S. military
military-industrial complex, xviii–xix, xxx, 26–27, 184, 186
Miller, Frank "Mr. Nuke," 20
mines, xi
mini-nukes, 48 49
MIRVs (multiple independent reentry vehicles), 82
missile defenses, xvi, xviii, 80
missile-defense shield, ix
missiles
  precision-guided, xxxii
  See also type of missiles
MITRE Corporation, xxxvi, xxxviii
Mobil, xxv
Mogadishu (Somalia), 158
Moon, 116–118
Moore, Mike, 127
morning-after pills, xlviii
Mortandad Canyon, 66
Moscow, 108
Mossadegh, Mohammed, xxvi
most exposed individuals (MEIs), 154–155
Mubarak, Hosni, xxxvii
mujahadeen, xiii
multinational corporations, xxxix, xliv

multiple independent reentry vehicles (MIRVs), 82
Murdoch, Rupert, xxi
mustard gas, xxviii
mutual assured safety, 21

NAFTA (North American Free Trade Agreement), 25
Nagasaki, 63
NAS, *see* National Academy of Sciences
NASA, *see* National Aeronautics and Space Administration
The Nation, xxxviii, xxxix
National Academy of Sciences (NAS), 64, 134, 151
National Aeronautics and Space Administration (NASA)
  and global mapping mission, 123–124
  and Mars missions, 131–132, 134
  and nuclear powered space probes, 138–142
  and space militarization, 119
"The National Ignition Facility and the Issue of Nonproliferation," 58
National Ignition Facility (NIF), 53–54, 58
National Imagery and Mapping Agency, 12
National Institutes for Health, 185
National Intelligence Council, 75
national missile defense (NMD) program, 4, 71–114
  background, 72–79
  and George W. Bush, 4
  definition of, 80
  and Europe, 182–183
  and France, 182
  and Great Britain, 181
  and Greenland, 182
  infrastructure of, 104–106
National Security Agency, xxxv
National Security Council, xxv, xxviii
Native Americans, 66
NATO, *see* North Atlantic Treaty Organization
Natsios, Andrew, xl, xli–xlii, xlv
Naval Theater Wide (NTW) Missile Defense, 92–94
Naval War College, 178
Navigation Warfare (NavWar), 128
NAVSTAR global positioning system, 98, 99
NavWar (Navigation Warfare), 128
NBC, xxiv
"near nuclear" weapons, examples of, x–xiii
neptunium, 148
Netherlands, 135, 159
neutron bombs, x, 49
neutron generator facility (NGF), 57
Nevada Test Site (NTS), xviii, xli, 37, 50–52, 54–55, 64, 65, 68
"New Europe," xxxii
New York City, medical description of Indian Point meltdown effecting, xv
New York Times, xxii, xxxi, xxxv, xliii, xlv
New York Times Magazine, xliii
New Zealand, 157
NGF (neutron generator facility), 57
NIF (National Ignition Facility), 53–54
Niger, xxiv
1984 (George Orwell), 15
Nisbet, Paul, xix
Nixon, Richard M., xii, xxv, xxvii, 72
NMD, *see* national missile defense program
Nolan, Janne, 19
Nortel Networks, xxxvii
North American Free Trade Agreement (NAFTA), 25
North Atlantic Treaty Organization (NATO)
  AWACS operated by, 89
  and cancer in Balkan War veterans, 158–161
  and cancer risks in troops, 153
  and Eastern Bloc countries, 37–39
  European dissatisfaction with, 182–183
  and Kosovo war, 122
North Dakota, 108
North Korea, 105
  in BM/C3 scenario, 107
  Bolton and, 171
  and economics of war, xxxiv
  nuclear reactors in, xli
  as nuclear weapons target, 4

in peace talks with South Korea, 77
as potential threat, 5, 28–29, 74–75, 79
as rogue state, 80
weapons supplied by, 78
Northern Alliance, x
Northrop Grumman, 27, 30, 90, 91, 102, 185
Northwest Territories (Canada), 137
Norway, 105, 112, 113, 135
NPT (Nuclear Nonproliferation Treaty), 43, 45, 47
NTR (nuclear thermal rockets), 141
NTS, *see* Nevada Test Site
NTW, *see* Naval Theater Wide Missile Defense
nuclear alert codes, ix
nuclear arms race, xvi
nuclear devices in space, 136–144
nuclear facilities, *see* facilities, nuclear
nuclear fusion, *see* fusion, nuclear
Nuclear Nonproliferation Treaty (NPT), 43, 45, 47
nuclear posture review, 20–21
nuclear power plants, 9–10
nuclear powered rockets, 141–142
nuclear powered space probes, 138–139
nuclear powered weapons, 142–143
Nuclear Regulatory Commission (NRC), xv
Nuclear Rites (Hugh Gusterson), 16
Nuclear Stockpile Stewardship Management Program, *see* stockpile stewardship management program
nuclear thermal rockets (NTR), 141
nuclear threats, examples of, xiv-xvi
nuclear war, 7–12
accidental, 11–12
and disease, 10
fallout from, 9
medical consequences of, 7–11
and nuclear power plants, 9–10
and nuclear winter, 10–11
nuclear waste, xli, 62–66, 149, 150
nuclear weapons
components of, 45–46
increase in funding for, xviii
new weapons, 55–57
test facilities for, 66
testing of, *see* testing, nuclear weapons
treaties for, 44
Nuclear Weapons in the Twenty-First Century (Stephen Younger), 48
nuclear winter, 10–11
Nunn, Sam, 116

O'Neill, Paul, 162
Oak Ridge National Labs
environmental hazards at, 64
manufacturing facilities at, 57
and nuclear space systems development, 140
Y-12 weapons plant at, 68
Oboe (subcritical test), 54
Ocean Spray Cranberries, 26
Office of Special Plans (OSP), xxiv
oil
and century of war in Middle East, xxv–xxx
in Kuwait, xxix
and planning for Iraq war, xxii
privatization of, xxxix
See also specific nation
Oil Nationalization Bill (Iran), xxvi
"Old Europe," xxxii
Oman, xxxii, 157, 185
Omega West reactor, 66
O'Neil, Tip, xl
100-TeraOPS computer, 56
Operation Desert Storm, xvi, xxix, 151–156, 160–161
Operation Iraqi Freedom
and economics of war, xxx–xxxviii
financing of, xxxi
justification for, xlvii
overview about, xxix–xxx
planning for, xxi–xxiii
selling of, to American people, xxiv–xxv
and the war Americans didn't see, xlvii–l
Option White TeraOPS computer, 56
Outer Space Treaty, 127, 141, 144
overpressures, 8
Owens, William, xxxvii, 22
ozone layer, 10, 143

PAC (political action committees) contributions, 163
Paducah Gaseous Diffusion Plant (Kentucky), 148–149
Pahlavi, Shah Reza, xxvi
Pakistan, 7
  and Afghanistan, xiii
  and arms race, 77, 78, 86
  foreign arms sales to, 185
  and international ramifications of U.S. behavior, xiii
  Muslim fundamentalists and military in, 176
  nuclear testing in, xviii
  as nuclear weapons nation, xiii, 44
  and political implications of George W. Bush administration behavior, xviii
  proliferation of uranium weapons in, 157
  U.S. relations with, xiii
Pakistani military, xiii
Paladin Capital Group, xxxvi
Palestinians, xxi, 158
Pantex plant (Texas), 50, 57
Parajito Canyon, 66
Paris Air Show, xxxi
Parsons Corp., xxxix
Patriot missiles, xxxii
Patriot (PAC-3) Army System, 86–88
Patriot (PAC-3) lower-tier system, xxxii, 73
PAVE PAWS (Perimeter Acquisition of Vehicle Entry Phased-Array Warning System), 101
Paveway II bomb, xxxii
Peeler, Bob, xliv
Pentagon, 17–23, 28–33
  and Afghanistan war, x
  al Qaeda attack on, xxi
  as America's largest company, 185
  Augustine and, 31–32
  budget for, xxxi
  and changing terminology, 85
  and Clinton administration, 20–23
  and corporate mergers, 29–30
  and economics of reconstruction, xliii, xlv, xlvi
  and economics of war, xxxi, xxxiv, xxxv, xxxvi, xxxvii
  and European dissatisfaction over NATO, 183
  "fight and win" policy of, xx
  and Iran-Iraq war, xxvi
  as Iraqi supporter, xxviii
  and Korean threat, 28–29
  and military spending, 5
  need for dismantling of, 186
  new space service in, 121–122
  pathological thinking of, 20
  and PNAC, xxiii
  and political implications of George W. Bush administration behavior, xvi, xix
  political role of, 18
  and post-September 11th spending, 184–185
  and prior knowledge of medical hazards, 154–156
  and rigged missile tests, 99–100
  SIOP planning by, 19–23
  and space shuttle, 123–124
  and weapons budget, 32–33
Perimeter Acquisition of Vehicle Entry Phased-Array Warning System (PAVE PAWS), 101
Perle, Richard, xvi–xvii, xxi, xxii, xxiii, xxiv, xxxiv–xxxvi, 169, 170
permanent normal trading relations (PNTR) status, 4
Perry, William, 29, 30, 39–40
Philip Morris Companies, xxxvii
Pike, John, 28, 32, 106, 124
Pine Gap (Australia), 105, 130, 180
pit production facility, 57
Pitt, William Rivers, xxii, xliii
planes, 3, 127–128
  See also type of plane
platforms, delivery, 49
plutonium 238
  health consequences of, 138–141
  production of, 139–141
  in space, 137–141
plutonium, 48
  behavior of, 51–52
  carcinogenic, xiv, xlix

and dirty nuclear devices, xiv
facilities working on, 56–57
and fire hazards, 67, 68
hazards of, 62–65
production of, 148
and safeguarding of Russian nuclear materials, xviii
in sphere of nuclear weapons, 45
in underground testing, 54
and U.S. support for Iraq, xxviii
plutonium pits
environmental hazards of, 63
Los Alamos manufacture of, 57
and weapons designs and modifications, 48–51
PNAC. *See* Project for a New American Century (PNAC)
PNTR (permanent normal trading relations) status, 4
poison gas, xxvii
political action committees (PAC) contributions, 163
politics, xvi–xix, 32–36, 163
Pollack, Jonathon, 174
polluted uranium, 148
polonium, 69, 149
Polycom, xxxvii
Portugal, 159
Postol, Ted, 99, 100, 112, 113
potassium iodide, xv–xvi
Powell, Colin
and China, 180
and coalition to fight terrorism, xvi
corporate ties of, 166–168
and economics of reconstruction, xxxix
and planning for Iraq war, xxiii
and political implications of George W. Bush administration behavior, xvi, xvii
SIOP review by, 18–19
precision-guided missiles, xxxii, xxxiii
preemptive strike, xxii, xxiii
Preston (England), 151
Prevention of an Arms Race in Outer Space (United Nations), 81–82
Price-Anderson Act, 141
privatization, xxxix, xliii–xliv
probes, nuclear powered space, 138–139
Project for a New American Century (PNAC), xxi–xxiii
proliferation, 45
proton radiography, 51
psychological operations (psyops), 117–118
Pueblo Canyon, 66
Puerifoy, Bob, 54
pulse-powered facilities, 51–52
purified uranium, 149
Putin, Vladimir, xvi, xix–xx, 29, 71, 109–110, 172–174, 184

Qasim, Abd al-Karim, xxv–xxvi
Qualcomm, xxxix

R&D facilities (research and development facilities), 56–57
radar, 89–90, 101, 102, 104–105, 108, 111, 112
radiation poisoning, 9
radioactive contamination, l
radioactive iodine, 62
radioactive materials, l
radioactive uranium, xxix
radioactive water, xlix
radiography, proton, 51
radium, 149
radomes, 130
radon, 149
RAND Corporation, xxxvii
Raytheon, 40
and Afghanistan war weapons, xxxiii
as contractor of Block-4A project, 88
as contractor for EKV, 97, 98
as contractor for NTW project, 93
as contractor for Patriot project, 87
as contractor for SIAP, 104
as contractor for THAAD project, 91
as contractor for TMD-GBR, 100
and economics of war, xxx
and foreign arms sales, 39
and Hughes Aircraft buyout, 30
and Long Range Plan, 119
as manufacturer of BMEWS, 101
as manufacturer of PAVE PAWS, 101
Operation Iraqi Freedom weapons supplied by, xxxiii
political clout of, xxxiii, 34, 35

Raytheon (*cont.*)
and post-September 11th Pentagon budget, xix, 184
think tanks funded by, 27
as third-highest defense contractor, 164
as war lobby, xxxiii
Readers Digest, 26
Reagan administration
defense buildup during, xix
and foreign arms sales, 39
and Iran-Iraq war, xxvi–xxvii
nuclear weapons buildup during, 3
and SBL program, 95
and Star Wars, 26–27, 71, 72
Reagan, Ronald, 184
Rebound (subcritical test), 54
"Rebuilding America's Defenses" (PNAC), xxii
reclaimed uranium, 148
reconstruction, economics of, xxxviii–xlvi
Red Terascale computer, 56
reliability, 46–47
rem, 69
Repacholi, Mike, 156
research and development (R&D) facilities, 56–57
Reykjavik (Iceland), 184
Rice, Condoleezza, xvi, 162, 168
Richard, Alain, 182
Richter, Burton, 84
Rio Grande River, 66
Robb, Charles, 130
rocket propellants, 60
rockets, nuclear powered, 141–142
Rockwell International, xxix–xxx, 27
Rocky Flats plant, 63
rodents, 10
rogue states, 80, 110
Romania, 38, 39, 159
ROTC (Reserve Officer Training Corps), xliv
Roving Sands 2000, 125–126
Rummel, John, 134
Rumsfeld, Donald
and Afghanistan war, x, xii, 49
corporate ties of, xxvii, 162, 165–166
and Defense Policy Board, xvii
and defense strategy, 85
and economics of reconstruction, xlvi
and economics of war, xxxiv
Hussein's meeting with, xxvii
Iraqi visits of, xxvii
and national missile defense report, 74, 75
Perle as advisor to, xxxiv
and PNAC, xxii, xxiii
and political implications of George W. Bush administration behavior, xvii, xviii
and September 11 as justification for policies, ix
and spy planes over China, 177
and think tanks, 27
Rumsfeld report, 74, 75, 113, 165
Russia, 105
and Afghanistan, xi, xiii
and George W. Bush administration, xvi, xviii, 172–174
and cancer in Balkan War veterans, 159
and China, 174
early-warning systems in, xx
enriched uranium in, xiv
false attack on, 11–12
and international ramifications of U.S. behavior, xiii
and International Space Station, 135
and Iraqi oil, xxvii
loss of nuclear weapons in, xiv
missile targets of, 7
and NATO expansion, 169–170
and new arms race, 86
nuclear alert codes of, ix
nuclear arsenal of, 81
and nuclear devices in space, 137, 138
nuclear testing in, xviii
and nuclear thermal rockets, 142
nuclear weapons facilities in, 12
and nuclear weapons treaties, 44
plutonium supply of, 139
as potential threat, 5, 75
and proliferation, 79
proliferation of uranium weapons in, 157
safeguarding of nuclear materials in, xviii
and START II Treaty, xx

strategic weapons of, 3–4
subcritical tests in, 55
and treaties, 108–110
and war against terrorism, xvi
Ryan, Michael, 122, 125

Sabri, Naji, xvi
safeguard, 72
safety, 46
Saido Arabia. proliferation of uranium weapons in, 157
SALT II, 166
Sánchez, Arias, 40
Sanders, Bernie, 30
Sandia Livermore Lab (California), 50
Sandia National Laboratory (SNL)
ASCI Red Terascale computer at, 56
defense program at, 44
Iraq support by, xxviii
Manhattan II project at, 4, 43
manufacturing facilities at, 57
microsystems and engineering sciences at, 57
nuclear facilities at, 50
nuclear weapons lab at, 14
university alliances with, 59, 61
uranium 238 contamination at, 156
Sandia Nuclear Weapons Lab (New Mexico), 37
"Satan" missile, xx
Saud family, xxxvii
Saudi Arabia
and AWACS, 89
depleted uranium used in, 151, 152, 154
oil in, xxxix
as purchaser of U.S. weapons, xxxii
Savannah River Nuclear Facility (Georgia), 154
Savannah River plant (SRP), 50, 57, 64, 139
SBIRS, *see* Space-Based Infrared System
SBIRS-High (High Orbit Space-Based Infrared System), 102
SBIRS-Low (Low Orbit Space-Based Infrared System), 103
SBL (Space Based Laser), 95
SBSS (science-based stockpile stewardship), 61
Scardaville, Michael, 78, 79
Schakowsky, Janice, xliii
Scheunemann, Randy, xxiii
Schlesinger, James, xxxvii–xxxviii
Schneider, William, x
Schrobenhausen (Bavaria), 158
Schultz, George, xxvi–xxvii, xxx, xlii
Schwartz, Bernard, 33
Schwartz, Nina, 99–100
Science Applications International Corporation (SAIC), xxxvii, xlvi
science-based stockpile stewardship (SBSS), 61
scientists, xxviii, 13–17
SCOPE, 11
Scud missiles, 86–87
SDI, *see* Strategic Defense Initiative
Seaborg, Glenn, 138
Searle Pharmacies, xxvii
Second Amendment, xviii
Sentinel, 72
September 11, 2001
and ABM treaty, 185
and economics of reconstruction, xlvi
and enemies of U.S., 4
as justification for George W. Bush administration
policies, ix
and nuclear meltdowns, xv
and Pakistan-U.S. relations, xiii
and Pentagon budget, xviii, 184–185
and planning for Iraq war, xxiii
and political implications of George W. Bush administration behavior, xvi, xvii, xviii, xix
and U.S. Russian relations, 5–6
Sha Zukang, 71
Shapir, Yiftah, 96
Shea & Gardner, xxxvii
Sheehan, Jack, xxxvi
Shell Oil, xxv, 131
Shelton, Henry, 74, 184
Shemya Island (Alaska), 105, 112, 113
Shulsky, Abram, xxiv
SIAP (Single Integrated Air Picture), 104
Silicon Graphics Corporation, 56
silicon-based microelectronics devices, 56
silicosis, 136

simulations, computer, 58–62
Single Integrated Air Picture (SIAP), 103
single integrated operational plan (SIOP), 3–4, 18–19
small-arms exports, xviii
"smart" bombs, xxxii, 145–146
Smith, Bob, 122
SMV (space maneuverable vehicle), 128
Snake River, 65
SNL, *see* Sandia National Laboratory
"soft kill" weapons, 116
solar space cells, 140
solid fuel, and ozone depletion, 143
Solway Firth (Britain), 158
Somalia, 158
Son of Star Wars (Bob Aldridge), 74
South Korea, 28, 77, 88, 89, 105
Southern Co., 34
Soviet Union, xix, xxv, 46. *See also* Russia
space, nuclear devices in, 136–144
Space Based Laser (SBL), 95
Space Daily, 126
space probes, nuclear powered, 138–139
space samples, 134
space shuttle, 123
space warfare, 115–144
space-based defense, 81–82
Space-Based Infrared System (SBIRS), 101–104
space-based infrared system-high, 130
Space-Based Integrated Flight Experiment, 126
Space-Based Laser Demonstrator, 126
Spain, 159
Sparta Corp., 119
Spectra-Physics, xxix–xxx
Spectrum Astro, 102
Spenser, Jack, 78, 79
Sperry, xxix–xxx
SRP, *see* Savannah River plant
SS & M, *see* stockpile stewardship and management program
SS-18 missile (Russian), xx
Stanford University, 59
Star Wars, 26–29, 71–114
  background, 72–79
  Congressional advocates of, 35
  Edward Teller s advocation of, 27
  evaluation of BM/C3, 106–111
  ICBM destruction mechanisms, 82–85
  international opinion of, 111–114
  legislation for, 29
  and think tanks, 28–29
  unilateral reductions proposal as ploy to divert attention from, xx
  weapon systems in, 85–106
Starmet plant (Concord, Massachusetts), 156
START, 48
START II, xx, 23, 48, 109, 110
START III, 11, 109
stereoscopic images, 51, 52
Stevedoring Services of America, xxxviii, xlv
Stevens, Ted, 113
Stiglitz, Joseph, 26*n.*
stimulus plan (George W. Bush), xl
stockpile stewardship and management program (SS & M), 14, 43–70
  agenda of, 44–45, 47
  building new nuclear weapons and
  environmental hazards of, 62–68
  facilities of, 50
  and fusion experiments, 52–54
  and government compensation, 68–70
  hazards of, 57–62
  infrastructure of, 45–46
  justification for, 46–47
  and nuclear weapons testing, 54–55
  and plutonium, 51–52
  and weapons development, 47–48
stockpiled weapons, xix–xx, 45–46
Strategic Arms Reduction Treaty, *see* START
Strategic Defense Initiative (SDI), 72, 108
Strengthening Transatlantic Security (Pentagon), 183–184
strontium, xiv, 62, 148
subcritical tests, 54–55
submarines, 3
subsidies, for armament industry, xxxi
sunlight reduction, 10
Swiss Federal Institute of Technology, 161
SYColeman, xlvi

Sydney Morning Herald, xlvii–xlviii
Symantec, xxxvii
Syria, xxxvii, 5, 78, 79

TA-2 plutonium facility (Los Alamos), 66
TA-18 plutonium facility (Los Alamos), 66
TA-41 plutonium facility (Los Alamos), 66
TA-55 plutonium facility (Los Alamos), 57
Tactical High Energy Laser (THEL), 95–96
Taepo-Dong missile, 74
Taiwan, 157, 170, 176–180
Taliban, xiii
Taylor, Ted, 13, 53, 84
technetium, 148
tectronics, xxix–xxx
TEF (tritium extraction facility), 57
Teller, Edward, 16, 27, 54
temperatures, subfreezing, 10–11
TeraOPS computer, 56
terminal phase systems, 85
terrorists
  aggressive militarization as defense against, ix
  low-tech threat of, 5
  and nuclear power plants, 10
  as U.S. enemies, 4
testing, nuclear weapons, xviii, xli, 50, 54–55, 66
Texas Instruments, 30
Textron, 38
THAAD (theater high altitude area defense project), 90–92
Thailand, 157
Thatcher, Thomas D., II, xxxviii
theater high altitude area defense project (THAAD), 90–92
  in national missile defense, 73
  and political donations, 34
theater missile defense ground-based radar (TMD-GBR), 91, 100
theater missile defense program (THD)
  definition of, 80
  and NMD, 85
theater missile defense program (TMD), 73
THEL, *see* Tactical High Energy Laser
think tanks, 24–27
  and military-industrial complex, 26–27
  and propaganda, 25–26
  role of, 24–25
30-TeraOPS computer, 56
Thompson, Loren, xix, 185
Thomson, Allen, 128
thorium, xlix, 69
Thorp, Frank, xlix
Thule (Greenland), 101, 112, 182
Ti-Coating, xxix–xxx
Tisdall, Simon, xx
TMD, *see* theater missile defense program
TMD-GBR, *see* theater missile defense ground-based radar
Tom Brown Inc. Oil company, 162
Tomahawk missiles, xxx, xxxiii
Tora Bora, xi
Total Information Awareness project, xxxiv
TotalFinaElf, xxv
Toupadakis, Andreas, 15
TOW missiles, xxxiii
Toynbee, Polly, 171
Transit 5BN-3 satellite, 138
transit phase systems, 83–84
treaties, 108–111
  ABM, *see* ABM treaty
  nuclear weapons, 44
  SALT II, 166
  space, 127, 141
  START, *see* START
"tree tops" propaganda, 25
Tribune Company, 166
Trident, xx, 36, 48
Trident D5 submarine ballistic missiles, xix
Trireme Partners, xxxv, xxxvi
tritium, 52, 53, 56
  environmental hazards of, 62
  in sphere of nuclear weapons, 45
tritium extraction facility (TEF), 57
truthout.org, xxii

TRW
as contractor for ABL, 94
as contractor for SBL, 95
and corporate mergers, 30
falsification charges against, 99–100
laser weapons developed by, 126
and Long Range Plan, 119
political clout of, 34, 37
think tanks funded by, 27
Turkey, 89, 157
two-stage gas gun, 52
The 2001 Quadrennial Defense Review (Pentagon), 179

ultraviolet light, 10
Umm Qasr, Iraq, xxxviii, xlv, xlvi
U.N., *see* United Nations
UN International Atomic Energy Agency, xiv
underground nuclear testing, 54
Union Carbide, 148
Union of Concerned Scientists, 100
Unisys, xxix–xxx
United Arab Emirates, 157, 185
United Defense, 30
United Kingdom, 101, 105, 111, 130, 151, 158, 181
and AWACS, 89
and BMEWS, 101
and George W. Bush administration, 181
cancer incidence in, 151
and century of oil and war in Middle East, xxv
and Comprehensive Test-Ban Treaty, 44
and International Space Station, 135
and Iraq, xxv, xxvi
and NMD concerns, 111–112
nuclear weapons tests in, 46
proliferation of uranium weapons in, 157
and recent international weapons development, xx
servicemen with Gulf War Syndrome, 156
Solway Firth, 158
and uranium weapons effects, 160
uranium weapons testing in, 158
United Nations (U.N.), xvi–xvii, xxvii, xxix, xlv–xlvi, 81–82, 127, 143–144, 157, 158
United States
enemies of, 4
global imperialism of, 180–184
and Iran-Iraq war, xxvi
Kuwait/Iraq policies of, 145
nuclear power plants in, xiv–xv
and nuclear satellite crash, 138
and nuclear weapons treaties, 44
number of nuclear weapons in, 46
resumption of nuclear weapons testing by, xviii
and satellite systems threats, 129
and space disarmament, 144
space warfare plans of, 118–121
and U.N. Arms Race resolution, 82
United States Tobacco Company, 34
United Technologies, 35, 39, 40, 91, 97
University of Chicago, 59, 60
University of Florida, 142
University of Illinois, 61
University of Illinois at Urbana-Champaign, 59, 60
university research, 59–61
University of Utah, 59, 60
unmanned drones, xii–xiii
upgrading facilities, 55–57
upper-tier defense (exo-atmospheric), 90–94
uranium
in B61-11, 47
characteristics of, 146–147
clean-up of, xli, 156–157
enrichment facility for, 57
handling of, 69–70
medical risks of processing, 149–151
in mini-nukes, 48
in R&D facilities, 56
in secondary mechanism of nuclear weapons, 46
in sphere of nuclear weapons, 45
uranium ammunition, 158

uranium weapons
in Bosnia and Kosovo, 158–161
components of, 147–148
in Gulf conflict, 151–156
history of, 146–147
and international concerns, 158–161
medical implications of, 151–156
proliferation of, 157–158
uranium weapons testing in Puerto Rico, 157–158
U.S. Agency for International Development (USAID), xxxix, xl, xlix
U.S. Air Force
bases in Guam and Wake Island, 180
and ICBM weapons, 22
laser weapons developed by, 126
and lower-tier defense, 89–90
and theater missile defense, 73
U.S. Army
and CEC, 104
and economics of reconstruction, xlvi
and economics of war, xxxi
environmental policies of, 157
and lower-tier defense, 86–88, 90
and theater missile defense, 73
and upper-tier defense, 90–91, 96
U.S. Congress
and Afghanistan war, x
anthrax letters to members of, xxxvii
and corporations, 24–25
design of new weapons authorized by, 48–49
and economics of reconstruction, xl
and economics of war, xxxi, xxxvii
and foreign arms sales, 40
and march to Operation Iraqi Freedom, xxv
and military spending, xxxi, 32–33
and military-industrial complex, 34–36, 184–185
and national missile defense program, 73–74, 79
and PNAC, xxiii
and political implications of George W. Bush administration behavior, xviii, xix
and selling of Iraq war to American people, xxv
and space warfare, 115–116
and worker compensation, 69–70
U.S. Freedom of Information Act, xxxviii
U.S. military, 17–23
budget for/spending by, xviii–xix, xxxi, 5, 184–186
buildup of, xix
interservice rivalry of, 17
morning-after pills for, xlviii
and PNAC, xxiii
privatizing by, xliii–xliv
and theater missile defense program, 73
see also specific branch
U.S. Navy
and CEC, 104
and lower-tier defense, 86, 88
presence in Pacific, 180
and theater missile defense, 73
and upper-tier defense, 90, 92–94
U.S. Secret Service, xxxv
U.S. Space Force, 121–123
U.S. State Department, xvi, xxxix, xlv
U.S. Trade Department, xxviii
USS *Abraham Lincoln,* Bush speech from, xlvii

Vandenberg Air Force Base (California), 98
Vardo (Norway), 105, 112
Vardo radar, 112
Vedrine, Hubert, 182
vertical proliferation, 45
ViaSat, xxxvii
Vieques (Puerto Rico), 157–158
Vietnam War, carpet bombing in, xii
Virginia class submarine, xix
virtual shock tube, 59–60
viruses, computer, 129
Vision for 2020 (U.S. space command), 118–119
Vista Technologies, 119
Voice of the New Iraq, xlvi

W-76 replacement warhead, 55
W-88 pits, 55

Wake Island, 180
Walpole, Robert, 165
war, economics of, xxx–xxxviii
war against terrorism, coalition for, xvi
Warburg Pincus LLC, xxxvii
warfare, space, 115–144
Washington Group International, xxxix
The Washington Post, xlii, 98
waste, nuclear, xli, 62–66, 149, 150
water supply, and nuclear meltdowns, xv
Waxman, Henry A., xl
weapons
  development of, xix–xx, 47–50
  foreign sales of, *see* foreign arms sales
  nuclear powered, 142–143
  reduction of, xix–xx
  stockpiled, xix–xx, 45–46
  See also type of weapon
weapons of mass destruction, xxiv, xxix–xxx
weapons systems, 85–106
The Weekly Standard, xxi
weightlessness, 132–133
Weinberger, Casper, xlii
Weiss, Steve, 163
Welch, Larry, 76, 92
Weldon, Kurt, 27, 185
West Nile Virus, xxviii
West Valley, NY, nuclear reprocessing plant in, xli
Westinghouse, 91
White House, and PNAC, xxiii
White House Office of Science and Technology Policy, 11
White Rock (New Mexico), 66
White Sands Missile Range (New Mexico), 91, 92
WHO (World Health Organization), xxix, xlix, 156
Wolfowitz, Paul, xvi, xvii, xix, xxi–xxii, xxiii, xxiv, 169–170, 177
Woods, Peter, 181
Woolsey, R. James, xvii, xxi, xxiv, xxxvi–xxxvii
World Bank, 25, 26*n*
World Health Organization (WHO), xxix, xlix, 156
World Trade Center, xiv, xxi, xxxvii
World Trade Organization (WTO), 26
Wright, David, 100
Wright, Eric, 161
WTO (World Trade Organization), 26
Wurmser, David, xxii
WWII, 8

X-1 machines, 50
X-I machines, 52
X-band radars, 104–105, 112, 113
X-rays, 46

Y-12 plant (Oak Ridge), 50, 57, 68
Y2K computer problems, 12
Yeltsin, Boris, 11
Yorkshire (England), 101, 105, 111
Young, Hugo, 112, 182
Younger, Stephen, 48
Yucca Mountain (Nevada), xli
Yugoslavia, 39
Yuma (Arizona), 150

Zakheim, Dov, 169
Zhu Bangzoa, 110
Ziehm, M. V., 155
Zoellick, Robert, 169, 170